AN EDITOR'S GUIDE
TO ADOBE® PREMIERE® PRO

SECOND EDITION

RICHARD HARRINGTON

ROBBIE CARMAN

JEFF I. GREENBERG

Peachpit Press

An Editor's Guide to Adobe® Premiere® Pro, Second Edition
Richard Harrington, Robbie Carman, and Jeff I. Greenberg

Peachpit Press
1249 Eighth Street
Berkeley, CA 94710

To report errors, please send a note to errata@peachpit.com

Peachpit is a division of Pearson Education
Copyright © 2013 Richard Harrington, Robbie Carman, and Jeff I. Greenberg

Senior Editor: Karyn Johnson
Development and Copy Editor: Kim Wimpsett
Production Editor: Danielle Foster
Keystroker: Pamela Berry
Proofreader: Bethany Stough
Composition: Danielle Foster
Indexer: Rebecca Plunkett
Interior design: Peachpit
Cover design: Mimi Heft

ISBN-13: 978-0-321-84006-6
ISBN-10: 0-321-84006-2

9 8 7 6 5 4 3 2 1

Printed and bound in the United States of America

To my parents, for teaching me hard work and persistence.

To my wife, your love makes all things possible.

To my children, you make me a better man.

—Richard Harrington

To all my teachers over the years, you've inspired me to teach others.

To my wife, your love and support allow me to do what I do.

To my daughter, your laugh and your smile make every day special.

—Robbie Carman

To my wife, whose love and understanding make it all worthwhile.

To my darling daughter, who gives me higher goals to reach.

To my brother, for getting family items off my plate and reminding me of who I am.

To my parents, for giving me a love of reading and learning.

—Jeff I. Greenberg

ACKNOWLEDGMENTS

The authors would like to thank the following people who made this book possible:

Gary Adcock	Jim Guerard	Kuhn	Jesse Schwab
John Barrie	Rod Harlan	Ron Lindeboom	Abba Shapiro
Pamela Berry	Mimi Heft	John Lytle	Colin Smith
Walter Biscardi	Dave Helmly	Chris Meyer	Karl Soule
Scott Bourne	Serena Herr	Kevin Monahan	Anne Marie Walker
Michael Coleman	Maxim Jago	Al Mooney	Jason Walsmith
Emmanuel Etim	Karyn Johnson	Jason Osder	Mark Weiser
Todd Evans	Mike Kahn	John Pascuzzi	Terry White
Chris Fenwick	Scott Kelby	Chris Phrommayon	Tim Wilson
Eric Fishback	Tim Kolb	Iva Radivojevic	Kim Wimpsett
Steve Forde	Todd Kopriva	Jack Reilly	Luisa Winters
Michelle Gallina	Ben Kozuch	Bill Roberts	Mitch Wood
Peter Getzels	Robert Lawrence	Jeff Rothberg	John Woody

The authors would like to thank the following companies for their support:

Adobe	National Association of Broadcasters
Authentic Records	The Nadas
Canon	Nikon
Creative COW	Panasonic
Future Media Concepts	RHED Pixel
Getzels Gordon Productions	Singular Software
The Kuhn Foundation	Vision III
Lynda.com	Zacuto

CONTENTS

ON THE DISC

INTRODUCTION

The first edition of this book was built out of a true need. We saw the rise of Adobe Premiere Pro and had a moment of clarity. Adobe Premiere Pro is a seriously powerful NLE that has some incredible strengths, and we don't know it as well as we should. What if a job arose or a freelance gig popped up? Were we prepared to leave money on the table?

Sure, as experienced editors and teachers, we'd used Adobe Premiere Pro for years. But we'd never taken the time to actually study the application to the same depth as Final Cut Pro or Avid. What became clear in early 2010 is that Adobe was 100 percent committed to making a kick-butt tool, and we'd be foolish to not give it proper respect. And that promise held true as the updates in CS6 and Adobe Creative Cloud have shown that Adobe Premiere Pro is now a major player in professional video editing.

At the same time, other nonlinear editing tools seemed to have a less clear future and upgrade path. Instead of being caught flat-footed, we decided to do something about it. It was time to master Adobe Premiere Pro so we could feel as fast at it as any other nonlinear editing tool and learn to take advantage of its unique strengths.

What you hold in your hands is a comprehensive guide to editing with Adobe Premiere Pro. The book was written because we were frustrated with so many of the existing training materials on the market. We wanted to learn the application at an accelerated pace and be able to use our existing Final Cut Pro and Avid experience as a launch pad to learning more quickly. For this reason, you'll find training videos, hands-on exercises, and shortcut guides throughout the book because we found that just reading wasn't enough.

Who This Book Is For

We wrote this book for you—just you. OK, you can tell your friends and colleagues about it. Whether you identify yourself as a professional editor or if video editing is a major part of your job, we welcome you.

The book makes the following assumptions in its teaching style:

- You have been editing video for at least a few years.

- You most likely have experience with another editing tool, such as Apple Final Cut Pro, Avid Media Composer, or Sony Vegas.

- You want to get the most out of Adobe Premiere Pro throughout your entire workflow. This includes tasks such as audio mixing, video compression, color grading, and visual effects. As such, you're able to turn to the Creative Suite toolset.

- You understand that editors are under pressure to be faster and more productive. As such, sarcasm and wit are natural side effects.

All three authors work in professional video (but with different areas of focus). We have experience cutting everything from broadcast to corporate as well as news to feature films. We know that different editors have different needs, but we try to address the most pressing needs with efficient workflows.

This book is designed so you can feel fully confident with Adobe Premiere Pro in a week's time. We know a new job or opportunity will pop up, and you'll need to be ready to go quickly. Be sure to keep the movies and shortcut guides on your laptop, tablet, or smartphone. You'll also want to work through all the hands-on exercises so you can master the skills needed to edit professionally with Adobe Premiere Pro.

What Gear Do You Need?

To complete the activities in this book, you'll need the following items:

- A qualified computer running a 64-bit version of the Macintosh or Windows operating system. You'll also need at least 4 GB of RAM (8 GB recommended) to properly handle HD video. You can see a detailed list of system requirements at www.adobe.com/products/premiere/tech-specs.html.

- A copy of Adobe Premiere Pro. If you want to get the most out of the book, you'll need a copy of Adobe Creative Suite Production Premium, Master Collection, or Creative Cloud to use the companion applications. If you don't already own the application, you can download a fully functional 30-day demo version from Adobe's Web site.

- A monitor capable of showing a minimum of 1280 x 900 resolution.

- A DVD-ROM drive to copy the files to your local computer.

- The latest version of Apple QuickTime.

- An MPEG-4 player, such as Apple QuickTime or iTunes, to view the video tutorials included on the disc. Both are free from www.apple.com.

- A PDF viewer application, such as Adobe Acrobat. A free version is available from Adobe's Web site.

- A fast hard drive rated for video playback. This can be an internal or external drive, but it should ideally be at least a 7200 rpm drive and not contain application or system files.

Iconography

Throughout the book you'll encounter several special symbols. These icons indicate a variety of ways that you can take the lessons deeper. Be sure to fully explore your options before moving to the next section of the book.

 Tip. You'll find tips that offer practical and advanced advice to improve your editing experience.

 Avid User Tip. These tips are designed specifically for those with Avid nonlinear editing experience as they transition to Adobe Premiere Pro.

 Final Cut Pro User Tip. There are also tips for those who've edited with Final Cut Pro as they transition to Adobe Premiere Pro.

 Noteworthy. These are "gotchas" to avoid, new terminology, or important skills.

 Training video. You'll find 73 training videos included on the accompanying DVD. These show advanced techniques and will extend your editing capabilities.

Meet the Authors

This book is a compilation of more than 50 years' experience with nonlinear editing. We set out to capture not only the best practices when working with Adobe Premiere Pro but also a solid workflow for any editor. What lies ahead is our collective experience to make adopting Adobe Premiere Pro a fast and efficient process. We've collaborated on each chapter to bring you the best of our collective knowledge.

Richard Harrington

Richard Harrington is a director/producer/editor with national PSAs and Ciné award-winning productions. He owns the visual communications company RHED Pixel (www.rhedpixel.com) in Washington, D.C.

Rich is also a Master Trainer for Adobe Premiere Pro. He has extensive experience with other editing tools and has held instructor certifications with both Apple and Avid. Rich consistently shares his knowledge as a regular contributor to Creative COW, *Photoshop User* magazine, and numerous industry blogs.

He has written and co-written a number of books including *Motion Graphics with Adobe Creative Suite 5 Studio Techniques* (Peachpit, 2010), *From Still to Motion* (Peachpit, 2010), *Photoshop for Video* (Peachpit, 2010), and *Video Made on a Mac* (Peachpit, 2009).

You can contact Rich at

- www.linkedin.com/in/richardharrington
- www.rhedpixel.com
- www.richardharringtonblog.com
- www.twitter.com/rhedpixel
- www.photofocus.com

Robbie Carman

Robbie Carman is a professional colorist who works on broadcast television series and independent films. Robbie is a Master Trainer for Adobe Premiere Pro. He's part of the first generation of certified Apple Final Cut Pro instructors and is certified in Final Cut Pro, DVD Studio Pro, and Color.

Robbie co-wrote *Final Cut Pro Workflows* (Focal Press, 2007) with Jason Osder, as well as *From Still to Motion* (Peachpit, 2010), *Video Made on a Mac* (Peachpit, 2009), and *Final Cut Studio on the Spot* (Focal Press, 2007) with Richard Harrington.

Robbie is a moderator in the forums on Creative COW and speaks nationally at conferences, such as the National Association of Broadcasters (NAB). Robbie is the co-owner of Amigo Media (www.amigomediallc.com), a boutique postproduction company located in Washington, D.C.

You can contact Robbie at

- www.linkedin.com/in/robbiecarman

- www.amigomediallc.com

- www.robbiecarman.net

- www.twitter.com/robbiecarman

Jeff I. Greenberg

Jeff I. Greenberg is a professional educator, editor, and consultant who has worked on projects at every level—from broadcast television to independent film. Jeff is a Master Trainer for Adobe Premiere Pro, is a Master Trainer for Apple, is certified for the entire Final Cut Studio suite, and holds numerous Avid Trainer certifications, including those for Media Composer, Symphony, and DS.

Jeff is a moderator in the forums of Creative COW and speaks nationally and internationally at conferences, such as the National Association of Broadcasters (NAB) and the International Broadcasting Convention (IBC). He has contributed to and technical edited numerous books and articles.

Jeff is the chair and program manager of the Editors Retreat, a yearly getaway that focuses on editing, aesthetics, business, and postproduction. He has video training materials available at Lynda.com and VASST.com.

You can contact Jeff at

- www.linkedin.com/in/jeffgreenberg

- www.JeffIGreenberg.com

- www.EditorsRetreat.com

- www.twitter.com/filmgeek

About the Disc or Downloads

In your hands is a book *and* a DVD (or a download link for those who bought the electronic version). These two pieces are of equal value and are meant to be used together for a complete learning experience. For the best results, we recommend watching the video clips and performing the exercises while reading or soon after reading the corresponding chapter.

What's Included

On the disc you'll find several useful items that are meant to bring the images in the book to life:

■ Hands-on lesson files and footage

■ Additional appendixes on advanced topics such as multicamera editing, DSLR video, tape workflow, stereo 3D and Final Cut and Avid interoperability

■ Comprehensive video training that explores additional topics

■ Template files and keyboard shortcut guides to enhance your postproduction workflow

What You Need

Welcome to a high-tech world. You won't need the latest and greatest, but we do have some strong recommendations. To use the DVD, you'll need the following items:

Copy Files First
We highly recommend you copy the files from the book's DVD to your local hard drive or media drive. The DVD media can't spin fast enough to play back HD video smoothly.

■ A Mac or Windows computer with a DVD-ROM drive.

■ The latest version of QuickTime installed to view the video files.

■ Adobe Premiere Pro CS6 or newer.

■ Additional creative software, such as Adobe Photoshop and Adobe After Effects, for specific exercises. Trial versions are available on Adobe's Web site.

■ A high-speed hard drive with a FireWire, SATA, USB3, or Thunderbolt connection for editing video files. Internal laptop or computer drives can work, but a performance drive (RAID) is highly recommended.

Working with Lesson Files

On the DVD, we've included project files and media for each chapter. These are designed so that you can follow along with the exercises throughout the book.

Copying Lessons and Media

From the DVD, simply copy the Lessons and Media and Appendixes and Media folders to a location of your choosing on your system. Inside this folder are folders for each chapter or appendix as well as a centralized media folder.

If you encounter a zip archive, you may need to unzip it to use it. On a Mac simply double-click the Zip archive to unzip it. On a Windows machine you may be able to simply double-click the Zip archive to open it. If not, be sure to download a free unzipping application. We've had good luck with the free Stuffit Expander, which you can download from www.stuffit.com/win-expander.html.

Accessing Lesson Files and Media

After copying Lessons and Media and Appendixes and Media folders, the next step as you follow along in each chapter or appendix is to open projects or access media as directed in the lesson.

You'll see in the exercises a step similar to the following, instructing you to open a project file:

Choose File > Open, and navigate to Lessons and Media > Lesson 07 > 07_essential_editing.pproj.

The Media folder should be copied in its entirety, and it contains the actual media used in the project files for a particular chapter.

In some exercises, you'll be prompted to import a file into Adobe Premiere Pro. When you're asked to import a file, the requested file(s) will be located in the specific lesson folder.

If you're following along with the lesson files and get stuck or are in a training center using this book, you'll also find finished lesson files for most of the chapters. We say most, because not all chapters have executable steps to make a finished file. One benefit that the finished lesson files have is that you can skip ahead to a finished version of a step-by-step exercise. While the finished versions of most exercises are available, we do encourage you to try individual exercises to really learn how Adobe Premiere Pro and other parts of the Creative Suite work.

Relinking Media

When opening project files, you may be prompted to relink media files. The reason that media doesn't automatically relink is because of the way Adobe Premiere Pro handles file paths in regard to project and media location. Adobe Premiere Pro uses a very literal path to specify a file's location.

In the relink dialog that appears, simply use the following path for each lesson to relink to media:

Lessons and Media > Media or Appendices and Media > Media

In some cases, media may be located in an individual lesson folder if it was manually imported into a project.

Be sure to select the Display Exact Name Matches Only check box. With this option selected, all you have to do is click the first file in the Media folder that is unlinked (it will be bold with all other files grayed out) and then click Open at the bottom of the dialog. All the media files for that exercise will then be relinked. After media has been relinked, save the project; then, if you want to return to an exercise at a later time, media will already be linked.

CHAPTER 1

The Adobe Workflow

THE JOB OF the modern-day video editor has evolved into a wide range of responsibilities. Seldom are we given the task of just cutting a project. Often, we are asked to tweak the audio, fix a dark shot, or animate a graphic. Because of the ever-expanding job description, we tend to own a lot of software. Most editors these days must have at least a rudimentary understanding of Adobe Photoshop for processing images and a basic understanding of Adobe Illustrator to deal with logos and artwork. The editors who are working the most usually know their way around a comp in Adobe After Effects as well.

The purpose of this book is *not to teach you how to edit* (we expect you're already skilled at that). Rather, our goal is to help you through some of the obstacles and speed bumps of transitioning to (or adding) Adobe Premiere Pro to your repertoire. We'll bring you up to speed quickly as well as explain the philosophy behind an efficient workflow.

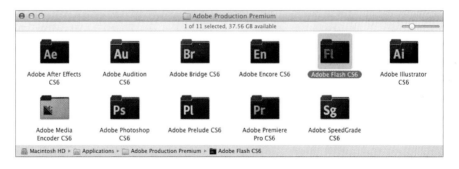

Meet Adobe Premiere Pro

Whether you're coming to Adobe Premiere Pro with experience in Apple Final Cut Pro, one of the Avid packages, or perhaps Sony Vegas, you'll see many familiar elements that are standard in modern nonlinear editing (**FIGURE 1.1**).

FIGURE 1.1 With Adobe Premiere Pro CS6, Adobe has streamlined the editing interface so all core functions are in the Editing workspace. You can access other features through the Window menu by choosing a specific workspace or a panel.

Our advice is that you come in with an open mind. Adobe Premiere Pro will seem both familiar and foreign, depending on the task at hand. Many of us have to learn multiple tools—think of Adobe Premiere Pro as a language with just a slight accent change. Although you may find changes (especially under a deadline) a bit stressful, remember that this is an opportunity to discover new ways to save time and enjoy editing. We've found that it takes a few weeks to get comfortable and perhaps a few months to become truly fluent.

Interface Philosophy

If you've ever changed from one edit system to another, you'll recall that at first it feels like you've walked into your home to find all the furniture rearranged. Initially, you're a little disoriented, but you can quickly learn to deal with the situation. Sure, you can move things back to where you like them, but you might just discover that you like some of the changes a bit better.

As you dive into Adobe Premiere Pro, you'll soon realize that there is very little you need to relearn to get a basic project out the door. Here is what you need to know:

- **Media management.** Getting media into your system is a primary concern, whether that means capturing from a tape source or importing digital media from any of the solid-state systems. The Adobe Premiere Pro support for native editing makes this task far easier than many competing systems (but very different).

- **Timeline operations.** Manipulating footage is the next task. You'll need to move files around, cut clips apart, and delete unused sections. If you can do that much, you're basically editing. Anything you learn beyond that just makes you more efficient. Many of the same keyboard shortcuts exist between editing apps (such as J-K-L keyboard shortcuts), and Adobe Premiere Pro offers a fully customizable keyboard so you can remap commands to the keys you already use.

- **Output.** Outputting a completed edit for final delivery concludes the process. Adobe offers more choices than any other nonlinear editing package we've worked with because this is an area in which it is a market leader.

If you can perform these three tasks, you can pretty much edit. So, take a deep breath and relax; we have lots of cool things to show you. By understanding the essentials, you can prioritize what else you need to learn and identify what will make you faster, better, and more efficient.

Interface Tour

After you launch Adobe Premiere Pro, you'll notice that it fills the entire screen (**FIGURE 1.2**). This approach keeps all the windows docked into an Application frame and makes it easier to keep your workspace organized. While in Adobe Premiere Pro, the screen is essentially one large Application frame. This is divided into a smaller series of nested frames that can hold a series of interconnected panels.

Let's open a project that's in progress to see the interface in context. From the Lessons and Media > Lesson 01 folder, please open 01_getting_started.prproj. You may need to relink media (see the Introduction in the section "Working with Lesson Files," if needed).

FIGURE 1.2 You can switch between workspaces to quickly reconfigure the interface layout by choosing Window > Workspace. In clockwise order, starting from the upper left, are the Audio, Color Correction, and Editing workspaces.

You'll find that all Adobe applications use the Application frame approach, so switching between applications is straightforward. Adobe applications minimize distractions to keep you on task.

Whether you like floating windows or docked panels is a moot point. You can easily switch between both methods as you choose.

To undock a panel, follow these steps:

1. Click a tab to select the desired panel.

2. Locate the panel menu for that panel in the upper-right corner of the panel. It is a small down-pointing arrow with four bars.

3. Click the panel menu and choose Undock Panel to free the individual tab. You can also choose Undock Frame to release the group of nested panels into a floating frame.

4. Drag the frame to a new position on the screen. It can be left floating over other windows, or you can dock it with other windows.

Before you start to rearrange panels and windows, however, it's best to familiarize yourself with the default interface arrangement. Like other edit systems, you'll need a few standard views (**FIGURE 1.3**). A quick tour of the major panels for the Editing workspace is included in the following sections, but you'll explore all of these panels in greater detail throughout the book and video lessons. After trying your hand at rearranging panels, reset your view by choosing Window > Workspace > Editing to continue the tour.

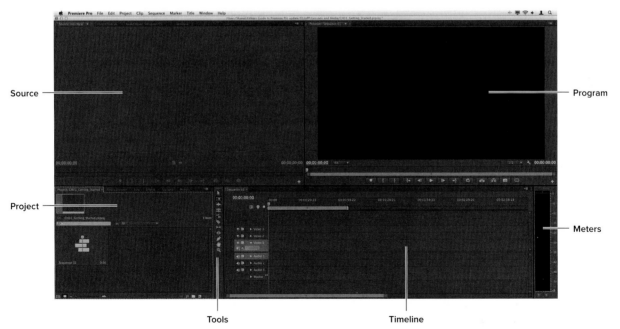

Source — Program

Project — Meters

Tools — Timeline

FIGURE 1.3 On the surface, the Adobe Premiere Pro user interface appears straightforward, but there are some customizable and useful features that are hidden from a novice user.

Project panel (Shift+1)

The Project panel (FIGURE 1.4) provides a centralized location to organize and navigate your media. Its primary role is to enable you to view and organize your assets into bins. You can use the Filter field (magnifying glass near the top) to quickly sift and sort your assets. You'll also find several controls across the bottom of the window to adjust how assets are displayed as well as create new media or content (such as color matte, bars and tone, and leader).

Double-click the clip 01015b.mp4 to load it into the Source Monitor.

Some or None?
You can change which buttons are visible by clicking the plus symbol in the bottom-right corner of the Source Monitor or Program Monitor. This will open the Button Editor where you can customize the layout of transport controls. If you don't need buttons at all, just click the panel menu and uncheck Show Transport Controls.

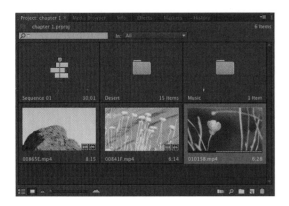

FIGURE 1.4 Seen here in thumbnail view, the Project panel is where you organize your sources.

Source Monitor panel (Shift+2)

The Source Monitor panel (FIGURE 1.5) serves the same function as the Source Monitor did for linear editors. You use this panel to load your clips for real-time viewing, mark In and Out points, and shuttle using transport controls. Be sure to explore all the controls at the bottom of the window on the Source Monitor panel.

FIGURE 1.5 The Source Monitor is the best panel to use to view clips before editing. Note the Drag Video Only and Drag Audio Only icons above the transport controls.

Most of the controls will look familiar, but here are a few notable controls you should know about (FIGURE 1.6):

- **Settings.** Use the menu under the wrench to switch what information is displayed including audio, scopes, and alpha channel details.

- **Export Frame.** You can quickly export a still frame based on the current-time indicator.

- **Button Editor.** Clicking this permits drag-and-drop customization of the buttons under the Source Monitor and Program Monitor panels.

Settings

Export Frame   Button Editor

In the upper-right corner of each panel is a small icon that indicates a panel menu. These menus allow you to control each panel. The contextual menu commands (FIGURE 1.7) will change depending on which panel you have selected.

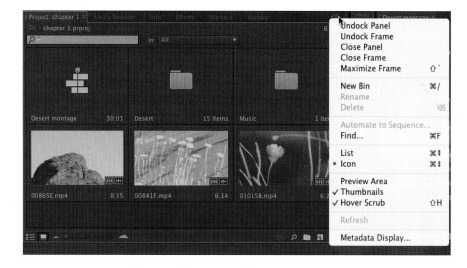

Cut Down the Playback Resolution!
Adobe Premiere Pro will play back with a reduced resolution if you right-click the Program Monitor. This is ideal on heavily compressed footage or when playback drops frames (depending on your system). It's hard to even notice a difference at ½ or ¼ .

Program Monitor panel (Shift+4)

The Program Monitor panel lets you visualize the Timeline, and as you move the playhead through your sequence, it will update. It can also control the quality of your view. If you're working with high-quality sources or lots of filters, you may need to render for final export.

In the meantime, Adobe Premiere Pro will let you adjust playback quality to improve real-time performance. Click the Selected Playback Resolution pop-up menu, and change the quality to Half (FIGURE 1.8). This affects only preview quality and not the final output.

FIGURE 1.8 The Program Monitor panel shows you the contents of your sequence. Note the mouse on the playback quality menu.

Timeline panel (Shift+3)

A timeline is a timeline, right? Right. But in Adobe Premiere Pro you may see audio tracks that contain multiple channels. Also, note the subtlety of the Track Targeting and Track Indicator artwork at the left side of the Timeline panel (**FIGURE 1.8**). If you are a "target-er," this should make perfect sense; if you're not, see Chapter 6, "Essential Editing Skills," for more in-depth coverage.

Got Several Sequences Open?
One unique element to the Program Monitor panel is the menu in the tabbed label in the upper part of the Program Monitor that allows you to access all the opened Timelines.

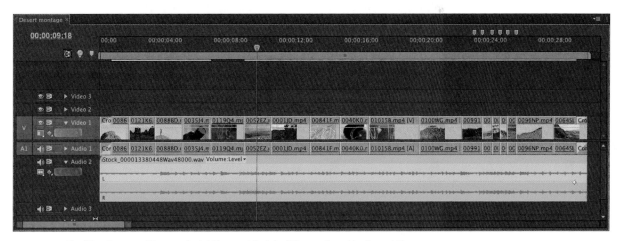

FIGURE 1.8 The Timeline panel is very straightforward, but don't be confused by the subtle gray highlights on the left end used for targeting.

Effect Controls panel (Shift+5)

The Effect Controls panel (**FIGURE 1.10**) is not just for controlling effects (although it does that quite well). Let's open the panel and put something in it to view.

1. Click the Effect Controls panel tab (it is docked with the Source Monitor by default).

2. In the Timeline, use the Selection tool, and click the first clip to activate it. This clip has a filter applied for color correction. Additionally, every clip you add to the Timeline will automatically have three built-in, intrinsic video effects (Motion, Opacity, and Time Remapping) and one audio effect (Volume) applied.

FIGURE 1.10 The Effect Controls panel contains controls for any effects along with the geometry aspects of a clip, such as Position, Scale, and Rotation.

You'll use the Effect Controls panel to adjust the geometry, speed, and opacity of a clip as well as its audio parameters. When you start adding additional effects (either video or audio), you will find those controls here as well.

Click the next tab to the right of the Effect Controls panel to open the Audio Mixer panel.

Audio Mixer panel (Shift+6)

The Audio Mixer panel (**FIGURE 1.11**) contains several useful controls. If you've ever experimented with ProTools or other digital audio workstations, you may be familiar with some of the controls in this panel. In addition to rudimentary record controls, you'll find the automation modes Read, Latch, Touch, and Write for each channel as well as channel effects inserts to add an effect to an entire track. Even programmable effects sends are available, and of course, all the controls are automatable.

Effects panel (Shift+7)

You'll find the Effects panel (**FIGURE 1.12**) docked with the Project panel. It unlocks a myriad of corrective and stylizing effects for both audio and video. Even if you're not "into effects," you'll still find this panel essential for color correction and audio restoration.

Although there is no menu system to access effects, you will find that the Effects panel offers some handy features. A search field at the top allows you to quickly find the effect you are looking for, and the building-block-style icons allow you to limit your effects to Accelerated Effects, 32-bit effects, and YUV effects (other third-party tools may also install buttons to enable quick filtering).

FIGURE 1.11 The Audio Mixer includes level controls, pan and master output controls, and channel effects inserts and effects sends via the disclosure triangle on the left side.

FIGURE 1.12 To quickly find an effect, you can type its name (or even a keyword) into the search field.

Media Browser panel (Shift+8)

The Media Browser panel (**FIGURE 1.13**) offers one way to browse your hard drives and connected volumes. It is a fast way to access your file-based assets. The Media Browser allows you to import files natively from many of the leading media formats (RED, XDCAM, DVCPRO-HD, and DSLR). By importing a file through the Media Browser, it will automatically become a clip in the Project panel. Although the Import command often works, the Media Browser is generally the best way to ensure a proper import with all metadata. The Media Browser is also capable of correctly merging spanned clips (long clips that get spread across two or more memory cards). You'll explore its functionality fully in Chapter 3, "Setting up a Project."

FIGURE 1.13 Be sure to expand the size of the Media Browser panel so you can see all of its features. You can press the grave accent (`) key to temporarily expand a window when the mouse pointer is over it.

Tools panel

As an experienced editor, you'll find that all your standard editing tools are available in the Tools panel (**FIGURE 1.14**). For example, you'll find tools like Track Selection, the Hand tool, and the Zoom tool for selecting and viewing Timeline elements. You'll also find standard editing tools like Ripple Edit, Roll Edit, and Slip. All of these tools offer standard keyboard shortcuts (**TABLE 1.1**). They can also all be customized by choosing Premiere Pro > Keyboard Shortcuts (Edit > Keyboard Shortcuts) and scrolling to the Tools section at the bottom of the list.

FIGURE 1.14 If you have trouble learning the Tools panel short-cuts, you can remap them to any key. In fact, Adobe Premiere Pro even offers presets that match Final Cut Pro 7 and Avid shortcuts.

Where's My Effects Menu?
Unlike Final Cut Pro 7, there is no way to access effects from the menu system. You must choose effects from the Effects panel. If you miss being able to quickly search for effects in a menu as opposed to the twirl-down bins of the Effects panel, try using the Find command at the top of the panel. You may find that this is actually a faster way to work.

TABLE 1.1   Default Shortcuts for Adobe Premiere Pro Tools Panel

Shortcut	Tool
V	Selection tool
A	Track Selection tool
B	Ripple Edit tool
N	Rolling Edit tool
X	Rate Stretch tool
C	Razor tool
Y	Slip tool
U	Slide tool
P	Pen tool
H	Hand tool
Z	Zoom tool

Info panel

With a clip selected in the Project panel, click the tab for the Info panel (it's docked into the same frame). The Info panel (**FIGURE 1.15**) provides a useful view into details of selected clips, graphics, or Timelines. You can find out frame size and rate, audio bitrates, and In and Out points. The Info panel also displays the number of video and audio tracks in an active sequence.

FIGURE 1.15 The Info panel is a great way to get detailed technical information about a clip.

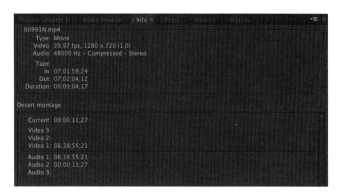

History panel

The History panel (**FIGURE 1.16**) is a clever way to track your progress as you work. It is essentially a visual representation of the available undos you have. Not only can you view the changes made to a clip, but you can also "go back in time" to any state along the way (up to 32 levels of undo). You'll notice that all of the steps you've taken so far in this project have been tracked.

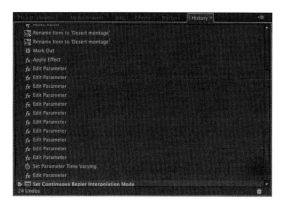

FIGURE 1.16 If you've used Adobe Photoshop, the concept of the History panel is identical.

Timecode panel

The Timecode panel (**FIGURE 1.17**) is a panel that many editors prefer to have visible. It can track the sequence timecode or the source timecode of a specific track

FIGURE 1.17 With the Timecode panel open, it can be resized as large as necessary; it's great for review sessions with clients!

Markers panel

The Markers panel (**FIGURE 1.18**) is a list of any markers that have been left on a clip. You can use markers in a number of ways, such as to choose where DVD chapters should be, to leave notes about specific clips, and even to trigger events in Adobe Flash.

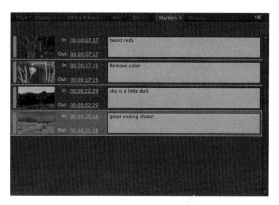

FIGURE 1.18 Markers have a variety of uses, from communicating to other tools in the suite to leaving messages or notes about what remains to be finished.

Using Workspaces

Customizing workspaces is the best way to quickly change the look of your user interface. To get you started, Adobe Premiere Pro offers prebuilt workspaces that inspire you to rethink your work environment.

Here are two ways to access workspaces:

- Choose Window > Workspace and then select from the menu.

- Press Option+Shift+1 (Alt+Shift+1) for the first workspace. You can use numbers for additional workspaces (they are numbered in alphanumeric order).

Let's try adjusting Adobe Premiere Pro so it looks even more like either Final Cut Pro or Avid Media Composer in its layout.

Continue working with the project Ch01_getting_started.pproj.

Choose Window > Workspace > Editing (CS 5.5).

- Adobe Premiere Pro 5.5 had a different default workspace than version 6. Many Final Cut and Avid editors may feel this workspace feels more comfortable because the project is in the upper-left corner of the screen. Effects in both software are also found in the upper-left area. Let's change it so that Adobe Premiere Pro does this too.

In the bottom-left frame are several tabs, Media Browser, Info, Effects, Markers, and History. Drag the Effects tab upward toward the Project panel. Release when the purple highlight is at the center section of the Project panel (**FIGURE 1.19**).

FIGURE 1.19 If you hit the edges rather than the center, the frame will be divided in half depending on the edge you hit, vertically or horizontally.

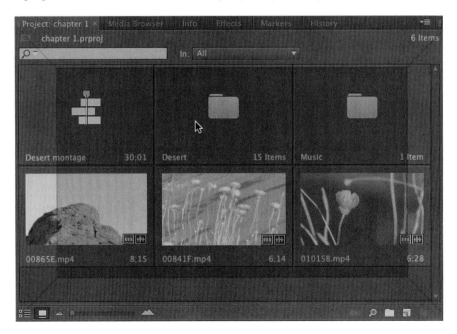

ARRANGING FRAMES AND PANELS ONSCREEN

The Adobe Premiere Pro application window is divided into frames, and several of those frames have multiple panels within them. Adobe tries to keep everything neat and tidy within the Application frame, but it doesn't force you to work that way. You can choose to view or hide any panel.

- To close a panel, select its tab, and then click the gray *x* next to its name.
- If you need to reopen a closed panel, just choose it from the Window menu.

If you want to rearrange frames, that's easy too. Essentially, the process of manipulating a panel involves learning how to separate it from its current frame location:

- You can click a frame's panel menu and choose to undock the highlighted panel or the entire frame.

- An even easier way to rearrange frames is to just tear them off. You can tear off a panel and float it separately from the rest of the main user interface by holding down the Command (Ctrl) key as you move it.

Any panel can be joined to another frame as well. This lets you create a customized grouping of panels and reduce the amount of time you spend clicking and navigating menus. To dock a panel into a frame, drag the panel from one location to another. After you drag a panel off and move it to a new frame, you have a few options.

- Look for the highlighted trapezoids along the edge of a frame. You can place the moving panel above, to the left, to the right, or below the current frame, making a new frame.

- You can also nest a panel into a frame by dropping it either in the tab area or in the center of the frame.

These techniques allow you to completely customize your workspace to suit your particular needs. If you'd like to capture a custom panel arrangement, be sure to store it as a workspace.

Create your own workspace by Choosing Window> Workspace > New Workspace... and saving the workspace with a name that makes sense to you (such as basic editing_yourname).

Be sure to fully explore workspaces because they are key to saving you time. Take a look at both the built-in workspaces and experiment with your own layouts. Find what works comfortably for you. For example, if you have two screens, you should consider using one screen for organization/bins and the other screen for the Source/Program/Timeline panels.

If you accidentally close something on-screen or your screen looks totally foreign, remember, you can always reset a workspace to its original state from the Workspace menu.

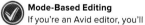 **Mode-Based Editing**
If you're an Avid editor, you'll find that workspaces are similar to the modes you use in Avid. Choosing one will quickly reconfigure the user interface for the task at hand.

Organizing Panels

In this video you'll learn the ins and outs of how to organize your panels into new frames as well as float them on-screen.

Which Suite Is Right?

Adobe offers several Creative Suite editions from which to choose. For video professionals, the most common choice is the Adobe Creative Suite Production Premium. If you also need print and Web design applications, choose the Adobe Creative Suite Master Collection.

It's in the Cloud

If you'd like to subscribe to software, the Adobe Creative Cloud combines the Master Collection (even more Adobe tools) with a collection of tablet and online collaboration tools for a monthly payment.

Creative Suite Production Premium

One of the main reasons that editors are attracted to Adobe Premiere Pro is because of its tight integration with other Adobe software applications. In fact, most choose to purchase Adobe Premiere Pro as part of a suite.

In the early days of bundled software packages, manufacturers did nothing more than shrink-wrap separate applications together or put them in one box. Other than getting a discount, you often faced great hurdles to get the applications to work well with each other. The Adobe Creative Suite, on the other hand, is a truly integrated suite:

- Applications often share code and resources, which makes for leaner installations and greater stability across applications.

- File formats are broadly compatible between applications. For example, you can use a layered Photoshop file in Adobe Premiere Pro as a source in your Timeline, in Adobe After Effects for a motion graphic, or as an interactive menu in Adobe Encore.

- Media can be sent via technology like Adobe Dynamic Link. You can hand off projects between Adobe applications through the postproduction process.

Because the Adobe Creative Suite Production Premium package is the best value for video professionals, it is the package on which we will focus. We'll explore some of these applications in more depth as we move through specific tasks such as titling, color correction, and audio restoration.

Adobe After Effects

After Effects is an industry-standard animation and compositing tool. The sheer number of projects that use this application is mind-numbing—everything from the simplest lower-third name key to finishing major motion-picture effects shots. The integration between After Effects and Adobe Premiere Pro through Dynamic Link makes it extremely easy to share elements and assets between the two applications.

As an editor, you'll turn to After Effects for a few core tasks.

- Advanced keying and compositing

- Animated type and motion graphics

- Advanced masking and rotoscoping

- Advanced retiming with optical flow

Adobe Photoshop Extended

 Photoshop is the leading choice for editing raster graphics such as photos. In fact, 98 percent of all video editors use Photoshop as a regular part of their video postproduction workflow. The current version of Photoshop significantly extends its nondestructive editing capacities, allowing for even greater control.

The Extended version of Photoshop included in the Production Premium package gives you the ability to edit video layers within Photoshop in much the same way you would a photo. This includes powerful filters like Adaptive Wide Angle Correction and Lens Correction. You'll learn about working with footage layers in Photoshop in Chapter 11, "Color Correction and Grading."

Photoshop also features a useful text engine. You can create logos, lower-thirds, and title graphics. We'll explore creating titles in Photoshop in Chapter 13, "Creating Titles."

Adobe Audition

 The Adobe Creative Suite includes Adobe Audition to help improve your sound editing and repair workflow. Adobe Audition is an all-in-one multitrack toolset for professional audio production. You'll use Adobe Audition to mix and record original audio on your computer. It also offers advanced controls for improving the audio in your Adobe Premiere Pro Timeline. We'll explore Adobe Audition in detail in Chapter 10, "Audio Mixing and Repair."

Adobe Media Encoder

 Adobe Media Encoder is an extremely fast compression utility that supports several file types. Whether you need to publish to a disc or the Web, it offers a wealth of output options. You can use it to do the following:

- Transcode files between formats, such as Flash, QuickTime, and MPEG. If you are using Windows, Windows Media support is also added.

- Optimize files for delivery via the Web or optical media (such as Blu-ray Disc)

- Transcribe interviews through speech analysis

- Automate tasks using a Watch Folder

You'll learn how to get the most out of Adobe Media Encoder in Chapter 15.

Adobe Encore

 Although Adobe Encore originally was just a tool to create DVDs, it has evolved into a multiformat authoring tool. Encore offers a suite of tools that allows you to author video and photos for deployment as a DVD, Blu-ray Disc, and SWF file. Encore accepts video files as well as photos, music, and sound. It also uses Adobe Dynamic Link to reduce the amount of time you spend exporting and managing files across projects and applications. Markers can also translate smoothly between Adobe Premiere Pro and Adobe Encore for navigation and Web links.

Adobe Bridge

 You will find that Adobe Bridge quickly becomes the center of a good Adobe Creative Suite workflow. It is a powerful media manager that provides centralized access to all your creative assets.

Once you begin to see its versatility, you will use it more to do the following:

- Visually manage your media

- Move, copy, and rename media files

- Create contact sheets or Web sites for client review for still images

- Browse text animation presets for After Effects

- Preview footage and listen to audio files

Adobe Prelude

 This new application allows easy handling, logging, and preparation of tapeless media to Adobe Premiere Pro. Its name derives from the idea that you'd prepare your materials before they'd get to Adobe Premiere Pro.

Prelude supports numerous file and card formats, can make copies to multiple locations, can transcode footage, can add markers, and even can build a quick edit for hand off to Adobe Premiere Pro, which is perfect for producers and other nontechnical types. It's perfect for properly handling loads of video material by an assistant (even if it's yourself!) or a producer, on- or off-set.

Adobe SpeedGrade

 The other "new" application in the suite is the addition of a dedicated high-end color finishing tool. Adobe purchased Iridas, which brought this previously extremely expensive tool down to a zero-cost addition to the suite. It's known for its powerful primary and secondary corrections, filters that mimic film processes, and an award-winning stereoscopic toolset.

Editing Workflow

As would be expected, Adobe Premiere Pro offers you the ability to work in a variety of ways. Whether you are still capturing from tape or are importing tapeless acquisition formats, Adobe Premiere Pro allows you to seamlessly mix frame rates and formats on the same Timeline with little to no performance hit. Adobe has also made it a priority to keep up with the latest in-camera technology including RED, Alexa, HDSLR, AVCHD, and more.

Native Editing Workflow

One of the big advantages of editing in Adobe Premiere Pro is native editing. Adobe Premiere Pro has the capability to natively ingest many digital acquisition formats without any special preparation. One of the easiest ways to do this is through the Media Browser (**FIGURE 1.20**).

FIGURE 1.20 The Media Browser is the simplest way to browse the contents of your hard drive.

Transcoding is the process of taking one file format and changing it to something with which your edit system can work. This is often done in another application like Adobe Media Encoder, Adobe Prelude, third-party apps like MPEG Streamclip, or possibly a utility that comes with your camera.

If you are a Final Cut Pro 7 user, you may be used to using the Log and Transfer command to ingest your media. Log and Transfer is often used to transcode media. But because you are transcoding inside the edit application, it doesn't feel like you are doing any file conversion (although the amount of extra time sure does feel that way). However, don't be fooled; Log and Transfer does take time. With Adobe Premiere Pro, you can avoid this step and get to your edit faster.

Here are the native formats supported by Adobe Premiere Pro:

- ARRIRAW

- AVC-Intra

- AVCHD

- Canon XF

- DVCPro 25, 50, HD (P2)

- HDV

- MPEG-2 (including a DVD's VIDEO-TS folder)

- Photo JPEG (as used by some DSLR cameras)

- RED R3D

- XDCAM, EX, 50, HD 422

Many editors believe you must transcode your media for color grading, but this is not accurate. The intermediate codecs that many are accustomed to using do not buy you any more dynamic range for color grading. Adobe Premiere Pro automatically up-samples media to 4:4:4 and 32-bit float upon import.

Transcoded Workflow

So, why would you ever want to transcode your footage?

The most common occurrence is that you want better performance on older hardware. Many formats, like H.264 files (common from DSLR cameras), are very taxing. Choosing to transcode provides a slight quality hit but better performance on slower machines.

Perhaps you want to cut in Adobe Premiere Pro, but you are working with other editors who are working in Final Cut Pro 7 or Media Composer. This is a good example of a situation in which you may want to transcode your footage (to a QuickTime-based codec such as ProRes or DNxHD) and export an XML for Final Cut Pro or AAF for Media Composer.

Some editors will also favor certain codecs because they allow for tighter media management. If you are working with native tapeless formats, the Project Manager command essentially copies or moves clips but cannot trim them. This is especially true for many of the long GOP or MPEG type formats. For this reason, third-party codecs can be used to create shorter source files for archiving.

If you decide you want to work with transcoded files, using Adobe Media Encoder and Prelude are the best ways to convert your files.

- In Prelude, it's easy to copy the contents of a card and transcode it in a single step.

- In Adobe Media Encoder, it's easy to set up a Watch Folder to just drop in those files that you want to transcode. As soon as you place a file in the Watch Folder, the transcoding process begins. In no time, all your media will be in a format that you can share between CS6 and other apps. In Chapter 15, "Publish Your Video," we'll cover everything you need to know about the Adobe Media Encoder.

Captured Workflow

Adobe Premiere Pro offers a wide variety of capture solutions that help you get video and audio into your system in a more traditional fashion, that is, from tape. Many hardware options have been tested and approved. For more information about the options, see the section "Monitoring and Capture Solutions" in Chapter 2, "Configuring Your Nonlinear Editor," and see Appendix C, "Capturing from Tape-based Formats."

Next Steps

In the next chapter, we'll discuss how to configure your system, including setting up your preferences and keyboard shortcuts. We'll also cover additional recommended hardware (such as graphic and capture cards) to really make your system sing.

A Note About Stock Music The music used in this exercise is from iStockphoto.com. They offer a wide selection of clips to choose from that are royalty-free. Thanks for allowing us to use the music in this book.

— Voicemail —
T-8 rim lights

(2)

11 Blitz 5 gal (fuel)

11 Wedco 5 gal (Diesel)
(yellow)

6PI
150S

Gear overhaul kit

CHAPTER 2

Configuring Your Nonlinear Editor

THERE'S A BIG difference between installing software and configuring it. It all comes down to power and control. By taking the time to get critical settings right and making some important decisions up front, you can get more tasks done (and feel more confident working with the application).

Being new to Adobe Premiere Pro, you may need to make tiny adjustments to feel comfortable transitioning to this tool (such as remapping keyboard short-cuts or rearranging the panels to your taste). In addition, you'll need to make choices relating to the software and supporting hardware to help you get the best editing performance. The techniques and choices we recommend in this chapter will work for most editors, but as with all configurations, you'll need to customize some of them to your needs and tastes.

FIGURE 2.1 The Preferences dialog offers several groups to make it easy to sort options. Click in the left column to jump to the desired category.

Notable Preferences

The default preferences in Adobe Premiere Pro (**FIGURE 2.1**) are optimized for two situations: First, they allow a new user to start using the tool with few to no adjustments. Second, they attempt to make the learning curve as easy as possible, providing obvious feedback for any user.

We encourage you to explore Adobe Premiere Pro's preferences by choosing Premiere Pro > Preferences (Mac) or Edit > Preferences (Windows). Let's explore the essential preferences that may need some adjustments if you're transitioning from another NLE.

Brightness

In the Appearance category, you'll find one incredibly useful preference, Brightness. This may seem trivial at first, but the Brightness setting really comes in handy. You can adjust how dark or bright the user interface is (**FIGURE 2.2**) by dragging the slider. Depending on what you're used to, you may want to adjust this slider because the Avid and Final Cut Pro interfaces are a different gray than Adobe Premiere Pro. You can also inverse the user interface to black text on white windows by dragging the slider to the left, resulting in a brighter interface. Some editors change the user interface to reduce eyestrain, as well as to accommodate for visual impediments, such as light pollution when editing on a laptop.

FIGURE 2.2 The default user interface (left) can be darkened (center) or lightened (right) to match the personal taste of the editor and accommodate for different lighting conditions.

Play Audio While Scrubbing

Located in the Audio group of the Preferences dialog (**FIGURE 2.3**), the "Play audio while scrubbing" preference is an ideal problem solver. Editors come down on one of two sides of the fence concerning this preference: They either hate having audio scrubbing on or hate having audio scrubbing off (and they'll argue ferociously about it either way).

FIGURE 2.3 Some editors find it useful to hear audio as they drag through a Timeline. This makes it easier to "spot" a clip. If it's distracting, you may want to deselect the "Play audio while scrubbing" option.

Audio Output Mapping

If you use third-party hardware, it's important to visit the Audio Output Mapping preferences. Adobe Premiere Pro can be set to output audio differently than the system default. This is perfect for those of you who are using USB-connected speakers or workstations with hardware monitoring cards, such as those from AJA or Blackmagic Design.

Media Cache Files

Media cache adjustments are found in the Media category. Certain video and audio formats are automatically cached (such as AVCHD, MPEG, and HDV). The cache improves performance for previews because the video and audio files don't need to be reprocessed each time. When you first import media, you may experience a delay while the media is being processed and cached.

A cache file is created for each clip. These cache files take up a small amount of space on your drive (but can add up over time). In the Media category in the Preferences dialog, you can choose to store the files next to the original media files or browse and select a folder (**FIGURE 2.4**).

Besides the individual cache files, Adobe Premiere Pro also keeps a database for its cached files, which is aptly called the Media Cache Database. This database links the cache to the media and speeds up performance when moving clips via Adobe Dynamic Link. If you'd like to clean your database, click the Clean button to remove conformed and indexed files from the cache, as well as remove their entries from the database. Clean removes files from only those clips that are offline.

TCache on Fastest Drive Consider putting your cache on the fastest drive. Putting this on a fast RAID or SSD can really improve project loading and redraws.

Quit If You're Not Using It Six Adobe applications in the CS6 Production Premium collection share resources. Don't leave them open if you're not using them. This will let your system devote as much horsepower to whichever one you're using at that moment.

FIGURE 2.4 If you want to clean up a drive at the end of a project, you should manually navigate to the cache files and delete them. Adobe Premiere Pro can re-cache files in the future when you open the project for revisions. This will eliminate cache files for both online and offline media files.

Memory Allocation

Longtime editors may remember configuring memory settings at the desktop or Finder level. With 64-bit applications, the process is a little different. Adobe Premiere Pro can utilize as much memory as your system can hold (or that you can actually buy). It's important to properly balance how much memory is used by Adobe Premiere Pro (as well as the other Adobe video applications) and other applications on your system.

The adjustment for memory is found under the Memory category. It's possible (and important) to reserve some RAM for other applications (**FIGURE 2.5**). If you need to run other essential applications simultaneously (such as a script application or a facility-wide media cataloging app), you should reserve extra RAM for these applications. Other applications that share memory management are Adobe Media Encoder, Encore, Prelude, After Effects, and Photoshop. This controls the shared memory management between the applications and can intelligently swap memory in the background.

FIGURE 2.5 A good rule of thumb is to install 2 GB to 3 GB of RAM per processor in your computer. RAM is useful when using the Mercury Playback Engine because it will boost your ability to play back video without rendering.

Equally important to your memory management is how rendering is handled. If you're working with a sequence that contains several high-resolution source videos or still images, be sure to set aside large amounts of memory to simultaneously render multiple frames. Leave the "Optimize rendering for" setting at Performance unless you get a Low Memory Warning alert.

Default Scale to Frame Size

In the General category, the "Default scale to frame size" setting is a tricky concept. Oversized stills and footage can be automatically resized to match your sequence frame size on import (**FIGURE 2.6**). There are two different ways Adobe Premiere Pro can behave. You should be aware of what each method does.

FIGURE 2.6 Adobe Premiere Pro automatically will down-sample a large still but rescale it to 100 percent if "Default scale to frame size" is selected.

- When "Default scale to frame size" is deselected (the default), imported oversized elements are left alone and *not* down-sampled when imported. Oversized stills and footage will be left at their original size and resolution. (This is our preferred method.)

- When "Default scale to frame size" is selected, imported oversized elements are set to "fit" the screen, *downsampling* the footage or stills to the size of your sequence.

Understanding Default Scale to Frame Size
In this video you'll learn how the "Default scale to frame size" option handles video and still images.

Why choose one method over the other? It's really a matter of workflow. When selected, you can import higher-resolution files (such as stills) and have them instantly fit the screen size (this is great for a quick slide show of stills). It's important to note that the images *have actually been down-sampled*. Anything more than a slight enlargement may make the images look soft. If you want to "pan and scan" your stills or push in quite a bit of footage, leave this option deselected so you have all the original pixels to work with.

Trim

The Trim category has the ability to refine the trim tools' behaviors. When using the trim tools, it's a common adjustment to trim by a single frame or by a larger offset (FIGURE 2.7). The default offset is five frames, but this can be changed to any number. This is really a personal preference based on your workflow. Most editors choose four frames if they are working with 24p material and five frames if they are working with 25 or 30 fps sources. Whichever number you choose, remember that you can always trim one frame at a time.

FIGURE 2.7 Adobe Premiere Pro lets you specify how many frames you want to trim when using the Large Trim Offset command. Depending on the frame rate of the sequence, four or five frames would be most common. Also note the Section Tool switch.

Roll/Ripple Trims

If you're a fan of quickly sailing down your Timeline and dragging the edge of clips to do a ripple trim, you probably want the choice of "Allow Selection tool to choose Roll and Ripple trims without modifier key" (FIGURE 2.8) turned on. Off is the default setting.

FIGURE 2.8 When this is activated, just position the mouse near the edges of an edit to activate the trim tools.

Player Settings

Very useful under here is the ability to target a second monitor for full-screen playback (FIGURE 2.9). On a two-screen system, turning this on globally uses the second screen to watch footage, which is great when circumstances dictate that hardware output isn't an option.

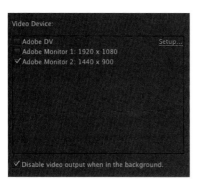

FIGURE 2.9 Turning this on allows the usage of a second screen solely for playback of either the Source Monitor or the Program Monitor.

Downsizing Danger
Because the "Default scale to frame size" option permanently discards pixels, we strongly recommend alternate workflows. Using the Image Processor script in Photoshop or Bridge is a much higher-quality way to scale a copy of your images to the right size.

Downsizing Advantage
On the other hand, by turning on "Default scale to frame size," renders are guaranteed to be faster for oversized elements because Adobe Premiere Pro won't have to push as many pixels.

Closed Captioning Workflow
In this video you'll learn how to sync closed-captioning data with a video project. You'll also explore the options for export.

Keyboard Shortcuts

The use of keyboard shortcuts quickly becomes an essential part of an experienced editor's workflow (**FIGURE 2.10**). The more you use the keyboard and the less you click buttons on-screen, the faster you will be with Adobe Premiere Pro (or any given piece of software). After all, you never see a concert pianist plucking notes one at a time using a mouse. You want to drive the editing system, and nothing does that faster than the keyboard.

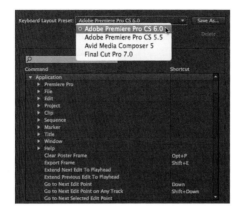

Keys to Smooth Migration Several companies, such as Bella USA (www.bella-usa.com) and Logic Keyboards (www. logickeyboard.com), make keyboards and skins that are colorized to help you learn and use Adobe Premiere Pro faster.

The Devil Is in the Details No matter how close the keyboard settings mimic the NLE you're comfortable with, there will be differences. They say the devil is in the details. It's likely that you'll be irritated when you find a keyboard behavior different from what you expect. When this happens, take a deep breath and remind yourself that you're working with a new tool. Sometimes different is better (with new opportunities for speed and efficiency), and sometimes different is just different.

Why Swap Shortcuts? The ability to swap the keyboard layout preset makes switching between NLEs more comfortable and convenient for many editors. You can choose between two Adobe Premiere Pro layouts, a layout for Final Cut Pro 7, or a layout for Avid Media Composer 5. Remember that these keyboards are a quick start, but they're not perfect!

The Default Keyboard Shortcuts

With Adobe Premiere Pro CS6, several of the keyboard shortcuts have been tweaked. What you'll find is that the new set takes several of the most used keys and updates them to close match common shortcuts used by other applications.

To view the keyboard shortcuts, choose Premiere Pro > Keyboard Shortcuts (Mac) or Edit > Keyboard Shortcuts (Windows).

Of course you'll need to learn Adobe's keyboard shortcuts. Or do you?

While writing this book, we had several intense discussions about whether those of you coming from a different NLE system should have to learn and adapt to the built-in keyboard layout preset for Adobe Premiere Pro. Or should you use one of the settings designed to mimic Final Cut Pro 7 or Avid Media Composer 5? Here are the two basic arguments concerning the use of the default keyboard shortcuts:

- **Using the native keyboard layout preset.** You should learn how to become an Adobe Premiere Pro editor, not a Final Cut Pro editor who happens to use Adobe Premiere Pro. By adapting to the tool, you can better dive into its deep use. You'll get the optimum advantage of learning which keys product designers thought were most important (and less important or not even mapped!).

- **Using a different keyboard layout preset.** If you're in a rush, the fastest way for you to get started and have the least amount of relearning to do is to choose the keyboard shortcuts that closely mimic an editorial application you feel more comfortable with. You can also use this as a starting point and continue to modify the keys as needed.

The grave accent (`) key is the single most important key (FIGURE 2.11), especially if you're using a laptop or a single screen. Press it, and whatever panel your mouse is on top of expands to full-screen. Press it again, and everything returns to normal.

This makes it quick and easy to toggle any panel—Project, Program, Timeline—to full-screen and back.

Starting with Premiere Pro CS6, if you hit Control+` (grave), it will make the Program Monitor or Source Monitor completely full-screen, which is fantastic on a laptop or with a client. This is called Cinema mode.

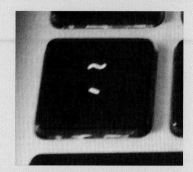

FIGURE 2.11 The ` is called the grave accent. And the squiggle? It's called a tilde.

Essential Keys
You'll find useful keyboard shortcut guides organized by task on the book's DVD-ROM or in the digital downloads folder.

Using an International Keyboard?
The grave accent shortcut isn't universal. If using a different language you may need to remap the key or look up the new assignment in the keyboard shortcut list.

Search for Shortcuts
In Adobe Premiere Pro CS6, a search box in the Keyboard Shortcuts dialog allows you to search for features. This is a great way to find a specific feature.

Remap with Logic
If you choose to map items to the keyboard, try to make them obvious. Using a sticker above the F keys on the keyboard with notes may be a way you've worked in the past, but it means you're still looking up the answer on the physical keyboard. Find a way for the keys to actually make sense. Think about customizing keys on the keyboard that are physically comfortable to access or that relate to a key's label with a mnemonic.

Print Your Shortcuts
Holding down Command+Shift (Ctrl+Shift) when opening the shortcuts dialog yields a clipboard button. You can then copy the keyboard and paste it into your text editor of choice, allowing you to search or print all the keys.

Customizing Shortcuts

As you work more and more in Adobe Premiere Pro, you'll desire more speed. This is why Adobe Premiere Pro offers a fully remappable keyboard. We suggest you keep a tally of how frequently you are forced to go to a menu or right-click for a given feature. If you find that you're using a feature frequently, then that's worth remapping.

To remap a keyboard shortcut, open the Keyboard Shortcuts or Keyboard Customization panel as discussed previously. Locate the command you want to customize. The search box at the top is a great way to find specific commands. Make sure you repeat your search in both the Application menu and Panels menu. You may find that common names for the interface that Apple and Avid use are different from those in Adobe Premiere Pro.

1. Select a command to remap. You can use the search field or scroll through the list, which is organized by menus, panels, and tools.

2. Double-click the field next to a shortcut.

3. Enter a keyboard combination. You can also use modifier keys such as Shift, Command (Ctrl), or Option (Alt). If you choose a shortcut already in use, Adobe Premiere Pro will warn you.

4. Click OK to save the set. You can also click Save As to give the set a new name that makes it easier to locate and permanently stores it.

Recommended Remapping for Final Cut Pro 7 Editors

Expert Final Cut Pro 7 editors are used to selecting tools by pressing a selection key multiple times. For example, in Final Cut Pro, you can press S multiple times to cycle between Slip and Slide. Adobe Premiere Pro *does not* have an equivalent behavior, so you'll want to give edit tools some special thought.

TABLE 2.1 contains the shortcut key remappings we recommend.

TABLE 2.1 Recommended Additional Final Cut Pro Remappings

Function	Shortcut	Function	Shortcut
Ripple	Shift+R	Timeline	Command+3 (Ctrl+3)
Slide	Shift+S	Project	Command+4 (Ctrl+4)
Set Editing Workspace (Workspace 3)	Control+U	Effects	Command+5 (Ctrl+5)
Paste Effects (Paste attributes)	Shift+V	Trim	Command+7 (Ctrl+7)
Remove Effects (Remove attributes)	Command+Option+V (Ctrl+Alt+V)	Capture	Command+8 (Ctrl+8)
Clip enable	Control+B	Audio Transition	Command+Shift+D (Ctrl+Shift+D)
Source Monitor	Command+1 (Ctrl+1)	Replace With Clip (From Source Monitor, Match Frame)	F11
Program Monitor	Command+2 (Ctrl+2)		

Recommended Remapping for Avid Media Composer Editors

Because Avid is a modal-based editor (you need to activate Effect mode or Trim mode to perform those functions), you'll find that you need to activate a given tool or window in Adobe Premiere Pro for the equivalent ability. Here are some suggestions to make the transition easier:

- **Become familiar with the tools.** The Selection tool acts like the Red/Yellow Segment modes, but it does quite a bit more.

- **There is no Effect mode.** Just click the clip and go to the Effects panel to add an effect.

- **There is no Trim mode.** Similarly, the closest you get to Avid's Trim mode is to use the Trim panel.

- **There is no Color Correction mode.** Color corrections effects have to be added manually to clips like other video effects.

Many of these remapped items aren't necessarily identical to the tools in Media Composer; instead, they try to approximate the best possible compromise. We suggest you use the changes in TABLE 2.2 to modify the default Avid keyboard layout that is provided. At times, the software will object that you're replacing a used key; take a good look at what the objection is and test the function, and then if you're confident that you won't need it bound to the key, feel free to ignore the objection.

TABLE 2.2 Recommended Additional Avid Remappings

Function	Shortcut
Selection tool	' (single quote) next to the Enter key
Trim	U
Toggle Trim Type	Option+U (Alt+U)
Mark Clip	T
Trim Backward	, (comma)
Trim Forward	. (period)
Trim Backward Many	M
Trim Forward Many	/ (forward slash)
Extend Edit	2
Ripple Trim Next Edit to Playhead (tail)	1
Ripple Trim Previous Edit to Playhead (top)	3

Backing Up and Moving Shortcuts

Whether you're a freelancer and floating between different suites or an individual user, you'll want to back up your keyboard layout that you use in Adobe Premiere Pro. Saving the keyboard shortcuts is straightforward; just click the Save button (**FIGURE 2.12**).

From the Keyboard Shortcuts panel, choose Save.

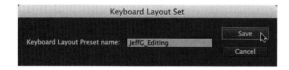

FIGURE 2.12 When you save your keyboard shortcuts, use a memorable name, such as *your full name_keyboard*. Adobe Premiere Pro will add the .kys extension.

Copying your keyboard layout and moving presets is a bit more complex. The file you need to look for has the extension .kys. You can find your keyboard settings on your machine by navigating to a specific folder. Its location depends on your operating system.

Finding the KYS File on a Mac

To find the Adobe Premiere Pro Custom.kys file, look in your User/Library/Application Support/Adobe/Premiere Pro/6.0 folder.

To get to this folder on your Mac, follow these steps:

1. In the Finder, choose Go > Go to Folder, or use the keyboard shortcut Command+Shift+G.

 Navigating to User Home Folder
If you're wondering why you can't navigate directly to your user Library folder via the Finder in OS 10.7, it's because Apple has hidden it! Using the Go to Folder command is the easiest way to access this hidden folder.

2. Type **~/Library/Application Support/Adobe/Premiere Pro/6.0** (the tilde [~] key is on the top left of your keyboard); see **FIGURE 2.13**.

FIGURE 2.13 You must type this path exactly or it won't work.

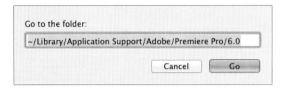

3. Copy the Adobe Premiere Pro Custom.kys file to wherever you like—a USB drive, a media drive, or even Dropbox.

Finding the KYS File on a Windows Machine

The Adobe Premiere Pro Custom.kys file is a little harder to get to on a Windows machine. It's in the User\AppData\Roaming\Adobe\Premiere Pro\6 folder. In Windows, this is a hidden directory. The AppData folder contains data and preferences for your Windows login and is normally hidden.

To get to this folder, follow these steps:

1. Start Windows Explorer.

2. On the left side, double-click the C: drive to open it, double-click the Users folder, and then double-click your username folder (**FIGURE 2.14**).

FIGURE 2.14 The folder with your username is where all your personal key preference files are in Windows.

3. Click in the Location bar and add **\AppData** (FIGURE 2.15). You'll then be able to see the hidden folder and continue navigating to the Adobe Premiere Pro data you need.

FIGURE 2.15
Click in the Location bar to be able to navigate to the hidden AppData folder.

4. Double-click each successive folder, namely, Roaming, Adobe, Premiere Pro, and 6 (**FIGURE 2.16**).

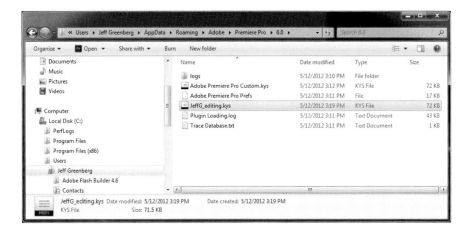

FIGURE 2.16 If you need to access the keyboard frequently, it's worth making a shortcut here in Windows.

5. Copy the Adobe Premiere Pro Custom.kys file anywhere you like—a USB drive, a media drive, or even Dropbox.

Once you've retrieved your shortcuts, all you have to do is copy that file to the equivalent location on another machine and your keyboard will appear in Adobe Premiere Pro.

No Buttons At All
Most professional editors are very keyboard-centric and feel that the buttons are a waste of space. They can be removed by going to the Program panel menu in the upper right and unchecking "Show Transport Controls."

Unhappy with Your Button Layout?
Don't forget there's a reset button, which will quickly reset the buttons to the default set.

Buy the Right Card
It is highly recommended that you consult the Adobe Premiere Pro system requirements and choose a graphics card that lets you utilize the CUDA/OpenCL technologies. A good resource for more information on the Adobe Premiere Pro requirements can be found at www.adobe.com/products/premiere/tech-specs.html.

Customizing Source/Program Buttons

A welcome addition to CS6 is the ability to customize the Source Monitor and Program Monitor panels. In versions prior to CS6, the Source Monitor and Program Monitor panels were cluttered, making it difficult for a novice editor to determine which buttons were most important. Worse yet, with the clutter, it forced the video to be scaled down quite a bit. This part of the user interface was a major improvement in CS6.

To adjust the buttons, find the small plus (+) sign button in the bottom-right corner of the Source Monitor and Program Monitor panels (FIGURE 2.17). This button permits drag-and-drop customization of the buttons underneath each monitor.

Let's customize the Program Monitor.

Navigate to Lessons and Media, and open the project called 02_settings.prproj.

After the project has opened, click the + button in the lower-right side of the Program Monitor panel (FIGURE 2.18).

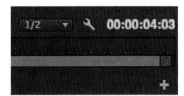

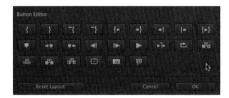

FIGURE 2.17 Press the small + in the lower-right corner to open the Button Editor.

FIGURE 2.18 Feel free to remove buttons that you'll never use. Do you really need a Play button if you're always going to use the spacebar?

You can customize these buttons to your liking; the two buttons that we find ourselves often adding are the Loop Playback and Safe Margins buttons. Let's add them now.

Drag the Safe Margins button (third row, fourth column) to the right of all the buttons already docked on the Program Monitor. It's a little tricky; dragging it too far to the right will place it on a second row.

Drag the Loop Playback button (second row, eighth column) to in between the Play button and the One Frame Right button. Optionally, you can also add a spacer to separate buttons a bit more.

The finished version looks like FIGURE 2.19.

FIGURE 2.19 A completed set of buttons. Don't forget the spacer in the bottom right; it'll let you add space in between buttons!

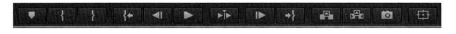

1. Click OK to store the new settings and close the Button Editor.
2. Try toggling on the Safer Margins overlay.
3. Turn on the Loop Playback option, and press Play. Let the sequence play to the end to see the loop.
4. (Optional) Reset the toolbar to the default settings. We reset ours so it'd resemble a default button bar for the rest of the text.

Mercury Playback Engine Performance

The 64-bit Mercury Playback Engine is the core technology that makes Adobe Premiere Pro fast and stable. When it's properly configured (and powered), you can mix several different formats together in the same Timeline and still achieve real-time playback. In fact, you can also get GPU-accelerated effects and transitions.

Although the graphics card plays a big role in the Mercury Playback Engine, it's important to note that the engine encompasses three features.

- **64-bit application.** To run Adobe Premiere Pro CS6, you'll need a 64-bit operating system. Make sure you're using at least the minimum supported version of OS X or Windows 7. See www.adobe.com/products/premiere/tech-specs.html for the system requirements to run Adobe Premiere Pro.

- **Multithreaded application.** Adobe Premiere Pro likes RAM (lots of RAM in fact). A good measuring stick is to have 2 GB to 3 GB of RAM per processor in your system. You can get by with less, but why starve a fire of oxygen?

- **Processes certain elements using Graphics Processor Unit (GPU) acceleration.** Adobe with Premiere Pro 5 and newer embraced Compute Unified Device Architecture (CUDA), which is NVIDIA's parallel computing architecture that enables dramatic increases in computing performance by harnessing the power of the GPU (graphics card) rather than the CPU. Starting with CS6, Open Computing Language (Open CL) is another technology that Adobe has adopted that accelerates even more hardware (at this time officially on a few Macintosh systems). This means that *the right video display cards* are optimized to handle the pushing of pixels, accelerating Adobe Premiere Pro effects significantly.

Even if you don't have a video card that takes advantage of these technologies, you'll still get significant performance improvement thanks to the Mercury Playback Engine.

Real-Time Workflow

Unfortunately, there's no magic formula to guarantee your system performance. The reason is that the more compressed codecs (such as HDV, AVCHD, and MPEG-4) require lots of horsepower, and uncompressed formats require a fast drive throughput. So, each combination of CPU, drive speed, GPU card, and RAM is unique. You'll find that the common Timeline colors mean slightly different things (**FIGURE 2.20**) and don't necessarily mean you're not going to get real-time playback.

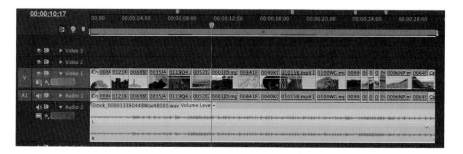

You Always Get Acceleration, Even Without a Supported GPU

A common misconception about Adobe Premiere Pro is that if you don't have the right video card, you don't get acceleration. The video card certainly helps the Mercury Playback Engine, but the engine is far more than just the video card.

NVIDIA Maximus

Want the maximum GPU acceleration? At the time of writing this book, NVIDIA has a technology called Maximus. To use it, you'll have to purchase a specific NVIDIA Quadro graphics card, along with a NVIDIA Tesla card (more or less it's a Quadro without the outputs). They get combined: the Quadro card draws the screen, and the Premiere Pro UI and the Tesla card do all the MPE acceleration. You'll need a PC configuration that supports slots (sorry, Mac users...sorry, laptop users), but this configuration makes Adobe Premiere Pro snappy even with H.264 footage.

AJA Test or Black Magic Disk Speed

AJA Video Systems and Black Magic Design both have excellent free tools to measure drive throughput specifically for video performance. You can download them at www.aja.com/products/software and www.blackmagic-design.com/support/.

FIGURE 2.20 Red colors in the Timeline do not mean bad things! You'll still often get real-time playback (but perhaps a few dropped frames). Adobe Premiere Pro will just render for final output, not Timeline playback. See the "A Word About Workflow in Adobe Premiere Pro" sidebar for greater detail.

Don't Panic
Many editors migrating to Adobe Premiere Pro become concerned when they see yellow and red bars in their Timeline. Don't worry: This does not mean your sequence won't play (or even that real time is disabled). See the sidebar "A Word About Workflow in Adobe Premiere Pro" for more information.

Reduce the Resolution
One great method of improving playback is especially relevant with non-GPU-accelerated systems. At the bottom of the Source and Record Monitors is a pop-up menu that looks like a wrench where you can choose Select Playback Resolution. You can change this resolution to 1/2 or 1/4. Other options are available depending on the resolution of the video. Because Adobe Premiere Pro doesn't have to compute all the pixels, performance is improved.

A WORD ABOUT WORKFLOW IN ADOBE PREMIERE PRO

Several times in this book you'll see this sentence repeated: Timeline colors don't mean what you think. This has very much to do with the fact that Adobe Premier Pro is designed to make significant dynamic adaptations on the fly to give you the best-quality playback possible.

Here's how to properly handle your final output:

- **Tape output.** If you go to tape, you may need to render. If available, the Mercury Transmit architecture helps, but you should test to see your system's capabilities.

- **Digital output.** When you go to other digital formats, Adobe Premiere Pro defaults to *bypass any render files* and directly renders in the output codec of your choice, although you have the option to utilize existing renders for faster output.

The three Timeline colors in Adobe Premier Pro are red, yellow, and green. These colors don't mean the same things as they do in other editing applications.

- **Green.** This segment has a rendered preview file associated with it. Playback will use the rendered preview file. Playback is at full quality and is certain to be in real time (as long as your drives are fast enough).

- **Yellow.** This segment doesn't have a rendered preview file associated with it. Each frame will be dynamically rendered just before the playhead reaches it. Playback at full quality will probably be in real time (but it might not be). Effects sections are typically being handled by the GPU accelerated graphics card, if available.

- **Red.** This segment doesn't have a rendered preview file associated with it. Each frame will be dynamically rendered just before the current-time indicator reaches it. Playback at full quality will probably *not* be in real time (but it *might* be).

- **None.** This segment doesn't have a rendered preview file associated with it. The codec used for the source media is simple enough that Adobe Premiere Pro can treat the media file as its own preview file. Playback at full quality is certain to be in real time but occurs for only a few codecs (including DV and DVCPRO).

The key concept here is to optimize the use of the Mercury Playback Engine. You can also adjust the resolution of the Program Monitor to half or quarter quality. Formats that are a struggle in other NLEs can be played back in real time without rendering. Just press Play and see what happens. A well-configured Adobe Premiere Pro system will often surprise you.

The guidelines listed on Adobe's Web site should be recognized for what they are—*the minimum* system requirements. Of course, the more you spend tweaking your system, the more it can handle. The key is to match your needs and budget. Don't overdevelop one area of your system (such as the graphics card) while neglecting another (like RAM).

Just like a good workout, you need to balance your system building.

The crucial elements to a real-time workflow include the following:

- **Using many cores.** Choose the fastest multicore CPU you can get your hands on that is supported by Adobe Premiere Pro. A hyper-threaded CPU is a must; each core gets two threads!

- **Increasing your RAM.** Although 4 GB of RAM is recommended, we suggest even more. A minimum of 8 GB of RAM is adequate, *especially* if you intend to use multiple applications in the Creative Suite simultaneously or work with HD video or RED footage. We've said it before, 2 GB to 3 GB per core is a good match for speed and performance.

- **Adding a GPU supported card.** Specific NVIDIA CUDA cards and specific OSX systems (OpenCL) will benefit with accelerated GPU performance. If your computer manufacturer doesn't sell cards supported by Adobe Premiere Pro, you may need to remove or upgrade the built-in card on a system and replace it yourself. For laptops, this is not an option.

- **Utilizing fast hard drives (7200 RPM or faster).** Make sure your drives can keep up with your data. Also, consider a RAID system for increased performance when you're working with uncompressed or high-bitrate formats. Multicamera editing also benefits from a RAID setup.

Measuring System Load

Just like racecar drivers need to see their tachometer and speedometer, so do editors need to see their system load (**FIGURE 2.21**). Closely monitoring performance makes it easier to balance the load by adjusting hardware or playback settings. A great way to learn what is stressing your system is to open the Activity Monitor (Mac) or the Resource Monitor (Windows).

- **Macintosh.** The Activity Monitor is found in Applications/Utilities/Activity Monitor.

- **Windows.** The easiest way to start the Resource Monitor (**FIGURE 2.22**) is to click the Start menu and search for *Resource Monitor* in the search box.

On either platform, you want to identify the culprits if you're having playback problems. Watch the CPU usage, memory usage, and disk usage when you play back video. If one or more values peak, it's likely that they're the weak links in your playback chain.

Speed Demon with an SSD Solid-state drives (SSDs) are becoming more and more common on systems; they're many times faster than the fastest hard drives. When they're built into a RAID, it's possible to get nearly maximum throughput when playing back your video. This hardware choice is particularly important in video formats with high data rates, such as RED or Alexa.

Dropping Frames? Editors tend not to worry about dropping frames while creating a story, but it's crucial to know whether your system drops frames during playback, because sooner or later it has to be addressed, especially with playout through an I/O card. Under the Settings menu (the wrench) of the Program Monitor is a dropped frames indicator. It's definitely worth turning on!

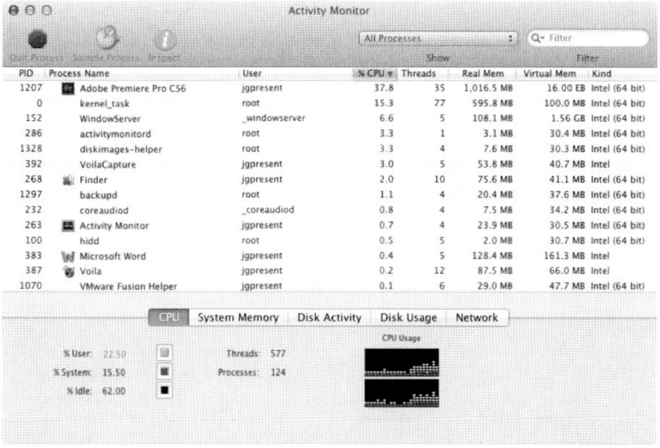

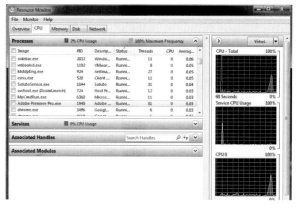

FIGURE 2.21 A CPU that's maxed out may mean your system is underpowered.

FIGURE 2.22 The Windows Task Manager is good, but the Resource Monitor is even better for monitoring your system performance. With it, the CPU is barely working.

Which Card? What Format?
You can find a full list of supported capture and monitoring cards at www.adobe.com/products/premiere/extend.html. You can also find a useful table of cards by format there.

A Note About Stock Music
The music used in this exercise is from iStockphoto.com. It offers a wide selection of clips to choose from that are royalty-free. Thanks for allowing us to use the music in this book.

Monitoring and Capture Solutions

Once upon a time the entire video world was tape-based. All input came in via a composite, component, or SDI (and later HD-SDI) connection. Expensive decks sat on the other end, and you'd control both the deck and the tape from within the software with machine control protocols.

Today, an increasing amount of footage is being captured from file-based sources and direct-to-disk or card cameras. You'll also find that more and more exports are to digital formats. However, certain video environments, such as the broadcast and educational worlds, are still very much tape-based.

Input/Output Cards

Input/output (I/O) cards and monitoring solutions are key components in tape-based workflows. They permit access and control of decks, as well as fully uncompressed output. I/O cards with a Broadcast monitor are necessary for professional monitoring. Some cards even permit cross conversion (between 1080 and 720) or down conversion (to SD) in real time.

Four major companies manufacture ingest/playback solutions.

- **AJA.** www.aja.com

- **Blackmagic Design.** www.blackmagic-design.com

- **Bluefish444.** www.bluefish444.com

- **Matrox.** www.matrox.com

Mercury Transmit

In earlier versions of Adobe Premiere Pro, GPU cards could not assist in output when using a third-party I/O card, like they could when playing back to the screen .

When you switched to the I/O card, all the effect-driven GPU benefits went away.

Starting in CS6, the Mercury Transmit architecture permits the GPU benefits of the Mercury Playback Engine to be leveraged to the I/O card, meaning that MPE-accelerated effects get the same benefit for output as they do to the screen.

When doing a playout to tape or playout server, make sure to test the system first. Many editors still render everything before mission-critical playback.

Next Steps

We've covered the major preferences, allowing you to understand and tweak Adobe Premiere Pro. Now that you have the application running and properly configured, it's time to start working with media. Let's get organized! You'll learn how to set up and configure new projects, as well as understand how to choose correct presets, modify project settings, and even bring in projects from other NLEs.

CHAPTER 3

Setting Up a Project

IT IS SAID that every journey begins with a single step. Postproduction is no different. Taking that first step blindly can lead to headaches and pain— no matter how good your footage or nonlinear editing (NLE) application. It's crucial that you choose an appropriate starting point. This generally means setting up an Adobe Premiere Pro project with the correct preset, but you may need to create a custom starting point as well.

In this chapter, you'll learn to set up a new project and how to turn that setup into a template. You'll explore the details of creating sequences and sequence presets, and you'll learn how to modify an existing project.

Using the New Project Panel

When you launch Adobe Premiere Pro from your Dock or Start menu (as opposed to double-clicking an existing project), you'll see the Welcome screen. This screen displays the five most recent projects you've opened. It also gives you the ability to start a new project, open an existing project, or just get help (**FIGURE 3.1**). Click the New Project icon to switch to the New Project dialog.

The New Project dialog offers several choices for your project (**FIGURE 3.2**). You need to make specific choices as to how video and audio details are displayed as well as what format (if any) to capture from. You can also specify where you'd like to store your capture and preview files. It's crucial to stay organized from the beginning of a project.

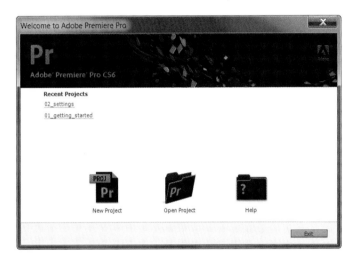

FIGURE 3.1 Starting a new project is just a click away. The most recent project list is also a quick way to open a recent project.

FIGURE 3.2 This is the first window you'll see when you start a project (top right). Don't forget to name your project! Untitled is a terrible name.

Video Rendering and Playback

If you're coming from using another NLE, it's likely that you're expecting to see something here about renders. At a certain level, the video and audio previews can act like render files.

But the Mercury Playback Engine (MPE) handles the need (or lack thereof) for renders a bit differently than you're used to.

Based on your system configuration (the CPU, RAM, drive type, and speeds), the MPE provides *software* acceleration. This is part of Adobe Premiere Pro being written as a 64-bit application to optimally utilize your hardware. It's referred to as Software Only Engine in the Renderer drop-down menu.

Adobe specifically supports certain video cards (based on CUDA and/or Open CL technologies) to provide extra acceleration to certain key effects, such as the Three-Way Color Corrector. These effects are handled by the graphics processing unit (GPU) for a hardware-accelerated system, shown as GPU Acceleration (CUDA) in the drop-down menu. You can find specifics on these cards at www.adobe.com/products/premiere/tech-specs.html.

Video/Audio Display Format

The Video Display Format and Audio Display Format settings offer different choices but several similar functions. Both control how Adobe Premiere Pro displays the counting method for video and audio.

Your options for Video Display Format include the following:

- **Timecode.** This option varies based on your sequence frame rate.

- **Feet + Frames 16mm or 35mm.** The 16mm and 35mm film options are for working with film-based projects.

- **Frames.** Animators tend to think in frames, because they constantly have to break down time into regular increments to create actions (such as a character moving). If you were an animator and wanted a ball to bounce over 4 seconds, you'd find that it's much harder to divide 4:00 seconds (at 30 fps) by 6 than by 120 frames (the equivalent of 4 seconds counting by frames).

Your options for Audio Display Format include the following:

- **Audio Samples.** Sound can be displayed in samples the way they're captured, such as 48 kHz (48000 samples per second).

- **Milliseconds.** Sound can also be measured in time—in millionths of seconds.

Capture Format Settings

When you choose to capture (as opposed to import), you must have a physical connection between your computer and a tape deck or camera. By default, Adobe Premiere Pro supports the use of the FireWire port on your computer (**FIGURE 3.3**). This allows for two types of capture, either DV or HDV. You can also add a third-party capture card to allow additional connection options, such as SDI, HD-SDI, HDMI, or component video.

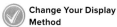
Change Your Display Method

If it ever becomes necessary, you can change the way Adobe Premiere Pro displays the video and audio information. Just choose Sequence > Sequence Settings and choose the desired display method.

FIGURE 3.3 FireWire connects cameras and decks to systems. As great as USB is, it can't transmit timecode information.

Keep Your Boot Drive Clean
You might feel comfortable storing your project files on your desktop, but we strongly advise against keeping your media on the startup or main hard drive of your computer.

Imports Are _Not_ Captured!
Imports are not moved into the captured video folder. This makes handling of file-based workflows a bit more complicated. Typically, footage from tapeless media will be transferred or transcoded to another drive and from there imported into Adobe Premiere Pro. Adobe Premiere Pro doesn't move this media to its scratch disk location. Also, keep in mind that in tapeless workflows you'll often end up with the camera original files (often as a disk image) and transferred or transcoded media on disk, essentially taking up double the amount of storage space.

Target Additional Drives When Possible
Ideally, your project assets and render files should exist on your media drives. Only in a pinch (such as in the field) should you store them on a laptop drive.

DEVICE CONTROL

Although the full Device Control settings are found in the Preferences panel, they work hand in hand with your Capture settings. For optimal deck or camera performance, be sure to check to see how Adobe Premiere Pro is handling the connected hardware (FIGURE 3.4).

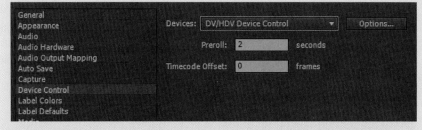

FIGURE 3.4 The Devices menu (found in the Preferences) contains the type of connections to Adobe Premiere Pro if you're using a hardware card; otherwise, it's DV (via FireWire).

Decks and cameras need a bit more time for tape to get up to speed and be usable. Change the pre-roll to at least four seconds, preferably six. HDV suffers because it's storing Long GOP MPEG-2 files on a tape, which are more difficult to capture. By making the pre-roll longer, Adobe Premiere Pro will have a chance to get a more stable stream from the tape.

You can attain better communication with your deck or camera by adjusting the Device Control options to specify your actual deck or camera (FIGURE 3.5). If your deck or camera is not listed, try the Generic setting.

FIGURE 3.5 Deck control is vital for capture and for recapture in the future.

Project Files

Toward the bottom of the General tab in the New Project dialog is an area where you save the project and name the project.

Be sure to specify a unique name for your project file. To choose a destination in which to store it, just click the Browse button. You can also click the menu next to Location to see a list of recently used locations.

Wherever your project is stored, Adobe Premiere Pro will also create interchange folders for working between different applications in the Creative Suite along with Auto Save folders. We recommend targeting a specific folder (ideally on a dedicated media drive) rather than your desktop to keep all these files together.

Scratch Disks

Also in the New Project dialog is a very important tab called Scratch Disks. As you work in Adobe Premiere Pro, it will create media. In some cases, that media can include captured video or audio. In all cases Adobe Premiere Pro will generate video and audio previews that speed up how clips load and cache, as well as the display of audio waveforms.

Where should you store your project? Where should you store your media? Well, there are two general philosophies about how to handle media:

- **Project-based setup.** All media and the project file are saved in the same place—in a dedicated project folder.

- **System-based setup.** Media is saved to one central location, and the project file is saved to another.

Using a project-based setup

By default, Adobe Premiere Pro will keep any created media together with the project file you create (**FIGURE 3.6**). Because this means that all files end up living in the same location, locating files is fairly simple. You can find all your render files and previews in one location (only imports and file-based media will need to be handled manually to specify where they'll live on your system).

FIGURE 3.6
Your project plus all created media stored in one location makes captured media well controlled.

Using a system-based setup

Some editors feel more comfortable knowing that all their media is stored in a single location. If you choose to store your Capture folders and Preview folders in a different location than your project, we suggest creating a folder named Adobe Media and storing it on the root of an external drive or on a dedicated media drive or array on your system and targeting new projects to that location.

File-Based Media? Two Times Is Better!
Every hard drive will eventually fail! In fact, each manufacturer provides the average fail time right on the side of the box! If you're in the field using a file-based camera, it's worth duplicating the media right there, just in case a drive dies. And solid-state drives? Having no moving parts makes that failure rate far, far smaller!

It turns out that various manufacturers take some very different approaches to how media is stored. Here's a quick summary to help you spot pitfalls in your workflow or correct some of the assumptions you might hold:

- **Adobe Premiere Pro.** With Adobe Premiere Pro, the default is to store the media with your project file. This simplifies backing up and moving projects. Because all the captured video and audio live in the same place as the media, it makes the essential media functions (such as copying) fairly straightforward. Because the media storage is set on a per-project basis, the media and project always live together. The only loose items you need to "wrangle" are imports (keep in mind that files in file-based cameras are considered imports).

- **Apple Final Cut Pro.** When using Final Cut Pro, you can choose to target scratch disks to store media. When acquiring footage from file-based or tape-based cameras, all files are stored in the capture scratch. The biggest struggle with this is that you still have to corral all of your imports such as graphics, music, and so on.

- **Avid Media Composer.** Avid is a little different. It keeps the projects (usually) in your shared folder on your main system and creates an Avid Media Files folder on each drive at its root. All media is stored here and catalogued in the database. Any files (especially stills) imported into Avid are reduced to video-sized resolutions. Avid *also* has a second method—called Avid Media Access (AMA), which is similar to linking, the way CS6 and Final Cut Pro works—meaning you have to keep an eye on where your imports are or face issues with media offline.

Creating a Sequence

After setting up a new project and clicking OK, you'll be prompted to create a new default sequence in the New Sequence dialog.

If you have no idea what to do here, don't panic—just hit Cancel. You can set up a sequence that matches your footage in several ways (covered next).

Meanwhile, the dialog contains a long list with several categories (FIGURE 3.7). At first, the choices might seem a little intimidating, especially when you're not sure of what kind of footage you have or what the final output will be. So, which sequence preset should you choose? Read on.

Choosing the Correct Preset

The Sequence Preset panel enables you to set up the specific format settings, previews, and the kind of video and audio tracks that will be created by default for a given sequence. Presets are available for virtually every camera format frame size and frame rate.

Sequence presets can be a bit overwhelming at first, because so many choices are available. The key is to understand what type of footage you have and use a preset (or build one) optimized to the kind of video you're handling.

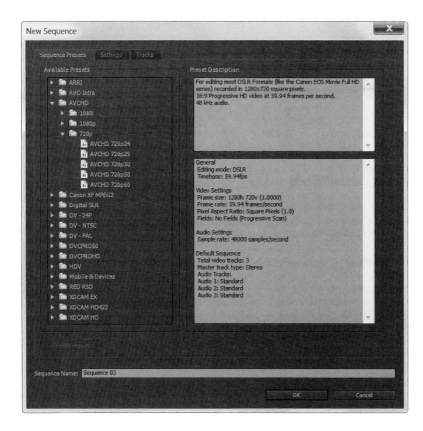

FIGURE 3.7 Although it seems like there is a multitude of choices, it really comes down to the frame size and frame rate. In Selecting a matching preset for your footage helps Adobe Premiere Pro perform optimally.

If you're not sure which sequence preset to choose after creating a project, there are three ways to create a sequence that matches your footage.

In the Lessons and Media folder, there's a project called 03_Choosing Presets that you can try all three of these methods with.

■ Drag either of the two clips to an empty sequence. You'll be presented with a Clip Mismatch Warning dialog. Choose Change Sequence Settings to match to your footage (**FIGURE 3.8**). This works only if the first clip you add is video. This is a new feature in Adobe Premiere Pro CS6.

FIGURE 3.8 The default for the Clip Mismatch Warning dialog (new to Adobe Premiere Pro in CS6) is to keep the existing settings (which is great when your sequence is correct). Be careful if you're used to pressing the Return key, which selects the default, because it won't convert the sequence to match your settings. Rather, it keeps the existing sequence settings.

■ Right-click any clip and choose New Sequence from Clip, building a sequence that matches your footage.

■ Drag an individual piece of footage onto the New Item icon (which looks like a pad of paper) at the bottom of the Project panel (this also works in Adobe After Effects).

Understanding the Makeup of Sequence Presets

Understanding how sequence presets work make choosing the right one quite a bit easier. Again, we really like the fact that Adobe's design team has made it possible for you to "just get to work" with your footage, by picking one of the three methods mentioned earlier to start working.

But we also understand that there's a technical need to understand what's going on here. Any given sequence can be defined by four properties:

- The *mode* is a combination of frame size, pixel aspect ratio, field dominance, audio sample rate, and preview codec that Adobe Premiere Pro should use to edit.

- The *frame size* includes which pixel aspect ratio to use (square or non-square).

- The *audio sample rate* includes common rates, such as 48000 Hz.

- *Video preview files*, which are the kind of preview files built, may act in some cases like render files.

If you're used to other NLE systems, you'll notice that one significant property is missing. A codec *isn't* part of the list. Adobe Premiere Pro handles the footage through the Mercury Playback Engine regardless of footage type.

This allows for seamlessly mixing codecs within the same sequence with little to no performance hit. Another thing to keep in mind with presets is that as you expand the functionality of your edit system, your sequence presets list will increase. If you add a third-party I/O card, for example, extra presets will be available just for that card.

In Adobe Premiere Pro prior to CS6, you could get your MPE acceleration *or* output through your I/O card. You couldn't get accelerated performance when you chose to send video to the I/O card.

In CS6, you now have that acceleration thanks to a technology that Adobe calls Mercury Transmit. Essentially, this technology "transmits" the MPE acceleration to the I/O card.

The selection process

Now that you understand how Adobe Premiere Pro works with sequence presets, choosing a specific sequence preset is straightforward. We recommend knowing the primary type of footage used in the sequence, because this is a quick way of correctly configuring settings (**FIGURE 3.9**) such as frame size and pixel aspect ratio.

FIGURE 3.9 If you had DSLR 1080p24 footage, this preset would be a perfect match.

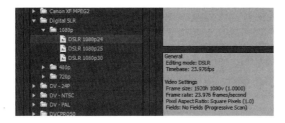

To choose a format from the presets, follow these steps:

1. Select the type of footage used most in the sequence (or the one you want to master to), such as XDCAM HD, DVCPROHD, or RED R3D.

2. Twirl down the Category folder for the selected format.

3. Select the frame size for the format. You may also need to choose whether the footage is progressive or interlaced.

4. Twirl down the frame size folder for the selected size.

5. Select the frame rate for the primary sources.

6. Enter a name for your first sequence and click OK.

   A new sequence is added to the Project panel.

Although choosing a preset is useful, you'll occasionally want to customize a preset to better fit your workflow. To do that, you need to go back to the New Sequence dialog. Choose File > New Sequence. In the next section, read about how to customize sequence presets.

Creating Custom Sequence Settings

Beyond presets lies the ability to modify the defaults or even create entirely new presets from scratch. This ability becomes very useful when building your own custom settings. Not everyone will need to, but not everyone works with just a singular format.

You can make very detailed choices about how Adobe Premiere Pro will handle formats as well as controls for the preview files.

The Settings and Tracks tabs in the New Sequence panel allow you to customize any of the presets, as well as save a preset for future use. You can even choose the default number of audio and video tracks for new sequences.

Customization can make sense for various situations such as the following:

■ When working with a news-sensitive editorial where changing the video preview format can speed up output.

■ When working with Final Cut Pro captured media using the ProRes codec family.

■ When working with nonstandard video sizes for output. Some examples we've seen include digital signage, where the sequence needed to be rotated for a sign that was vertical (720 x 1280), a science museum where the video was going to be three images horizontally (1280 x 2160), and an Android tablet with a nonstandard display size (1024 x 768).

Settings tab

On the Settings tab of the New Sequence dialog is where all of your horsepower lies for creating a new sequence, so let's start there (FIGURE 3.10). Here you can build almost any sort of sequence you need, from turning the second display into a playback monitor to creating unique custom composition sizes. The Settings tab is broken up into a few main areas; let's first look at the editing mode section.

Working with Apple's ProRes?
You can download a set of ProRes presets from http://labs.adobe.com, specifically optimized to work with ProRes.

Custom Is an Open Book
If you want to build a custom preset from scratch, choose Custom > Editing Mode. You'll then be able to specify almost every adjustment on the Settings tab. However, a custom setting can also hinder the performance of your system. With a custom setting, it's best to start by using settings that almost match your desired configuration.

- **Editing Mode.** You can adjust two elements in this option. The first element is the editing mode, which refers to exactly what kind of methods Adobe Premiere Pro will use to handle your footage. You'll see existing listings for DSLR, RED, XDCAM, and so on—essentially all the major video formats. This choice dictates how Adobe Premiere Pro handles video previews. The second element, Timebase, lets you choose a standard frame rate (several nonstandard rates for multimedia and digital signage are also offered).

FIGURE 3.10 The Settings tab is divided into four areas: Editing Mode, Video, Audio, and Video Previews.

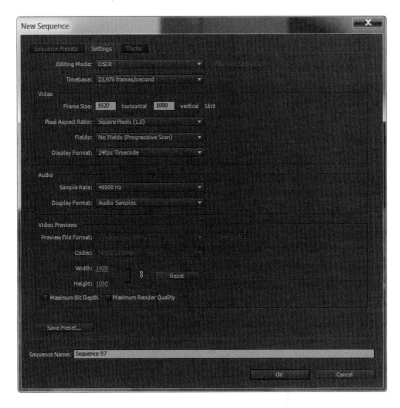

Start with a Preset
When customizing a setting, it's best to start with one of the Adobe system presets and adjust it as needed. If you adjust options such as fields or pixel aspect ratio incorrectly, you may struggle to get your footage to play back correctly.

Forget Rendering
Between the Mercury Playback Engine and fractional resolution playback, it's possible to have a real-time response, especially if your system is optimized for the Mercury Playback Engine with the proper video card.

TABLE 3.1 contains a comprehensive list of the presets for the Editing Mode setting on the Settings tab. Because the custom editing modes must be flexible enough for multiple formats, any settings prior to switching to Custom will propagate into the Video, Audio, and Video Previews areas (for example, if you select any of the 720p settings such as DSLR 720 and then Custom, it'll inherit 720p settings).

Depending on the preset you've selected, you may find several of the choices here grayed out because their values are often determined by the preset chosen.

Generally, frame sizes and fields are linked to specific formats and frame rates (especially if you're shooting interlaced or progressive video). All HD video is upper field first; if you're shooting progressive video, both fields are displayed simultaneously.

Frame size can be *any size*, but most of the time you'll want to choose a size that matches the kind of video you'll be working with.

TABLE 3.1 A Guide to Editing Modes

Editing Mode	Frame Size	Pixel Aspect Ratio (PAR)	Field Order	Preview Format	Preview Codec
ARRI Cinema	adjustable	adjustable	adjustable	I-Frame Only MPEG	MPEG I-Frame
AVC Intra 100 1080i	1920 x 1080	Square (1.0)	Upper First	I-Frame Only MPEG	MPEG I-Frame
AVC Intra 100 1080p	1920 x 1080	Square (1.0)	Progressive	I-Frame Only MPEG	MPEG I-Frame
AVC Intra 100 720p	1280 x 720	Square (1.0)	Progressive	I-Frame Only MPEG	MPEG I-Frame
AVC Intra 50 1080i	1440 x 1080	HD Anamorphic (1.33)	Upper First	I-Frame Only MPEG	MPEG I-Frame
AVC Intra 50 1080p	1920 x 1080	HD Anamorphic (1.33)	Progressive	I-Frame Only MPEG	MPEG I-Frame
AVC Intra 50 720p	960 x 720	HD Anamorphic (1.33)	Progressive	I-Frame Only MPEG	MPEG I-Frame
AVCHD 1080i Anamorphic	1440 x 1080	HD Anamorphic (1.33)	Upper First	I-Frame Only MPEG	MPEG I-Frame
AVCHD 1080i Square Pixel	1920 x 1080	Square (1.0)	Upper First	I-Frame Only MPEG	MPEG I-Frame
AVCHD 1080p Anamorphic	1440 x 1080	HD Anamorphic (1.33)	Progressive	I-Frame Only MPEG	MPEG I-Frame
AVCHD 1080p Square Pixel	1920 x 1080	Square (1.0)	Progressive	I-Frame Only MPEG	MPEG I-Frame
AVCHD 720p Square Pixel	1280 x 720	Square (1.0)	Progressive	I-Frame Only MPEG	MPEG I-Frame
Canon XF MPEG2 1080i/P	1920 x 1080	Square (1.0)	Upper/Progressive depending	I-Frame Only MPEG	MPEG I-Frame
Canon XF MPEG2 720p	1280 x 720	Square (1.0)	Progressive	I-Frame Only MPEG	MPEG I-Frame
DSLR	adjustable	adjustable	adjustable	I-Frame Only MPEG	MPEG I-Frame
HDV 1080i	1440 x 1080	HD Anamorphic (1.33)	Upper First	I-Frame Only MPEG	MPEG I-Frame
HDV 1080p	1440 x 1080	HD Anamorphic (1.33)	Progressive	I-Frame Only MPEG	MPEG I-Frame
HDV 720p	1280 x 720	Square (1.0)	Progressive	I-Frame Only MPEG	MPEG I-Frame
P2 1080 i/p	1280 x 1080	DVCPro HD (1.5)	Upper/Progressive depending	P2 1080i/p DVCPro HD	DVCPro100
P2 720p	960 x 720	HD Anamorphic (1.33)	Progressive	P2 720p DVCPro HD	DVCPro100
P2 DVCPro NTSC 50	720 x 480	D1/DV NTSC (.9091) or D1/DV NTSC WS (1.2121)	Lower/Progressive depending	P2 DVCPro50	DVCPro50
P2 DVCPro PAL 50	720 x 576	D1/DV PAL (1.094) or D1/DV PAL WS (1.4587)	Progressive	P2 DVCPro50	DVCPro50
QuickTime DV 24p	720 x 480	D1/DV NTSC (.9091) or D1/DV NTSC WS (1.2121)	Progressive	QuickTime DV NTSC	DV25 NTSC
QuickTime DV NTSC	720 x 480	D1/DV NTSC (.9091) or D1/DV NTSC WS (1.2121)	Lower/Progressive depending	QuickTime DV NTSC	DV25 NTSC
QuickTime DV PAL	720 x 576	D1/DV PAL (1.094) or D1/DV PAL WS (1.4587)	Lower/Progressive depending	QuickTime DV PAL	DV25 PAL
RED Cinema	Varies	Square (1.0)	Progressive	I-Frame Only MPEG	MPEG I-Frame
Sony XDCAM EX 1080i	1920 x 1080	Square (1.0)	Upper First	I-Frame Only MPEG	MPEG I-Frame
Sony XDCAM EX 1080p	1920 x 1080	Square (1.0)	Progressive	I-Frame Only MPEG	MPEG I-Frame
Sony XDCAM EX 720p	1280 x 720	Square (1.0)	Progressive	I-Frame Only MPEG	MPEG I-Frame
Sony XDCAM HD 1080p	1440 x 1080	HD Anamorphic (1.33)	Progressive	I-Frame Only MPEG	MPEG I-Frame
Sony XDCAM HD/ EX 1080i (SP)	1440 x 1080	HD Anamorphic (1.33)	Upper First	I-Frame Only MPEG	MPEG I-Frame
Sony XDCAM HD422 1080i/p	1920 x 1080	Square (1.0)	Upper/Progressive depending	I-Frame Only MPEG	MPEG I-Frame
Sony XDCAM HD422 720p	1280 x 720	Square (1.0)	Progressive	I-Frame Only MPEG	MPEG I-Frame

Customizing Sequence Settings for Fast Renders

In this video you'll learn how to adjust sequence settings in order to speed up rendering fast previews when offline editing.

Tape-Based Workflows

If you're working with a tape-based workflow, your render settings do count in regard to output. If you build a custom sequence, you have the option of adjusting your video previews to a higher-quality codec (or even uncompressed). This allows you to render instead of just previewing as you work. For time-sensitive output, such as news workflows, this is an optimal way to work.

Advantages with 32-Bit Processing

Adding effects that are 32-bit provide a marked advantage when processing. Other effects are 8 bits per channel. When you mix the two, Adobe Premiere Pro handles each in their appropriate bit depth.

Here are some notes about video formats:

- Frame size and pixel aspect ratio are interrelated. All full HD video (1080 x 720) and computers utilize square pixels.

- A number of compressed HD formats, such as 1440 x 1080, 1280 x 1080, 960 x 720, require non-square pixels. These "thin raster" sizes require a non-square pixel like standard-definition video.

- Standard-definition video, both NTSC and PAL, has two sizes: a 4:3 pixel and a wide-screen 16:9, or anamorphic, pixel.

- Fields are relevant to the source. You're labeling your sequence so Adobe Premiere Pro can accurately handle the mixing of different formats.

- **Audio.** For most formats, the audio is set correctly at 48000 Hz. Some DV formats work only at 32000 Hz. One day you may be working at higher sampling rates, such as 96000 Hz.

- **Video Previews.** One of the ways Adobe Premiere Pro is significantly different from other tools is in the way it previews or renders footage. Footage is pushed through the Mercury Playback Engine. When you export a file, you can choose whether to utilize the existing previews (great for speed) or discard them and have Adobe Media Encoder encode them in the background. You'll learn more about this in Chapter 15, "Publish Your Video."

At the bottom of the Video Previews area are two check boxes for video previews that require a bit of extra explanation.

- **Maximum Bit Depth.** Adobe Premiere Pro handles video in 8-bit depth, unless you select this check box. It's crucial to select this option in 10-bit (and beyond) formats like RED, Alexa, and HDCAM SR. By processing the extra bit depth, Adobe Premiere Pro will handle all of the video data in 32 bits per channel.

- **Maximum Render Quality.** Maximum Quality maintains sharpness when you're doing up-converts (from SD to HD) or down-converts (from HD to SD). Be careful with its use; it requires more memory (especially to render).

Setting initial tracks

Next to the Settings tab is the Tracks tab, which has three sections. Two are about creating default video and audio tracks. One section (in the middle of Audio) is for the Master output, and the details about that option are discussed in the next section.

You'll find that you almost *always* need a fixed initial number of tracks to get your work done, which you can easily configure using the Tracks tab (**FIGURE 3.11**).

Video is the easiest to understand. For Video, we like to work with at least three to four video tracks by default. Usually, primary footage, such as interviews, are on Video 1, and often B-roll is on Video 2. For flexibility, we usually leave titles on the fourth track with the empty one for other composites or graphics. Try to be controlled and specific as you use video tracks; working in later phases of postproduction (such as color correction) can be painful if you just throw footage anywhere on any track for no specific reason.

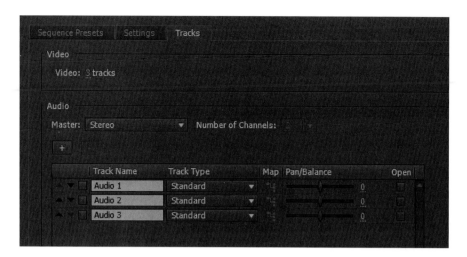

Audio is a bit more complex but straightforward once you know what's going on. Unlike other tools you may have used, the Adobe Premiere Pro track types dictate what happens to audio that's placed on them.

Adobe Premiere Pro has four kinds of audio tracks (**FIGURE 3.12**). Each track type is designed to handle certain kinds of audio; note that some, such as standard tracks, can handle multiple audio types. What's neat about audio tracks in Adobe Premiere Pro is that it's possible to name the tracks to help segregate audio and stay organized. And you can even choose to have them set to Open so you can see the waveforms as well. Here are the different types of audio tracks you can use in Adobe Premiere Pro:

Stereo Clips Don't Mean Two Tracks
Often, editors are confused by what a stereo clip is. It's a single element that has two waveforms—one panned left, one panned right. This type of clip needs to take up only a single track. Final Cut Pro treats these types of clips as two individual mono clips, taking up two tracks, when they're actually a single item. Only recently, with newer versions of Media Composer, has the idea of a stereo track been available.

FIGURE 3.12 Standard tracks are the most similar track type to other editorial tools like Final Cut Pro or Avid.

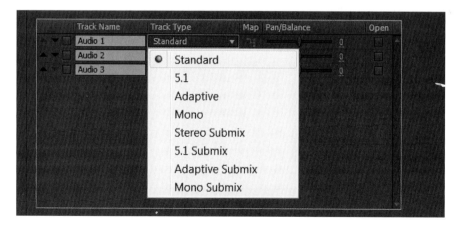

- **Standard.** This is the new default (and the most common) type of track in Adobe Premiere Pro. Clips that are mono (one waveform) or stereo (two waveforms in one clip) can go on this type of track. If you used previous versions of Adobe Premiere Pro, you'll be excited you no longer have to have separate stereo and mono tracks.

- **Mono.** Any type of clip placed on a mono track becomes "mixed down" to a mono output automatically (the track can still be panned).

FIGURE 3.13 It's possible to have an output greater than the type of playback capabilities you have. For example, you can generate surround sound sequences even if your system supports only stereo monitoring.

- **5.1.** This track is specifically meant for clips that source from 5.1 materials, such as a surround Dolby Digital (.ac3) file ripped off a DVD.

- **Adaptive.** Adaptive tracks are new to Adobe Premiere Pro CS6. They permit the routing of any input audio track to any output of the Master track (such as when a multitrack XDCAM clip comes in and you need to route the channels to four separate master outputs).

Adobe Premiere Pro also has submix track types that you probably noticed in the list of available tracks. It's possible to send (combine) multiple tracks (such as several tracks of music or effects) and mix them together as a single entity. This results in the ability to lower or raise these elements (the submix) with a single fader, rather than multiple faders, and also allows you to do things such as add effects to the submix rather than individual tracks.

You may have worked around this need in other applications by nesting or mixing down complex audio tracks. A submix eliminates this need. Submixes are discussed in detail in Chapter 10, "Audio Mixing and Repair."

Master track configuration

The Master drop-down menu refers to what sort of output you want your sequence to generate. The default is Stereo (**FIGURE 3.13**). You also have the ability to output 5.1 (surround sound), mono, and multichannel output.

Once the sequence is created, the master output is set in stone. It dictates how Adobe Premiere Pro will output your audio and cannot be changed.

The Master track output works like this:

- **Mono.** All audio output will be a single channel regardless of how many speakers are attached.

- **Stereo.** All audio will output as two channels: Left/Right. This is the most common format for output. You can pan tracks within the stereo sound field.

- **5.1.** With the right audio setup, this output is commonly known as *surround sound*. With this option chosen, you'll have six tracks in the master output. You can use a joystick-style panner to pan tracks within the surround sound field. This option is perfect for mixing standard, including mono or stereo, mono only, and 5.1 tracks, in true surround sound. Keep in mind that for monitoring you'll need a setup that is capable of monitoring in surround. You can configure audio hardware in Preferences.

- **Multichannel.** This output choice is used for routing tracks to specific outputs. A common example would be creating a "split master" where specific tracks need to route to specific output tracks. You can choose between 1 to 16 tracks depending on your needs (16 tracks of audio is what HD-SDI can handle). The new adaptive track options in Premiere Pro CS6 also make the task of routing to a multichannel output extremely easy. This routing will be discussed more in Chapter 10.

Setting Sequence Start Time

Especially in broadcast workflows, having your sequence start at a specific time is very important. You can choose to set the start time of a sequence to any starting timecode. Although this has become less critical in the days of digital output, it is still *crucial* when outputting to tape. A sign of a professional (for ease of other people in the production pipeline) is to have the first frame of your work on the 1:00:00:00 mark rather than the zero mark. Bars and tone often start at 58:30:00 or 59:30:00 minutes, with slates and countdowns preceding the one-hour mark, where the show begins.

Here's how to change the starting timecode:

1. Open a sequence so it is loaded in the Timeline panel.

2. Go to the panel menu or right-click the tab of the sequence and choose Start Time (**FIGURE 3.14**).

3. Enter a start time for the sequence, and click OK.

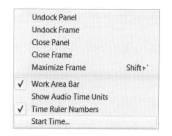

FIGURE 3.14 Choose an appropriate start time, for example 58:30:00 if you need to have bars plus a slate before your output.

Creating Your Project Template

Regardless of how you handle your media, you can still save time by creating a project template at the desktop level that you'd duplicate at the start of a project.

You likely have only a few formats you regularly work with, so if you take the time to set up and then save the project, that setup can become an ideal starting point for future projects.

To be clear, we're not talking about creating sequence presets; we talked about that earlier in the section "Creating Custom Sequence Settings." Rather, we're talking about taking a prebuilt project and duplicating it to save some time.

By setting up a project template, you can just duplicate and rename the template, and *everything* is set up the way you need. Let's set up a project template.

1. Configure a project in a way you like to work. Adjust the settings described in this chapter to match your needs.

2. Add any extra elements to the project to make your workflow easier.

3. For example, you can include bins already laid out, frequently used music, sound effects, client graphics, and stock footage that you need for a client or show.

4. Choose File > Save, and name the project with a logical name (such as XDCAM 1080p24).

5. Instead of creating a new project each time, you can just duplicate the project template file. You'll then have a perfect starting point for future projects—no configuring necessary!

You can find a finished example of this (along with some useful bins) in Lessons and Media > Lesson 03 > 03_Example_Template_XDCam1080_24p_Finished.

Creating a Preset from an Existing Sequence

If you have a sequence (like the one we created) that you're currently using with the tracks/output that you prefer, you can use the Load from Sequence button to replicate that specific sequence type and then save it as a preset for future use!

SAVING A CUSTOM PRESET

If you've customized a preset, it's a smart choice to save the preset so you can quickly reuse it again in the future (FIGURE 3.15). This will accelerate your workflow because each time you will be at a starting point of your own choice by using a preset that you've saved and that is specific to your needs rather than one of the stock presets.

For example, this would be particularly useful if you *always* need a set number of tracks. Combine this with creating your own custom project template as discussed earlier in the chapter, and you have every future project already prepared *exactly to fit your needs*.

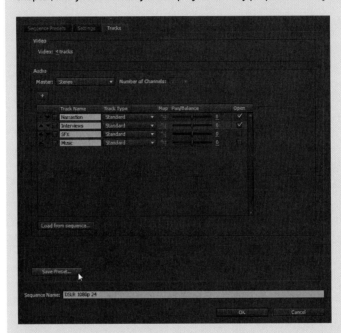

FIGURE 3.15
Custom presets make your work easier.

Here's an example of optimizing a custom preset in Adobe Premiere Pro to work with a DSLR camera, with four video tracks and four named audio tracks:

1. Start with a new sequence. On the sequence Presets tab, we chose DSLR 1080p 24 because it's a popular way to shoot DSLR video.
2. Change to the Settings tab. Change the video to four tracks.
3. Press the plus button below the Master Audio output.
4. Name the tracks, in order, as follows: Narration, Interviews, SFX, Music.
5. Set the first two tracks to open (because seeing their waveforms will make editing easier).
6. Click the Save Preset button.
7. Name the preset DSLR 1080p24 documentary setup.

You can find a finished version of this type of sequence in the project in the Lesson 03 folder called 03_Choosing Presets_Finished.

Modifying an Existing Project's Settings

After you've properly configured a project, you'd like to think that it'll be smooth sailing.

The truth is that there will be times when you've already started the project and you need to make minor adjustments. The process of modifying existing settings is very similar to the project setup steps.

To change settings for an existing sequence, choose Project > Project Settings.

It's important to be aware of which settings you can change. You'll then have a number of options you can alter, which we'll describe in detail in the following sections. Note that both General and Scratch Disks open the same dialog, but depending on the option you choose, a different tab will be selected.

General Tab

If you need to switch the display format of the video from timecode to frames or switch the audio settings from samples to milliseconds, you'll adjust those timings on the General tab. It's also where you can adjust the action and title-safe areas. You can also switch the Mercury Playback Engine from utilizing a GPU (if you have a supported CUDA-enabled card) to a software-only system, or vice versa (**FIGURE 3.16**).

Scratch Disks

Scratch disks fill up. That's the downside to all the video you're creating (often with less discretion than in the past because drives have gotten cheaper). Every time you render and every time you capture (but not import), you create media.

If this happens in the middle of a project, you might have to make a tough decision, which is whether to store the newly captured media and previews somewhere else on your system (**FIGURE 3.17**). Changing this option won't change where the existing media is, only where new media is stored.

> **Future Media Creation**
> Changing your scratch disks settings won't modify any existing media files. Only future media creation is impacted. Changing this setting midproject is mildly hazardous; it could leave you with media in two or more locations.

FIGURE 3.16 Do you have a card that can take advantage of the Mercury Playback Engine with GPU acceleration? Try switching its mode on this menu and then check your computer's processor load to see how well your system works without the acceleration.

FIGURE 3.17 There are two setups: project-based (as shown here) where the media lives with the project and system-based where you always target a specific drive, as mentioned earlier in the chapter.

Importing Existing Projects

So, you need to import your work from a *different* NLE. Experienced editors know that NLE systems are tools (not religions!). It is *very* common to have multiple editing systems and even platforms within the same facility.

Not every show starts (or finishes) in Adobe Premiere Pro. Projects are collaborative processes. You may receive from your client a simple log file or edit decision list (EDL) that you need to import from an older editing system. Or your client might have worked with Final Cut Pro or Avid Media Composer to assemble a rough cut, and you want to import that work rather than rebuild it.

Adobe Premiere Pro allows you to access all this information, even when there's nothing beyond a simple shot list.

Importing an EDL

While EDLs are still used quite a bit (with Adobe SpeedGrade, for example), it's getting less and less common to ever touch one.

Once upon a time, EDLs were the way to exchange Timelines between an offline NLE and a tape-to-tape suite.

Nowadays, EDLs are the lowest common denominator to get a sequence from one editorial tool to another, usually because they have no other level of compatibility. Just keep in mind, EDLs translate only a sequence, not a project or bins.

When they are used, they're almost always a last resort because they are often problematic. Typically, you can have only one track of video and four tracks of audio in an EDL. If your Timeline has more than that, you'll have to export (and therefore import on your target system) separate EDLs and assemble them manually.

The only flavor of EDL that Adobe Premiere Pro recognizes is the CMX 3600. Formats that are often used these days such as eXtensible Markup Language (XML) and Advanced Authoring Format (AAF) are the grandchildren of EDLs.

Let's import an EDL. Note that these steps are for reconnecting to existing media files. You could also recapture material from tape if you imported the EDL and then, with the offline clips selected, choose File > Batch Capture. The EDL you're about to import sources from 720p60 material, which will cause an interesting wrinkle.

1. Open any project, or choose Lessons and Media> Lesson 03 > 03_Choosing Presets.

2. Choose File > Import.

3. Choose File > Lessons and Media > Lesson 03 > desert_montage.edl.

4. Select the appropriate timebase. In this case, it's NTSC (29.97fps) **(FIGURE 3.18)**.

5. Actually, it's really 60fps, but since there's no 60fps, 29.97 is the appropriate choice and works. In NTSC, there are 60 distinct moments split across two fields, yielding 29.97 interlaced frames in SD; we happen to call it 59.94 in HD, but they're interlaced. In 720, there's no interlacing, so 29.97 is actually 59.94.

FIGURE 3.18 EDLs are limited to a single frame rate.

XML Defined
Like HyperText Markup Language (HTML), eXtensible Markup Language (XML) is essentially a text file that is marked up with "tags" that give attributes to the text. It is a popular format for exchanging complex data between applications and even manufacturers.

Importing a Final Cut Pro Project
Learn how to exchange data from Apple Final Cut Pro to Adobe Premiere Pro in this video.

6. Select a matching sequence type. For this example, since it was shot with a DSLR at 60fps at 720, use Digital SLR, 720p60.

7. (Optional) Select the bin, right-click, and choose Link Media, or click the Project menu and choose Link Media. Navigate to Lessons and Media > Media > Footage if you're asked to reconnect to an MP4; or, navigate to Lessons and Media > Media > Footage > Audio if you're asked to reconnect to a .wav file. Keep going until you've relinked all the footage. Choose Display Only Exact Name Matches to make this faster.

Importing Final Cut Pro Projects

For whatever reason—cost, convenience, familiarity—someone you're working with is bound to be using Apple's Final Cut Pro 7. Thanks to XML, Adobe Premiere Pro is able to transfer a project from Final Cut Pro 7. Alternately, by reversing the process, you can export an XML file from Adobe Premiere Pro and import the XML into Final Cut Pro.

By using XML, you can go back and forth to and from Final Cut Pro. It should be no great surprise that not every effect or transition is going to come across. Major items, such as clips and sequences, are successfully translated with the proper metadata.

The basic process is to export an XML file, open the XML file in Adobe Premiere Pro, and then link back to the QuickTime files—or the reverse to go to Final Cut Pro from Adobe Premiere Pro.

You'll find full details and gotchas in Appendix D, "Working with Final Cut Pro." Also be sure to watch video #05 for more information.

Importing an Avid Project

Learn how to exchange data from Avid Media Composer to Adobe Premiere Pro in this video.

Importing Avid Projects

Thanks to AAF, Adobe Premiere Pro is able to import sequences from Media Composer as well as export sequences to Media Composer.

Basic edits and some transitions come across, but only for a single sequence. You can't transfer an entire project.

The basic process is to export an AAF project from Avid, import the AAF into Adobe Premiere Pro, and then relink or recapture your media. To go to Avid, you export the AAF and then link back to your media.

You'll find full details and gotchas in Appendix E, "Working with Avid Media Composer." Also be sure to check out video #06 for even more information.

Next Steps

Now that you have your project set up (and set up for future projects), it's time to get footage into your system. Whether you are using a tape or tapeless workflow or capture cards, you need to know how to best get footage into Adobe Premiere Pro and work with the rest of the suite. In the next chapter, we'll talk about capturing and importing along with the basics of dynamic linking between different applications in the Adobe Creative Suite 6 Production Premium.

Importing Media

THE FIRST STEP to starting a project is getting your media into Adobe Premiere Pro. No matter what kind of project you're doing, if you can't import media, you're stuck. Adobe Premiere Pro offers different paths to importing including an Import command, Media Browser, and Adobe Dynamic Link. The one you choose will be based on the source material and your objectives.

Of course, not everything will come in the way you expect it. So, it's essential you know how to modify clips. Adobe Premiere Pro also doesn't work alone: It's crucial you understand the real "superpowers" of the suite. You can draw assets from the rest of the Adobe Creative Suite components, including Adobe After Effects, Adobe Photoshop, Adobe Audition, and even Adobe SpeedGrade. In this chapter, you'll learn about importing files and the effect it will have on your system.

Importing Files into Adobe Premiere Pro

Overall, Adobe Premiere Pro behaves the way most other editorial systems do. It provides a link from the original media to a pointer that lives inside your project. After you've imported media files, moving them outside the application can break links.

You can directly import assets into Adobe Premiere Pro in four ways:

- Standard importing by choosing File > Import

- The Media Browser panel

- Adobe Prelude

- Adobe Bridge

Whichever way you use Adobe Premiere Pro, it will create a link to your media, whether the media consists of videos, stills, or audio files (or even a dynamic project from one of the other Adobe Creative Suite apps, such as After Effects).

Standard Importing

Standard importing is probably the most straightforward type of importing you can do, and you've been doing it for years. To import any file, choose File > Import. If you prefer to use keyboard shortcuts, press Command+I (Ctrl+I) to open the standard Import dialog for Macintosh (**FIGURE 4.1**) or for Windows (**FIGURE 4.2**).

FIGURE 4.1 The Standard OS X Import dialog; note the search box in the upper-right corner.

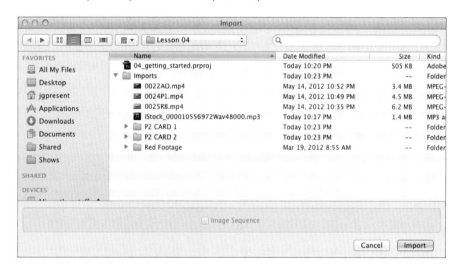

Let's import a clip to see this process.

1. Choose File > Open, and navigate to Lessons and Media > Lesson 04 > 04_getting_started.prproj.

   This is is an empty project that's set up for the media in use.

2. Choose File > Import.

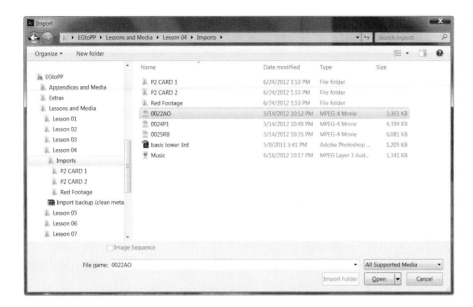

3. Navigate to the Lessons and Media > Lesson 04 > Imports folder on your local drive.

4. Select the first clip (0022AO.mp4), and click the Import button.

5. Click the New Bin button at the bottom of the Project panel or press Command+/ (Ctrl+/).

6. Name the bin File Menu Imported, and drag the clip into the new bin.

7. Repeat these steps for the two other clips in the Lesson 4 folder (0024P1.mp4 and 0025RB.mp4).

The Common Media Folder
We have a standard template we like to use for all new projects. It's a series of folders that you can use to get and stay organized at the desktop level. In this video, you'll explore the common media folder approach to media management.

BEST PRACTICES WITH MEDIA

It's said that you are your worst enemy. Nowhere is that statement more true than when you're importing footage. Who knows exactly what corners you cut last month (or last year). Good editors start organized and stay organized from the beginning to the end of the edit.

Here are a few key techniques to remember:

■ **Always create a disk image.** Be sure to create a verified copy or disk image of your tapeless media in your project's folder. You'll be able to go back to the "virtual tapes" if you ever need to reload.

■ **Stay organized.** Although Adobe Premiere Pro can import files and footage from anywhere, it's best to copy files and footage into a folder within the project. Any external materials to Adobe Premiere Pro will then live with the project.

■ **Clearly label old files.** There are too many stories of different versions of a graphic and editors being unsure of which one was being used. Consider renaming or removing old files at the desktop level. If you replace an old file with a newer one (and match the name), Adobe Premiere Pro can connect to the new asset. Just make sure there is no difference in the new asset, such as duration or frame size.

Using the Media Browser

Our favorite import method, by far, is the Media Browser (**FIGURE 4.3**). Its flexibility makes it superior to the standard file system import. Not only does it display the files in a straight list, but it also adjusts the view using the metadata. Being able to see this metadata makes it far easier to select from long lists of files or shots.

By default, you'll find the Media Browser in the lower-left corner (if your workspace is set to Editing). You can also quickly access it by pressing Shift+8. Because it's a dedicated panel in Adobe Premiere Pro, you can save it to a specific workspace or move it around so it lives in a different part of the interface.

FIGURE 4.3 The Media Browser has the capability to display clips and cards from popular formats like P2, XDCAM, RED, and even Arri.

The major benefits of the Media Browser include the following:

- Auto sensing of camera data—AVCHD, Canon XF, P2, RED, Arri, Sony HDV, and XDCAM (EX and HD)

- Narrowing the display to a specific file type, such as JPEG, TIFF, XML, AAF, and more

- Viewing and customizing the display of metadata

- Spanned clips appear as a single element

Once the Media Browser is open, you'll find that it is not significantly different from browsing using the OS. You can navigate through the folders on the left side and use the up, down, left, and right arrows in the upper-right corner.

Camera media

Adobe Premiere Pro's Media Browser (**FIGURE 4.5**) automatically recognizes camera media, meaning that if you navigate into a directory of XDCAM, P2, or RED files (among others), it will autorecognize the footage. This makes it easy to use and adjust metadata from the field.

FIGURE 4.5 P2 card import in the Media Browser

> ! **Manually Sift**
> Sometimes you'll be looking in a folder that contains a copy of a media card along with other files. When this happens, Adobe Premiere Pro will automatically assume the files are camera media, ignoring other elements you might want. You'll need to manually switch the folder view back to a standard file listing to see those files.

> ✓ **Sometimes a Thousand Words Are Better Than a Picture**
> We're huge fans of the thumbnail view in CS6 because of hoverscrub. But there are times where we really want to see more information than just the picture. To see this information, you must switch to the list view in the bottom left of the Media Browser.

Let's use the Media Browser to import the clips from a copy of a P2 card.

1. Start with the same project from the preceding exercise.

2. Click in the Media Browser, or press Shift+8.

3. Press the grave accent (`) key to display the Media Browser full-screen.

4. Navigate to Lessons and Media > Lesson 04 > Imports > P2 CARD 1.

   Try hoverscrubbing by moving your mouse across the images.

WHAT IS THE MEDIA CACHE?

To improve playback and lessen the load on the CPU, some formats—particularly the more compressed HD formats—will need indexing and caching. As you import these files, Adobe Premiere Pro takes a moment and builds an internal index to lessen stress on the system.

Configure the settings for the media cache by choosing Preferences > Media.

FIGURE 4.4 It's suggested that you clean the media cache database on a regular basis.

Cache files are generally small. You have the option to move them (as mentioned in Chapter 2, "Configuring Your Nonlinear Editor") to live somewhere else. The main advantage of this would be to offload these files from the internal hard drive to your fastest drive.

The media cache database should never be moved, but on a regular basis, it should be cleaned (**FIGURE 4.4**). How frequently you do that depends on your facility. If you're a news organization, you probably should clean this on a monthly basis at a minimum.

Want to Transfer Manually?
Later in this chapter, we talk about the idea of creating a clone of your card-based media and offer other thoughts on file-based workflows.

5. Change from the thumbnail view to the list view by clicking the list icon in the bottom left of the Media Browser.

6. Select the three clips (002AO, 0024P1, 0025RB), and choose File > Import from Media Browser.

7. Press the grave accent (`) key to return the Media Browser to normal size.

8. Click the Project panel to make it active, create a bin called From Media Browser, and move all the clips you just imported into that bin.

Narrowing file types

Being organized in the editorial process is a key skill, both within and outside of Adobe Premiere Pro. Yet, sometimes you'll find yourself scanning a long list of files for a specific format (**FIGURE 4.6**). An easy way to reduce the number of files you're looking at is to limit the file types to the specific format you need.

FIGURE 4.6 Not only can you limit the files to a specific format, but you can also select multiple formats, such as stills, which makes finding just the stills in a directory quick and painless.

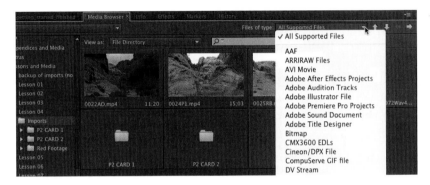

CUSTOMIZING THE METADATA IN THE MEDIA BROWSER

Having a complete view of metadata information is ideal, especially if you work with XDCAM or P2 or other formats with rich metadata, where you can set information such as scene number and ratings while you're out in the field. But metadata isn't very valuable unless you can access it. Fortunately, the Media Browser permits that. Adobe Premiere Pro maintains a custom directory view for each format.

Here's how to access the different directory viewers.

1. In the top right of the Media Browser panel, click the panel menu and choose Edit Columns. You *must be in list view for this to work.*

2. Select a directory viewer to customize, such as P2 (**FIGURE 4.7**).

3. Add or remove columns by selecting them relevant to your needs.

4. Use the Move Up or Move Down button to rearrange the order of columns.

5. Click OK to store your column settings.

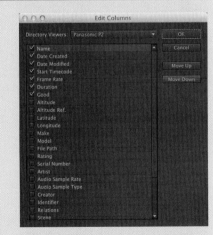

FIGURE 4.7 Remember that each directory viewer is unique; customizing P2 doesn't customize XDCAM (or any of the others).

Adobe Prelude

New in the CS6 family is Adobe Prelude. Think of Prelude as a "preprocessor" for your file-based media. It will allow you to preview your media, choose which clips you want, and even allow a logger or producer to do some basic editing.

Most important, Prelude can copy your media from one location, such as the card that came from your camera, to a specific set location, helping you stay organized. And it's even possible to make extra backups of your media at the same time. The best part? The data with these copies is verified, which ensures that every bit is successfully copied and backed up.

Ingesting

The first step to working with Prelude is to ingest the media. Ingesting means adding the media to your drives. By ingesting to the right location, such as your media drive, you'll end up quickly organized for future editing.

Let's ingest some media.

1. Launch Adobe Prelude, and then click the New Project icon on the Welcome screen (FIGURE 4.8).

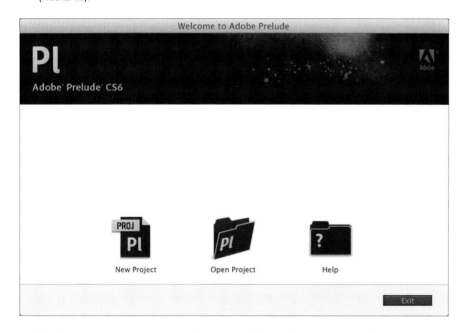

Ingesting into Adobe Prelude
This video goes over the basics of launching Adobe Prelude, starting a project, and ingesting some media.

FIGURE 4.8 You can quickly start a project in Adobe Prelude; the method is nearly identical to Adobe Premiere Pro.

You're going to capture the media to your desktop. Realistically, you'd pick your own media location for this. You're creating this folder so you have an easy time finding (and later deleting) the media you're creating on your machine.

2. In the dialog box, navigate to your desktop folder.

3. Create a folder called Card Media.

4. Name the project Desert P2 footage, and save it in the newly created folder.

   You're now looking at the Prelude interface (**FIGURE 4.9**). There are four buttons in the top left to help focus on the streamlined workflow.

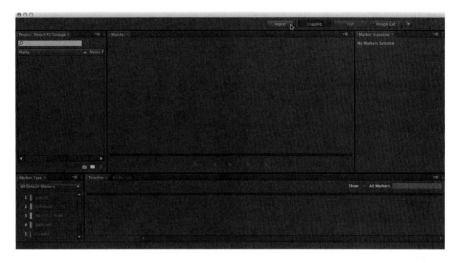

FIGURE 4.9 The four major steps in Prelude are echoed by the buttons Ingest, Logging, List, and Rough Cut.

 Copy First or Directly from Card
In this exercise, the media was already copied to your drive. Adobe Prelude can work directly from a media card and can transfer that safely to a destination drive for you.

5. Click the Ingest button.

   A drive/file list comes up that resembles the Media Browser in Adobe Premiere Pro.

6. Navigate to Lessons and Media > Lesson 04 > Imports > P2 Card 2 (**FIGURE 4.10**).

7. Click the Check All button (along the bottom of the window).

FIGURE 4.10 Similar to the Media Browser, the Ingest dialog box has the ability to switch from List to Thumbnail in the lower-left corner.

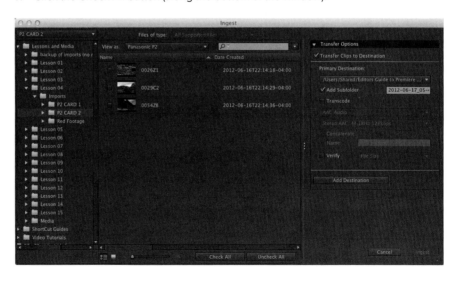

8. Make sure to select the Transfer Clips to Destination button.

   Change the primary destination to the folder Card Media on your desktop that you created in step 4.

   You have these options at this point:

   - Transcode the footage

   - Add subfolders (creating an organized structure)

   - Verify that the copy occurred without errors

   - Add a destination to create a copy somewhere else

   - You're not going to do any of those now, but know that you have the option to adjust how and where Prelude ingests your footage.

9. Click Ingest to start the transfer of the media.

   The footage is copied and placed on the left side of the Project panel. You can double-click any clip and use J-K-L In and Out points and other basic editorial tools to prepare for the edit in Adobe Premiere Pro. You can also add descriptive markers that speed up the editorial process. Be sure to check out videos #09 and #10 for more information on these tasks.

Sending your ingested media to Adobe Premiere Pro

Once your footage is ingested, copied, and possibly marked and edited together, all that remains is the hand-off. Fortunately, the process of moving from Adobe Prelude to Adobe Premiere Pro couldn't be easier.

Let's send our ingested video to Adobe Premiere Pro.

1. Create a new bin called P2 Media from Prelude.

2. Select all the clips in your Adobe Prelude project, and place them in the new bin.

3. Select the new bin.

4. Choose File > Send to Premiere Pro to transfer to the Adobe Premiere Pro project that's currently open (you must have a project open).

5. Switch to Adobe Premiere Pro. The files appear in the Project panel ready for you to use.

   In your own projects, be sure to give the bin a more discrptive name that matches the content and role of the footage.

6. You can now quit Adobe Prelude and close the project.

Subclipping and Rough Cuts with Adobe Prelude

In this video you'll learn how to use the subclipping rough cuts features of Adobe Prelude.

Markers and Metdata with Adobe Prelude

Learn how to organize your media and create descriptive markers that will travel to Adobe Premiere Pro.

What's Wrong with Adobe Bridge?
Adobe Bridge has come quite a distance since the first edition of this book. It now handles all sorts of file-based camera material (such as P2, XDCAM, and RED). It's not as flexible for transcoding or adding markers the way Adobe Prelude is.

FIGURE 4.11 Adobe Bridge is a versatile program in its own right. Notice Filtering on the left side and Video Metadata on the right side.

Adobe Bridge

Most people encounter Adobe Bridge (**FIGURE 4.11**) via Adobe Photoshop. In case you've never used it, it's a dynamic media browser—think of it as a file browser on steroids. It's a media browser that is optimized mostly for still photography, but it has loads of power for video users.

You can manually open Adobe Bridge by clicking its application icon. You can also choose File > Browse in Bridge in Adobe Premiere Pro to automatically launch Adobe Bridge and point it to the same directory that the Media Browser is viewing.

Adobe Bridge has a few killer features you should know about. They are optional uses but are very powerful in and out of the video workflow, acting as a significant replacement for your native OS file system. The features we'll focus on are adding metadata (such as a rating), batch renaming, and collections (on the accompanying DVD).

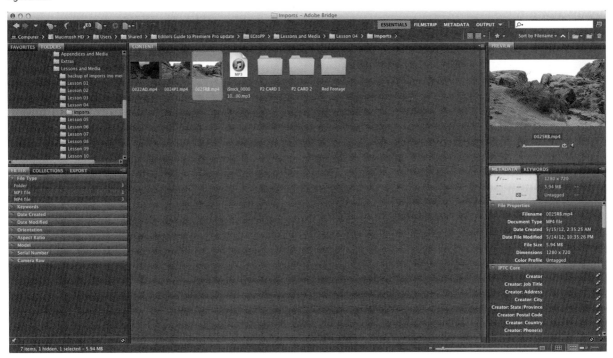

Adding Metadata with Adobe Bridge

What Is EXIF?
The EXchangeable Image File (EXIF) format specifies additional data for stills and audio but unfortunately not video.

Metadata is additional data about the actual video in the shot. It could include information such as the frame size of the shot or the scene number. With stills, metadata can include all sorts of common EXIF data, such as aperture, location (if the camera has a GPS chip), and camera model or lens.

You imported material earlier in this chapter. By adding the metadata to the QuickTime files, you'll be able to contrast your existing imported files by importing the same files *after* you've added metadata. The choice to add metadata offers additional organizational ability in Adobe Premiere Pro, such as being able to sort on information such as shot type. Because the metadata stays with the clips, the media will be easier to organize in the future if you bring the clips into a new project.

1. Continue working with 04_getting_started.prproj.

2. Launch Adobe Bridge by choosing File > Browse in Bridge.

3. Navigate to the Lessons and Media > Lesson 04 folder.

4. Select all three MP4 video clips (0022AO.mp4, 0024P1.mp4, and 0025RB.mp4).

5. Select the Metadata tab (in the lower-right corner), and scroll down to browse the categories.

6. Find the Video category, click Scene, and add the scene number 15 (**FIGURE 4.12**).

   If you see a pencil icon, it means the field can be adjusted. After the metadata has been added to the clips, the clips are permanently modified.

FIGURE 4.12 Customizing the Scene metadata. You can change any field that has a pencil next to it.

Viewing metadata from Adobe Bridge

You'll now directly import these clips in Adobe Premiere Pro. Earlier they were imported without the new metadata. Those previously imported clips don't have metadata. You're now going to import them again; the difference is that now there's new metadata. Both clip imports will exist in the same project, but you can see the metadata difference. Let's make a quick comparison of this information.

1. In Adobe Bridge, select the three clips you just added metadata to.

2. Choose File > Open, or press Command+O (Ctrl+O). The clips should now be imported into the Project panel in Adobe Premiere Pro.

3. Create a bin called From Bridge, and move all the clips into that bin.

 Before and After Comparison

You'll modify the metadata and reimport the same clip as earlier in this chapter. If you didn't complete the earlier sections, it's not an issue. You just won't be able to compare the new import, which has extra metadata, with the old imports.

 Stars and More

You can add other metadata like ratings and get them to show up in Adobe Premiere Pro. Once you add them in Bridge, you need to go to the Metadata display in the Project panel menu in the upper right. The easiest way to find a field, such as Ratings, is to type its name in the search box at the top of the window.

11 Rating Clips in Adobe Bridge

In this video you'll learn the workflow of how to rate clips and add keywords, quickly sifting through your material.

 12 Building a Collection in Adobe Bridge

In this video you'll expand on learn how to use ratings and keywords from the prior video by having Adobe Bridge build collections to help you locate footage quickly. This video shows you how to sift, sort, and then move the data at the desktop level or into an Adobe Premiere Pro bin for organization. You can even create dynamic smart collections that will automatically gather footage that meets your key criteria.

Batch Renaming Clips in Adobe Bridge

In this video you'll learn how to use the Batch Rename command to quickly add the date and time to a series of clips, providing each with a unique name. You can even preserve the original filename in the clips so you can cross-reference your archived media from the shoot. The Batch Rename command is particularly useful for cameras such as DSLRs that don't assign unique clip names.

FIGURE 4.13 Note the differences in the Project panel between the two lists of identical files. Adobe Premiere Pro can display only the metadata that was embedded in a file prior to its import.

4. Click the Project panel to select it, or press Shift+1 and then click the grave accent (`) key to view the Project panel full-screen.

5. Switch the Project panel to list view by clicking the list view icon in the bottom-left corner.

6. Click the disclosure triangle to open the File Menu Imported bin and the From Bridge bin.

   You should see the same clips in both folders.

7. Scroll to the right until you see the Scene column.

   Note that the items in the File Menu Imported bin *do not* have the scene number, yet the ones that were imported from Adobe Bridge do. The only reason the newer clips have this data is that they were imported *after* you added the data in Adobe Bridge (**FIGURE 4.13**). If you were to import them now via the Import command or via the Media Browser, the new import would also have this metadata.

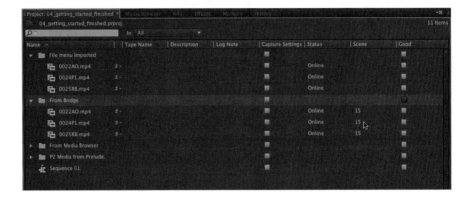

Tape-Based Workflows

For decades, videotape was *the* format for most individuals choosing to edit. The original tapes could be stored on a shelf and be available for recapture if they were ever needed in the future.

The downside of using videotape has always been the cost of the consumables—videotape—along with the restriction that acquisition was forced to be real time (compared to tapeless, which can be faster than real time).

For more information on tape-based workflows, see Appendix C, "Tape Workflows," on the DVD or with the downloadable files.

Tapeless Workflows

It used to be that most of the media you dealt with was recorded on tape. The beauty of tape-based formats is that there is a raw tape that can be stored and retrieved as needed. However, most productions are going tapeless (FIGURE 4.14). The advantage of being able to ingest footage faster than real time is the killer feature, but other advantages of tapeless workflows include working at higher resolutions than HD, mixing different frame types and rates on a card, and even (on some cameras) being able to access the raw sensor data.

When to Transcode?
Some workflows still require transcoding with Adobe Premiere Pro. These mainly include scenarios where you want to hand off your edited material and a project to another system, such as Apple Final Cut Pro or Avid Media Composer. These workflows are discussed in the appendixes of this book on the DVD.

FIGURE 4.14 A Panasonic P2 card

What makes Adobe Premiere Pro particularly amazing is its ability to work with tapeless formats without any transcoding or rewrapping. Yes, you'll need a robust system and, preferably, a system with the GPU-based Mercury Playback Engine. The ease of the workflow on your system to handle media natively means that you don't need to waste time; you can start editing immediately.

Mounting a Card

To load the tapeless media onto your system, you'll need the appropriate card reader or drive. For many formats, this will mean an approved hardware device from the manufacturer (such as a P2 card reader or XDCAM drive; see FIGURE 4.15). In other cases, you may be able to use a generic third-party device (such as a CF card reader). Some cameras and hard drive recorders will require you to hook up the actual device to transfer the media. In any workflow, be sure that you attach the device to the fastest port and connection protocol supported by your machine.

FIGURE 4.15 A Sony XDCAM deck reads XDCAM media.

The following camera workflow guides may be useful:

- **RED.** http://bit.ly/K72lh1
- **DSLR.** http://bit.ly/IlwNCh
- **XDCAM.** http://bit.ly/K72MNW
- **Canon.** http://bit.ly/KErmR7
- **P2.** http://bit.ly/KATgnl
- **AVCCAM.** http://bit.ly/L5r1JX
- **JVC.** http://bit.ly/IH2f01

Creating a Clone and a Copy

In a Hurry? Don't Forget to Back Up

If you're in a rapid turnaround environment (such as news), you may choose to edit directly from the tapeless media. Just remember that neither the Import command nor the Media Browser actually copies the footage to your drive. Before you hand the cards back to a videographer (or erase them), be sure to use the Project Manager to copy the used media to one of your media drives.

Although it's possible to work directly from a card or field disk, it isn't a permanent solution. Because tapeless media is expensive, you'll probably want to reuse it! Therefore, you need to make sure the content on your tapeless media is archived. The footage coming in from tapeless sources should be moved to at least two locations (not on the same drive).

That's how Adobe Prelude fits in. It was primarily designed for copying media from file-based storage systems to multiple locations with the option to transcode.

Storing your media can be done by using two separate but related methods.

- **Transfer the media.** Whether it's by unwrapping or simply copying the footage contained on a tapeless media device, the first step in archiving is to make sure you have a "live" version of the footage.

- **Back up the media.** After footage has been transferred from the tapeless media, the next step is to create a backup of the tapeless media on your computer. In the world of tape, this process is akin to putting tape back on the shelf after you've captured it.

When you make a copy of your media, *it's not enough to just drag and drop files*. In most cases, it's *crucial* to maintain the file structure of the original tapeless media when copying to a backup device and your media drive. If you discard the metadata and folder structure on the card, you can lose important information and face challenges when importing spanned clips.

We're big fans of cloning the disks. These clones are *bit for bit* verified copies of the originals. You'll find this capability built into Apple's Disk Utility tool, which allows you to create a disk image (.dmg) file. Unfortunately, Windows 7 doesn't offer the same built-in feature, but there are third-party tools that allow creation of ISO files.

For those of you on set, this job is often performed by a digital imaging technician (DIT). Aside from being responsible for the transferring and extra copies of footage, a DIT might also check the footage for exposure and possibly apply a LUT or use a tool like Adobe SpeedGrade to check the footage.

Spanned Clips

Some formats will create multiple spanned clips to represent a single video file. A *spanned* clip divides the material into separate files to keep the length of any one file under a threshold (such as 4 GB). Although spanned clips are physically stored as separate files, they should be handled by Adobe Premiere Pro as a single clip.

Here are some important tips concerning spanned clips:

- **Select only one clip.** The key to importing spanned clips is to select only one of the clips in the span. If you select more than one spanned clip, you will end up importing duplicate copies of the media.

- **Keep the XML.** The reason you cloned the entire card was to retain all of the metadata. Without this data, spanned clips typically cannot be reassembled.

- **Both cards.** If the clip spans two P2 or XDCAM cards, it's important to copy the entire directory for both cards to your drive. The copies should be at the same level in a media folder.

- **Favor the Media Browser.** The most reliable way to import spanned clips is with the Media Browser. However, you can also use the Import command (File > Import) in most cases.

NATIVE SUPPORT FOR RED AND ALEXA FOOTAGE

The RED cameras and the ARRI ALEXA have caused quite a revolution in filmmaking. The camera and the images it produces rival what's possible with physical 35mm film. In the future, there are likely going to be similar new formats. Adobe has a section of its website designed for this; visit http://labs.adobe.com.

The unique part of the Adobe workflow is the focus on a truly native raw workflow. This means that the footage stays as close as possible to what was shot on set or in the field. You never need to transcode the footage (which essentially "bakes" the color and exposure into the clips). This lets you freely adjust the look and feel of your footage all the way through post.

The following RED R3D file permutations are supported:

- 2K
- 3K
- 4K
- 4K HD
- 5K

The following ALEXA sizes are supported:

- 2880 x 1620
- 1920 x 1080

The RED R3D Source Settings dialog (FIGURE 4.16) offers extensive controls over RED footage. You can change color settings, create your own presets, and even modify multiple clips at once. The Source Settings permit you to adjust the RED footage prior to any other adjustments (such as applying the Three-Way Color Corrector) in Adobe Premiere Pro. ALEXA footage also uses the Source Settings menu choice.

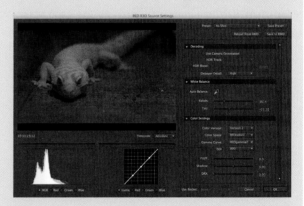

FIGURE 4.16 The RED R3D Source Settings dialog (right-click a RED clip in the Project panel and choose Source Settings) allows for adjustments on the curve, to the ISO, and more. A very short RED clip is available in the Lesson 04> Imports folder for you to experiment with.

Supported File Types

Clients throw everything at us. It's rare that they understand that certain formats aren't optimized for video editing. In their heads, video is video, photos are photos, and audio is audio regardless of where it came from.

It's always best to work with the least compressed file type, with the XDCAM files instead of the Flash file that was posted to the Web, and with the TIFF rather than the JPEG from your client's smartphone. Realistically, we don't always get these choices. Fortunately, Adobe Premiere Pro handles almost everything.

You can find the full list of supported formats at http://adobe.ly/supportedformats.

For all supported formats, remember that they're imports, not captured footage. Adobe Premiere Pro merely links to them. If you move them (or eject the card), you'll no longer have access to the footage (it'll then be offline). You need to copy or clone the desired media to your media folder at the operating system level.

Footage Files

Adobe prides itself on keeping up with the latest changes in camera technology in Adobe Premiere Pro. As such, you'll often see "dot" updates available that add support for new cameras. You can find the full list of supported formats at www.adobe.com/products/premiere/native-tapeless-workflows.html. These formats can be read by Adobe Premiere Pro, providing access to their metadata. Some manufacturers provide drivers to mount their material on your system. Some also have their own players or utilities that allow you to examine the footage, assign card names, and adjust metadata. We strongly suggest you visit your manufacturer's Web page and stay abreast of the latest information for your camera.

The major tapeless formats supported by Adobe Premiere Pro include the following:

- Any DSLR camera that shoots H.264 directly into QuickTime
- ARRI ALEXA
- Panasonic P2
- RED ONE, RED EPIC, RED SCARLET
- XDCAM (disc based or card based)
- Sony HDV (when shot on removable media)
- AVCHD cameras
- Canon XF
- AVC-Intra Frame (50/100 Mbs)

Graphics Files

Adobe Photoshop is a graphics tool used by 98 percent of all video editors. Fortunately, Adobe has also integrated a lot of its image-handling features into Adobe Premiere Pro. You can import most formats, including JPEG, TIFF, PNG, and PSD files.

With that said, here are a few key points to keep in mind when importing graphics into Adobe Premiere Pro:

- **PDF files won't work.** Perhaps it's because PDF files span multiple pages that they won't work. It's a concept that just doesn't make any sense in the video world. You can open a PDF in Photoshop and crop or extract images.

- **Develop DNG/Camera Raw files.** You should process any raw still images using Adobe Lightroom or Adobe Photoshop. We recommend developing and saving 16-bit TIFF files.

- **Stick to RGB.** Make sure your graphics are in RGB mode. In Photoshop, choose Image > Mode > RGB. In Adobe Illustrator, choose File > Document Color Mode > RGB. CMYK and even grayscale will cause weird color shifts or even incompatibility. Keep in mind that Adobe Illustrator files will be flattened.

- **Go big if you want.** Unlike other editing tools, which may limit their graphics to 4 KB, you'll have greater range in Adobe Premiere Pro. The maximum still or movie image frame size that can be imported is 256 megapixels. There's also a maximum dimension of 32,768 pixels in either direction. Of course, keep in mind that bigger images use more RAM and need faster disk speeds to display.

Photoshop (.psd) files

One of the best features that illustrates how well the Adobe family communicates is the ability to import a layered Photoshop file into Adobe Premiere Pro (a workflow we explore in Chapter 12, "Essential Effects"). When you import a layered Photoshop file, the dialog in **FIGURE 4.17** appears. Here you have four choices; each gives you a slightly different result.

FIGURE 4.17 The Photoshop Import dialog. Good naming conventions in Photoshop equals ease of knowing what to import to Adobe Premiere Pro.

Image Sequences
Even cameras/systems that can't output QuickTime or AVI files often can produce an image sequence. Image sequences are also often used with time-lapse cameras. These sequences are a number of sequentially numbered stills. Either import via the File > Import command (and click the Image Sequence button) or via the Media Browser (where you'll find the switch under the panel menu).

Codec Packs Warnings
If you're a Windows user and you want to use a codec pack, be forewarned. Be very, very careful about installing any codecs not from professional video manufacturers (such as the K-Lite Codec pack). Depending on how they instruct Windows to work, Adobe Premiere Pro and other video tools may no longer correctly play back.

Understanding Bits per Channel
Video professionals describe how many steps per channel as bit depth. Most video has 8-bits per channel ($2^8 = 256$), which equals 256-steps per channel. Because there are three color channels on a computer (Red, Green, and Blue), they yield millions of colors. Some video formats support 10 and even 12 bits per channel. If you're working with still images or rendered computer graphics, they can be brought in at 16-bits per channel.

Understand the Creative Suite Graphics Workflow
If you want to fully understand how to use the Adobe Creative Suite to build video graphics, we can recommend a great book; *Motion Graphics with Adobe Creative Suite 5 Studio Techniques* (Adobe Press, 2010) explores Photoshop, Illustrator, After Effects, and Adobe Premiere Pro.

- **Merge All Layers.** This option brings in a single file and merges the layers based on *what was visible* when the file was saved in Photoshop. The new file will occupy one track in your Timeline panel.

- **Merged Layers.** This option allows you to bring in a single merged file. You can choose which layers you want to be visible. The new file also occupies only a single track.

- **Individual Layers.** This option lets you bring in each layer as an individual file. You can choose which layers you want to import.

- **Sequence.** This option is similar to the Individual Layers option. The difference is that you get a sequence that matches the Photoshop file's appearance. This makes it easy to animate layers with keyframes (see Chapter 12). You can place the sequence as a nested item inside another sequence.

If at any point you want to force a graphic to update in Photoshop (such as to adjust exposure or use the Clone Stamp tool to remove something), it's easy. Select the clip in your sequence or Project panel and choose Edit > Edit in Photoshop.

Illustrator (.ai) files

Unlike Photoshop, Illustrator stores most graphics as mathematical vectors. The benefit is infinite scaling to size for specific applications, such as when printing or when working with vectors in After Effects. No matter how much a vector file is scaled up or down, the graphic remains crisp in Illustrator (or After Effects).

When you import a vector graphic from Illustrator into Adobe Premiere Pro, it will rasterize (be converted to pixels). If you scale it larger, the image will become pixelated. An Illustrator file comes across only as a "flattened" item—all the layers are combined.

If you intend on scaling up the graphics more than 125 percent, it's best to open them in Illustrator and adjust the scale there. Simply choose Edit > Edit Original from within Adobe Premiere Pro to open the vector file. When you're finished, close the file and save your changes. The linked file will update within Adobe Premiere Pro.

CREATING SPECIAL CLIPS (SYNTHETICS)

A number of elements, such as black video or color bars, can be created in Adobe Premiere Pro. These elements are referred to as *synthetics*—clips that don't have associated media but are synthetically created by Adobe Premiere Pro. To create any of these synthetic clips, choose File > New and then select the element you want from the menu.

The synthetic elements include the following:

- **Bars and Tone.** Test generators to help calibrate your system and elements specified in some deliverables for calibration needs.

- **Black Video.** An opaque black piece of video.

- **Color Matte.** Essentially identical to black video but with color.

- **Universal Counting Leaders.** A standard countdown video.

- **Transparent Video.** A clip similar to black video or color matte but transparent. This is perfect for adding an effect like timecode, lens flare, and other effects that need a transparent background.

Audio Files

Pretty much every audio format you'll encounter will work in Adobe Premiere Pro. You can toss in MP3, AAC (MP4), WAV, and AIFF. With that said, it is *far* better to work with uncompressed audio files. Otherwise, you'll be forcing your system to work harder than necessary, which can lead to dropped frames and drifting sync during playback.

Modifying Clips

Sooner or later, footage will be captured incorrectly, imported wrong, or just plain need modification. There will be lots of times when you'll need to break the rules (such as when dealing with overcranked footage). This section explains exactly how to make important changes to how your footage plays back and is used.

Adjusting Audio Channels

As you learned in Chapter 3, "Setting Up a Project," Adobe Premiere Pro has four track types: Standard, Mono, 5.1 and Adaptive. A standard track is a single track where you'd put a mono clip (like narration) or a stereo clip (like music).

You may be familiar with other editorial tools that use a pair of tracks to handle stereo (usually a pair of mono tracks). A cool feature of Adobe Premiere Pro is that you're able to handle the audio easier because it's a single element. Prior to CS6, it was crucial to understand how to modify audio channels in a clip, but it's a skill that is nearly no longer necessary.

Switching incorrectly set stereo elements

If an imported stereo clip was incorrectly interpreted as a pair of mono tracks, it's possible to fix it pretty quickly.

In the 04_getting_started project, we intentionally imported the Mono music.mp3 clip by forcing it to be a pair of mono clips in the Audio preferences by setting the Default audio tracks (on import) to be Mono. If this clip was dragged to a Timeline, it'd take up two tracks.

To fix it, all you have to do is choose Clip > Modify > Audio Channels and choose the Stereo preset (FIGURE 4.18). If you then drag the clip to a Timeline, it will take up only one track.

Uncompress It!
The best way to lessen the stress on your computer's CPU is to transcode. Modern systems are pretty fast. But often it's considered wasteful to use computing power on dynamically converting audio that can quickly be converted into an uncompressed file. You can transcode audio from either Adobe Premiere Pro or Adobe Media Encoder.

Transcoding Audio in Adobe Media Encoder
In this video you'll learn how to build a Watch Folder to convert any MP3 files to uncompressed audio with the Adobe Media Encoder.

Recording a Narration Track
In this video you'll learn how use the Audio Mixer to record a scratch track. This is perfect if you need to edit now before the voice-over artist is available (or you're the voice-over artist!).

Change Early
You can change the audio channels for imported items only before the clip has been added to a sequence.

FIGURE 4.18 Choose Clip > Modify > Audio Channels to change the audio information. Just remember that if the audio clip is already used in a Timeline, that version of it won't be changed.

Forcing an audio track override

When you import audio, Adobe Premiere Pro uses the default interpretation based on the clip. This happens *based on the Audio preferences*. You can resolve 99 percent of improper audio imports by setting the Adobe Premiere Pro Preferences correctly.

1. Choose Premiere Pro > Preferences > Audio (Mac) or Edit > Preferences > Audio (Windows).

2. The default is Use File. If desired, adjust the setting to your needs.

   In situations in which you're bringing in audio with multiple mono tracks, such as an interview where each person has a microphone, it might be warranted to override a stereo recording to be interpreted as a pair of mono tracks.

Interpreting Footage

There are some very good reasons for reinterpreting your footage. They include graphic files or footage that is missing a flag for pixel aspect ratio correction or correctly removing extra frames from 24p material.

Of course, any time you monkey with the way Adobe Premiere Pro interprets the footage, you're taking the chance that your footage might not look right. Choose the wrong setting and your alpha channel may be reversed or a video file won't play back because of an incorrect frame rate.

But sometimes you'll have to tweak these settings, if, for whatever reason, they were interpreted incorrectly.

For this section, you'll be looking at the footage in Lessons and Media > Lesson 04 > 04_getting_started.

Assigning a frame rate

The footage frame rate is set in the camera, but the sequence frame rate is set by you when you create it. You can of course cut footage of differing frame rates together into the same sequence, and Adobe Premiere Pro will automatically blend the frames so the proper speed is maintained.

But what if that's not what you want? Perhaps you shot footage at 60 frames per second to conform it to play back at 30 frames per second. This technique works only with cameras that have a high frame rate (like 720p60 cameras). Otherwise, your best bet is to choose Clip > Speed/Duration to change the speed of the clip, which is mentioned in Chapter 7. With this technique, you'll get a nice, slow-motion effect.

Let's slow down a clip that has been shot at 60 frames per second.

1. Open Sequence 01 Frame Rate.

2. Play back the footage and observe the speed of the woman walking through the frame (Clip 0097SJ_60.mp4).

3. In the Clips to be Adjusted bin, select 0097SJ_60.mp4, and choose Clip > Modify > Interpret Footage (**FIGURE 4.19**).

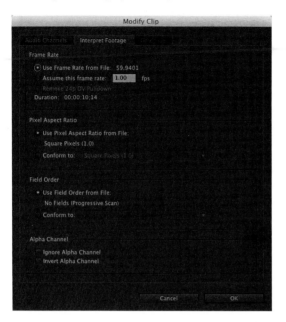

FIGURE 4.19 It's possible to reinterpet the frame rate, pixel aspect ratio, field order, and alpha channel.

No Undo for Interpret
The Interpret Footage dialog allows you to modify the way Adobe Premiere Pro handles your clips. Be careful; there is no easy reset.

4. Select the "Assume this frame rate" option, enter **29.97** frames per second, and click OK.

5. Drag the right edge of the clip to extend the shot.

6. Play back the sequence and watch it to see the impact of the frame rate change.

Interpreting pixel aspect ratio

There are headaches and then there are Headaches. When your files have the wrong pixel aspect ratio, they will look distorted. Computers have square pixels; the height and width are the same. Video pixels are often non-square; that is to say, they have a different width than height. Being able to interpret non-square pixels correctly is a technical necessity because so many cameras can shoot multiple sizes and frame rates (while preserving affordable recording options).

You'll see non-square pixel aspect ratios most often in standard-definition files. Both wide-screen (16x9) and "normal" (4x3) video files have the same number of pixels. It's the shape of the pixels that makes the difference. The 16x9 pixels are wider (and hence fill out the television frame).

The pixel aspect ratio information is stored in the raw media file. When interpreted incorrectly, it looks like FIGURE 4.20.

FIGURE 4.20 Both clips are the same video. The pixel aspect ratio of the one in the Source Monitor (left) is incorrectly interpreted, whereas the shot in the Program Monitor (right) is correct.

Hip to Be Square
A good rule of thumb is that if the file is 1920 x 1080 or 1280 x 720, it is full HD and should be square pixels. Every other sizing (1440 x 1080, 1280 x 1080, 960 x 720) should have a pixel aspect ratio other than square.

View all the information
It's hard to see anything wrong on a progressive display. But even when viewed, you should set the Program or Source Monitor panel to view at 100% (or 200%) size to see all the information. Additionally, you need to go to the panel menu and show both fields. Keep in mind that it's likely to see some field discrepancy on screen if you're viewing interlaced information on computer screens (which are always progressive.) Oddities can only be truly obseved on a broadcast monitor.

Let's fix a clip that's incorrectly flagged as square pixels.

1. Open the sequence 02 Bad PAR. The sequence contains two clips. The red clip is being interpreted incorrectly as being D1/DV NTSC (0.9091).

2. Play the sequence and compare the frame sizes.

3. Right-click the Red clip, and choose Reveal in Project.

4. Choose Clip > Modify > Interpret Footage. Click the Pixel Aspect Ratio Conform To button, and choose the D1/DV NTSC Widescreen 16:9 (1.2121) option.

5. Click OK. The footage conforms to the correct pixel aspect ratio and fills the frame.

6. Watch your sequence to see the impact of the change.

Field order

Video can be recorded in fields, usually 1/60 or 1/50 of a second apart. They're stored together as a single frame. The term for this is *interlacing*. Although interlacing is a depreciating technology, you'll still encounter it.

Should Adobe Premiere Pro store the field order (and retrieve it) as the first field, the top field? Or should the field order be retrieved by the second field (lower field) first? Some cameras shoot progressive where both fields are shot at the same time and stored together to make up a frame.

Generally, unless you're shooting progressive, high definition is generally upper field first. Video is generally lower field for standard definition. If you see "tearing" or "sawtooths" when you play back the video, that may be a sign of a field problem. It's easiest to see when the video is output on a broadcast monitor and jitters oddly during playback.

If you need to fix a clip that's incorrectly flagged with the wrong field order, follow these steps:

1. Select the clip

2. Choose Clip > Modify > Interpret Footage.

3. Select the Field Order Conform radio button and choose the appropriate field choice (**FIGURE 4.21**)

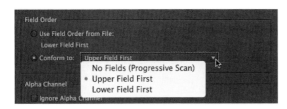

FIGURE 4.21 There are three different options for field choices: Progressive, Upper Field First, and Lower Field First.

Alpha channels

Alpha channels determine the visibility of parts of a clip. However, transparency can be confusing because of how the term alpha channel is used. The term *alpha channel* is used when it's on a clip, but when you view only the alpha channel, it's typically called a *matte*.

Two alpha channel settings are available in Adobe Premiere Pro.

- **Ignore.** This option disables the alpha channel (meaning no transparency).

- **Invert.** This option can be used if the transparency is reversed; you'll see the background, not the foreground (**FIGURE 4.22**).

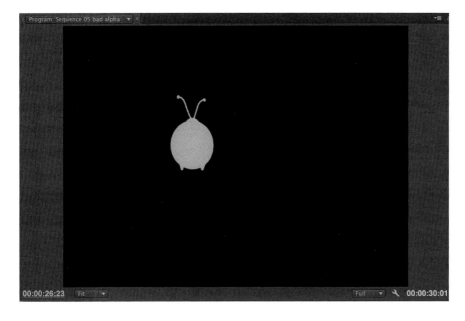

FIGURE 4.22 When the alpha channel is reversed, as in this example (a figure is animated on a gold matte background), you see the background, not the element.

Straight vs. Premultiplied Alpha

If your footage has slight glows or color shift at its edges, it may be that the alpha channel is not correctly set (it'll be obvious when it's skewed). Unfortunately, Adobe Premiere Pro lacks the ability to modify the interpretation rules. When the alpha channel interpretation is incorrect, your best bet is to bring the footage to After Effects where it can be repaired.

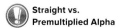

Let's fix a clip that has its alpha channel incorrectly inverted.

1. Open the Sequence 04 Bad Alpha. Go to frame 25;11.

   The sequence contains two clips. The top clip is being interpreted incorrectly over a gold matte.

2. Right-click the top clip (Bad Alpha), and choose Reveal in Project.
3. Choose Clip > Modify > Interpret Footage. Select the Alpha Channel option, and deselect the Invert Alpha Channel option.
4. Click OK. The footage shows the correct areas of transparency.
5. Watch your sequence to see the impact of the change.

Modifying Timecode

Modifying the timecode means the clip will no longer line up with the original media it was sourced from, making it nearly impossible to retransfer or recapture. So, be careful when you do this.

However, you might want to modify timecode for a couple of reasons: to sync by timecode or to assign timecode to a clip like a DSLR clip or an audio track meant to be used in multicamera editing.

To modify the timecode, follow these steps:

1. Select any clip in the Project panel.
2. Choose Clip > Modify > Timecode.
3. Enter the new timecode, and then select Set at Beginning or Set at Current Frame (FIGURE 4.23).

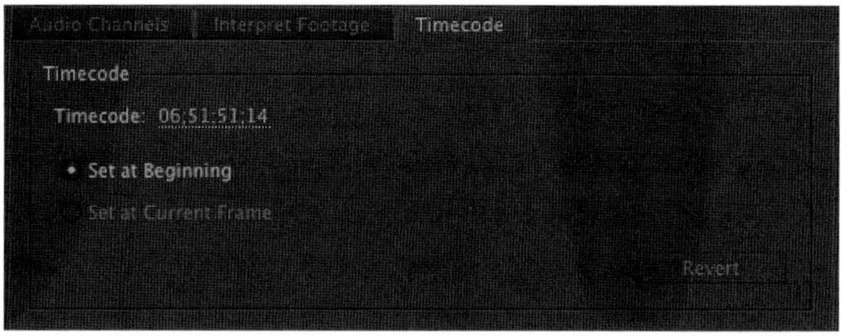

FIGURE 4.23 The Timecode adjustment window. Be aware that when you modify the timecode, you may be causing a mismatch if you ever need to relink to the nonmodified original source.

4. Click OK to make your adjustment.

An Introduction to Adobe Dynamic Link

The principal goal with Dynamic Link is to minimize time lost from rendering or exporting. The beauty of Dynamic Link is that you can pass elements between applications in the Creative Suite and minimize your need to create extra media and renders. The functionality exists between several applications but behaves a little differently depending on the pair of apps being used. Dynamic Link is currently supported by the following Adobe products:

- After Effects
- Audition
- Encore

Pro Importer
You'll find that the previously sold Automatic Duck is now bundled with After Effects. Just choose File > Import > Pro Import After Effects. You can now import Final Cut Pro and Avid projects with great accuracy. Be sure to click the Modify Settings button to adjust how tracks and media are handled.

Linking to and from Adobe After Effects

There are several ways to integrate Adobe Premiere Pro and After Effects to easily exchange projects in both directions. This seamless ability to exchange files is driven by the role each application serves. After Effects provides Adobe Premiere Pro with advanced titling, compositing, and special effects. Adobe Premiere Pro adds robust audio controls and video capture to After Effects. Here are a few workflows worth trying.

You can work with After Effects in three general ways.

- **Replace with After Effects Composition.** You can select clips in a sequence and then choose File > Adobe Dynamic Link > Replace with After Effects Composition. The clips are exchanged with After Effects, and a new linked composition is created. We explore this workflow in Chapter 12.

- **New After Effects Composition.** If you need a blank canvas (for example, to create an animated title), you can choose File > Adobe Dynamic Link > New After Effects Composition. An empty composition will open in After Effects. Save your content in After Effects when you're done, and the Adobe Premiere Pro link will update the content in your project or sequence. We explore this workflow in Chapter 13, "Creating Titles."

- **Import After Effects Composition.** In Adobe Premiere Pro you can choose File > Adobe Dynamic Link > Import After Effects Composition to bring an After Effects composition into an Adobe Premiere Pro project. Once added, the After Effects composition will look and behave like any other clip. If you make changes in After Effects, they'll automatically update in the Adobe Premiere Pro sequence.

You can work with Adobe Premiere Pro material in After Effects in two ways.

- **New Premiere Pro Sequence.** This creates an empty "clip" in After Effects. You can switch to Adobe Premiere Pro and add multiple files and even tracks into the sequence. When you switch back to Adobe Premiere Pro, you can treat the clip as a single video file. Any updates in Adobe Premiere Pro will appear in After Effects as well.

- **Import Premiere Pro Sequence.** In After Effects, you can choose File > Adobe Dynamic Link > Import Premiere Pro Sequence. This allows you to use a sequence as a single layer in your After Effects composition without having to render or export. If you make any changes in Adobe Premiere Pro, they will be automatically reflected in your After Effects comps.

Linking to and from Adobe Encore

As you finish your work, one common distribution format is disc, either DVD or Blu-ray Disc. You can take any sequence and send it to Adobe Encore. Simply choose File > Adobe Dynamic Link > Send to Encore. This method allows you to pass a sequence to DVD, Blu-ray Disc, or Flash without having to render it first.

Encore will open and let you choose the kind of disc you'd like to make (**FIGURE 4.24**) as well as what sort of default transcoding you should do. Encore will also recognize chapter markers from the Adobe Premiere Pro sequence, which allows for more precise chapter markers. Similarly, you can dynamically link an After Effects composition to an Encore project.

FIGURE 4.24 In the Encore New Project window you can choose the type of disc you'd like to build as well as the basics for transcoding.

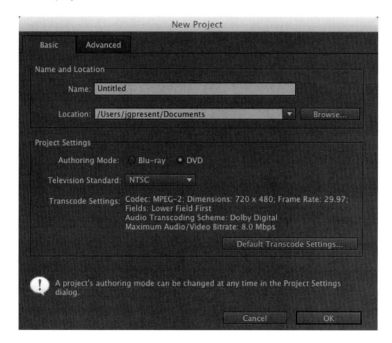

Linking to and from Adobe Audition

Starting with Adobe Production CS5.5, Adobe Audition is included in the suite. Check out Chapter 10, "Audio Mixing and Repair." Adobe Audition permits adjustment fixes of single audio clips to Adobe Audition for multitrack mixing and audio restoration.

To send a single clip, select a clip either in the browser or in a sequence. Choose Edit > Edit in Adobe Audtion > Clip. The clip will be replaced by an extracted audio clip. There is also a method of sending a sequence (see Chapter 10) that isn't a dynamic link.

DYNAMIC LINK DOESN'T MEAN IMPORT

Adobe Dynamic Link exists only for specific workflows, but it's important to remember that you can use it only for special purposes. The goal of Dynamic Link is to allow content to update easily (such as a video track in Encore after changes are made in Adobe Premiere Pro) or to make it easier to exchange files (such as between Adobe Premiere Pro and After Effects).

Besides Dynamic Link, you can almost always import files from one application to another and retain editability.

- For example, Photoshop and Illustrator graphics can be easily modified by choosing Edit > Edit Original in After Effects.

- Although Adobe Premiere Pro can't access raw camera formats, After Effects can. If you open a raw file in After Effects and save the project, you can dynamically link to the project in Adobe Premiere Pro.

Be sure to fully explore the documentation with each application to learn even more ways to use Dynamic Link. Plus, in the world of Adobe, it never hurts to just try importing a project file and see what happens.

TABLE 4.1 contains the available relationships between applications in the Creative Suite.

TABLE 4.1   Relationships Between the Tools in the Creative Suite

From	Pr	AE	Au	En	Ps	AI	Fl	AME
Adobe Premiere Pro	■	DL Export	DL Export	DL Export	Export	NA	NA Import	Export
After Effects	DL Export	■	Import	DL Export	Export	NA	Export XFL	Import
Audtion	DL Export	Export	■	Import	NA	NA	NA	NA
Encore	NA	NA	NA	■	NA	NA	Export	NA
Photoshop	Export/ Import	Export/ Import	NA	Export/ Import	■	Export/ Import	Export/ Import	NA
Flash	Export	DL	DL	Export	Export	Export/ Import	■	Export
Adobe Media Encoder	Export	Export	Export	NA	NA	NA	NA	■

DL = Dynamic Link   Import = Import project file   NA = Not applicable
Export = Export or save compatible files   XFL = XML-based Flash Exchange format

Next Steps

Now that you've managed to get hundreds of different footage types into Adobe Premiere Pro, you need to do your due diligence as an editor and "get organized." In the next chapter, we discuss adding and customizing bins and analyzing clips for face detection and speech recognition (with or without scripts attached). In addition, we'll review best practices to help your edits run smoothly.

CHAPTER 5

Organizing Media

EDITORS ARE GIVEN the task of sifting through too much footage in too little time. Toss in the challenge of making difficult delivery dates, and you'll soon see the cracks in the foundation. The greatest secret for success is to be organized and *stay organized*. Developing this discipline means you can find footage when you need it, today and in the future.

There's only one thing worse than coming back to a project that's six months (or six years) old and wondering, what is all this stuff and who did this? It's realizing that the person who did it *was you*.

In this chapter, we'll show you how to minimize this frustration, show you the power of working in the Project panel, and show you how to look at and find footage in the most effective manner.

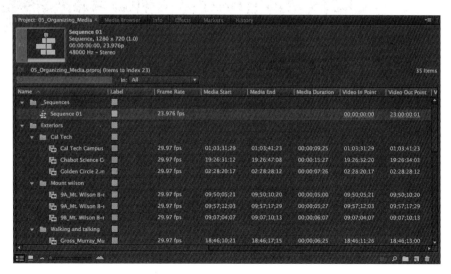

FIGURE 5.1 A well-organized project makes it easy to handle any amount of footage.

Closer To Truth
Some screen shots and footage for this chapter are from the PBS series Closer To Truth: Cosmos, Consciousness, God. © The Kuhn Foundation. Robert Lawrence Kuhn: creator, executive producer, writer and host; Peter Getzels: producer and director. Find out more about the series by visiting www.closertotruth.com.

Open/Close Everything
If you add the Option (Alt) key and click the triangle next to a bin to twirl it open (or closed), every bin will open (or close).

FIGURE 5.2 The information on this QuickTime movie indicates it's a 720p clip.

Understanding the Project Panel

The Project panel holds all your media (captures and imports), any synthetics (like titles), and sequences. It's the heart of your project; it has a record of every clip being used within a project (**FIGURE 5.1**).

There are several ways to navigate the Project panel quickly.

- When you want to select an element (clip, sequence, bin), all you have to do is click the icon. Clicking the name tells Adobe Premiere Pro that you want to edit the name.

- If you want to quickly switch between icon and list views in the Project panel, just use the shortcut Shift+\ or click the List View or Icon View buttons at the bottom of the Project panel.

- To change the size of your thumbnail icons, use the shortcut Shift+] to make them larger and the shortcut Shift+[to make them smaller. You can also use the slider at the bottom of the Project panel to manually adjust the size to your liking.

- To navigate around the Project panel, you can use the keyboard. The up and down arrow keys permit movement up and down the Project panel. The left and right arrow keys twirl open/twirl closed bins when in list view.

- When working in list view, you can see several columns of information. Each column has fields that contain important metadata about your clips. Some are prefilled with information such as Duration and Pixel Aspect Ratio. Other fields (such as Description and Log Note) can be filled in by you to hold important details. To quickly switch fields, press the Tab key to go forward or Shift+Tab to cycle backward.

- If you want to sort by a property (such as Duration or Name), just click the column heading. Click it a second time to toggle and reverse the sorting order. You can also drag columns to rearrange them left to right.

- If you'd like to see extra information for a clip, you can turn on the Preview Area at the top of the Project panel. Click the Project panel menu and choose Preview Area. You'll now see a poster frame for any selected item at the top of the Project panel. You can click the Play button or press the spacebar to view the thumbnail in full motion. It will also show any details about a clip, such as the duration of a clip, whether it's video or audio, and the frame rate/size of the clip (**FIGURE 5.2**). Many editors find the Preview Area inefficient and disable it (especially on smaller screens).

- If a clip is in the Source Monitor, Timeline panel, or Project panel, you can select it and choose File > Get Properties For > Selection to see additional information about a clip. You can also press Shift+Command+H (Shift+Ctrl+H) to see that information.

- Along the bottom row of the Project panel are a series of icons that are mostly shortcuts for elements like searching and creating new bins, sequences, or synthetics.

- In the upper-right corner (like most of the panels in Adobe Premiere Pro) is a panel menu, which contains commands that allow you to customize that panel, as well as other crucial customizations and shortcuts.

Working with Bins

As an experienced editor, you're used to using bins to organize the files in your project. Adobe Premiere Pro behaves in the same way as other nonlinear editing (NLE) tools because it lets you use bins to collect and hold elements (clips, stills, sequences, and other bins) in whatever structure you find useful.

Creating Bins

Having multiple bins is a *good* thing. It goes back to the idea that you should be (and stay) organized. You can add as many bins as you need to your project. You can create a new bin in four ways.

- Choose File > New > Bin.

- Right-click in the Project panel and choose New Bin.

- Click the New Bin icon at the bottom of the Project panel.

- Press Command+/ (Ctrl+/).

Opening Bins

When you open a bin, you have a few choices. You can open it in its own stand-alone window, open it as a separate tab in the Project panel, or open it in place.

- **Open in new window.** Simply double-click a bin to open it in a new window. This is a separate window that can be docked or moved anywhere onscreen.

- **Open new tab.** Hold down the Option (Alt) key when double-clicking to open the bin in a new tab in the Project panel.

- **Open in place.** Hold down the Command (Ctrl) key when double-clicking to open the bin in place. When you do this, it navigates the view *inside* the bin (hiding the rest of the project). By clicking the project name or the folder at the top of the window, you can navigate out of the bin (FIGURE 5.3).

FIGURE 5.3 The Exteriors bin has been opened in place. By clicking the folder with the up arrow (where the cursor is), you can move upward and back to the rest of the project.

Smart Sorting
There are some quick sorting options that might not occur to you. Try Sort by Media Duration to find the longest clips. Try Sort by Tape Name to get a listing of all the media based on which tape it came from. Try Sort by Media Start to get a list of the order in which the footage was shot.

Make Room to Organize
Be sure to try out the Metalogging Workspace (Window > Workspace> Metalogging) to arrange your panels for media-management tasks. You can also press the grave accent (`) key with your cursor over the Project panel to make it temporarily larger.

The History of Bins
The term bin goes back to actual film editing. A bin was essentially a trash can with wheels and a rack at the top with nails. You'd hang your film from the nails. As you cut up the film, you'd store the pieces in these bins—one per scene to stay organized.

Nested Bins
If you press the keyboard shortcut Command+/ (Ctrl+/) or click the New Bin icon twice, Adobe Premiere Pro will nest a new bin inside the prior bin automatically. You can also drag a bin inside another to create a nested organization structure.

Change the Opening Methods
Adobe Premiere Pro allows you to customize all three methods of opening a bin. Open the Preferences dialog and choose General. The Bins section lets you adjust the modifier key behaviors for opening bins.

Recommended Standard Bins

We use certain bins in nearly every project. In Chapter 3, "Setting Up a Project," we showed you how to build a default project. In our default project, which we duplicate, these bins are premade and ready to go.

The following are some common bins you'll likely need:

- **Sequences.** You might choose to create separate sequences for different parts of your work. When working on narrative productions, it's common to have a sequence (and bin) per scene. When working in documentary/industrial productions, it's common to have at least one bin per section that you're working on.

- **Old Sequences.** We recommend duplicating your active sequence twice a day. The reason is that you'll get a "super" undo to deal with major changes in direction by the client or producer.

- **Outputs.** Every time we output a digital file or tape, we duplicate the sequence and specify all the information such as about who the sequence is going to. Make sure you add the date (and possibly color code) to the sequence to make it easy to identify the project when the client calls with questions.

- **Imports.** We differentiate imported stills, video, and audio from camera material (which is also imported). We'll usually split the variety of non-camera-based imports into separate nested Audio, Video, and Still bins. You could also create additional folders such as Music and SFX.

- **Selects.** We recommend you duplicate your favorite shots and then move them into a bin (or series of bins) based on content. This makes it easier to find your shots in a way that's similar to your thought process.

- **Interviews.** Aside from a single interview bin, try adding a bin for each person interviewed.

- **Raw footage from tapes/cards.** We recommend one bin per tape or card. Instead of dragging out clips, copy them into your Selects folders. This virtual copy takes up no extra space and will let you search the bins based on media cards or tapes in a linear fashion based on time of day or shooting order.

Feel free to adapt this list of standard folders to your own needs. If you work in a highly specialized environment, you may find you want a few more bins to keep things organized. Just be sure to update your project template and make the change globally for all future projects. This will ensure that it's easier to find what you are looking for.

Customizing Bin and Clip Views

Once you have bins for all your media, you'll need to be able to view your media in a dynamic fashion. It's valuable to be able to survey your footage (and easy) when each shot is represented by an icon.

Sometimes it's useful to be able to view metadata of a shot, such as when you need to determine which camera the shot came from. Occasionally, you'll want to add to the metadata, such as including a description of the shot.

To begin learning what you can do, let's start by changing the view you're looking at.

Changing Views

Two different views are available for a bin: list and icon views. Most editors work in list view the majority of the time, because they can see more clips on the screen at once. However, the icon view also offers many benefits, including a storyboard view, hover-scrub, and the ability to sort visually quickly.

To switch between list and icon views, you can click the buttons found in the lower-left corner of the Project panel (**FIGURE 5.4**). You can also switch between the two views by pressing Command+Page Up (Ctrl+Page Up) for list view and Command+Page Down (Ctrl+Page Down) for icon view.

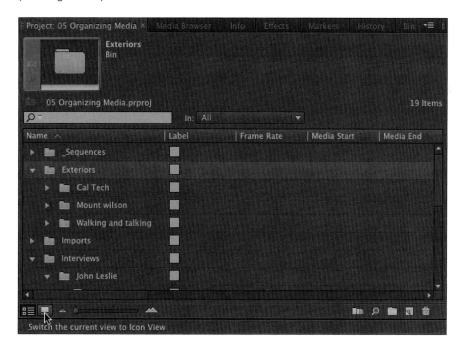

FIGURE 5.4 The Project panel in icon view with the icon button highlighted by the cursor.

List view

The list view is where most editors eat, breathe, and live on a project. It's a straightforward list with the most important ingredient, the name of the clip, listed at the left. The reason that this view is the most useful has to do with the amount of material that can be displayed as well as the sorting options mentioned earlier in the chapter.

It's possible to display a list and still view thumbnails of the shots (**FIGURE 5.5**). Use the Project panel menu to customize icon size and the display. Click the Project panel menu, and choose Thumbnails. You can also make the thumbnails larger and smaller with the same keys in icon view, Shift+[and Shift+].

FIGURE 5.5 The project being displayed in list view with thumbnails *on* and thumbnails made larger with Shift + [.

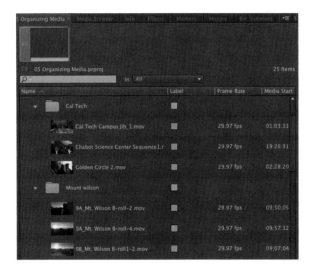

Icon view

New in Adobe Premiere Pro CS6 is a feature known as *hoverscrub*, which is the ability to hover with your mouse and scrub over a clip seeing the footage dynamically. This method of quickly scrubbing your clips, especially when thumbnails are large, has become a hit with us. It doesn't eliminate the need for the Source Monitor, but it certainly makes it faster getting to know footage, especially when you've made the bin full-screen.

The benefits of icon view include the following:

- Viewing by icon means you're able to see the clip without loading it into the Source Monitor (**FIGURE 5.6**).

- Hoverscrub lets you skim a clip's contents quickly by just dragging the mouse pointer across a clip.

- It's the foundation of editing via storyboard (see Chapter 7, "Additional Editing Skills").

- It's a great way to become familiar with footage you haven't viewed before.

- Many file-based cameras (still or video) produce clip names that are a series of numbers. Icon view is a perfect way to see what the clips are without changing their camera-assigned names.

FIGURE 5.6 The Exteriors > Cal Tech bin in icon view set to Large icons. Notice how easy it is to distinguish between wide shots and close-ups. Scrubbing your mouse over clips in icon view shows the footage thanks to hoverscrub.

Select the Filter Bin Content Box
Any time you're working in the Project panel, press Shift+F to select the Filter Bin Content box.

Where Did My Clips Go?
If the Project panel shows (filtered) next to the name of your project and you can't see your clips, it means that there's some text in the Filter Bin Content box. Clear the text, and your clips should reappear.

Searching for Clips

The primary reason and use for all the metadata is finding a clip when you need it. Being able to access a clip quickly when you have tens, hundreds, or even thousands of clips is part of an editor's skill. Adobe Premiere Pro offers two types of controls to sort through your material: filtering and finding.

Filtering Your View

When you filter your view, Adobe Premiere Pro reduces the number of clips it displays. The process is as simple as typing in the Filter Bin Content box near the top of the Project panel (**FIGURE 5.7**). Just enter a name (or other metadata) for the clip(s) you're looking for.

Based on what you type in the Filter Bin Content box, the Project panel will display only the clip information that matches your criteria. You can even have the Project panel search the transcript data (if there's a script attached to the shot).

Let's explore the filtering process.

1. Launch Adobe Premiere Pro.

2. Choose File > Open, and navigate to Lessons and Media > Lesson 05> Ch05_ Organizing_Media.prproj.

   Although the project is pretty organized, we'll use a filtered view to quickly locate clips. In this case, let's find all the interview shots of Max Tegmark.

3. In the Filter Bin Content box, start to type **Max**.

   As you type, the area below the text field starts to show you have many clips that match that keyword (currently in all the data).

4. Scroll through and look at the other data. Notice that you can still sort with this filtered view.

5. When you're finished, make sure to clear the filtered view by clicking the X in the filter area.

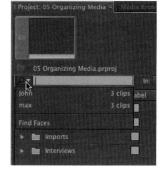

FIGURE 5.7 Click the magnifying glass to see a list of recent searches.

Using the Find Command

If you'd like to perform a more advanced search, simply invoke the Find command by pressing Command+F (Ctrl+F) or clicking the magnifying glass icon at the bottom of the Project panel. This command opens the Find dialog (**FIGURE 5.8**), which permits searches in the Project panel. This technique shares the same concept as using a Find command in a word processor or spreadsheet. By specifying identifiable criteria, you can find elements that match.

FIGURE 5.8 Each time you click the Find button, the next clip that matches the search criteria is found.

1. In the Find dialog, select the name of the columns to search from the Name menus under Column.

   Although it's not as quick as the Filter Bin Content box, the Find menu command has the extra ability to do searches based on the "AND" condition as well as searches based on the "OR" condition. To search via the "OR" condition, change the Match menu from All to Any.

2. Choose the appropriate operation (such as Contains or Starts with) from the menus under Operator.

3. Enter text to describe what you want to find in the specified columns in their respective Find What fields.

   Here's an example:

   Find ALL the clips named David that have CU (close up) in the Description field.

   Find all the clips named Princeton or Wilson to find footage that occurred at both those locations.

4. If you're searching for two criteria simultaneously, be sure to specify the relationship between the two searches.

   The Match menu allows you to switch the search from "all the criteria—this AND that" to "any of the search criteria—this OR that."

5. Click Find to start the search.

6. Click Find again to go to the next result. Click as many times as needed.

7. When you've found what you're looking for, click the Done button.

Viewing Thumbnails

Whether you're using icon view or list view with thumbnails enabled, you'll see a representative frame for the clip (called a *poster frame*). Sometimes this frame may not be very useful because it can contain a slate with no reference or lack any critical action that helps you know the content of the shot.

You can easily change a clip poster frame.

1. Select a clip in the Project panel.

2. Scrub to see the desired frame in a clip. You can use the hoverscrub feature or select the clip and use J-K-L or the clip playhead.

3. Set the poster frame by right-clicking the thumbnail viewer when it is stopped on the desired frame and choosing Set Poster Frame or pressing Cmd+P (Ctrl+P).

Assigning a Label Color

Adobe Premiere Pro automatically assigns colors of the different elements based on their type when imported. At its most basic level, this means you can look in a bin or at a timeline and know what each element is (**TABLE 5.1**).

Here's how to change a label color:

1. Make sure the Project panel is set to list view.

2. Select one or more items and choose Edit > Label.

TABLE 5.1 Default Label Assignments

Element	Color
Bin	Mango (Orange)
Sequence	Forest (Green)
Video (only)	Violet (Purple)
Audio (only)	Caribbean (Light Blue/ Green)
Movie (video + audio)	Iris (Blue)
Still	Lavender (Pink)
Adobe Dynamic Link	Rose (Red/Pink)

BEST PRACTICES FOR BIN ORGANIZATION

Although bin organization is a very personal process. You don't need to adopt all of these techniques, but think about making them part of your workflow.

- **Organize by shoot.** Consider organizing your source footage by when you actually shot the footage. This chronological order will make it easier to locate clips (especially when notes get thin from the field). Identify where footage is hidden. Searching chronologically is also useful to many producers and directors as they recall details from a shoot or want to explore different takes.

- **Duplicate clips.** Remember that you can duplicate a clip within a project with virtually no impact on disk usage. We duplicate clips all the time, especially in long-form projects. This lets us keep everything organized by shoot and then break down our clips by type, such as scene-based clips for a narrative or interview-based clips for a corporate/industrial shoot. You can use word-processor-type commands such as Copy and Paste to duplicate clips from one bin to another. You can also choose Edit > Duplicate to make a copy of a selected clip.

- **Name clips.** Because Adobe Premiere Pro knows the name of the original media (in its metadata), you can call the clips anything you want. We'll often rename duplicate copies to something more descriptive to help when browsing bins. Consider adding the initials of anyone you interview or naming a clip based on its camera move (pan L to R, dolly in) or B-roll content. If we're working on a scripted piece, we'll rename a clip based on its scene, setup, and take information.

The use of label groups makes it easy to select similar items. This is a useful way to add metadata or arrange a category of clips.

1. Select an item that represents the label or category you want in your Project panel.

2. Choose Edit > Label > Select Label Group.

   All of the similar items are now selected in the Project panel.

Using Subclips

Back in the days of tape, it was very easy for editors or assistants to split up a long tape with accurate logging before the tape was captured. These days, it's not uncommon to get a clip that's 20 or more minutes long.

These long clips are difficult to navigate with a mouse—even the smallest movement is tens of seconds. Likely, a long clip doesn't have just a single shot but multiple shots and takes. It would make your life and the project less complicated if you could divide it into piece. That's what a subclip is—a section of a clip with its own unique In and Out points. It can also have its own custom name (which can refer to the original media) (**FIGURE 5.9**).

FIGURE 5.9 This illustrates how several subclips can be taken from the same clip. Note: it's impossible, of course, to make multiple In/Out points on a single clip.

subclip 1   subclip 2   subclip 3

Creating a Subclip

The use of subclips is essential because it improves your project organization by splitting larger clips into smaller clips.

Here's how to make a subclip:

1. Select a clip and load it into the Source Monitor.

2. Mark an In point to define the start of the subclip.

3. Mark an Out point to define where the subclip ends.

4. Choose Clip > Make Subclip. A new dialog appears.

5. Give the clip a more descriptive name, and click OK. A new subclip will appear in the Project panel. Note that it has a different icon compared to a regular clip (FIGURE 5.10).

When to Subclip

A general rule is to start subclipping when a clip is longer than one minute. Of course, you might still take the time to subclip shorter clips because you can speed up the editing process when you need to audition takes and separate different takes of B-roll quickly.

Here are some situations in which subclipping is ideal:

■ Divide interviews into *just* the interviewee's responses.

■ Separate different takes in an actor's performance.

■ Break continuous camera movements into individual elements.

■ Split long B-roll shots into smaller clips so it's easier to avoid using the same shot multiple times in a project.

■ Create subclips to identify best takes and then hide the original clips in a bin labeled Do Not Use.

The Logic of Subclips

Subclips link to the original piece of media. They take up no extra room in a project. Whether a master clip or a subclip, they both point to the same media. The other major concept to keep in mind about subclips is that they're initially limited to the length you created them.

Here are some rules you should know about subclipping:

■ Subclips can't be extended beyond the initial In and Out points unless you modify the subclip (FIGURE 5.11).

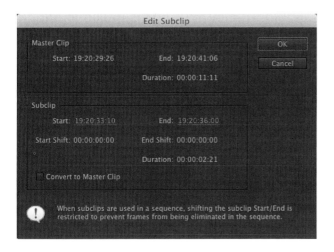

FIGURE 5.10 The subclip icon looks like an icon with an In and Out point. You can see this icon only if you turn off clip thumbnails under the panel menu.

Subclip by Dragging
Make an In point and an Out point in the Source panel. You can then Command-drag (Ctrl-drag) by clicking the video in the Source panel and dragging to a bin or the Project panel. You'll create a subclip between the In and Out points of the loaded clip.

Effective Subclipping
If the mechanics of subclipping in Adobe Premiere Pro are still a little foggy to you, check out this video to see how to create and work with subclips.

FIGURE 5.11 Notice the warning at the bottom of the Edit Subclip dialog. Your options to modify a subclip that's already in use are limited.

- To modify a subclip, select the subclip and choose Clip > Edit Subclip. If a subclip is on a timeline, you can't make it shorter than the original subclip.

- Subclips refer to the original clip unless you make them a master clip, which makes the subclip completely separate from the original.

- To turn a subclip into a master clip, select the subclip and choose Clip > Edit Subclip. Select the Convert to Master Clip check box, and click OK. Do this to completely separate the subclip from knowing the master clip it came from, essentially turning it into a duplicate.

Get Organized with Metadata

Technically, labels and columns are just a type of metadata. They're fields of data that describe a clip. Descriptions, such as the type of audio or video, the height, and the frames per seconds, are also types of metadata. At its simplest, metadata is information about your file that describes the audio, video, and technical aspects of a clip.

Some cameras add their own metadata, such as the time of day for a shot or location via GPS. Some cameras allow you to add metadata while shooting, such as a "good" rating, or user-assigned information such as camera name or angle.

Viewing Metadata

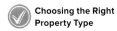
EXIF Data
Exchangeable Image File Format (EXIF) data is a standard set of data that still cameras (particularly DSLRs) use. This fantastic information includes f-stop, type of lens used, and very camera-specific items, such as distance to subject.

Choosing the Right Property Type
Adobe Premiere Pro has several classes of metadata. Text is standard alphanumeric text that sorts A–Z. Integers are whole numbers. Real refers to fractional numbers (numbers with decimal places). Boolean displays a check box (on/off).

Adobe Premiere Pro permits you to see existing metadata based on broad category types. Even more valuable is that you can add your own metadata. You can easily view this information within the Project panel (in list view) or Metadata panel (**FIGURE 5.12**). When viewing the metadata in a project, it's easy to see multiple elements along with select metadata. When viewing metadata in the Metadata panel, you see every piece of metadata for a specific selection.

Here's how to change which metadata is displayed by default. Let's enable the Comment field.

1. Option-click (Alt-click) the disclosure triangle next to the bins in the Lesson 5 project to open all the bins.

2. Maximize the Project panel by mousing over it and pressing the grave accent (`) key to switch the window to full screen.

3. Locate the Panel Options menu at the top right of the panel, and choose Metadata Display.

4. Expand the Premiere Pro Project Metadata category (**FIGURE 5.13**).

5. Select the Comment check box.

6. Click OK.

7. In the Project panel, you now can scroll horizontally to see (and fill out!) the Comment column. Experiment and add some metadata about the clips.

FIGURE 5.12 (Left) The Metadata panel, normally hidden when using the Editing workspace, can be displayed by choosing Window > Metadata.

FIGURE 5.13 (Right) Numerous other pieces of Adobe Premiere Pro–specific metadata are normally hidden.

Customizing Headings in the Metadata Display

To really maximize metadata, it's crucial to know that you can add your own metadata based on your needs and based on your specific workflow to an existing category of metadata (also called a *schema*). The Metadata display allows you to create your own fields for data in an existing schema and even lets you create your own schema, which we'll discuss in a later section. When you add your own fields or create a new schema with new fields, they'll be visible in the Project panel.

You can add any sort of field you want or need by clicking the Add Property button (**FIGURE 5.14**) next to an existing schema. Some properties that we've added in the past include the following:

FIGURE 5.14 The Metadata display with the cursor over the Add Property button. By clicking it, you can create your own custom metadata properties.

- **Framing Composition.** Identify the shot composition, such as CU, MS, or WS.

- **Speaker Name.** Who's talking? Also, get the correct spelling of the name of the person in the shot.

- **Summary.** Paraphrase the question or answer from each response in an interview.

- **Take.** For scripted pieces, be sure to identify the number of the performance (such as take 1, take 2, and so on).

Let's add the Frame Composition property to all the shots in the Exteriors bin. To make it easy, you'll change the thumbnails so they're visible and large.

1. With the same project still open, twirl down the Exteriors bin. Then twirl down the Cal Tech, Mount Wilson, and Walking and Talking bins.

2. Click the Project panel menu, and choose Metadata Display.

3. Locate the yellow hyperlinked text labeled Add Property next to the schema called Premiere Pro Project Metadata. Click the link to open the Add Property dialog (**FIGURE 5.15**).

FIGURE 5.15 By clicking the Add Property link, you can add your own custom metadata. In this case, we've added a custom field to the Premiere Pro Project Metadata schema.

4. Change the name to Frame Type.

5. Change the Type menu from Integer to Text.

6. Click OK to store the change.

7. At the end of the Adobe Premiere Pro Project Metadata schema list is a new field called Frame Type.

8. Click OK to add the field to the Project panel.

9. Drag the Frame Type column all the way to the left so it's next to the Name column.

10. Go to the Frame Type Column and fill in the shot types (**FIGURE 5.16**).

FIGURE 5.16 Common frame types are WS (wide shot), MS (medium shot), and CU (close-up).

Saving Schema

So far, you've learned how metadata can help you get organized, whether it's the ability to show or hide metadata fields or the option to add metadata that is unique for your needs. The final step to using metadata is to control it through the use of categories.

Adobe Premiere Pro offers you the ability to create a separate metadata category called a *schema*. This is a custom category of metadata based on your needs. If your work requires a range of proprietary metadata, such as an internal cataloging system or an address book such as a database, a schema permits you to have a custom grouping of your custom metadata.

To build your own schema, do the following:

1. Click the Project panel menu, and choose Metadata Display.

2. Click the New Schema button to create your own category (**FIGURE 5.17**).

FIGURE 5.17 Creating a new schema can be done in the Metadata display.

3. Enter a descriptive name for the new schema, and click OK.

4. Now notice next to your new schema there is the yellow Click the Add Property hyperlinked text that you saw before when you added a field to the Premiere Pro Project Metadata schema. Clicking this option will open the Add Property dialog.

5. Create custom fields, and be sure to specify their types.

   The steps are identical to how you created the Frame Type field previously. It's likely you'd create more than just one field for your own custom schema.

Using the Metadata Panel

Separate from the Project panel is the Metadata panel. This panel is devoted to showing *all the metadata* for whichever clip (or clips) is selected. This panel makes it possible to add or adjust and view metadata beyond what's visible in the Project panel, and because it needs more screen real estate, it has its own separate panel (see the sidebar "Getting Organized with a Second Monitor").

To open the Metadata panel, choose Window > Metadata (**FIGURE 5.18**). You can also access the Metalogging workspace by choosing Window > Workspace > Metalogging (**FIGURE 5.19**).

 Clip vs. File and Modification Dates
Notice there are two areas that have some similar data: the Clip section and the File section in the Metadata panel? If you change anything in the File area, it will permanently modify the file itself.

FIGURE 5.18 (Right) The Metadata panel displays all the data Adobe Premiere Pro has about a clip.

FIGURE 5.19 (Below) The Metalogging workspace switches the primary focus of Adobe Premiere Pro to viewing and modifying metadata.

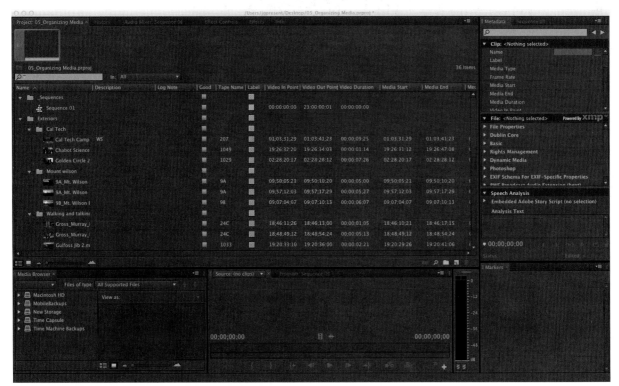

GETTING ORGANIZED WITH A SECOND MONITOR

Originally, editing system screens were such low resolution that it was necessary to have two screens to get work done. Organization took place on one screen, and the other was used for the editorial interface.

Even though screens are getting wider, we're still huge fans of using two screens (FIGURE 5.20).

FIGURE 5.20 Two monitors really make handling of medium and long-form projects easier with the additional real estate.

To increase the available screen space, use multiple monitors. When you work with multiple monitors, the application window appears on one monitor, and you place floating windows on the second monitor. Monitor configurations are stored in the workspace. Create your own workspaces for two-screen flexibility beyond the built-in ones.

To make any panel into a floating window, choose Undock Panel from any panel menu. To make any frame (a collection of panels) free-floating, choose Undock Frame from the panel menu.

With all this metadata, the second screen is devoted to both our Project panel and the Metadata panel. The extra real estate really eases handling the amount of information and organization in our projects.

Here are some important details when using the Metadata panel:

- You can choose any one element and view its metadata.

- You can select multiple items to view or modify several elements simultaneously.

- You'll often need to view and modify multiple clips, especially in long-form projects. Be sure to use the Metalogging workspace to see all of your media organization and metadata tools at once.

- When the Metadata panel is visible, you're able to work in both the Project panel and/or the Metadata panel to access and modify your metadata information.

Where's the Metadata?
If you perform speech analysis, the metadata is added to the media file. This means the data will stick with the clip even as it moves between projects and users.

Organizing Clips with Speech Analysis

It seems like more and more media is being pushed at editors. This is caused by the convenience of tapeless media as well as the lower cost of field-production equipment. To combat this steady rise in shot ratio (the amount of footage shot versus the amount used), you'll find a useful analysis methods to make finding the right clip faster: speech search. Speech analysis is game-changing as an editor. When paired with a transcript, it makes selecting a sound bite as easy as selecting text.

For speech analysis, you have the ability to send any clip to Adobe Media Encoder. Adobe Media Encoder will generate a transcript using speech analysis. Since the results vary too much, we prefer attaching a professionally created transcript. After the metadata is either created or attached, you'll have the ability to search for specific text in the speech.

Speech analysis technology is a bit of a mixed bag. It works very well on some subjects (especially those who speak clearly and enunciate). It doesn't work as well for those who tend to slur their words or speak with strong accents. A poor microphone or bad audio recording can also complicate its results.

Analyzing a Clip

Let's analyze the speech of a clip. To give you more choices, we suggest you first download all of the available languages from Adobe.com. To download all languages from Adobe's Web site, visit http://j.mp/otherlang.

1. Select the clip 0007B-John Leslie_Mt. Wilson Observatory_Leslie-4.mov in the Interviews > John Leslie bin.

2. Choose Clip > Analyze Content.

   A new dialog opens (**FIGURE 5.21**).

FIGURE 5.21 With the numerous varieties in English, it's useful to pick the closest native version for the speaker.

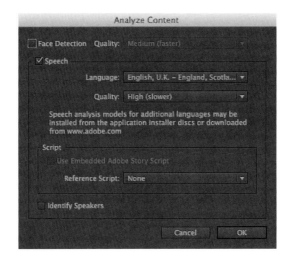

3. Deselect Face Detection, and select the Speech option.

4. Choose English – U.K... for Language, and set Quality to High.

5. Click OK.

   Adobe Media Encoder will launch (if it's not already open) and will analyze the speaker's voice. When the clip is finished, switch back to Adobe Premiere Pro. You can continue to edit while speech analysis is running. The metadata will be added as each clip completes the analysis process.

6. In Adobe Premiere Pro, choose Window > Metadata to open the Metadata panel.

7. Select the clip again in the Project panel.

8. In the Metadata panel, under the Speech Analysis area, you can see the results of the speech analysis (**FIGURE 5.22**).

FIGURE 5.22 The Speech Analysis panel permits marking In and Out points and direct editing from the text. It did OK but not great. In a later section we'll show you how to improve the results.

Although the text isn't perfect, we'll show you how to refine accuracy with a transcript. The rough transcript may be good enough to spot a sound bite or talking point. You can click a word to cue the sound bite and move the Current Time Indicator. And if desired, you can click and edit the text.

After analysis is performed, speech is visible in the Metadata panel. You can also click a word to edit it to improve the accuracy of the transcript.

Improving Accuracy with a Transcript

Speech analysis can be markedly improved by referencing a document of what was actually said. For interviews, the ideal item to use to help the quality of the analysis is a transcript. Often, corporate and documentary productions have interviews transcribed. This helps with scriptwriting and can help an editor to quickly find a sound bite from an interview.

Transcripts are usually generated by exporting an MP3 audio file, which can be sent to a transcription service. The service will return a text document with each speaker separated. To take advantage of this document, you need to link to a text file (.txt) in the Analyze Content dialog.

Let's use a transcript to get decent analysis from a speaker with a difficult accent.

1. Continue working with the current project.

2. Locate the clip 0257A-Juan Maldacena_Princeton_Maldacena-4.mov, and load it into the Source panel. You'll find it in the Interviews > Juan Maldacena bin.

 Go High or Go Home
Given that Adobe Premiere Pro performs speech analysis with no per speaker training, we feel that the only Quality choice worth using is High.

 What About Face Detection
Face detection technology looks through your clips and sets a flag (yes or no) if a clip has a face in it, allowing you to quickly narrow down your clips. It's possible to filter a project for just clips with faces. Just choose this option in the Analyze Content dialog and stick with the Medium quality choice.

 Follow the Bouncing Ball
Arrange the Metadata panel so you can see the Source panel at the same time (this is a great time to use the Metadata workspace!). Now when you play back a clip that's had speech analysis performed, each word becomes highlighted as the clip plays. You can also click a word to cue up text.

 Timecoded Transcripts
There's no need to pay for timecode transcripts because the analysis feature will sync the transcript and make speech search very functional.

Speech Search
After you have performed speech analysis on your interviews, you can then use the Filter Bin Content box to specifically filter for a given word spoken by a speaker. With this feature, you can quickly filter through your project, finding clips with specific phrases that you're looking for.

Improving Speech Analysis with a Text File

Check out this video for more on using speech analysis and then adding a "phrasionary" to improve analysis.

FIGURE 5.23 Reference scripts have the option to match recorded dialogue. It's possible to just add common jargon that'd be difficult to recognize (see the following video).

If You Don't Have Transcripts

You can try giving Adobe Premiere Pro a document that has difficult words or phrases (often referred to as a phraseology) to improve analysis.

Try and Try Again

If you're working with transcripts and you don't want to wait for them to analyze speech, you can perform speech analysis in Adobe Premiere Pro twice: right away when you first get the clip(s), and then again after you've received the transcript.

3. Click Play to listen to the clip; you'll notice a strong accent.

4. In the bin select the shot 0257A-Juan Maldacena_Princeton_Maldacena-4.mov, and choose Clip > Analyze Content.

5. Select the option for Speech analysis.

6. Set Language to English-U.S. and Quality to High (Slower).

7. In the Script portion of the dialog, in the Reference Script menu, choose to add a reference script (**FIGURE 5.23**).

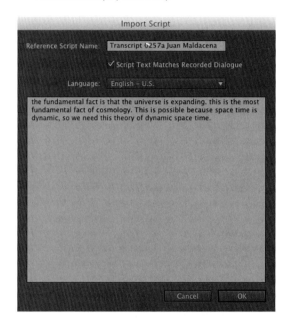

8. Choose File > Open, navigate to Lessons and Media> Lesson 05, and choose the text file Transcript 0257a Juan Maldacena.txt.

9. Because this is a transcript, in the Import Script dialog, select the Script Text Matches Recorded Dialogue check box and click OK. This has to be a plain-text file.

10. Click OK to start Adobe Media Encoder speech analysis.

11. When it finishes, play the clip with the Metadata panel visible and compare how the interviewee's speech compares with the speech analysis.

A reference script, list of talking points, or key phrases can improve translation, too. Just be sure not to select the Script Text Matches Recorded Dialogue check box.

Improving Accuracy with a Script and Adobe Story

For narrative scripts, Adobe Story (FIGURE 5.24) is a great screenwriting application that tightly integrates with the Creative Suite. There are two versions: Adobe Story Free and Adobe Story Plus (see the "Adobe Story Free vs. Adobe Story Plus" sidebar).

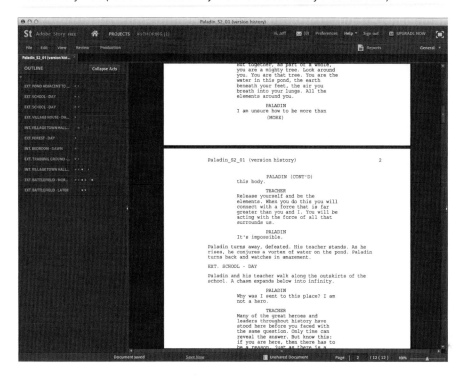

FIGURE 5.24 Adobe Story can help you create more organized scripts. It also translates that information into searchable meta-data which is helpful for a speedy postproduction workflow.

You can choose to create an entirely new script or just to convert a script created in other software (such as Final Draft or Microsoft Word) to the Story format. When a script, such as a screenplay, is used, a slightly different workflow occurs.

The actual script should be processed with Adobe Story. It can then be attached to the footage. Here are some rules about using Adobe Story for improved analysis:

- Scripts must be generated in Adobe Story. You can import an existing file from other scriptwriting software or a text file. You can also create entirely new scripts.

- For best results, assign scene numbers to the script.

- Adobe Premiere Pro must have the scene metadata filled out with matching scene information for a clip.

- A script is attached by selecting a clip and choosing File > Adobe Story > Attach Script File.

- Scripts created with other tools *must* go through Adobe Story first so they can be saved in the .astx format.

The Adobe Story Workflow
Check out this video to learn the essentials of integrating Adobe Story with Adobe Premiere Pro.

A Safer Backup
Instead of "versioning" your project by choosing File > Save As, choose File > Save as Copy to create a duplicate of the project but continue working in the project with the existing name.

Next Steps

Now that you're comfortable with the Project panel and metadata, you're ready to hone the essential editing skills. In the next chapter, we'll discuss editing and how to load footage into the Source Monitor. Then you'll learn how to make In and Out points, selecting the footage you consider important. We'll also explain how to get that footage into the Timeline panel to make further edits.

CHAPTER 6

Essential Editing Skills

UP UNTIL THIS point, we've spent a great deal of time focusing on getting organized for editing. As an experienced editor, you know that properly configuring and organizing an edit is essential to a successful project. Of course, it's not as much fun as *actually* editing video.

After all, you probably didn't get into this business because you like organizing files with folders or knowing the finer points of how a video codec works. You want to create compelling stories—stories that entertain, inform, or even inspire! Without further ado, let's get to the fun stuff, editing in Adobe Premiere Pro.

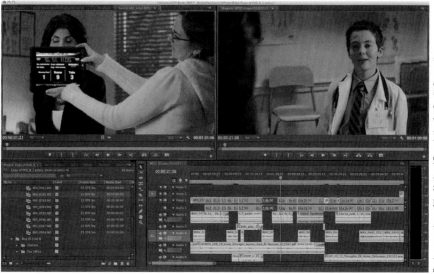

Footage courtesy of the National Foundation for Credit Counseling (www.DebtAdvice.org)

Source vs. Sequence Clips
It's important to understand the relationship source clips have to sequences. Every time you add a source clip to a sequence, a new instance is created in the Timeline (called a sequence clip). By double-clicking a clip, you will load it into the Source Monitor panel, where you can edit the effects and properties of sequence clips individually with no effect on the source media file. When loaded in the Source menu, sequence clips are identified by including the sequence name before the clip name and a time-code reference at the end.

Using the Source Monitor

In the previous chapter, you mastered ways to organize your media and quickly locate clips (if you skipped Chapter 5, please go back and read it now). Although there are many ways to edit, most pros agree that using the Source Monitor offers far greater precision than any of the drag-and-drop methods. By accurately selecting which parts of a clip to use before the clip hits the Timeline, you'll have less editing and clean up to do.

Loading a Clip

To use the Source Monitor, you simply need to load a clip into it. However, there are multiple ways to have clips appear in the Source Monitor, depending on the task you're choosing. Here are the two most relevant methods to load a single clip:

- Double-click a clip in the Project or Timeline panel.

- Drag a clip from the Project panel to the Source Monitor.

Once you've added a clip, the Source Monitor opens (**FIGURE 6.1**). Its name is also added to the Source menu. When you click the menu (**FIGURE 6.2**), you'll see that clips are listed in the order in which you load them (with the newest clips at the bottom of the list).

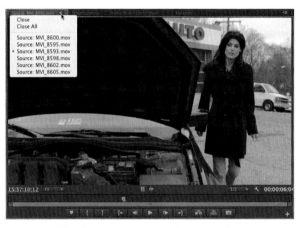

FIGURE 6.1 The Source Monitor's primary controls are located along its bottom edge. You can toggle their visibility by clicking the Settings menu and choosing Show Transport Controls.

FIGURE 6.2 The Source menu places the newest clips at the bottom of the list.

Long List of Sources
The Source menu can get so long that it extends to the bottom edge of your screen. At that point, the old items will drop off the list. If there are too many clips to sort through, just click the Source menu and choose Close All.

Let's practice loading a clip.

1. Launch Adobe Premiere Pro.

2. Choose File > Open, and navigate to Lessons and Media > Lesson 06 > 06_essential_editing.prproj. You'll use this project for all the exercises in this chapter.

3. Open the project bins and try loading individual clips into the Source Monitor.

   You'll find two bins called Card 01 and Card 02 nested in the Footage bin.

4. Click the Source menu, and switch to previously loaded clips.

With a little customization, you can use keyboard shortcuts to navigate clips in the Source Monitor. This is a great way to quickly switch between loaded clips and activate sources.

1. Choose Premiere Pro > Keyboard Shortcuts (Edit > Keyboard Shortcuts). The Keyboard Shortcuts dialog opens.

2. Scroll to Panels and click the disclosure triangle next to Source Monitor Panel to reveal the customizable commands for that panel.

3. Click to set keyboard shortcuts for any of the commands that begin with *Source Clip*. We suggest the mapping as indicated in the following table.

4. Click Save As, and give your keyboard shortcut set a custom name.

5. Click OK.

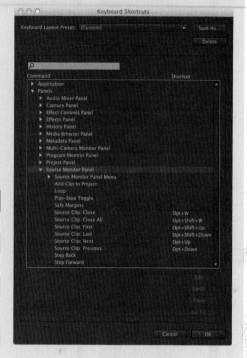

Command	Mac	Windows
Source Clip: Close	Option+W	Alt+W
Source Clip: Close All	Option+Shift+W	Alt+Shift+W
Source Clip: First	Option+Shift+up arrow	Alt+Shift+up arrow
Source Clip: Last	Option+Shift+down arrow	Alt+Shift+down arrow
Source Clip: Next	Option+up arrow	Alt+up arrow
Source Clip: Previous	Option+down arrow	Alt+down arrow

Loading Multiple Clips

You can quickly populate the Source Monitor with several clips. This is a useful way to stay organized, because you can load the next group of shots you intend to work with. Let's load several clips. You'll continue to use the same project as before.

1. Switch to the Project panel, and locate the bin called Footage. Open it and locate Card 01.

2. Select multiple clips in the bin.

   You can hold down the Shift key to select a range of clips or press the Command (Ctrl) key to select noncontiguous clips. You can also drag an entire folder at one time.

3. Drag all of your selected clips into the Source Monitor.

   All of the clips load into the Source Monitor, but only one is visible. The order in which clips load is based on the order you originally selected them. The last clip you choose will be active in the Source Monitor. To switch clips, just click the Source menu.

 Want More Timecode?
Timecode numbers in time ruler are not visible by default in Adobe Premiere Pro CS6. You can click the Settings menu (the wrench icon) and choose Show Time Ruler Numbers. Remember, the yellow text on the left edge indicates the current timecode, so you can probably get by without using the continuous scale. It's all about reducing clutter in CS6.

Source and Program Monitor Controls

The Source Monitor has many controls (**FIGURE 6.3**). There is no "right" way to work with your footage. Rather, you can choose which features you'd like to use. Here are some of the most useful controls that you have to choose from when it comes to navigating through a clip:

21 **Controlling the Source Monitor**
In this video you'll learn how to load and control clips in the Source Monitor.

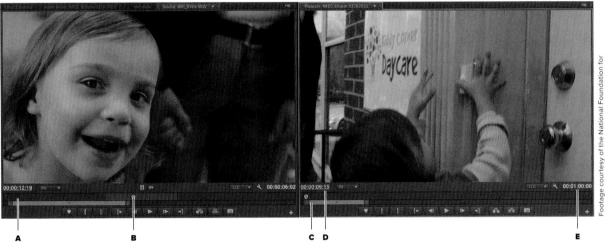

A   B   C D   E

Footage courtesy of the National Foundation for Credit Counseling (ww.DebtAdvice.org)

FIGURE 6.3 Pay close attention to how the Source and Program Monitors differ. The most important differences lie in which information is displayed as timecode.

 More (or Less) Controls
Don't like the buttons you have? Then change them! You can open the Button Editor for the Source and Program Monitors by clicking the plus-shaped icon in the lower-right corner. You can now drag new buttons to add them as well as rearrange them. Change your mind? Just click the Reset Layout button to go back to the default set.

A Time ruler. The time ruler is useful for measuring where you are within a clip. The tick marks equate to the unit of time. You can also see the In and Out points for the clip (which can also be dragged and repositioned). Timecode numbers are off by default but can be enabled by clicking the Settings button and choosing the Time Ruler Numbers option.

B Playhead. The playhead shows you the current frame in the monitor. Older documentation may refer to this as the current-time indicator (CTI).

C Horizontal zoom bar. Adjusting the horizontal zoom bar controls the level of detail you'll see in the time ruler. You can drag the end handles to change the scale or press the plus (+) or minus (-) keys. You can also drag the center of the bar to scroll through the time ruler.

D Current time display. The time display in the lower left of the video frame shows the timecode for the playhead. The Source Monitor shows the time of the current clip, and the Program Monitor shows the sequence's current time. To switch the measurement method, Command-click (Ctrl-click) the current time display.

E Duration display. The duration display in the lower right of the video frame shows the duration between the In and Out points set. When no In point is set, the start of the clip or the sequence is used. When no Out point is set, the Source Monitor uses the end of the clip, and the Program Monitor uses the end of the last clip in the sequence to calculate duration.

22 **Editing Directly from a Bin**
Thanks to the new viewing options for clips, it's possible to view very large thumbnails for your clips right in a bin. In fact, you can set In and Out points as well as view clips in real time without ever using the Source Monitor. Some prefer this style of editing, and it's worth checking out how it works in this video.

Playback Resolution

Playing back certain video formats can require a great deal of processing power. This is especially true for both highly compressed formats (such as DSLR) and formats that require mathematically difficult debayering such as RED's .R3D files). Fortunately, the Source and Program Monitors let you lower the playback resolution (**FIGURE 6.4**).

FIGURE 6.4 If you are editing off an internal drive on a laptop, lowering the playback resolution can improve playback for HD footage.

Let's change the playback resolution for a sequence. You'll continue to use the same project as before.

1. Switch to the Project panel.

2. Open Bin Sequences.

3. Locate the sequence called 03 Doctor Reference. Double-click to load the sequence.

4. Click the Playback Resolution menu in the Program Monitor and set the quality to ½.

5. Click Play to view the change in performance and quality. See how the performance of your system varies with the resolution.

Paused Resolution

For both the Source and Program Monitors, you can also choose a separate Paused Resolution display. This offers great control over your ability to monitor video. Many editors choose to set the playback resolution to a lower setting (such as ½ or ¼) but will leave the Paused Resolution setting at the default, set to Full. To access the controls, just click the Settings menu (the wrench icon) and choose Paused Resolution (**FIGURE 6.5**).

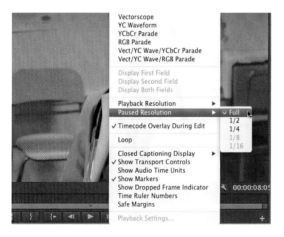

FIGURE 6.5 The Paused Resolution setting should typically be set to Full quality.

Full-resolution display when paused (the default) makes it easier to check for critical areas such as focus and edge detail. This extra level of information is also helpful when performing tasks such as keying and color correction. Just keep in mind that scrubbing uses the playback resolution, not the Paused Resolution setting.

Resolution Shortcuts
Use the following shortcuts to switch the resolution of the Program Monitor or Source Monitor.

Full   Cmd+0 (Ctrl+0)
½   Cmd+2 (Ctrl+2)
¼   Cmd+4 (Ctrl+4)
⅛   Cmd+8 (Ctrl+8)

Unlimited RT
Using a lower playback resolution is very similar to using the Unlimited RT features in Final Cut Pro 7. You are decreasing the load on the system by reducing the playback resolution during the creative editing stage.

Draft Mode
Using a lower playback resolution is very similar to using Draft Quality or Best Performance in Avid's Video Quality menu. You are decreasing the load on the system by reducing the playback resolution during the creative editing stage.

50 Percent = 75 Percent
Setting the playback resolution to half quality significantly lowers the load on your system. Half quality loads half the data for the width and half for the height (25 percent of the information). In other words, 75 percent of the overhead is reduced. You'll hardly notice the difference because your Source and Program Monitor panels are likely not full-screen. Why waste the resources to play pixels you can't see?

Which Resolution?
Not all playback resolutions are available for all sequence types. Most standard-definition sequences offer Full and ½. Many HD sequences allow for ¼ resolution. Larger formats like R3D and ARRIRAW can go as low as ¹⁄₁₆.

Viewing Fields

If you're working with interlaced sources (such as SD or 1080i), you can choose how the Source Monitor and Program Monitor display fields (**FIGURE 6.6**). You can choose to see the first (upper) field, second (lower) field, or both fields to check interlacing. Just click the Settings menu in the Source Monitor or Program Monitor and choose the desired option. Note that this option is disabled for sequences that use a progressive preset.

FIGURE 6.6 Many users choose to view only a single field when viewing interlaced video on their computer displays. The interlaced settings are typically supported by third-party output cards.

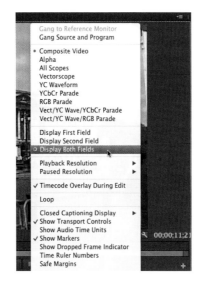

False Errors
If you're working with compressed footage, especially AVCHD and other H.264-codec-based media, you may see artifacts. These appear in the Source Monitor or Program Monitor when you lower the playback resolution. When set below Full resolution, these formats have error correction turned off. The artifacts are not really there and will not appear in exported media.

Change the Magnification Level

Chances are you'll need to shrink the display size of a video clip to see it edge to edge in both the Source and Program Monitors. The most commonly used option is Fit, which scales the window so the entire clip is visible (**FIGURE 6.7**).

1. Select either the Source or Program Monitor.

   Make sure a video clip is displayed beneath the playhead.

2. Click the Select Zoom Level menu and choose a desired size.

   The Fit option is most common. For critical image analysis, consider viewing actual pixels at 100% (you'll likely need to adjust the size of the panel to accommodate the picture). The scale of the Source Monitor is a percentage of the original media. The Program Monitor is a percentage of the sequence's frame size.

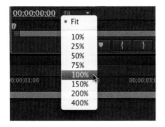

FIGURE 6.7 The Fit view lets you see your entire image in the Source or Program Monitor.

Which Scale?
The 100% scale option is the most visually accurate. The Fit option is most popular but is the least accurate because it often scales using decimal values to fit your screen. A better choice in many cases is 50%.

3. Expand the size of the panel as needed.

   In some cases, such as when animating with the Motion effect, you may want to decrease the scale and increase the panel size. This will enlarge the pasteboard (the empty area around the video) and give you more room for keyframes and manipulating the image. Use the monitor's scroll bars to adjust the visible area of a monitor. Scroll bars appear only when the image is too big for a monitor. Alternately, use the Hand tool (H) to pan around the screen.

Changing Frames in the Program or Source Monitor

As a skilled editor, you know there are many ways to move around your media. Whether by clicking buttons or dragging with a mouse, the user interface provides obvious and familiar tools that match the conventions used by other nonlinear editing (NLE) software packages. What's less obvious is the many keyboard shortcuts available (**FIGURE 6.8**). **TABLE 6.1** contains the default navigation keys (which can of course be modified with the Keyboard Shortcuts panel).

FIGURE 6.8 To help you learn keyboard shortcuts, you can get a color-coded keyboard with many of the shortcut keys labeled. This one is from Logickeyboard (www.logickeyboard.com).

TABLE 6.1 Default Navigation Shortcuts

Command	Shortcut
Play backward (tap for acceleration)	J
Pause	K
Play forward (tap for acceleration)	L
Advance one frame	Hold down the K key and tap the L key, or press the right arrow key
Advance five frames (or amount specified as large trim in preferences)	Shift+right arrow key
Jump back one frame	Hold down the K key and tap the J key, or press the left arrow key
Jump back five frames (or amount specified as large trim in preferences)	Shift+left arrow key
Go To Next Edit Point button	Down arrow with a Timeline panel or Program Monitor active
Go To Previous Edit Point button	Up arrow with a Timeline panel or Program Monitor active

Want Slow-Mo?
Just hold down the K key and then press J or L to play in slow motion. J will play backward at a reduced rate, and L will play forward.

Modifying Tracks While Editing

A quick way to modify tracks while editing is to simply right-click an audio or video track in the targeted track headers. You can then choose to rename, add, or delete tracks, as well as indicate where the new tracks should be located. You might decide that renaming is a good option. For example, you can identify audio tracks by their role, such as Music, SFX, Dialog, and so on. No one said you had to be limited to the classic V1 and A1 structure, which really relates to traditional decks or NLE timeline structure.

Targeting and Patching

In this video you can see the different ways that targeting tracks can be accomplished using both track targeting and patching.

Navigating the Timeline

Now that you've mastered clip navigation, it's time to start putting things all together (literally). The Timeline panel should feel quite familiar to an experienced editor. There are a few subtle differences, however, that are worth exploring, as well as a powerful feature worth noting.

Opening a Sequence in a Timeline Panel

When you first launch Adobe Premiere Pro, the Timeline panel is visible (even if no sequence is loaded). A few important features are useful for additional control over sequences.

- Double-clicking a sequence is the fastest way to load it into the Timeline panel.

- You can open as many sequences as you like in the Timeline panel. If you have several open, a thin scroll bar appears at the top of the panel, which you can drag to navigate horizontally through the open tabs.

- You can drag a sequence tab and drop it into another docking area. This will create another Timeline panel that can have sequences added to it as well. This is useful for comparing two sequences at once.

Targeting Tracks

It's essential that you target where you want an edit to occur in a sequence. This can be done through targeting specific tracks so they are highlighted. It is possible to edit in new content as well as overwrite existing content with empty space as you make an edit without targeting. Editing is very much about precision, and this ability to precisely target a specific track is an essential skill (**FIGURE 6.9**).

FIGURE 6.9 You can edit media in your Timeline in several ways. Dragging (left) lets you drop the media into place. Pasting (center) lets you copy or cut media that's in the Timeline and paste it into a new location (controlled by targeting tracks). Patching with the Source Monitor (right) and a three-point edit is the most accurate method.

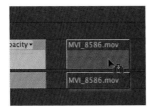 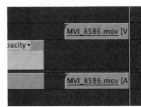 

The technique you choose will vary based on your editing approach.

- **Dragging.** If you prefer to edit by dragging clips, you can target tracks by simply dropping a clip where you want it. This method is the least accurate and can lead to clips ending up in unintended places.

- **Pasting.** If you choose to paste clips from one part of your sequence to another, you must specify target tracks first. You can select more than one target track using the track headers. The lowest track targeted will always be used if multiple tracks are targeted.

- **Source Monitor.** The most precise way to edit is with the Source Monitor. You can use both audio and video source track indicators as well as target where you want the edit. You can target multiple tracks at one time. Then using a three-point edit, you'll have an accurate edit.

In and Out Points

You'll find that the In and Out points feature in Adobe Premiere Pro behaves similarly to other editing tools. The standard shortcuts of I and O are used to mark an In and Out point, respectively. A few additional shortcuts and commands are related to In and Out points that are worth mentioning.

- **Reposition In and Out points.** If you hold the Option (Alt) key, you can drag the In/Out Grip (the textured area at the center of the shaded span between the In and Out points) to reposition the In and Out points simultaneously (**FIGURE 6.10**). This allows you to set a new range in the Program Monitor or Timeline panel without changing the duration marked. This technique is called *slipping* and is covered in depth in Chapter 9.

FIGURE 6.10 You can hold the Option (Alt) key to switch to the hand tools and make it easier to drag the In/Out Grip.

- **Remove In and Out points.** If you Option-click (Alt-click) the In or Out button, you'll clear the In or Out point (**FIGURE 6.11**). We also recommend customizing your keyboard shortcuts so Option+I (Alt+I) and Option+O (Alt+O) clear the In and Out points.

FIGURE 6.11 When creating a three-point edit, you may need to clear a fourth mark from the Source or Program Monitor.

- **Go to In and Out points.** You can also use the keyboard shortcuts so Shift+I and Shift+O go to the In and Out points (**FIGURE 6.12**).

FIGURE 6.12 Be sure to keep the Go to In and Go to Out mapped on your keyboard for maximum speed.

 Video Only or Audio Only Edits While Dragging
If you really like dragging and dropping, you can take more control. When a clip is loaded into the Source Monitor, two small icons (next to the Zoom level menu) represent video and audio. By dragging just one icon (instead of the whole clip), you can select just video or audio for an edit.

New Audio Behavior
A welcome addition in CS6 is that you no longer need to precisely match mono sources to mono tracks or stereo to stereo tracks. You can place a mono or stereo clip on the same "standard" track. You can see the number of channels indicated by clip color or when you expand the track and view its waveform.

 Targeting Shortcuts
Most of the track targeting commands can have custom keyboard shortcuts assigned if you prefer using the Keyboard Shortcuts menu.

WORKING WITH MIXED-FORMAT SEQUENCES

It's essential to remember that although you can mix clips with different frame rates, frame sizes, and aspect ratios, there's no reason to make your machine work harder than needed. Always take the time to set your sequence settings to match your primary format during the creative editing stage (if needed, you can switch the settings to render for final output if a different mastering codec is desired). For more on sequences, be sure to read Chapter 3, "Setting Up a Project File."

Here are a few more details to remember:

- **HD and SD mixing.** If you mix clips with different frame sizes and aspect ratios, Adobe Premiere Pro can automatically scale the video appropriately. If needed, clips will be letterboxed or pillarboxed when the edge of the frame is reached. Just right-click a clip and choose Scale to Frame Size.

- **Mixed frame rates.** If the frame rate of a clip differs from the sequence frame rate, it will play back at the sequence's rate.

- **Don't panic when you see red.** Although red and yellow render bars accurately communicate the need to render before final output, they are no guarantee that media won't play back. We recommend rendering during downtime or better yet final output. During the creative edit, try to play back all clips as is (often your system will be robust enough to handle the footage).

Using Markers

The use of markers is likely part of your editing approach already. Some editors use markers to quickly identify parts of a clip (such as action or a selected sound bite). Others use markers to position and align elements in a Timeline. Adobe Premiere Pro has a versatile marker system, one that even supports Web interaction.

Adding Markers to Clips

Many editors choose to add markers to clips. Clip markers are useful for attaching notes to clips or creating points that can be used to align two or more clips. Markers can be added using the Source Monitor panel.

1. Open the Footage bin in the Project panel and choose any clip. Double-click to load it.

2. Position the playhead where you want the marker to appear.

3. Click the Marker button or choose Marker > Add Marker (M) (**FIGURE 6.13**).

FIGURE 6.13 Click the Add Marker button once to add a marker. Do not double-click it, or you will add an additional marker.

 CS6 Markers Are a Big Change
The use of markers in Adobe Premiere Pro CS6 have been dramatically simplified and consolidated. You'll no longer find dedicated markers for sequences or clips. The numbered markers are also gone. What's left is a unified marker system that performs all of the same functions without unique types.

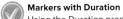 **Markers with Duration**
Using the Duration property is a useful way to make a detailed comment about a particular clip. Markers with duration have a bar extending from the marker to show a time range. Any comment entered will display next to the marker; if no comment is entered, the marker name data is displayed.

4. To modify a marker, press Option+M (Alt+M) and enter details using the Marker dialog (FIGURE 6.14).

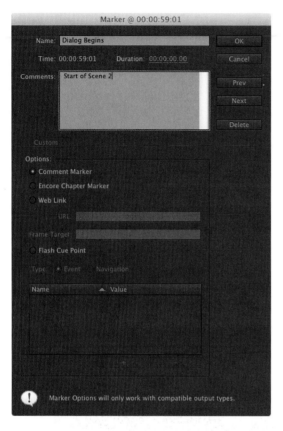

FIGURE 6.14 The Marker dialog box contains several options for modifying the content and behavior of a marker.

 Semi-permanent Markers
Adding a marker to a clip permanently modifies the media. It will travel with the clip when you add it into a sequence or when the clip is imported into a new Adobe Premiere Pro project.

Viewing Markers Easily
You can see an easy-to-navigate list of markers in the new Markers panel (docked with the Project panel by default). This is also a great way to edit the marker's comment as well as In and Out points. If you want to name a marker or change its type, you still need to double-click it in the Makers panel, Timeline panel, or Source or Program Monitor panels.

Add a Marker to a Timeline Clip
If you need to add a marker to a clip that's already in the Timeline panel, you'll need to double-click it to load it in the Source Monitor panel. Any markers added in the Source Monitor will show up in the Timeline as well applied to the version of the clip in the Timeline panel.

5. Click OK when finished.

Adding Markers to Sequences

If you're working in the Timeline or Source Monitor panel, any marker you add will be to the sequence only. When Snap (S) is turned on, any element you drag will automatically snap in place to that marker, which is a nice way to quickly align clips and other elements in a Timeline.

Let's give it a try.

1. In the Sequences bin, double-click to open the sequence 01 Markers Start.

2. Move the playhead to a desired frame in the Timeline panel. You can also position the playhead in the Program Monitor.

   In this case, position the playhead where the actress turns her head (approximately 00:00:02:21).

3. Click the Add Marker (M) button in the Program Monitor or the Timeline panel. A new marker is added (**FIGURE 6.15**). Let's test snapping with a marker.

4. Move the playhead later in the Timeline panel. Make sure Snap is enabled (**FIGURE 6.16**).

5. Drag the second clip in the Timeline panel so it aligns with the newly added marker (**FIGURE 6.17**).

FIGURE 6.15 A marker in the Timeline panel is not attached to any one clip. It can be used for precise alignment of different Timeline elements.

FIGURE 6.16 The magnet-shaped button indicates whether Snap is turned off or on. It is a useful way to align items when dragging.

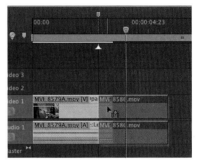

FIGURE 6.17 The marker provides a precise point to align the dragged clip.

Markers on the Fly

Press the M key to add a marker while a clip or sequence plays. Playback will continue, and you can go back and edit the markers later. This works well because of the new uninterrupted playback performance in CS6.

More on Markers with Duration

Use markers with duration to add comments or notes to help throughout the postproduction process. For example, you can mark out an entire sound bite so it stays marked (even if In and Out points change). You can also add comments about audio mixing or color correction for an assistant editor or colleague.

USEFUL MARKER SHORTCUTS

Here are useful shortcuts to speed up your use of markers in your clips and sequences:

Shortcut	Mac	Windows
Add Marker	M	M
Go to Next Marker	Shift+M	Shift+M
Go to Previous Marker	Cmd+Shift+M	Ctrl+Shift+M
Clear Current Marker	Option+M	Ctrl+Alt+M
Clear All Markers	Option+Shift+M	Ctrl+Alt+Shift+M

Syncing with Markers

You can use markers to sync footage. This type of workflow is particularly useful for synced sound workflows. In this case, audio is recorded separately from the camera. This is a common practice for DSLR, R3D, and other camera systems that aren't great at recording audio.

Syncing in a bin

Let's try syncing two clips. Once aligned, a new clip can be created and merged.

1. In the Project panel, open the bin Sync Footage.

2. Double-click to load the file Sync_Video.mov.

3. Drag through the video clip, and locate the white flash of the slate. You can also listen to the reference audio to help spot the point. Position the playhead where the slate flashes (**FIGURE 6.18**).

Footage courtesy of the National Foundation for Credit Counseling (www.DebtAdvice.org)

> **Audio Timecode**
> If the audio file you're using when creating a merged clip has timecode (such as a Broadcast WAVE format), you can specify that it become the new timecode for the clip. This is very useful when working with formats that lack timecode (like many DSLR models). Just choose the Use Audio Timecode From Clip option in the Merge Clips dialog box.

FIGURE 6.18 The iPad app *DSLR Slate* makes a useful digital slate. The white flash is one frame long and makes a great sync point. The slate also displays other useful data about the scene that can help when editing. The app is completely configurable.

4. Press M to add a marker, and then press Option+M (Alt+M) to open the Marker dialog.

5. Name the marker Sync 1, and click OK.

6. In the Project panel, double-click to load the file Sync_Audio.wav.

7. Drag through the video clip and locate the large spike near the beginning, which indicates the beep generated by the slate. Position the playhead where the waveform spikes (**FIGURE 6.19**).

FIGURE 6.19 The large spike indicates the sync point.

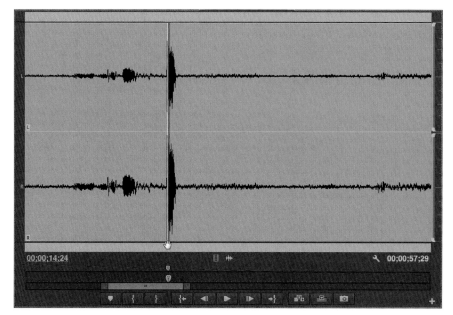

8. Press M to add a marker, and then press Option+M (Alt+M) to open the Marker dialog. Name the marker Sync 1, and click OK.

9. Select both Sync_Video.mov and Sync_Audio.wav in the Project panel.

10. Choose Clip > Merge Clips. A new dialog box opens.

11. Name the clip Synced Clip Demo.

12. Choose the Clip Marker option, and use the markers named Sync 1.

    If you don't have identical markers in both clips, this option will be grayed out.

13. Choose the Remove Audio from AV Clip option (**FIGURE 6.20**).

14. Click OK to create a newly merged clip and add it to the Project panel.

    This clip behaves as a new clip, but it links to two source files on your media drive.

FIGURE 6.20 Check your settings carefully when merging clips.

Merge Clips Workflow
Learn how to create merged clips for use in a project with markers.

Syncing in a sequence

You can also align two clips in a sequence using markers. Remember, if you want to attach a marker to a sequence clip, you need to double-click the clip in the Timeline panel to load it into the Source Monitor. In this case, markers were added in the previous exercise.

Sync A Lot?
If you need to sync a lot of clips, be sure to check out Plural Eyes from Singular Software (www.singularsoftware.com). It can automate this repetitive task.

1. In the Project panel, locate the bin Sync Footage, and double-click the sequence named 02 Sync Start to load it.

2. In the Timeline panel, Shift-click to select both clips (**FIGURE 6.21**).

FIGURE 6.21 Select both tracks you want to sync in the Timeline panel.

FIGURE 6.22 Adobe Premiere Pro offers multiple ways to synchronize clips.

3. Choose Clip > Synchronize. A new dialog opens (**FIGURE 6.22**).

4. Choose the Clip Marker options, and choose marker Sync 1.

5. Click OK; the two clips are precisely aligned (**FIGURE 6.23**).

FIGURE 6.23 Aligning clips with markers is a very accurate way to synchronize clips.

6. Disable the original audio track and listen to the synced sound and video track.

Interactive Markers

You can also use markers to exchange information or add interactivity when outputting to certain file formats. In fact, you can place markers in an Adobe Premiere Pro Timeline and exchange them with Flash Video, DVD, or Blu-ray Disc projects thanks to the tight integration of the Adobe Creative Suite. Simply double-click a marker and choose the desired option (**FIGURE 6.24**).

FIGURE 6.24 Markers can add rich interactivity to DVD, Blu-ray, and Flash outputs.

Three interactive marker types are available. This style of authoring is typically done with Adobe Flash Professional (which is included with the Master and Production Premium Creative Suite collections). You can also use Adobe Encore to create disc-based and Flash projects. The three interactive markers are as follows:

- **Encore chapter marker.** If you'd like to add cue points or chapter markers for use in a DVD or Blu-ray Disc project, add Encore Chapter Markers. These markers will come over when you exchange a sequence with Adobe Dynamic Link to Adobe Encore or compress the sequence using Adobe Media Encoder.

- **Web Link.** Certain formats like Flash Video support the use of Web Links. You can add a marker at a specific point in time to trigger the loading of a Web site into a targeted frame or window. In Adobe Premiere Pro, you can precisely time the marker and specify its destination. This feature can also work with DVD and Blu-ray Discs on Web-enabled players and computers.

- **Flash Cue Point.** You can add markers that can serve as navigation points for Flash authoring. These points can also act as triggers to load content into a frame.

Essential Editing Commands

The core functionality of editing in Adobe Premiere Pro should closely match your experience with other nonlinear editing applications. You can make two primary types of edits once you've determined which clip you want to use and what portions you want to use (and where to place it).

- **Overwrite.** The overwrite edit is the default editing method. Frames (or empty space) in the sequence are replaced with new frames.

- **Insert.** An insert edit adds the clip to your sequence and shifts the existing material later in the sequence (to the right).

Although there are other specialty edits (such as the replace edit) and many other ways to approach editing, these two commands encompass how you'll work 99 percent of the time.

Overwrite Edit

The overwrite edit is a fast way to quickly assemble your edit. The key to the overwrite edit is to remember to accurately patch your tracks from the Source Monitor so the targeted (highlighted in the sequence) tracks line up. If you've targeted a track for editing but have no source indicator patched (targeted), the empty track background will overwrite any media for the duration of the source clip. This type of edit can be useful (such as when you want to create a hole to fill later), or it can be destructive because you may unintentionally remove material from your sequence.

For this exercise, use the sequence 04 Doctor Start and media in the bin Card 02 to practice. Watch the sequence 03 Doctor Reference to see one way that the scene can play out. Because you are an experienced editor, we won't walk you through a long exercise. Instead, you'll use the media in the bins to cut a short scene.

Here's how to create an overwrite edit:

1. Open a sequence with which you'd like to edit.

   The sequence 03 Doctor Start is properly set up with the right frame rate and frame size for the media in the Card 02 bin.

2. Load a clip into the Source Monitor. Mark a duration that you'd like to use (**FIGURE 6.25**).

Footage courtesy of the National Foundation for Credit Counseling (www.DebtAdvice.org)

FIGURE 6.25 Be sure to precisely select the dialogue you want to use.

Insert and Overwrite in Action
In this video you'll see how the Insert and Overwrite edit commands function.

Overlay = Overwrite
Earlier versions of Adobe Premiere Pro refer to an overlay edit. In CS5.5, the term was renamed overwrite, which is a closer match to industry conventions. You'll still see the old term pop-up in some dialog boxes from time to time.

Add a Track While Adding a Clip
If you drag a clip from the Project panel or Source Monitor to the empty space above the topmost video track, a new video track will be added. For audio-only files, simply drag to the empty area below the lowest track. The correct track type will be added based on the source clip.

Which Range?
Dragging a clip to the Timeline uses the clip's In and Out points. However, using the Insert or Overwrite command will use any In or Out points set in the Timeline.

Lock it Down

In this video you'll learn the difference between track locks and sync locks and how they'll impact your insert edits.

FIGURE 6.26 Patching tracks requires precision. Make sure you have accurately targeted both the source and destination tracks.

FIGURE 6.27 The overwrite edit will replace any existing material in the Timeline with new frames.

How Do Locks and Targets Work?

If a track is either targeted or sync locked, an insert edit will affect it. Only nontargeted tracks with Sync Lock disabled will be unaffected when the new clip is added to the Timeline.

Quickly Lock

If you need to lock all the video or audio tracks, simply Shift-click a lock icon in the Timeline panel. It is in fact often faster to lock all tracks and then selectively unlock any tracks you don't want to use.

FIGURE 6.28 By default, all Sync Locks are enabled for a sequence.

3. Place the playhead in the sequence where you'd like to add the media. A manually marked In point can also be used.

4. Click to select the headers of the tracks where you want the overwrite edit to occur. In this case, make sure Video 1 and Audio 1 are selected.

5. Drag the source clip track indicators so they map to the headers of the tracks where you want to overwrite the media. This is often called *patching* (**FIGURE 6.26**).

6. In the Source Monitor, click the Overwrite button, or press the period key (**FIGURE 6.27**). The audio and video media are overwritten to the targeted tracks at the playhead.

Insert Edit

The insert edit is best used when you want to preserve previously edited content but need to make an addition. For example, you might need to add an extra sound bite or add a shot to a B-roll series. When you create an insert edit, you need to pay close attention to your use of locks.

■ If one or more tracks are locked, an insert edit affects only clips in unlocked tracks. All media will move on the unlocked tracks.

■ If you'd like to control which tracks are affected by an insert edit, you can also use Sync Locks. Deselect the Sync Locks for any tracks you want to leave unaffected.

Here's how to create an insert edit:

1. Open a sequence with which you'd like to edit.

2. Load a clip into the Source Monitor. Mark a duration you'd like to use.

3. Place the playhead in the sequence where you'd like to insert the media.

   Typically, this will be between two clips, but you can also split an existing clip.

4. Click to select the headers of the tracks where you want the insert edit to occur.

5. Drag the source clip track indicators so they map to the headers of the tracks where you want to overwrite the media.

6. Select the Sync Lock boxes in the track headers for any tracks that you want to shift as part of the edit (**FIGURE 6.28**).

7. In the Source Monitor, click the Insert button, or press the period key (.) (**FIGURE 6.29**).

   The edit occurs. The audio and video of the source clip are added to the sequence. If a track has no source track indicator (or is targeted because its Sync Lock is enabled), an edit impacts that track's contents. In this case, an empty track background is inserted on the track at the playhead for the duration of the source clip.

FIGURE 6.29 The insert edit will ripple items in your sequence and is affected by both Sync Locks and which tracks are targeted.

Three-Point Editing

Knowledgeable editors know that the most precise edit they can make is a three-point edit. Ultimately, the three-point edit is defined by using three marks in both the Timeline (or Program Monitor) and Source Monitor (**FIGURE 6.30**). You choose either two In points and one Out point or two Out points and one In point. There is no need to set a fourth point, because Adobe Premiere Pro can determine it for you.

Footage courtesy of the National Foundation for Credit Counseling (www.DebtAdvice.org)

FIGURE 6.30 An In and Out point have been set in the Source Monitor to indicate which footage will be used. An In point in the Timeline panel (or Program Monitor) shows where the newly added media will begin.

Backtiming Clips
A useful three-point editing technique is backtiming a clip. Mark an In and Out point in your sequence to define the range. Then use just an Out point in the source. Adobe Premiere Pro will calculate where the new clip should start. This is useful if you want to place a B-roll just before a critical sound bite.

The Danger of Dragging Clips
We are not known for frequently soapboxing on a particular topic, but for this we'll make an exception. DO NOT drag and drop media into your Timeline when you need a precise edit. Taking the time to master a three-point edit ensures that you've accurately chosen both source frames and a destination. Dragging and dropping, on the other hand, leads to a disorganized Timeline and can easily lead to unwanted gaps and flash frames.

When setting the range for the edit, you'll use an In point and an Out point. The most common choice is to set these points inside a source clip. However, there may be times when you want to define that range in the Timeline (such as if you have a sound bite to cover with B-roll).

You then must specify where you want the third point to be. Again, this can be on either the source or program side. Most find it easiest to place the In point to define where a clip should start. You can also use just an Out point to specify where a clip should end.

Here's how to use a three-point edit:

1. Open a sequence with which you'd like to edit.

2. Load a clip into the Source Monitor. Mark a duration you'd like to use.

3. Click to select the headers of the tracks where you want the insert or overwrite edit to occur.

4. Drag the source clip track indicators so they map to the headers of the tracks where you want to overwrite the media.

5. In the Source and Program Monitors, use any combination of three In and Out points.

6. Click either the Insert or Overwrite button in the Source Monitor.

    The edit is made.

Next Steps

Now that you've regained your confidence in the Timeline, it's time to take even more control. The next chapter explores several additional controls for editing. You'll learn to create four-point edits, retime clips, spot edits with waveforms, and replace clips. You'll also gain additional control over creating sequences using specialized editing commands such as Automate to Sequence and storyboard editing.

CHAPTER 7

Additional Editing Skills

FOR THE BULK of your editing, you'll use the Overwrite and Insert commands, but there are other ways to get the job done. Adobe Premiere Pro offers several advanced editing commands as well as automation features to speed up the editing process.

In this chapter, you'll explore how you can retime footage. Whether it's the Fit to Fill option or variable-speed Time Remapping option, Adobe Premiere Pro has you covered. You can also precisely swap out footage in a Timeline or even a project with the Replace command.

In addition, we'll show you several editing techniques that help you save time and avoid mistakes. You'll try powerful automation techniques to quickly storyboard and edit a sequence. You'll then assemble those shots automatically in the Timeline. You can also nest sequences to create easy-to-manage sections for a big project.

Let's move your editing skills up a notch or two.

Four-Point Editing

In the previous chapter, we discussed the standard editing technique of using three points to define an edit. The use of three points (a combination of In and Out points) split between the Source Monitor panel as well as the Program Monitor or Timeline panel can accurately describe an edit.

But what happens when you have four points defined?

The truth is that you have problems (or at least a discrepancy). The most likely scenario is that the clip loaded in the Source Monitor panel will have a different duration than the marks in the Timeline panel or Program Monitor. At this point, Adobe Premiere Pro alerts you to the discrepancy and asks you to make an important decision.

Editing Choices with Four-Point Edits

When four points are defined (two in the Source Monitor panel and two in the Program Monitor or Timeline panel), you'll need to choose a method to resolve the four points. Adobe Premiere Pro offers five choices (**FIGURE 7.1**) on how to make a four-point edit.

FIGURE 7.1 When making a four-point edit, you can either ignore one of the points or change the speed of the clip.

- **Change Clip Speed (Fit to Fill).** The first option assumes you chose four points for a reason. The In and Out points for the source clip are preserved, but the clip's speed is adjusted to match the duration set by the sequence's In and Out points.

- **Ignore Source In Point.** The In point in the source clip is ignored and dynamically determined by Adobe Premiere Pro. The new duration will match the duration determined by the sequence's In and Out points. This option is available only if the source clip is longer than the range set in the sequence, and this option will back-time the edit.

- **Ignore Source Out Point.** The Out point in the source clip is ignored and dynamically determined by Adobe Premiere Pro. The new duration will match the duration determined by the sequence's In and Out points. This option is also available only if the source clip is longer than the range set in the sequence.

- **Ignore Sequence In Point.** This choice will ignore the sequence In point you set and perform a three-point edit. If the clip is shorter than the duration defined, you can end up with unwanted video left behind in the sequence from the shot you were trying to cover.

- **Ignore Sequence Out Point.** This option is similar in that it will ignore the sequence's Out point you set and perform a three-point edit.

Making a Four-Point Edit

The act of creating a four-point edit is just like three-point editing except you've defined one more point. This may be on purpose because you want to change clip speed, or it may be an inadvertent error as your fingers fly across the keyboard.

Let's practice.

1. Launch Adobe Premiere Pro.

2. Choose File > Open, and navigate to Lessons and Media > Lesson 07 > 07_essential_editing.pproj. You'll use this project for the entire lesson.

3. Open the Sequences bin and make sure the sequence 01 Key Grab is loaded.

    This sequence contains a rough edit that you want to cut a new shot into. The clip you'll use is a different duration than what's needed for the cutaway angle.

4. Scroll through the sequence and locate a marker near the 13:00 mark.

    This marker defines an area where there is a slight jumpcut in the scene because of differences in the actor's performance between takes. The duration of the marker is a suggested range for the cutaway shot.

5. Mark an In point and an Out point in the sequence around the marker duration (**FIGURE 7.2**).

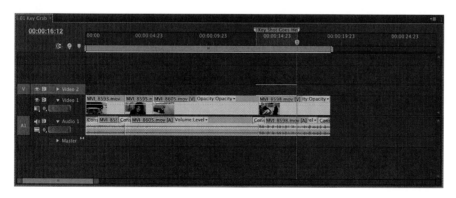

FIGURE 7.2 Once marked, the In and Out points will create a highlighted range in the Timeline panel.

6. Load the clip MVI_8602.mov from the Project panel into the Source Monitor panel.

    You can use the search field to locate the clip or manually find it by choosing Footage > Card 01.

7. A range should already be set in the clip (**FIGURE 7.3**). If not, use the clip marker to guide you in setting your In and Out points.

8. Click the headers of the tracks in the Timeline panel to properly patch and target them (**FIGURE 7.4**).

   For this edit, target the edit so it writes video only to Video 2 (the upper track).

FIGURE 7.4 The B-roll shot will be laid on top of the action by being patched to track V2.

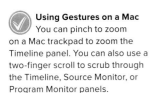

Using Gestures on a Mac You can pinch to zoom on a Mac trackpad to zoom the Timeline panel. You can also use a two-finger scroll to scrub through the Timeline, Source Monitor, or Program Monitor panels.

9. Click the Overwrite button to make the edit. Adobe Premiere Pro prompts you for input since the durations specified are different.

10. In the Fit Clip dialog, choose the Change Clip Speed (Fit to Fill) option.

    The edit is made in the Timeline. You'll see numbers in the edited clip that indicate the speed change.

11. Watch the sequence to check your edit. Adjust it to taste as needed by redoing the edit or dragging to reposition the clip.

Retiming Clips

If only editing were as simple as putting the right pieces in the right order. So often you'll also have to deal with time, whether it's the inflexible duration of a :30 commercial or the need to force fit a longer piece of footage into a shorter hole.

Adobe Premiere Pro offers additional ways to change the speed of a clip (besides four-point editing). The standard way in which video speed changes is through the omission or addition of source frames. This makes the clip play faster or slower. If you change the speed of a clip, it results in a corresponding change in duration.

Changing the Speed/Duration of a Clip

There are two ways to approach changing the speed of clips. You can precisely change the duration of a clip to reach a certain time. Alternately, you can change the percentage of playback (such as 50 percent to slow down a clip).

For practice, you can use the sequence 02 Speed Changes to adjust the timing of clips. This sequence is just three shots roughly assembled for illustrative purposes.

Here's how:

1. Select one or more clips in the Timeline panel or Project panel.

    You can Shift-click to select multiple clips in a Timeline panel or a contiguous group in a Project panel. To select a noncontiguous group of clips in a Project panel, Command-click (Ctrl-click).

2. Choose Clip > Speed/Duration or press Command+R (Ctrl+R).

3. You now have several options to control how the clips play back. Do any of the following:

    -   Leave Duration and Speed ganged together (a chain icon between them). You can then enter a new duration (**FIGURE 7.5**) or speed. Entering data in one field impacts the other.

    -   Click the Gang button so it shows a broken link (**FIGURE 7.6**). You can then enter a new speed for the clip without changing its duration (if the clip isn't long enough, empty frames are inserted).

    -   With unganging, you can also change duration without changing speed. Shortening a clip will leave a gap in the timeline. If the clip has another after it adjacent in the timeline, making the clip longer has no effect, because the clip cannot ripple by default. In this case, select the Ripple Edit, Shift Trailing Clips option.

FIGURE 7.5 The Clip Speed/Duration dialog offers several controls that allow you to precisely manipulate time.

FIGURE 7.6 Unganging a clip for a speed change lets you modify its speed or duration independently.

Frame Rate Differences
When mixing source frame rates in a sequence, Adobe Premiere Pro will still maintain the original speed of the footage so it plays back at 100 percent. If needed, frames will be duplicated or removed to maintain the new frame rate while still preserving motion and audio sync.

Force Fitting a Selection
If needed, you can adjust multiple clips at once. This is a useful way to force a group of clips to match a specific duration. Just select multiple clips and choose Clip > Speed/Duration. Enter a new playback duration for all the clips. This is a great way to create highlight reels timed to music where key shots need to time out to musical beats. Just limit yourself to the video portion because the audio may sound distorted due to the speed change.

Using the Speed/ Duration Command
Learn how to use the Speed/ Duration command to precisely control a clip's speed and duration in this video.

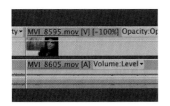

FIGURE 7.7 A negative number indicates a clip has been reversed.

Better Blending
If you are changing the speed of a clip, you can smooth out the effect with frame blending. Just select a clip and choose Clip > Video Options > Frame Blend.

FIGURE 7.8 When changing a clip with the Rate Stretch tool, the clip's In and Out points are preserved, but its playback speed changes.

28

Variable-Speed Effects
In this tutorial, you will explore creating variable-speed effects. You'll learn to speed up, slow down, rewind, and freeze a video clip using the Time Remapping effect and keyframes.

Time-Remapped Audio?
When using Time Remapping, the audio and video tracks are unlinked. Speed changes are applied only to the video track. This can result in out-of-sync audio.

- To play a clip backwards, select the Reverse Speed option. You'll see a negative symbol next to the speed value in the Timeline panel (**FIGURE 7.7**).

- If your clip has audio, consider selecting the Maintain Audio Pitch check box. This will attempt to maintain the clip's current pitch while the speed or duration changes. Without this option enabled, you get a chipmunk or slow-motion audio effect.

4. Click OK to apply the change.

Changing Speed and Duration with the Rate Stretch Tool

If you have two clips that need to match durations, the Rate Stretch tool (X) is the easiest way to make the edit. Unlike the Speed/Duration command, there is no guessing for the correct value. You simply drag the clip's edge to manually set it to the correct duration. Adobe Premiere Pro does all of the math for you.

1. Select the Rate Stretch tool (X) in the Tools panel.

2. Drag either edge of a clip in the Timeline panel (**FIGURE 7.8**).

The Rate Stretch tool changes the speed and duration of the clip.

Changing Speed and Duration with Time Remapping

The Time Remapping effect lets you create variable-speed effects. By default, Time Remapping is an intrinsic effect that is applied whenever you add a clip to a sequence, but you must modify it to see speed changes. The effect is useful for selectively retiming shots in a Timeline. For example, you can retime a reaction shot to adjust how long it takes for an actress to turn her head.

Let's practice.

1. With the same project open as in the previous exercise, open the Sequences bin and load the sequence 02 Speed Changes (if it's not already opened from the previous exercise).

2. Move the playhead so it is over the fourth clip in the Timeline (colored orange).

3. Click the Show Keyframes button in the track header (**FIGURE 7.9**). If it is not selected, select Show Keyframes.

4. Click the Clip Effect menu triangle, which is located next to the name of the clip on the clip icon in the sequence, and choose Time Remapping > Speed (**FIGURE 7.10**).

   Increase the Zoom level so the clip fills the Timeline panel. You can also adjust the height of the track to make it easier to see the clip controls. A horizontal rubber band is visible across the center of the clip. It is used to control the speed of the clip.

FIGURE 7.9 To control the Time Remapping effect, be sure to select the Show Keyframes option.

FIGURE 7.10 There's only one option for Time Remapping; be sure to choose Speed to see the controls.

Why Can't I Adjust the Effect?
You may notice that the Speed and Velocity values for the Time Remapping effect appear in the Effect Controls panel. These are for reference only. You cannot directly edit these properties in the Effect Controls panel; you must do so in the Timeline.

Reposition Time Remapping Keyframes
If you want to move an unsplit speed keyframe, just Option-click (Alt-click) and drag it into a new position. If you've split the halves apart, just drag the gray-shaded area of the speed transition into a new position.

5. You can drag the rubber band up and down to change the speed. A tooltip shows you the speed change (**FIGURE 7.11**). Although this kind of adjustment is useful, it doesn't show the true power of the tool. Set the speed back to 100%. Let's add keyframes.

6. Command-click (Ctrl-click) the rubber band to add a keyframe.

   In this case, click and add a keyframe just as the actress turns her head. A keyframe is visible in the Timeline panel as well as on the Effect Controls tab in the Source panel.

7. Move the cursor over the front section of the rubber band (before the keyframe). It changes shape.

8. Drag downward to set the rubber band to 50% speed (**FIGURE 7.12**).

9. Play back the clip. The speed change is present (but abrupt).

   Speed keyframes can be split in half to create a smooth transition between speeds (which can be refined with adjustment handles). A ramp appears indicating the transition.

10. Drag the speed handles apart to smooth the transition (**FIGURE 7.13**).

11. To further refine the effect, click the gray area between the two speed keyframe halves. A blue curve control appears in the gray area, which offers Bezier handles (**FIGURE 7.14**).

FIGURE 7.13 The greater the distance between the handles, the smoother the transition.

FIGURE 7.14 You can adjust the Bezier control handles to create additional ramping between speed changes.

FIGURE 7.12 The speed change is effective but sudden.

FIGURE 7.11 The yellow tooltip shows you any changes in the clip's speed.

Removing the Time Remapping Effect

Retiming Audio with Audition

If you need to change the duration of an audio clip with great precision, check out Adobe Audition. In fact, its pitch shifting is some of the best in the business and has been used for years by radio pros to condense audio into shorter durations with little effect on pitch. We'll discuss the technique in full in Chapter 10, "Audio Mixing and Repair."

Automatic Speech Alignment

Learn how you can do dialogue replacement while retiming clips and syncing clips with Adobe Audition. This is great for ADR work or for swapping out a scratch track with a final recording.

The Time Remapping effect cannot be toggled on and off like other effects. It is either applied or removed. Although this is a useful way to remove an effect, just be certain you want to proceed.

Here's how to remove Time Remapping:

1. Select a clip in the Timeline panel that has Time Remapping applied.
2. Select the Effect Controls tab in the Source Monitor panel.
3. Click the triangle next to Time Remapping to open it.
4. Click the Toggle Animation button (stopwatch) next to the word *Speed*. This sets it to the Off position.

    A warning dialog opens to alert you that keyframes will be removed.

5. Click OK to entirely remove the effect.

    If you want to reapply Time Remapping, you must click the Toggle Animation button and restore it to the On position. No keyframes are present, but you can begin anew.

Replacing Clips

At some point in the editing process, you'll need to replace a clip in your project. It might be a global replacement, such as replacing one version of an animated logo with a newer file. You may also want to swap out one clip in your Timeline for another in a bin. Depending on the task at hand, you can use a few methods to swap shots or media.

Replacement Techniques

You can replace clips in a Timeline in a few ways. The method you choose will depend on the accuracy level needed when replacing a clip. Whichever method you choose, the replaced clip will retain any effects that were applied to the original clip in a Timeline. Here are the methods you can use:

■ You can replace any clip in the Timeline using an Option-drag (Alt-drag) technique. Simply select the replacement clip and hold down the modifier key as you drag. When the Option (Alt) key is pressed, the In point of the new clip will be used to define the starting point of the edit.

■ If you'd like to use the In point of the original clip (not the replacement), hold down Shift+Option (Shift+Alt) as you drag. This method works best for multicamera footage that was shot simultaneously (with matching timecode).

■ The easiest and most accurate method is to use the Replace Clip command. This command lets you target a clip in your bin or Program Monitor for replacement. This works particularly well because you can precisely sync the edit using the playhead. We'll try this technique next.

Making a Replace Edit

Now that you understand the role of the Replace Edit command, it's time to try it. In this case, you'll continue to work with the file 07_essential_editing.prproj. One clip has a flat performance, so you will swap it out for a better line read.

Let's practice.

1. Open the Sequences bin and load the sequence 03 Doctor Intro.

   This sequence contains a rough edit. We've already created L-cuts and overlapped the performance and dialogue.

2. Play the sequence and watch the performance.

   The middle clip (colored orange) lacks energy. A better performance is in the bin. Let's create a Match Frame replace edit.

Match Frame Replace Edit

In this tutorial, we explore using the playhead and the Replace Edit command to precisely replace a clip in the Timeline.

Remapping Suggestions
Consider mapping the Audio Waveform option for the Source Monitor in the Source Monitor panel menu to Shift+W. To switch back, map the Composite Video option to Shift+Q.

3. Place the playhead in the sequence on the doctor's first word ("Hey") at approximately 00:04:05 (**FIGURE 7.15**).

FIGURE 7.15 Precisely place the playhead over the clip you want to replace.

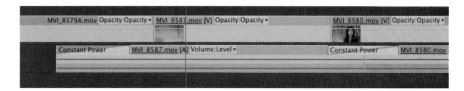

4. Load the replacement clip MVI_8588.mov into the Source Monitor panel.

This clip has been set to show an audio waveform using the Settings menu to make it easier to spot the edit point.

5. Play the clip and find the doctor's first word ("Hey") in the Source Monitor.

A clip marker helps you find the correct spot (**FIGURE 7.16**). Put the playhead on the marker.

FIGURE 7.16 You can use the arrow keys to scrub and listen to a clip's audio.

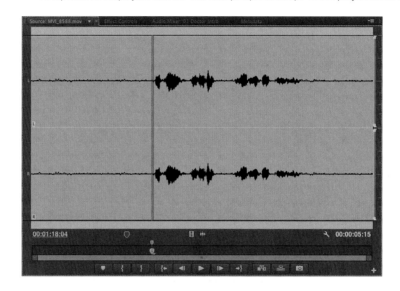

6. Use the Selection tool (V) to make sure the orange clip is selected in the Timeline (when selected, the clip will be highlighted) (**FIGURE 7.17**).

FIGURE 7.17 A clip must be highlighted to use the Replace With Clip command.

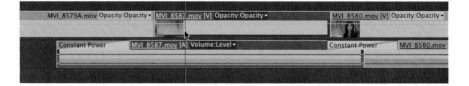

7. Choose Clip > Replace With Clip > From Source Monitor, Match Frame.

The clip is replaced.

8. Watch the newly edited sequence to check the performance.

EDITING WITH AUDIO WAVEFORMS AND TIME UNITS

As you work with source clips, it's important to know how to view audio waveforms. By looking at the details, it's often much easier to spot sync points or even dialogue breaks. Here are a few ways to better examine audio waveform details:

■ **Display audio waveforms in the Program Monitor.** Whether you're working in the Source or Program Monitor, audio waveforms are a handy way to edit. Click the Settings button (FIGURE 7.18) near the bottom of the panel and choose Audio Waveform.

■ **Show Audio Time Units.** If you'd like to view the audio waveform at the sample level, just click the Settings menu for the Source or Program Monitor panel and choose Show Audio Time Units. You can now zoom to greater detail (up to the individual sample level).

■ **Zooming audio waveforms horizontally.** If you'd like a closer look at audio waveforms in the Program Monitor, you can zoom your magnification level. You can zoom horizontally by dragging either end of the horizontal zoom bar, which runs below the time bar in the Source Monitor (FIGURE 7.19).

■ **Zooming audio waveforms vertically.** You can also zoom vertically by dragging the vertical zoom bar that runs next to the decibel ruler (located to the right of the Source Monitor) (FIGURE 7.20). Even though the waveforms appear taller, you are adjusting only their display (not playback volume).

■ **Viewing waveforms in the Timeline.** If you want to view audio waveforms for a track in the Timeline, just click the triangle to the left of the audio track name. Click the Set Display Style icon and select Show Waveform (FIGURE 7.21). You can drag the bottom edge of the track to expand it vertically to see more waveform data (FIGURE 7.22).

■ **Play Audio While Scrubbing.** To actually hear the audio as you navigate it, be sure to check your preferences. Open the Adobe Premiere Pro Preferences dialog and choose the Audio category. Make sure the Play Audio While Scrubbing option is selected for easier editing.

FIGURE 7.18 Click the Output button to see several choices for viewing a clip.

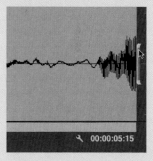

FIGURE 7.19 Dragging the zoom handle will magnify the waveforms.

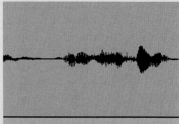

FIGURE 7.20 If you hold the Shift key when dragging, both channels will zoom for a stereo track.

FIGURE 7.21 Be sure to enable the Show Waveform option to see audio data.

FIGURE 7.22 You need to drag the handle to view audio wave-forms in the Timeline.

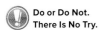

**Do or Do Not.
There Is No Try.**

The Replace Footage command cannot be undone. So, be sure to think about your choice. Choosing Edit > Undo will not work. Fortunately, you can *choose Clip > Replace Footage again to relink to the original file.*

Replacing Footage in a Project

You can replace any clip in the Project panel with new media. When you use the Replace Footage command, the source footage in a clip is replaced with media from a new source file. The benefits of this method are that all instances of a clip (as well as subclips) plus any edits made are retained in both the Project panel and the Timeline panel.

The replacement footage you use should have the same duration as the source footage to avoid potential problems. This method is ideal when you want to replace footage in the following circumstances:

- A watermarked stock footage clip needs to be reconnected to a clean file after licensing.

- A draft render animation is replaced with a final render.

- Offline resolution footage needs to be connected to high-quality footage.

- You've transcoded footage to a new codec and want to reconnect.

- To replace a clip in your project, follow these steps:

    1. Select a clip in the Project panel that you want to replace with new footage or a new version of the clip.

    2. Choose Clip > Replace Footage.

    3. In the Replace Footage For dialog, navigate to the new file that has the replacement footage.

        You can rename the clip with the replacement footage's filename by selecting the Rename Clip To Filename option.

    4. Click Select.

        The footage updates throughout your project.

Timesaving Editing Techniques

As you continue to work with Adobe Premiere Pro, you'll find several new ways to increase the pace and accuracy of editing. Techniques like storyboard editing and using the Automate to Sequence command help you organize your edit quickly. You can also use nested sequences and gap detection to keep a Timeline running smoothly.

Storyboard Editing

One technique to visually organize an edit is to use storyboard editing. You can quickly assemble a rough cut by lining up clips in a bin. The clips can be added to a new or an existing sequence based on their selection order.

1. Open the Sequences bin, and load the sequence 04 Storyboard.

2. Open the bin called Storyboard by double-clicking.

3. Click the Icon View button at the bottom of the bin (**FIGURE 7.23**).

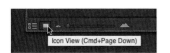

FIGURE 7.23 Switching to Icon View provides you with large icons and thumbnails to help you select clips.

4. Click the Zoom In button (if needed) at the bottom of the bin and resize it so the clip thumbnails are easy to see.

5. Use Hover Scrub (Shift+H) to preview the clips. Just drag the pointer from left to right (or back) over the clip's thumbnails (**FIGURE 7.24**).

6. Click the first clip so it is selected.

7. Play the clip using J-K-L keys to review it.

8. Adjust the clip's In (I) or Out (O) points as needed directly in the bin (**FIGURE 7.25**).

   For these four clips, you can use their existing points or adjust them as desired.

9. Arrange the clips in the Project panel by dragging them to a new order (**FIGURE 7.26**).

   Alternatively, you can Command-click (Ctrl-click) to specify the order in which the clips are selected. You can click each clip to specify the order (like you're tapping it on its head to stand in line).

FIGURE 7.24 (Top Left) Hover Scrub makes it easy to see the content of a clip. The left edge is the start of the clip, and the right edge is the end.

FIGURE 7.25 (Top Right) Setting In and Out points directly in the bin makes it easy to control which parts of a clip are used for an edit.

FIGURE 7.26 (Bottom Left) Arrange the clips into the desired order for editing by dragging. Here the clips are in the order the director intended.

10. Select all of the clips in the bin by choosing Edit > Select All.

11. Click the Automate to Sequence button at the bottom of the bin (**FIGURE 7.27**). This will take all of the selected clips and add them to your open sequence.

12. Choose from the following options in the Automate To Sequence dialog (**FIGURE 7.28**):

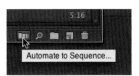

FIGURE 7.27 The Automate to Sequence command uses all of the selected clips for a single editing operation.

FIGURE 7.28 The Automate To Sequence options can be used to quickly assemble a rough cut based on the clip order in a bin.

 Automate to Sequence Goes Low

The Automate to Sequence command disregards target tracks. Instead, it will always use the lowest available video and audio tracks. You can omit a track by locking it.

- **Ordering.** This menu specifies the method used to determine clip order. You can select Sort Order to use the order in the bin. You can also choose Selection Order to build a sequence based on the order in which you selected the clips.

- **Placement.** There are many ways to determine how clips are ordered in the Timeline. The Sequentially option places clips one after another. You can also select the Unnumbered Markers option to use any sequence markers you've added (you'll try this method later in the chapter).

- **Method.** You can choose between two methods for adding the clips to your Timeline. Select an Insert edit to add the clips at the In point (or playhead) and shift the remaining clips down the Timeline. You can also select an Overlay (which is actually an overwrite) edit to replace clips already in a sequence.

- **Clip Overlap.** If you'd like to create a montage with dissolves, you can select the Clip Overlap option. This lets you specify the duration of the transition and how much to adjust the clips' In and Out points. The specified overlap will be divided equally between the incoming and outgoing clips (centering the transition on the edit). You can specify a duration in frames or seconds.

- **Apply Default Audio Transition.** This option creates a crossfade between audio clips.

- **Apply Default Video Transition.** This option creates a cross dissolve between video clips.

- **Ignore Audio.** This option ignores audio in the selected clips and adds only video tracks.

- **Ignore Video.** This option ignores video in the selected clips and adds only audio tracks.

13. Click OK to create the edit.

Editing with Markers

The use of Timeline markers can quickly speed up editing. You can listen to your audio track in real time and tap out markers that match the beat of music at key points in the narration.

You can add a marker to a sequence on the fly in two ways: You can click the Set Marker button in the Source Monitor panel, and you can also press the M key.

Let's give it a try.

1. Open the Sequences bin, and load the sequence 05 Automate.

2. Click the Timeline panel, and position the playhead at the start of the sequence.

   The music track has been offset a small amount to allow a little ramp-up time to add a marker for the first beat.

3. Click the Play button, and listen to the track once to familiarize yourself with the music.

4. Rewind the playhead to the start of the Timeline.

5. Click Play again, but this time click the Set Marker button (M) for every major beat.

   Markers are added to your sequence (FIGURE 7.29).

FIGURE 7.29 Be sure to listen to the track at least once to familiarize yourself with the major beats. Markers added at key points in the music will tightly sync the edit to the music.

6. Move the playhead to the start of the sequence, and lock Video 1 so it is not modified by the Automate to Sequence command. This will force the Automate to Sequence command to use the next higher track.

7. Open the Birds bin by double-clicking. If desired, rearrange the order of the birds by dragging their thumbnails.

8. Choose Edit > Select All.

9. Click the Automate to Sequence button.

10. Choose the following options for the edit:

    Ordering = Sort Order

    Placement = At Unnumbered Markers

    Method = Overlay Edit

11. Click OK to make the edit (**FIGURE 7.30**). Remove any extra shots after the music ends.

FIGURE 7.30 You may have a few extra clips (or not enough) depending on how you added your markers. You can adjust the Timeline as needed.

12. Make sure all of the clips on Video 2 are selected. If not, drag to select all of the video clips on track Video 2.

13. Choose Sequence > Apply Default Transitions to Selection to apply a dissolve between all of the clips.

    Transitions are added to all of the clips (except for the start and end).

14. Move the playhead to the start of the first clip and press Command+D (Ctrl+D) to add a transition.

15. Move the playhead to the end of the last clip and press Command+D (Ctrl+D) to add a transition (**FIGURE 7.31**).

FIGURE 7.31 A cross dissolve is added to all of the clips by default. If you'd like an effect other than a dissolve, you can right-click any effect in the Effects panel and choose Set Selected as Default Transition.

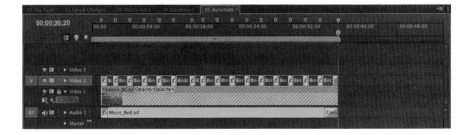

16. Watch the sequence to review your work.

Nested Sequences

As you work with a sequence, you can choose to nest items to create complex groupings. When you nest a sequence, it appears as a single, linked video/audio clip. You can select a nested item as well as move and trim it. Nests are also a useful way to apply a transformation to several clips at once.

Why create a nested sequence?

There are several reasons to create a nested sequence. These include both technical and organizational benefits. Here are some reasons to use nests:

■ **Create complex groupings and nested effects.** You may need to globally apply an effect to several shots. For example, you can nest several clips and then create a picture-in-picture effect. The shots can transition between each other, but the nest can be scaled and positioned as a group.

Mixed Nests
You can nest a sequence into another and mix settings as needed. A nest can have a different editing time base, frame size, and pixel aspect ratio settings than the sequence it's placed in.

Nested Changes Propagate
If you make a change to a source sequence, it will be reflected in any nested instances created from it.

- **Apply different settings to copies of a sequence.** You may want to quickly apply a colorization effect to heavily stylize a series of shots. Using nests lets you reuse footage but treat it differently each time.

- **Streamline your Timeline.** If you've built complex effects or multilayered sequences, you can nest the shots together. This can reduce the chance of accidentally moving only part of a multilayered clip. It also makes it easier to create transitions and trim shots.

Limitations of a nested sequence

Because there are relationships between clips in a sequence, you will find that nesting has some limitations. For example, you cannot nest a sequence within itself. Rather, you'll be prompted to give the nested portion a new name.

When you create a nest, the source items set the duration. If you have empty space at the start or middle of a sequence, that will be included in the nest. Empty space at the end of a range of clips is ignored when creating a nest.

You can trim the contents of clips within a nest. Although this can be used to lengthen a nest, problems arise when the source clips are shortened. When the duration is reduced, you may find instances of black video and silent audio, which can be trimmed as needed in the Timeline panel.

Create a nest from a selection of clips

The easiest way to create a nested clip is to precisely select clips you want to nest. This can be done by using the Track Selection tool or by Shift-clicking multiple clips in the Timeline panel. Let's give it a try.

1. Continue working with the 05 Automate sequence from the previous exercise.

2. Drag to select all of the clips on the track Video 2.

3. Choose Clip > Nest (**FIGURE 7.32**).

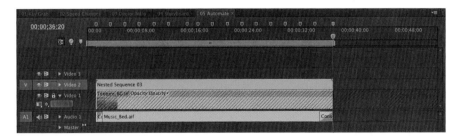

A nest replaces the clips in the current sequence. A new sequence is also added to the Project panel.

4. In the Effects panel, search for the Drop Shadow effect (Video Effects > Perspective > Drop Shadow).

5. Apply the effect to the nested clips by dragging the effect onto track Video 2.

6. In the Effect Controls panel, adjust the Scale property to 80%.

Nesting by Dragging
A quick way to create a nest is to drag a sequence from the Project panel into the appropriate track or tracks of the active sequence. You can also load a sequence as a source in the Program Monitor and use the standard Insert and Overwrite (Overlay) commands.

Open the Source of a Nest
If you need to see the source for a nested sequence, simply double-click a nested sequence clip. If a track is targeted, you can also press F to match frame and open the original clip that was placed in the nested sequence.

FIGURE 7.32 Nesting makes it easier to treat several clips as one in the Timeline panel.

7. In the Effect Controls panel, adjust the Drop Shadow properties to taste (**FIGURE 7.33**).

FIGURE 7.33 Two effects were combined to create a picture-in-picture look over the texture background.

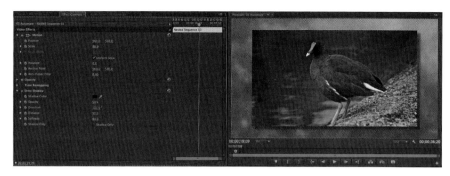

Find Gaps in Sequences and Tracks

Nothing ruins a show quicker than flash frames caused by gaps in a sequence. Dragging media around without having the Snap function turned on typically causes these little one-frame gaps. Fortunately, Adobe Premiere Pro makes it easy to spot gaps. Because you've been quickly editing with automation commands, it makes sense to quickly check for inadvertent gaps.

Let's try detecting gaps in a sequence.

1. Open the Sequences bin, and load the sequence 06 Gaps.

2. Choose Sequence > Go to Gap, and choose one of the following options:

   - Next in Sequence. This finds the next gap to the right of the playhead. The gap must span all tracks to be seen.

   - Previous in Sequence. This finds the next gap to the left of the playhead. The gap must span all tracks to be seen.

   - If one or more tracks are targeted, you can choose one of these options:

   - Next in Track. This finds the next gap to the right of the playhead but only on the selected tracks.

   - Previous in Track. This finds the next gap to the left of the playhead but only on the selected tracks.

Once a method is selected, the zoom level of the Timeline panel remains unchanged. You may find it useful to zoom the level of the Timeline panel to better view any detected gaps.

Next Steps

In the next chapter, you'll explore how to manipulate elements once you've added them to a Timeline. You'll learn how to quickly select and move clips within an edit. You'll also master techniques for Timeline operations such as Lift, Extract, and Ripple Delete. In addition, you'll explore the finer points of transitions.

Avoid Gaps
Dragging and dropping clips into a Timeline is one of the leadng causes of gaps. Four out of five advanced editors recommend the use of three-point editing for an organized Timeline.

CHAPTER 8

Timeline Operations

ONCE YOU START assembling clips in a row, you will undoubtedly need to make changes. It might be because an irksome client or a producer can't make a decision. Or it could be because of a change in direction for the story or a new interview that suddenly needs to be integrated. For whatever reason, you need to be in total control of the Timeline panel.

In this chapter, you'll explore many ways for making selections in the Timeline panel—whether you need to select part of a clip or several clips. You'll also learn several techniques for moving clips around a sequence, including the use of the clipboard and special commands like Lift and Extract. In addition, we'll help you smooth out your cuts with the proper use of video and audio transitions.

Let's put that Timeline to work.

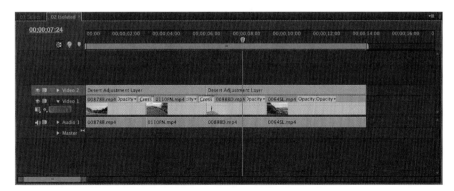

Selecting Clips

Several editor tasks, such as applying effects and transitions and even moving clips, all have the same starting point. Before you can perform any action that affects a clip as a whole, you'll need to properly select the clip. Several selection tools are available to you in the Tools panel, and you need to know which ones to use in specific circumstances.

For this section, you'll use a practice project. It contains simple clips that are lettered in order. This will make it easy to see the different tools and test their uses.

1. Launch Adobe Premiere Pro.

2. Choose File > Open, and navigate to Lessons and Media > Lesson 08 > 08_timeline_operations.prproj.

3. Open the Sequences bin, and load the sequence 01 Select.

   You'll use this sequence to practice selections.

Selecting a Clip

The easiest method of selection is just a single clip, and the best tool to use is the Selection tool. The quickest way to access the tool is by pressing its shortcut, V (think of the shape as matching the tip of the arrow for the tool). Simply click the middle of an individual clip to select it (**FIGURE 8.1**).

FIGURE 8.1 Be sure to avoid clicking on an edge of a clip or the Selection tool will switch to the Ripple Edit tool. Also, don't click the line in the middle (that adjusts the volume or the selected effect).

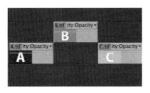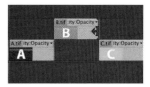

Even if you don't have the Selection tool active, you can often select single clips. Clicking in the middle of a clip with the Ripple Edit tool or Rolling Edit tool will also select the clip. The same holds true for the Rate Stretch tool. In fact, if you click with the Slip or Slide tool, you can also make a selection (just be careful not to drag, or you'll adjust the visible contents or position of the clip).

Selecting a Range of Clips

Another common scenario is the need to select several clips. This may be driven by the use of a common effect or the need to quickly move a section of your video to another location. Either way, Adobe Premiere Pro offers a few ways to select a range of clips.

You can do any of the following to select multiple clips:

- Click in an empty area of the sequence (under the time ruler), and then drag to create a selection. A rectangular marquee appears that lets you select any part of the clips that you'd like to select (**FIGURE 8.2**).

FIGURE 8.2 The Selection tool switches to a Marquee Selection tool if you click and drag in an empty area of the Timeline panel.

- To add additional clips, hold down the Shift key. You can Shift-drag with the marquee to add any additional clips to the selection.

- To remove items from the selection, just Shift-click previously selected items.

Selecting All the Clips on a Track

Adobe Premiere Pro offers a special tool to select clips based on their track level. The Track Select tool (A) selects all of the clips on a single track that are forward of the click point. In other words, you can select all of the clips on a track by clicking the first clip you want to select on that track (**FIGURE 8.3**). If you want to isolate a selection, just click a later clip (**FIGURE 8.4**), and the selection will be made from that clip forward.

Select All Clips on All Tracks A quick way to select all the clips on all video tracks is to Shift-click with the Track Select tool. This forces the tool to choose all clips on all tracks from that point forward.

FIGURE 8.3 The Track Select tool uses the keyboard shortcut A, which you can think of as Select All for that track.

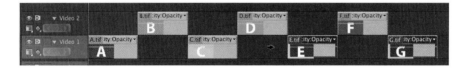

FIGURE 8.4 By clicking later in a Timeline, you can select all the clips from that point forward.

Selecting Noncontiguous Clips

Sometimes you'll need the ability to select clips on multiple tracks in different positions or track levels. We find this particularly useful when applying preset color corrections based on subject or to select multiple audio tracks for filtering. To select multiple clips, use the standard Selection tool (V), and then Shift-click to select items as needed (**FIGURE 8.5**).

FIGURE 8.5 Keep holding down the Shift key as you click to add more clips to your selection.

Select Audio or Video by Track

The Option (Alt) key modifier also works with the Track Select tool. When you click, you can select all of the clips in an audio or video track independently.

Selecting Audio or Video Only

You may find the need to independently select the audio or video in a clip. Common scenarios include replacing sync sound material as well as unlinking audio to reposition it for drift or delay. You may also want to remove the audio from an edited clip entirely if the background sound is too distracting.

Let's try it out.

1. Open the Sequences bin, and load the sequence 02 Isolated.

2. Choose the Selection tool (V).

3. Hold down the Option (Alt) key and click on an item to make a selection (**FIGURE 8.6**). By holding down the Option (Alt) key, you temporarily unlink audio from video.

FIGURE 8.6 When clips are linked, the Selection tool will select both tracks by default (left). Using the Option (Alt) key modifier (right) lets you isolate audio or video selections without unlinking clips.

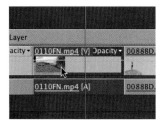
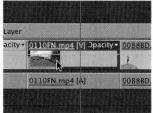

The Effect of Splitting

When you use the Razor tool to split a clip into two clips, it creates a new and separate instance of the clip in the Timeline panel. The two new clips are both full versions with handles intact that connect to the original media. Each clip will have different In and Out points, however.

Splitting a Clip

If you want to split a clip into two clips, you'll find a few ways to do this in Adobe Premiere Pro. Splitting a clip is useful if you want to remove part of an audio or video track while leaving other parts behind. It also works well when you want to split a sound bite or b-roll clip to rearrange its order.

Continue to work with the 02 Isolated sequence, and try these techniques to split a clip:

- Use the Razor tool (C) to split a single or linked clip. Wherever you click, the clip will be its split point (**FIGURE 8.7**).

FIGURE 8.7 The Razor tool will work on clips or linked clips (unless a track is locked).

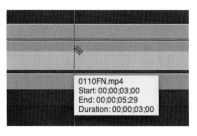
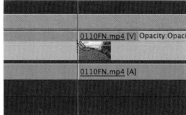

- To split only the audio or video portion of a linked clip, Option-click (Alt-click) with the Razor tool.

- To split all tracks, Shift-click with the Razor tool. This works regardless of track selection (but does respect locked tracks) (FIGURE 8.8).

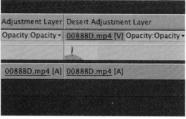

FIGURE 8.8 The Razor tool can split several tracks with the Shift key. The benefit here is that you do not need to select tracks to split them (but you may lock tracks that you don't want affected).

- If you want to control which tracks are split, use the Add Edit command (formerly called Razor All Tracks in CS5 and earlier). Just click the headers for the targeted tracks. With the playhead in position, choose Sequence > Add Edit. You can also press Command+K (Ctrl+K).

- If you want the Add Edit command to work regardless of track selection, just press Command+Shift+K (Ctrl+Shift+K).

Linking and Unlinking Clips

After you add a video clip to a sequence, the clip's audio and video will route to different tracks. By default, there is a link between the audio and video pieces so that when you select or drag one, the other follows. In this case, the audio/video pair is called a *linked clip*.

If you want to break this link, you can unlink the two parts. There are reasons for unlinking—for instance, when you want to fix drift in an audio track or relocate the audio from a clip.

Let's try unlinking and linking.

1. Open the sequence 03 Sync, and choose the Selection tool.

2. Click on the video clip in the Timeline panel, and choose Clip > Unlink (FIGURE 8.9).

3. Drag the audio a few seconds to the right.

4. Play back the clip. The audio is very far out of sync.

5. Select both the audio and video clips by Shift-clicking.

Don't Split for Effects
You'll discover in Chapter 12 that all effects offer keyframes. This means you can change an effect's properties over time. Do not split a clip just to modify its effects.

When to Link
If you've created a sound bed of several sound effects, you can link them together. You may also have synced sound that gets added to a video clip. Both of these are good uses for manually linking.

FIGURE 8.9 When a clip is unlinked, you'll notice that the [V] and [A] track labels disappear from the clip. Also, the name of the clip is no longer underlined.

6. Choose Clip > Link.

   The clips are relinked, and you can easily see how much an item may have slipped out of sync (**FIGURE 8.10**).

 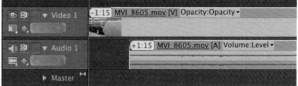

FIGURE 8.10 The numbers on the clips on the right indicate how far out of sync the audio and video tracks are.

Unlink Several
You can choose *to unlink video and audio from multiple clips. Just select the clips and choose Clip > Unlink.*

7. Right-click on the numbers that appear at the In point of the clip in the Timeline panel, and choose a sync method (**FIGURE 8.11**).

   ■ **Move Into Sync.** This method shifts the selected portion in time to regain sync. The move disregards adjacent clips and can result in overwritten media.

   ■ **Slip Into Sync.** This method slips the media content to restore sync. It preserves the clip's In and Out points in the Timeline panel. This method requires adequate handles of unused media to slip.

FIGURE 8.11 The original media is out of sync (left). It can be moved into position (center) or slipped into sync (right) by right-clicking on the number.

Moving Clips

Like a musical composer, you'll often need to shift the notes and bars around (except in your case, they are sound bites and B-roll). A big part of editing is experimenting with the order of clips and how they juxtapose with footage. Adobe Premiere Pro lets you place clips into any order you need; you can also change the order of clips in the Timeline panel in many ways.

Dragging Clips

A Better Drag
To see how to take control when dragging, be sure to watch this video tutorial.

FIGURE 8.12 The small numbers are a useful way to judge position when dragging a clip.

As you drag clips in the Timeline panel, you should pay careful attention to the translucent rectangle that represents the clip's duration (**FIGURE 8.12**). This image will help you place the clip. A small window near the rectangle also displays a positive or negative number to show forward or backward movement in the Timeline. You can use the sequence 04 Dragging & Rearranging to practice these techniques.

Here are a few important notes to keep in mind when dragging a clip:

- The default method when dragging is an overwrite edit.

- Hold down the Command (Ctrl) key when dragging to perform an insert edit.

- To duplicate a clip instance when dragging, hold down the Option (Alt) key.

- You can drag a clip vertically to a new audio or video track. Leave the Snap option turned on to help keep the track aligned to its original horizontal position (**FIGURE 8.13**).

- To unlink an audio and video clip when dragging, press the Option (Alt) key, and then click and drag the audio or video track. The video and audio will lose sync. You can release the modifier key and drag the clip into place (**FIGURE 8.14**).

Move with the Keypad
If you have a full-size keypad, you can use the numeric section for quick movement. Just select a clip in your Timeline panel, make sure Num Lock is on, and then press the plus (+) key and a number to indicate the number of frames you want to move. Press Return (Enter) to move the clip. You can also use the minus (-) key to move a negative position.

FIGURE 8.13 Using the Snap option will keep clips precisely aligned when dragging.

FIGURE 8.14 Releasing sync lets you adjust natural sound independent of B-roll.

- You can move both the audio and video with one operation. After dragging the video portions of a clip into place, press and hold the Shift key. Continue holding the Shift key and drag downward past the dividing bar to position the audio clip. Release both the mouse and Shift key when the items are correctly positioned (**FIGURE 8.15**).

FIGURE 8.15 After dragging the item into place (left), hold down the Shift key and drag downward (center) to reposition the audio clip (right).

Rearranging Clips in a Sequence

When dragging clips, it's possible to avoid gaps using a rearrange edit. The Rearrange command is similar to both extract and insert edits in that clips are moved and over-written, yet they are swapped and positioned into a new order at the same time. Many editors refer to this as a *swap edit*.

1. Open or continue working with the sequence 04 Dragging & Rearranging.

2. Select the second clip (B) in the Timeline panel.

3. Drag the clip to the left and press and hold down Command+Option (Ctrl+Alt). The Rearrange icon appears (**FIGURE 8.16**).

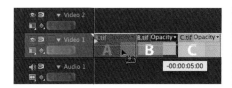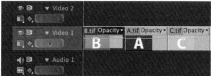

FIGURE 8.16 A rearrange edit is useful for repositioning clips quickly.

4. Release the clip to perform an insert edit that shifts clips in the destination tracks only. The clips are now swapped.

Using the Clipboard

Although its use may feel more like you are working with a word processor instead of a tape deck, using the clipboard is still a relevant technique. Often overlooked for their simplicity, there is still a lot of power when it comes to the Copy and Cut commands.

Copying

The Copy command lets you duplicate a selection and repeat it in your Timeline panel. If you're using multiple clips, the relative spacing (both horizontal spacing in time and vertical spacing in tracks) of clips is maintained. The copied clips can be pasted to a new position or track based on the playhead and track selection targets.

Let's give it a try and create a layered effect with blending modes.

1. Open the sequence 05 Copy and Paste.

2. Option-click (Alt-click) the video portion of the clip to select just the video track.

3. Choose Edit > Copy, or press Command+C (Ctrl+C).

4. Move the playhead to the start of the clip (**FIGURE 8.17**).

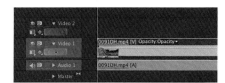

FIGURE 8.17 Carefully position the playhead to control the pasting of clips.

5. Use the track selection targets to untarget V1 and A1. Instead, aim the pasting to track V2.

6. Choose Edit > Paste or press Command+V (Ctrl+V) to add the footage into your sequence (**FIGURE 8.18**).

FIGURE 8.18 The track targets control where the footage is pasted.

7. Select the top video clip in your Timeline panel.

8. In the Effects panel, type **blur** into the search field to locate the Gaussian Blur effect (FIGURE 8.19).

Paste Insert
If you'd like to create an insert edit with the clipboard's contents, simply choose Edit > Paste Insert. The playhead will be treated as the In point, and the clips will be added at the targeted tracks.

FIGURE 8.19 The search field in the Effects panel is a useful way to quickly find effects.

9. Drag the Gaussian Blur filter onto track V2.

10. Double-click the video clip on V2 to load it into the Source Monitor panel.

11. Click the Effect Controls tab. Twirl down the controls for the Gaussian Blur effect, and set Blurriness to 50 pixels and select the Repeat Edge Pixels box (FIGURE 8.20).

FIGURE 8.20 You will fully explore the controls for effects in Chapter 12.

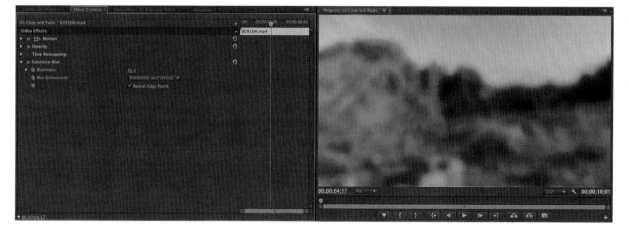

12. Set Opacity to 50%. Twirl down the Opacity controls, and set Blend Mode to Soft Light (**FIGURE 8.21**).

FIGURE 8.21 The technique of blending a blurred copy of footage with itself is often used to create a "film look."

Cutting

The Cut command is similar in function to the Copy command. Simply select one or more clips and choose Edit > Cut or press Command+X (Ctrl+X) to move the clip to your clipboard. The key difference between Cut and Copy is that the Cut command leaves an empty space between the clips when executed (**FIGURE 8.22**).

FIGURE 8.22 The Cut command preserves the relative spacing between the clips. It is similar to the Lift command, which we'll cover in the next section.

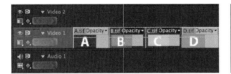

 Need to Find a Clip in Your Project?
If you need a quick way to locate a clip inside a bin, just right-click a clip in your Timeline panel and choose Reveal In Project.

Extracting and Deleting Segments

A good editor knows that editing is more often about taking away the right parts rather than just adding pieces together. You may need to discard some frames that detract the viewer's eye or expunge the "umms" and "ahhs" from a sound bite to add a few IQ points. It's important that you know the many ways to remove media from a sequence because each has certain benefits that will impact your workflow.

Lift

The Lift operation lets you remove or *lift* the selected frames from your sequence. Left behind will be a visible gap in the Timeline (as determined by the In and Out points you've set). The benefit of the Lift command is that the removed frames are placed on your clipboard so they can be added back into your sequence. This last step is optional, because many prefer to simply leave a visible gap to alert them to a need for B-roll or coverage.

Here's how to perform a Lift:

1. In the Timeline or Program Monitor panel, mark a range for lifting using In and Out points.

   You can use the practice sequence 07 Lift, which already has points set.

2. Use the track selection buttons (the headers of tracks) in the Timeline to specify which tracks should be subject to the Lift command (**FIGURE 8.23**). Be sure the tracks you want to lift are highlighted.

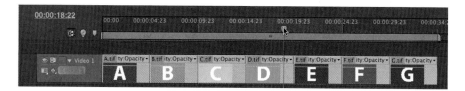

FIGURE 8.23 Be sure to be precise when marking a range for lifting.

3. Click the Lift button in the Program Monitor (**FIGURE 8.24**).

   The frames are lifted and placed on your system's clipboard. Adding the material back into the sequence is an optional step.

4. Click the header of the track for which you want to paste the lifted frames.

5. Move the playhead to specify where you want the lifted frames to begin.

6. Choose Edit > Paste or press Command+V (Ctrl+V) to add the frames back into your sequence.

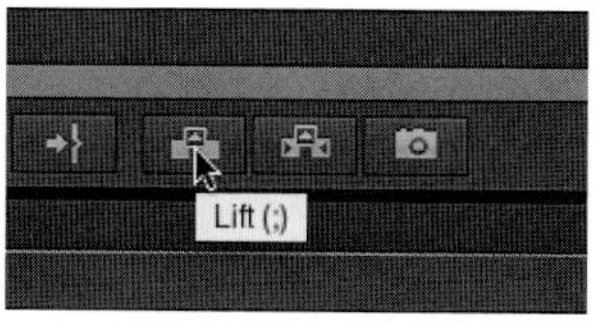

Extract

The Extract command is similar to the Lift command except it leaves no gap where the selected frames once lived. Instead, a ripple delete occurs (where the clip is removed and the gap is closed). You set In and Out points just like the Lift command to select the frames. We find the Extract command to be most useful when tightening up interview clips because unwanted bites can be removed and the sequence runtime adjusts downward.

1. In the Timeline or Program Monitor panel, mark a range for lifting using In and Out points.

   You can use the practice sequence 08 Extract, which already has points set.

2. Use the track selection buttons (the headers of tracks) in the Timeline panel to specify which tracks should be subject to the Extract command (**FIGURE 8.25**).

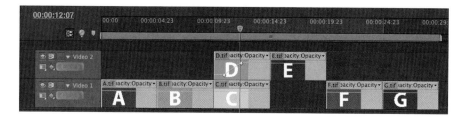

FIGURE 8.24 You can also press a semicolon (;) to perform a lift.

Uninterrupted Playback
In Adobe Premiere Pro CS6, the Timeline will continue to play in most circumstances (unless, of course, you click Stop). The following options can be modified while playback continues:

- Switching to a different application
- Making basic editing operations such as trimming
- Adding a title while playing
- Keyframing or modifying an effect while playing back a clip for evaluation
- Modifying audio parameters during playback
- Entering metadata in a bin

FIGURE 8.25 You need to use targeting to specify which tracks to extract as well as sync locks to indicate which tracks to move clips to when the Extract command is executed.

FIGURE 8.26 You can also press the apostrophe (') to perform an extract.

FIGURE 8.27 The Extract command's selection is determined by using In and Out points in conjunction with targeted tracks.

3. Click the Sync Lock boxes in the headers of all the tracks you want to be shifted when the Extract button is clicked. This will force the gaps to close for all sync locked tracks.

4. Click the Extract button in the Program Monitor (**FIGURE 8.26**).

   The frames are extracted and placed on your system's clipboard (**FIGURE 8.27**). Adding the material back into the sequence is an optional step.

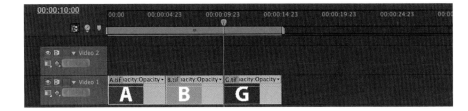

5. Click the header of the track into which you want to paste the extracted frames.

6. Move the playhead to specify where you want the extracted frames to begin.

7. Choose Edit > Paste to add the frames back into your sequence.

Delete and Ripple Delete

If you just want to remove a clip, it's simple. Select one or more clips in the sequence with the Selection tool or a marquee selection and press the Delete key. This works when you've clearly selected clips. Unlike Lift and Extract, which use In and Out points, the Delete and Ripple Delete commands use the Selection tool. If you want to merely delete part of a clip, use the Lift command (but do not paste the material back into the sequence).

Similar to the Delete command is Ripple Delete, which also removes tracks, but it will close the gap as well. All unlocked tracks will shift according to the amount of material you've selected for deletion. If you want to prevent an item from moving, lock the track (or turn off Sync Locks).

Here's how to perform a ripple delete:

1. In the sequence, select the clip or clips you want to delete.

2. Choose Edit > Ripple Delete.

   You can also press Option+Delete (Alt+Delete) to perform the command.

Deleting gaps in a track

If you have gaps in your Timeline panel that you'd like to close up, that's simple too. You can use the Ripple Delete command as well to remove unintended gaps.

In a Timeline, do one of the following:

- Right-click the gap between two clips, and choose Ripple Delete (**FIGURE 8.28**).

- Select the gap between two clips, and choose Edit > Ripple Delete.

- Select the gap between two clips, and press Delete.

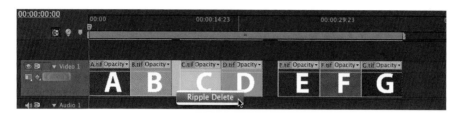

FIGURE 8.28 The Ripple Delete command is an effective way to close a gap in a sequence.

Deleting all clips on a track

If you'd like to delete all the clips on a given track, you just need to make an accurate selection. This method will remove all media but still leave the track behind.

1. Choose the Track Select tool (A) from the Tools panel.

2. Choose one of the following options:

   - To delete both the audio and video for linked clips, click the first clip in the track. You'll need to click only the video or audio part of the clip to make a selection.

   - Deleting only part of a track's clips (not the linked counterparts) is pretty straightforward. Just Option-click (Alt-click) in the Timeline panel to select just that track's clips.

3. Press the Delete key or choose Edit > Delete.

Deleting a track

If you decide you do not need an entire track, you can delete it and all of its contents. This is a useful way to clean up a sequence of unused audio and video tracks.

1. Open the sequence 09 Delete.

   This sequence has several empty audio tracks and one empty video track.

2. Right-click one of the audio tracks, and choose Delete Tracks.

   A new dialog opens with precise controls.

3. Select the Delete Audio tracks option, and choose All Empty Tracks; do the same for Delete Video tracks (**FIGURE 8.29**).

4. Click OK to clean up your Timeline panel.

   All empty tracks are removed (except for one audio track, which is a required element of a sequence).

FIGURE 8.29 Several options are available within the Delete Tracks dialog for precise control.

Disabling a Clip

As you start to stack your Timeline, there will be times when disabling is a better option than deleting. For example, you may have multiple B-roll shots laid in for a producer to review. By disabling a clip, you can see options without having to keep multiple versions of the sequence. A similar technique is useful when you want to audition multiple music tracks for an edit or to swap out scratch narration with final takes.

Here's how to disable a track:

1. Select one or more clips in your sequence. You can use the sequence 10 Disable to compare the before and after states of the effect.

2. Choose Clip > Enable or right-click a clip in the Timeline panel.

   A check mark next to the Enable command indicates that the clip is enabled. If a clip has been disabled, it will appear dimmed in the Timeline panel.

Adding Transitions

A wise man once said, "If you can't solve it, dissolve it." Although that may seem a little trite, the use of transitions can be important to an editor. The proper use of wipes and dissolves can smooth the transition of time and space for two video clips. You can also use audio dissolves to help clean up edits or smooth over sound beds.

The key to using transitions, however, is (and will always be) restraint. We do not subscribe to the belief that transitions are like sprinkles to pour all over your editing ice cream sundae. The number-one transition you'll use most often is a cut, followed by cross dissolves and a Dip to Color transition.

Edit Points and Handles

If you plan on using transitions, you need to understand the concept of handles. When you create an edit, you've ideally been using In and Out points to define your shots. The handle between a clip's Media Start time and In point is called the *head material*, and the handle between a clip's Out point and Media End time is called the *tail material* (**FIGURE 8.30**).

The unused portions of the clips provide an overlap area for transitions to occur (**FIGURE 8.31**). For example, if you apply a two-second, cross-dissolve transition centered between two video clips, you'd need a one-second handle on both clips.

If you apply a transition to a clip that doesn't have enough frames as handle, the transition appears but has diagonal warning bars through it (**FIGURE 8.32**). In this case, Adobe Premiere Pro is extending the handles using repeated head or tail frames (essentially creating a freeze-frame midtransition).

FIGURE 8.30 A video clip with handles. The ghosted area in the Timeline simulates the handle area and would not be visible normally.

A Media Start
B Handle
C In point
D Out point
E Handle
F Media End

A B C

D E F

FIGURE 8.31 If you select a transition, you can view it on the Effect Controls tab (nested in the Program Monitor panel). This makes it easier to see how the handle areas overlap.

FIGURE 8.32 The striped area of the transition indicates that frames are being repeated during the transition. You can shorten the transition, slip the shot, or accept the repeated image (which is not usually desirable).

Adding Video Transitions

Adobe Premiere Pro offers two types of video transitions. One category of transitions is found in the Video Effects group in the Effects panel. These transitions are meant to be applied to an entire clip and can be used to reveal the footage (typically between its In and Out points). The more traditional style of transitions is found in the Video Transitions group. These are organized into six categories based on style (**FIGURE 8.33**).

FIGURE 8.33 Category folders make it easier to find just the transition you are looking for.

Applying a single-sided transition

If you have a single clip on its own (such as the first or last clip in a sequence), you can apply a single-sided transition. This type of effect will transition the video clip to or from black or can be used to reveal a video clip or graphic on a lower track in the Timeline panel.

Let's give it a try.

1. Open the sequence 11 Transitions.

   This sequence is a montage of three clips. The clips do have adequate handles for transitions.

2. In the Effects panel, find the Cross Dissolve effect.

   You can use the search field to locate it by name or open folders of presets.

3. Drag the effect onto the start of the first video clip. You can set the effect to Start at Cut only for the first clip (**FIGURE 8.34**).

4. Drag the effect onto the end of the last video clip. You can set the effect to End at Cut only for the last clip (**FIGURE 8.35**).

5. To preview the added transitions, play back the sequence.

Apply a Transition to All Clips

If you want to find a similar way to apply a transition to all clips between the In and Out points, you won't have to look far. With the Selection tool, Option-drag (Alt-drag) to select the audio or video clips that you want to affect. Then choose Sequence > Apply Default Transitions to Selection. The command works only with double-sided transitions, however.

Review a Transition

Want to take another look at a transition? Just press Shift+K to preview around the current position of the playhead.

Quickly Replace a Transition

You can drag a new video or audio transition from the Effects panel on top of an existing transition in your sequence. This will preserve the alignment and duration of the transition and is a great way to swap out transitions or experiment.

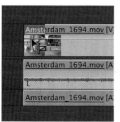
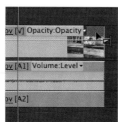

FIGURE 8.34 The Start at Cut icon indicates that this is a single-sided transition.

FIGURE 8.35 The End at Cut icon looks slightly different than the Start at Cut icon. It clearly shows that the Cross Dissolve transition will fade out the clip without extending the duration of the last clip.

 Looking for More Transitions?
Adobe offers a Web page with links to several options to extend the power of Adobe Premiere Pro. Just visit www.adobe.com/products/premiere/extend.html and click the Plug-in tab.

 Customizing Default Transitions
In this video you'll learn how to apply default video and audio transitions. You'll also learn to customize which transition is used as well as its properties.

Applying a transition between two clips

A common use of some transitions is to create an animated change between two clips. These transitions are used for stylistic effects in certain editing genres. You'll find a targeted collection of approximately 20 transitions to choose from (most of them are fairly restrained).

1. Continue working with the sequence 11 Transitions.

   You'll now add two interior transitions between clips 1 and 2 and between clips 2 and 3.

2. In the Effects panel, find the Dip to White effect.

   You can use the search field to locate it by name or open up folders of presets.

3. Drag the effect onto the edit point between clips 1 and 2 (**FIGURE 8.36**).

   Place the transition so it is centered at cut.

Force a Single-Sided Transition
If you want a transition to be single-sided (even when it is applied between two clips), Command-drag (Ctrl-drag) it into place. You can make one clip fade out while the adjacent one cuts in.

FIGURE 8.36 Depending on where you drag, the effect can be set to End at Cut (left), Centered at Cut (center), or Start at Cut (right). You can also drag the transition to freely place it for a custom start point.

4. Drag the Dip to White transition onto the edit point between clips 2 and 3.

   The only option you have here is Start at Cut because there is not enough handle for the incoming clip (the third in the Timeline). Let's apply the effect, and then you'll modify the clip to make it work in the next section (**FIGURE 8.37**). Notice the zebra stripes, which indicate that frames have been extended.

FIGURE 8.37 The transition could be placed only to start at the edit point. Although your options are initially limited without proper handles, you can modify the effect afterward to achieve the desired results.

Take Total Control of Transitions

The Effect Controls panel offers several options. In this video you'll learn to build custom effects and control their speed, position, and properties.

Modifying transitions with the Effect Controls panel

After you've applied an effect, you can take precise control over how it performs using the Effect Controls panel. Some transitions will have more choices than others, but there are some typical controls. The major benefit of the Effect Controls panel is that clips are displayed in an A-roll/B-roll format. This makes it easy to adjust the positioning of an effect or even to trim sources.

Let's modify a transition.

1. To start, double-click the Dip to White transition you just added to the previous sequence.

   The Effect Controls panel opens with the transition loaded (**FIGURE 8.38**).

FIGURE 8.38 Depending on the transition applied, some fields may appear empty or be hidden. Most of the controls are fairly easy to use, however.

2. Make sure the Show Actual Sources option is selected to view frames from the actual clips. This makes it easier to judge changes you make to the transition's source clips.

3. Click the alignment menu and switch it to Centered at Cut to match the earlier Dip to White effect (**FIGURE 8.39**).

FIGURE 8.39 You can force an effect to change its alignment, even if there are not proper handles.

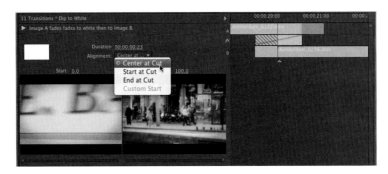

The transitions icon switches to show the new position. The striped bars in the transition indicate that frames are being repeated within the effect. This means that a freeze frame is being used for the incoming clip. This can be resolved using basic trim tools right in the Effect Controls panel.

4. Click the Play the Transition button to play back the transition in the panel (FIGURE 8.40).

FIGURE 8.40 Playing back an effect in real time is important before you start to modify its properties.

In this case (because of the transition through a color), it's hard to notice the repeated frames.

5. Click the duration field and enter **2:00** for a two-second duration effect.

Playback the transition and judge its effectiveness.

6. If you want to resolve the repeated frames, there are a few methods you can use:

■ You can drag the transition in the Timeline panel or the Effect Controls panel to change its alignment to a custom start (FIGURE 8.41). As you drag, you'll see the striped bars appear or disappear indicating a change in how frames are being repeated.

FIGURE 8.41 Dragging the transition lets you create a custom alignment to refine the timing and placement of the transition.

■ You can click in the middle of the transition and drag its position to perform a rolling edit (FIGURE 8.42). This changes where the edit happens in the actual sequence.

FIGURE 8.42 You'll explore the Ripple and Roll commands in greater detail in the next chapter.

■ You can click and drag the handles of the incoming or outgoing clips in the Effect Controls panel. In this case, you can lengthen or shorten the clip (which affects the handles). This type of edit is typically referred to as a single-sided trim, and it will result in items shifting in your Timeline (FIGURE 8.43). You can also drag the transition's handles to change its duration.

7. When you're finished tweaking, play back the effect.

Watch in True Full-Screen
If you'd like to see either the Source or Program Monitor panel in a full-screen (Cinema) mode, just press Command+` (Ctrl+`) with either panel selected. Press Esc to exit the full-screen view.

FIGURE 8.43 Through a series of drags, you can trim the clips to fix insufficient handles in a transition.

A The outgoing clip is a few frames short.

B Dragging the clip until the stripes are removed creates a trim and resolves the repeated frames.

C The incoming clip is several frames short, and many frames are being repeated.

D Dragging to the left trims the clip and resolves the handle issue.

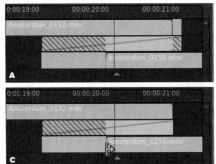
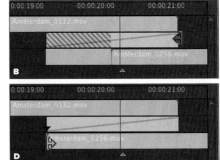

Adding Audio Transitions

The use of audio crossfades is a useful way to smooth out an audio track. Whether it's resolving an abrupt upcut between two sound bites or the slow fade in of a natural sound bed, transitions are essential to a good mix. There are three audio transitions to choose from.

- **Constant Gain.** The Constant Gain crossfade, as its name implies, transitions audio by using constant gain (volume) between the clips. Although often useful, this type of crossfade can sometimes sound very sudden as the outgoing clip fades out and the incoming clip then fades in at an equal gain. The Constant Gain crossfade is most useful in situations where you do not want much blending between two clips but rather more of a dip out and in between the clips. Other applications may call this a *+0 audio dissolve*.

- **Constant Power.** The default audio transition in Adobe Premiere Pro creates a smooth, gradual transition between two audio clips. The Constant Power crossfade is probably the crossfade you're most accustomed to in other editing applications. Similar to how video dissolves work, when applied, the outgoing clip at first slowly fades out and then fades out a faster rate toward the end of the clip. On the incoming clip, the opposite occurs. Audio level increases quickly at the start of the incoming clip and slower toward the end of the transition. This crossfade is useful in most situations where you want blending between clips.

- **Exponential Fade.** Similar to the Constant Power crossfade, the Exponential Fade transitions audio in a smooth manner. The way it works is that it uses a logarithmic curve to fade out and fade up audio. This results in very good natural blending between audio clips. Some editors prefer the Exponential Fade transition when performing a single-sided transition (such as fading in a clip from silence).

Creating a crossfade

Let's try creating a crossfade.

1. Continue working with the sequence 11 Transitions.

   You'll now add four audio transitions between the clips to smooth out the audio track.

2. In the Effects panel, find the Exponential Fade crossfade transition.

   You can use the search field to locate it by name or open up folders of presets.

3. Drag the transition onto the first edit point.

   Repeat for the second audio track (**FIGURE 8.44**).

4. You can double-click a transition to load it into the Effect Controls panel.

5. Enter a duration of 2:00 (**FIGURE 8.45**).

FIGURE 8.44 When dragging transitions, you'll need to apply them to each track separately.

FIGURE 8.45 You can easily change the duration of a transition as well as its placement in the Effect Controls panel. You can enter a new number or drag the handle to change duration.

Using the Apply Audio Transition command

If you want to quickly apply an audio transition, you have two ways to do so. The effect applied will be the default audio transition. If you haven't changed it, this will be the Constant Power crossfade with a one-second duration.

1. Move the playhead to an edit point.

2. Make sure the tracks you want to affect are targeted.

3. Press Command+Shift+D (Ctrl+ Shift+D) to apply the default audio transition (**FIGURE 8.46**).

4. You can press the Down or Up keys to quickly move to the next or previous edit point.

5. Repeat adding transitions for the next three edit points.

6. Watch your sequence to see and hear the effect of the transitions you've applied.

> **Need More Audio Control?**
> You can always use the Pen tool and a clip's audio volume keyframe graph to manually adjust the mix for a clip.

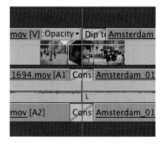

FIGURE 8.46 By using targeted tracks and the Apply Audio Transition command, you can quickly add crossfades. This is much faster than dragging and dropping from the Effects panel.

Next Steps

In this chapter, you were introduced to many ways to move clips around your Timeline panel. The next chapter is a natural progression because it tackles trimming. Experienced editors have come to rely on trimming to quickly shift their edit points. Whether you're trying to edit to music or just want to finesse the rhythm of the edit, trimming is an essential skill that separates the true editors from the assemblers.

CHAPTER 9

The Power Is in the Trim

TRIMMING IS THE most powerful part of editorial as well as the most misunderstood. We continue to encounter editors who don't know how trimming works. If you're a "razor and delete" editor, we hold nothing against you. If your clients are happy and you deliver shows on time, then you're a great editor!

But there is truth to the statement "Shows aren't ever finished; they're abandoned." There's always something more that can be done; edits adjusted for timing and rhythm, and shots slipped to create better synchronicity. *Great editors* know the ins and outs of trimming so they can quickly finesse their timelines.

Some editorial systems are primarily mouse based—and become finicky when it comes to subtle changes in the Timeline. With Adobe Premiere Pro CS6, there have been huge strides in improving its trimming abilities.

Closer To Truth
Some screen shots and footage for this chapter are from the PBS series Closer To Truth: Cosmos, Consciousness, God. © The Kuhn Foundation. Robert Lawrence Kuhn: creator, executive producer, writer and host. Peter Getzels: producer and director. Find out more about the series by visiting www.closertotruth.com.

Basic Trimming

You'll find multipurpose trim tools, such as the Ripple Edit, Rolling Edit, Slip, and Slide tools, a key part of your workflow. All of these tools can be overkill, however, if you just need to make a simple trim (such as adjusting a clip's In or Out point) without affecting other clips or sequence length.

Trim in the Source Monitor

Perhaps the easiest way to trim a clip in your Timeline is by using the Source Monitor panel. Load a clip from the Timeline panel into the Source Monitor by double-clicking it. Once it's loaded, you can easily adjust its In and Out points as well as perform other types of edits such as a slip (which we'll talk about later in this chapter). Let's take a look at how this works.

If you'd like to practice these techniques, feel free to open the project 09_trimming. prproj which can be found in Lessons and Media > Lesson 09. Once the project is loaded, open the sequence called 01_triminsource. This sequence contains a few shots with which you can practice these techniques.

With a clip loaded into the Source Monitor from a sequence, you can trim a clip in two basic ways.

- **Marking new In and Out points.** To trim a clip, you can simply update its In or Out points on a clip by pressing I or O (or using the Mark In and Mark Out buttons at the bottom left of the Source Monitor) at a new location in a clip. After you update an In or Out point, the clip on the sequence will update. Keep in mind that if there are clips located adjacent to the clip you just trimmed in the Timeline, there will be gaps on one or both sides. Also, if there are clips located after the clip, you can only shorten (not lengthen) the clip with this technique.

- **Dragging In and Out points.** If you're more of a drag-and-drop type of person, you can drag to trim a clip. On the mini Timeline in the Source Monitor, simply place your cursor over an In or Out point (or at the start or end of a clip). The cursor changes into a bracket-like tool with arrows pointing to the left and right (**FIGURE 9.1**). This is either the Trim-in or Trim-out tool (depending on what point you're on), which we'll explore more in the next section when trimming a sequence. Once the tool appears, drag left or right to update the In or Out point of the clip. Just like marking a new In or Out point, the clip will update on the sequence.

FIGURE 9.1 Positioning the pointer over an In or Out point in the Source Monitor changes the cursor to the Trim tool, which you can use to drag In and Out points to a new position.

Basic Trim in a Sequence

If you've used other editorial packages, you're aware that one of the fastest ways to trim is directly on a sequence. As you play back a sequence, you'll often discover points at which a cut would benefit from a trim. Here's how it works in Adobe Premiere Pro:

1. With the project 09_trimming.prproj loaded, open the sequence called 02_trimonsequence. This sequence has a few clips that you can use to make a basic trim on the sequence.

2. With the Selection tool active (V), move the pointer over the In or Out point of a clip on the sequence.

When you do, you'll notice that the pointer changes between the Trim-in or Trim-out tool; you can tell by which way the directional arrows point (**FIGURE 9.2**). You'll be trimming the Out point when the bracket icon/arrow is open and pointed to the left, and you'll be trimming the In point when it's open and pointed to the right.

3. Click to select either the In or Out point of a clip. If you're trying to select one side or the other of an edit, you'll select the side to which the bracket/arrow is pointing. Notice now there is a red indicator bar highlighting the point you selected—either in or out (**FIGURE 9.3**); this selection indicates that you'll be doing a regular trim.

4. Now that you've selected an edit point, you can create a basic trim in three ways.

   ■ **Dragging.** Of course, you can drag the selected point to make a trim. As you drag, below the clip on the sequence, you'll see a yellow timecode box showing you how much you've trimmed the clip (forward or backward). Likewise, as you drag, in the Program Monitor you'll see the In or Out point you've selected to trim dynamically update. You'll also see in the Program Monitor a source timecode overlay on the clip that is useful if you need to trim to a specific timecode. Additionally, in the Program Monitor on the lower-left and right corners, you'll see two timecode displays. The left one is like the yellow timecode box you see on the sequence, which indicates how much you've trimmed. The timecode on the right indicates the new duration of the clip (**FIGURE 9.4**).

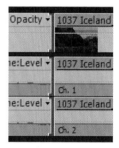

FIGURE 9.2 Similar to the Source Monitor, when you place the pointer over an edit in a sequence, the cursor changes to the Trim-in/out tool. Depending on what side of the edit you're over, you'll trim either the Out point of the outgoing clip or the In point of the incoming clip.

FIGURE 9.3 In Adobe Premiere Pro CS6, you can select edit points with the Selection tool. The red color of this selected point indicates you'll be doing a normal trim.

FIGURE 9.4 When you make a trim in a sequence, the Program Monitor changes to display the new In/Out point as well as timecode information about the resulting edit.

Audio Goes Too?
You may have noticed that when you selected an edit point and the clip you clicked has linked audio, the audio is also selected. This is a normal behavior because most of the time you'd probably want to trim both elements. You can override this behavior by using the modifier key Option (Alt) when you click to select a point. This allows you to quickly make L and J cuts.

Watch Those Waveforms!
When you start trimming, you might find it helpful to look at the audio waveforms of the clips you're trimming. The more you look at the waveforms, the easier it will be to quickly identify words and phrases as you trim a clip, which can be very helpful while trimming dialogue.

You Can Ripple Only So Far
When you ripple an edit, it's important to remember (as with other edits) that you can lengthen a clip only by using the Ripple Edit tool to the media's limits—you can't invent media you don't have! If a clip is still too short, explore the speed change options you learned in Chapter 7.

Sync Locks—The Exception to the Rule on Rippling
In sequences with multiple tracks, sync locks become important. Generally you'll have Sync Lock enabled for all tracks, but if you disable it on a track and make a trim on another track, you could move clips out of sync. We mentioned before that rippling makes a sequence longer or shorter; this is generally true, but in sequences with multiple tracks and Sync Lock disabled on a track, you might not change the sequence duration but rather just the duration of the track you're rippling a clip on.

- **Nudge.** With a point selected, you can use the keyboard shortcut Option+left/right arrow (Alt+left/right arrow) to trim the selected point forward or backward one frame at a time. By pressing Shift+Option+left/right arrow (Shift+Alt+left/right arrow), you can trim multiple frames at a time. The default for a multiframe nudge is five frames, but you can adjust this in Preferences > Trim > Large Trim Offset.

- **Numeric entry.** With a point selected, if you have a numeric keypad on your keyboard, you can also type in plus or minus and then the amount of frames by which you'd like to trim. Simply press the Return (Enter) key to commit to the trim. Like when dragging, when making a trim, if you're using numeric entry, you'll also be left with a gap.

Rippling Edits

As you've seen, you can trim a clip on a sequence by either its In point or its Out point. However, this can cause some problems because you can be left with a gap between clips after the edit. It can also be problematic because you cannot make a clip longer by adjusting the clip's In or Out point when it's adjacent to another clip.

Enter the ability to ripple (cue fanfare). Rippling lets you trim a clip while closing gaps or pushing everything else down the sequence. It can often be a huge time-saver because it performs a couple operations at once. Just remember that when you ripple an edit point in a sequence, you'll likely change the overall length of the sequence.

For example, if you rippled a clip's Out point to the left on a sequence (making that clip shorter), your entire sequence would become shorter. Likewise, if you rippled a clip's Out point to the right (making that clip longer), your entire sequence would become longer. This behavior (shortening or lengthening) assumes you have Sync Lock enabled for all tracks in a sequence, which we recommend you do most of the time. If you've disabled Sync Lock on a track, it's possible you'd make only the track, which you trimmed a clip on, shorter or longer and not adjust the overall sequence length. Generally speaking, we like to work with all of our tracks having Sync Lock enabled. We'll discuss sync locks more in several tips in this chapter.

One last thing to keep in mind about ripple edits—they're one-sided, meaning that when you ripple a clip, you don't change the corresponding In or Out point of the clip next to the one you're trimming.

Let's dive in and take a look at how you can ripple in Adobe Premiere Pro.

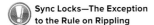
Rippling Edits with the Selection and Ripple Edit Tools

Earlier in this chapter we talked about doing a basic trim on a sequence. You can use the same basic methodology to make ripple edits quickly and efficiently, and you don't need anything more than the Selection and Ripple Edit tools.

1. From the current project, open the sequence called 03_ripple. This a short sequence containing a few clips you can use to practice ripple edits.

2. Play back the sequence. Notice in this interview that there are a couple of instances where the edits don't seem quite right. You can fix these issues using ripple edits.

3. Play back the sequence again, this time paying special attention to the first edit point. You should notice that the first interview bite (the person being interviewed) seems to get cut off while he is still speaking. That is, the edit cuts to the interviewer while the person being interviewed is still talking. To fix this, you need to extend the Out point of the first clip. In this exercise, you want to extend the Out point of the first clip so that the person being interviewed can complete his thought.

4. With the Selection tool, select the Out point of the first clip.

5. The selection is red, indicating that you'll be doing a basic trim. Right-click the red indicator line, and you're presented with a menu of different types of trims you can make based on your selection (**FIGURE 9.5**) including Ripple Trim In, Ripple Trim Out, Roll, and Trim In and Trim Out (trim is the default operation). For this exercise, be sure to choose Ripple Trim Out. Notice that the selected point changes to a yellow indicator; yellow means you'll be performing a ripple edit.

6. For even quicker access to the different trim methods, you can use the keyboard shortcut Ctrl+T (Shift+T) on Windows to cycle through the different trim types (**FIGURE 9.6**).

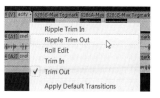

FIGURE 9.5 With a edit point selection made, right-clicking the indicator line brings up a menu of different types of edits that you can make.

The Importance of Sync Lock
When trimming with multiple tracks on a sequence, Sync Lock on a track comes into play. With this option enabled on a track or tracks (you can toggle it on/off in a track header), when you make a trim on another track, Adobe Premiere Pro will keep other tracks in sync by adjusting those tracks in a corresponding amount to the trim you made. With Sync Lock on all four tracks, rippling an edit would make the entire sequence longer or shorter. With Sync Lock disabled, however, on a track or tracks, when making a trim on another track, Adobe Premiere Pro will not attempt to keep clips on other tracks in sync, which could result in out-of-sync material as well as the sequence duration not changing.

No Toggle—No Sweat
If you're in a rush, you can use the modifier key Command (Ctrl) to quickly turn the Selection tool into the yellow ripple indicator when you click. This will also allow you to quickly select a roll edit. If you add the Option key, you can temporarily break the link between audio and video, so when you click, you'll be selecting only audio or video. If you want to go even faster, choose Preferences > Trim > Allow Selection tool to choose roll and ripple trims without a modifier key. With this option on, Adobe Premiere Pro intelligently chooses the correct tool.

A

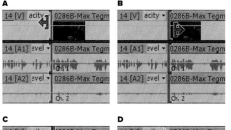

B

FIGURE 9.6 By using the keyboard shortcut Ctrl+T (Shift+T), you can toggle different trim modes.

A Trim outgoing clip's Out point
B Trim incoming clip's In point
C Roll
D Ripple outgoing clip's Out point
E Ripple incoming clip's In point

C

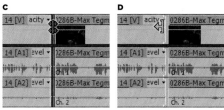

D

E

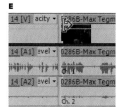

Be Careful of the T
If you're going to toggle a trim type on the Timeline, be careful to use the modifier Ctrl (Mac) or Shift (Windows). If you don't, you'll end up in the new Trim Edit mode (the Program Monitor looks different). If that does happen to, you can simply press T again to get out of the Trim Edit mode.

The Radio Edit
As you start to trim a sequence, one of the first things you should focus on is that all of the audio (interview bites, narration, and so on) is cut together well. This is often referred to as a radio edit. The Ripple Edit tool is a versatile tool that helps you do this. Later you can go back and refine video with ripple and roll edits or even create split edits to better match action between video clips.

Nudging and Timecode to Ripple
Fast editors know dragging can be slow; instead of dragging to make a ripple, you can nudge an edit point that has been selected as a ripple edit by using the keyboard shortcut Option (Alt)+left/ right arrow to go frame by frame. Adding the Shift key allows you to nudge by multiple frames. You can also ripple by timecode by typing in the amount of frames or timecode value you'd like to trim by on a numeric keypad. Just remember to press the Enter key to confirm the ripple.

Navigating Edit Points Using the Keyboard
To reduce the amount of clicks you need to make, many editors find it useful to click to select an initial edit point and then, using the keyboard, navigate to other edit points in the sequence. You can do this easily in Adobe Premiere Pro by clicking to select a point with the Selection tool and then using the up and down arrows to navigate to another edit. Remember once on an edit, you can use Ctrl+T (Shift+T) to toggle the edit type.

7. With the edit point now selected as a Ripple Trim Out, click and begin to drag right but don't let go. What you should notice is that the Program Monitor has changed to a two-up view.

- The left side showing the Out point of the outgoing clip and the right side showing the incoming clip. In this case, because you have the outgoing clip's output selected, as you move, the mouse only the left side updates. Ripple trims, like normal trims, are one-sided. So, in this case, you're not affecting the right side or incoming clips in point.

- Also notice several timecodes in the Program Monitor (**FIGURE 9.7**). First, each clip is labeled with source timecode, making it easy to ripple to a specific point. In the lower-left corner, you'll see by exactly how much you're rippling the selected point (this matches the yellow timecode box you see in the Timeline while dragging).

- Finally, in the lower-right corner, you'll see sequence timecode—meaning that if you were to release the mouse, that timecode would be where the new edit point would happen.

FIGURE 9.7 As you ripple an edit, the Program Monitor updates to show you several pieces of timecode information so you can make accurate edits.

8. Drag to the right until the subject looks like he's finished his thought.

9. We rippled forward +00:03;00 where the subject says "...my death is just the end of the...." Let go of the mouse button to perform the edit.

10. Back up the playhead and play through the edit, and you should now notice that the edit is much cleaner, and the subject doesn't get cut off. If needed, refine the trim to taste.

11. Navigate to the second edit point in the Timeline. Play through the edit a few times to familiarize yourself with the cut.

The person being interviewed trips up and doesn't make a complete thought at the end of the second clip. In the previous step, you rippled an Out point forward, but in this case, you'll ripple it backward to cover up the misspoken thought. To do this, you'll use the Ripple Edit tool.

12. Choose the Ripple edit tool (B) (**FIGURE 9.8**).

13. With the Ripple Edit tool active, place the tool over the second edit point and drag from one side to the other.

14. When you do, you'll notice that the Ripple Edit tool, and its directional arrow changes to face one direction or the other. With the bracket open and the arrow pointing to the left, you'll be rippling the Out point of the outgoing clip when you click. With the bracket icon open and the arrow pointing to the right, you'll be rippling the In point of the incoming clip (**FIGURE 9.9**).

FIGURE 9.8 If you prefer a dedicated tool for rippling an edit point, you can use the Ripple Edit tool, which you can find in the Tools panel or by activating it using the keyboard shortcut B.

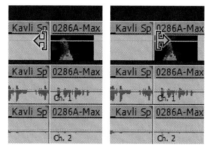

FIGURE 9.9 The direction of the Ripple Edit tool determines what point you'll be rippling—either the Out point of the outgoing clip (left) or the In point of the incoming clip (right).

15. Make sure the open side of the Ripple tool shape is open and pointing to the left so you can adjust the Out point of the second clip.

16. Click and drag to the left until you see the person being interviewed put his arms down in the two-up display of the Program Monitor.

17. Ripple this Out point back by -00:01;03, just to the point where the person being interviewed says "...it's all there and...."

18. Play back that part of the sequence; the edit is much cleaner.

If you play back the rest of the sequence, you'll see that there are similar problems throughout. Feel free to practice rippling on all of these different edits with either the Selection tool method or the dedicated Ripple tool. To help you out, we've placed sequence markers to let you know which direction you should be rippling; it's up to you to decide which side of the edit to ripple.

 Up and Down, Mind Your Targeted Tracks

One thing to be aware of when selecting an edit point and then navigating to other edits using the up and down arrow keys is that track targeting comes into play (targeting is when a track is selected or highlighted in the track header). If a track is not targeted when you use the up or down arrow key, when you arrive on the new point, the untargeted track won't take place in the edit.

 Play Around

When doing any sort of trim, it's imperative that you watch and listen to the edit. Often, though, you'll want to preview that edit point multiple times to get a good feel for whether things are working.

An easy way to do this is by using the keyboard shortcut for Play Around (Shift+K). When you invoke this shortcut, the playhead will back up and then play through the closest edit. How much the playhead backs up and plays through is determined with the Pre/Post Roll options in Preferences > Playback. Adding looping to Play Around allows to you keep watching. The cool part? You can make trims while playback is looping around and the edit updates—called dynamic trimming.

 I Can't Hear My Audio While Rippling!

When performing a ripple edit in the Timeline, you can't hear the audio of the clip. This can make it difficult to be exact when trimming sound bites. To get around this problem, we're fans of using In and Out points or the playhead on the sequence to first "spot" where you want the trim (the edit point) to line up. Then, with snapping on when you make the ripple edit, the new edit point will snap to that point. If snapping is off, just click the magnet icon in the upper-left corner of the Timeline panel or press S on the keyboard.

Rolling Edits

When you made a ripple edit in the previous section, you trimmed either the In or Out point of a clip. This didn't actually affect the In or Out point of the adjacent clip. However, there are often times you'd like to change where an edit point falls without changing the overall duration of the sequence.

A roll edit is a two-sided trim, meaning that you affect both points (Out and In) on both sides of the edit. Roll edits are perfect for when you're trying to match action between two angles or when you need to adjust an edit so that a cut happens at different points in time but doesn't affect the overall duration of a sequence. Roll edits can also be used to create split edits (where audio or video have different In and Out points). Let's look at using roll edits in Adobe Premiere Pro.

Rolling Edits with Selection Tool and Rolling Edit Tool

Making rolling edits in Adobe Premiere Pro is easy, and the best part is you have multiple methods at your disposal. Which one you use is up to you. Let's take a closer look at making rolling edits.

1. Open the sequence called 04_roll. This a short sequence containing a few clips you can use to practice rolling edits.

2. Play back the sequence. Everything seems to work OK, but on each clip, the audio and video end at the same place, making the edits feel a touch harsh. Since the audio is working, this is a perfect opportunity to roll the video clips to finesse the action.

3. Play through the first edit, and then position the playhead on the second clip (right after you hear the interviewer say, "Some people call…").

   This is one second forward of where the edit is currently. Make sure you've enabled snapping (S), which will make the edit you're about to do easier.

4. With the Selection tool active, Option-click (Alt-click) either side of the first edit (it doesn't matter which side). Using Option (Alt) temporarily disables the link between audio and video. When you do, an edit point will be selected. You can see this with the red indictor line that appears. As discussed, this red line indicates a normal trim.

FIGURE 9.10 Toggling a selected edit point until both sides are selected with a thick red indicator indicates that you'll perform a roll edit.

5. Using the keyboard shortcut Ctrl+T (Shift+T), toggle the selection until you see a thick red bar covering both sides of the edit (**FIGURE 9.10**). This bar indicates you'll be performing a roll edit. Note you can also right-click the selection and choose Roll from the menu.

6. Click the edit and start moving the edit point to the right, but don't let go. You'll notice that the Program Monitor changes to a two-up view. Both sides of the edit move as you drag, because a roll is a double-sided edit.

7. Continue to drag to the right until the edit point snaps to the playhead that you previously positioned in step 3. Release the mouse and play back to review the edit by pressing Shift+K.

The edit should feel a little smoother since audio and video are not cutting at the same time. You've also created what's known as a *split edit* in the process. Note you could also use the nudge and timecode methods for moving this edit point, which we detailed earlier in this chapter.

8. Navigate to the next edit point (between the second and third clips).

9. Play through the edit a few times.

    As in the previous example, this edit could benefit from a roll edit to smooth the transition between the clips out.

10. Position the playhead to the point in the third clip right after you hear the person say, "I met....".

11. Activate the Rolling Edit tool by using the keyboard shortcut N (**FIGURE 9.11**). You can also select the Rolling Edit tool from the Tools panel.

12. Option-click (Alt-click) the video edit (to choose just video and ignore linked audio), and drag the edit point to the playhead position (about ten frames).

    Back up the playhead and play through the edit; you should notice a much more solid edit.

13. Skip over the edit between the third and fourth clips—this edit already works. Go to the last edit point in the sequence between the fourth and fifth clips and preview the edit. Another way to make a rolling edit is by using the Extend Edit command.

14. For this edit position, position the playhead in the last clip so it's right after the word *thought* and right around the word *was*. Then Option-click (Alt-click) to select the edit point and toggle the trim type until you've selected a roll edit.

15. Press the shortcut E to extend the edit to the playhead. This will move the edit point forward to the playhead's position (about 15 frames).

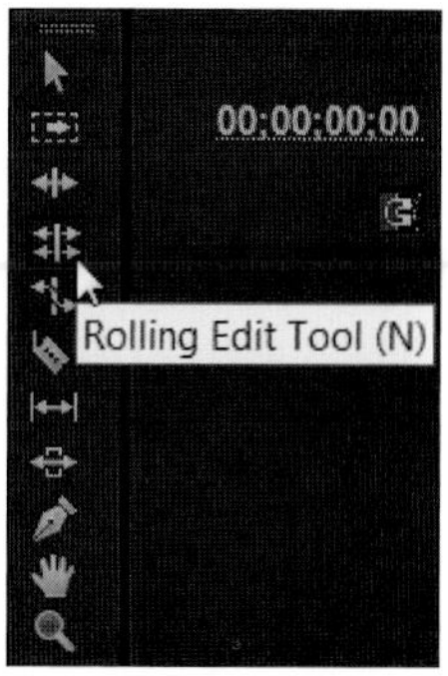

Trimming in the Program Monitor

Trimming on the Timeline is fast and quick, but it has two issues. It can be difficult to see exactly what is going on visually on both sides of the edit, and you don't get to hear audio while trimming. When trimming on the Timeline, Adobe Premiere Pro, like every editor, shows you only the frame your playhead is on. When you grab one of the edits, only then are you able to see both sides of a trim (in the two-up displays in the Program Monitor). In addition, when you trim from the keyboard, you miss out on these visual cues, because the playhead remains in place while you trim! It's a catch-22 for sure.

What's really needed is a specialized view where you can see and hear both sides of an edit simultaneously. Adobe Premiere Pro has you covered with the Trim mode in the Program Monitor panel (**FIGURE 9.12**). This feature is a way to temporarily convert the Program Monitor into a dedicated workhorse tool built to optimize trimming. So, what's the big deal with this new mode?

FIGURE 9.11 Like the Ripple tool, there is a dedicated tool in the Tools panel for performing rolling edits; it's aptly called the Rolling Edit tool, and you can activate it by using the shortcut N.

Roll for Montages
Probably the most common uses for a roll edit are for action matching in montages as well as doing tasks such as lining up an edit to a beat in music.

What About the Trim Monitor Panel?
If you're a fan of the old Trim Monitor from CS5.5 and prior, have no fear, because it still exists. You'll still find the legacy Trim Monitor (which is actually a separate floating panel) by choosing Window > Trim Monitor. This panel is still very usable and even provides a few additional features that the new Trim mode doesn't have. With that said, we've found the new Trim mode functionality to be much faster than the classic Trim Monitor.

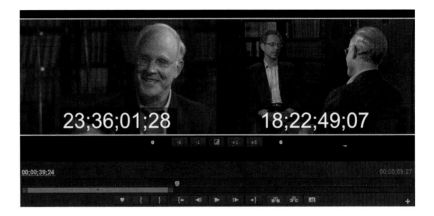

FIGURE 9.12 The Trim mode in the Program Monitor is a new and very functional addition to Adobe Premiere Pro CS6.

For one, it cleans up the interface considerably; instead of a floating window, you can perform visual trims directly in the Program Monitor, along with the added benefit of functionality like J-K-L trimming and audio scrubbing as you trim. In this section, we'll delve into this new functionality.

Launching Trim Mode

Before performing an edit in the Trim mode in the Program Monitor, it'd probably be a good idea to know how to actually open this view. There are three basic ways to enter into Trim mode.

- **Double-click.** With the Selection, Ripple Edit, and Rolling Edit tools, you can double-click an edit point to launch the Trim mode in the Program Monitor. Just keep in mind depending on the tool you use to launch the Trim mode with, by default it will become the type of trim enabled initially (you can always change the type).

- **Marquee.** With the Ripple Edit and Rolling Edit tools, simply drag a marquee around an edit point to launch a trim edit. Like double-clicking, depending on which tool you used, that edit type will be autoselected in Trim mode. You may want to hold down the Option (Alt) key to temporarily unlink audio and video tracks.

- **Press T.** With an edit point selected, with any of the trim tools, press T on the keyboard to launch Trim mode in the Program Monitor. Again, which tool you selected an edit point with will be the type of edit that the Trim mode launches with. You can also simply position the playhead near an edit point and press T by default; this will launch the Trim mode with a rolling edit enabled.

Making Ripple Trims Using the Trim Mode

The best way to learn trimming is to try it. Getting hands-on with this visually rich interface can make trimming seem much more understandable.

1. From the current project, open the sequence called 05_trimedit. This sequence is a combination of the ripple and roll sequences you worked with earlier.

   The sequence is not meant to be a complete and coherent sequence but rather a collection of clips to practice using the Trim mode of the Program Monitor.

2. Look at the first edit point. As you did earlier in the chapter when you rippled this edit, you needed to fix this edit point. But this time, we'll jump into the Trim mode of the Program Monitor panel.

3. Make the Ripple Edit Tool active (B), and then double-click the Out point of the first clip to launch the Trim mode of the Program Monitor.

4. When the Trim mode view opens, notice that the blue line above and below the left side? This indicates that you'll be performing an edit on the outgoing clip (**FIGURE 9.13**). In this case, since you launched Trim mode by double-clicking with the Ripple Edit tool you'll be performing a ripple edit; however, if you had double-clicked this edit point with the Selection tool, you'd still see the same line but would be performing a simple trim on that side of the edit. Remember, you can use Ctrl+T (Shift+T) to cycle through the different types of edits.

5. To perform a ripple trim in Trim mode of the Program Monitor, you have a few choices.

   ■ You can place your cursor over the side of the clip you're trying to ripple—in this case the left or outgoing clip—and drag in the direction you want to trim. Notice the cursor changes to the yellow Ripple tool you saw in the Timeline. The very cool part about this method is that you'll hear audio while rippling, which is a functionality that you don't have while rippling in the Timeline.

   ■ All of the keyboard options that we discussed earlier will work. Hold the Option (Alt) key and tap the left or right arrow to ripple by a single frame. Just add the Shift key to the previous combination, and it will trim by multiple frames (by default five frames). Of course, if you can use those shortcuts, you can also use a numeric keypad to ripple by specified frames.

   ■ You can use the trim buttons (either the multiframe buttons or single-frame buttons). In this case, you'd use the positive (+) multiframe or single-frame buttons. Remember, the multiframe button value can be adjusted by choosing Preferences > Trim > Large Trim Offset.

   ■ If you're more of a keyboard person (we are, especially when editing interviews/ sound bites), you can also use the J-K-L keyboard commands. The thing to understand is that J-K-L not only control playback but also, when you press K or pause, commit you to the edit at the position you stop playback.

Targeted Tracks Affect Your Trim
Before invoking the Trim mode in the Program Monitor, be sure you target (select) the tracks you want to work with by clicking the track headers. If you don't say, for example, target one track in a linked pair of audio, you won't be able to make an edit correctly.

FIGURE 9.13 In the Trim mode of the Program Monitor, the blue line over the left clip shows that you'll be performing an edit on the outgoing clip. Since we launched Trim mode by double-clicking with the Ripple Edit tool, you'll be performing a ripple edit.

Be Aware of Sync Lock
Just like when trimming directly on the Timeline, when you use the Trim mode of the Program Monitor, sync lock comes into play. For example, with Sync Lock on for track 1, making a trim to a clip on track 2 will keep everything in sync on track 1. Turn Sync Lock off, however, on track 1, and when making the same trim on track 2, items may be forced out of sync.

Trim Mode: Ripple
Check out this video to see using the new Trim mode functionality in Adobe Premiere Pro to make a ripple edit.

FIGURE 9.14 In Trim mode in the Program Monitor, the blue line over both sides of the edit indicates you'll be performing a roll edit. Just like rippling, you can roll this edit in a number of ways.

6. Using the method of your choice, ripple the first clip forward so the person being interviewed doesn't get cut off.

   We rippled forward +00:03;00. That's the point where the subject says "...my death is just the end of the...." Notice after you make the change that the edit point in the sequence has also been updated.

7. Press the spacebar to review the edit; the Trim mode in the Program Monitor changes back to the normal Program Monitor view while playing. When you stop playback, it switches back to the Trim mode view. If you're not satisfied with the results, ripple the clip again until the edit feels correct to you. To exit the Trim edit mode, simply click in the gray area of the Timeline or press T.

Making Rolling Trims Using the Trim Mode

You've probably guessed it, but if you can make ripple edits using the Trim mode in the Program Monitor, you can also make rolling trims. In this section, we'll check out making a rolling trim using the Trim mode in the Program Monitor.

1. While still working on the sequence called 05_trimedit, navigate down to the edit point between the third and fourth clips and preview the edit.

   This edit could be smoothed over just like you did previously by rolling just the video forward.

2. Position the playhead near the third edit, and Option-click (Alt-click) with the Selection tool (this temporarily unlinks audio and video).

3. Toggle the trimming mode by pressing Control+T (Shift +T) until you've selected a roll (a thick red line); then press T to launch Trim mode in Program Monitor.

   Notice the blue line above and below both the outgoing and incoming clips? This indicates you'll be performing a rolling edit, which affects both the Out point of the outgoing clip and the In point of the incoming clip simultaneously (and in equal amounts) **(FIGURE 9.14)**.

4. To perform a rolling trim in Trim mode of the Program Monitor, you have a few choices.

   - You can place your cursor between the two clips in the Trim mode view; notice that the cursor changes to a double roller just like you saw when rolling in the Timeline. Drag to the left or right to perform a rolling edit.

   - All of the keyboard options that we discussed earlier will work for rolling. Hold the Option (Alt) key and tap the left or right arrow to roll by a single frame. Just add the Shift key to the previous combination, and it will roll by multiple frames (by default five frames). You can also use timecode on a numeric keypad to roll by frames or timecode.

- You can use the trim buttons (either the multiframe buttons or single-frame buttons). In this case, you'd use the positive (+) multiframe or single-frame buttons to invoke a roll.

- As with a ripple, you can also use the J-K-L keyboard commands.

5. Using the method of your choice, roll the edit to the right so that the edit happens after you hear the interviewer say, "Some people call." This is about one second forward of where the edit is currently. Notice that after you make the change, the edit point in the sequence has also been updated.

6. Press the spacebar to review the edit; the Trim mode in the Program Monitor changes back to the normal Program Monitor view while playing. When you stop playback, it switches back to the Trim mode view. If you're not satisfied with the results, roll the clip again until the edit feels correct to you. To exit the Trim mode of the Program Monitor, simply click in the gray area of the Timeline or press T.

Making Split Edits

You do realize you've already done some split edits, right? Calling out this idea directly is warranted. A *split edit* is when the edit of linked video and audio don't line up in a straight cut.

Starting audio before video or visa versa, gives the illusion of a give and take with dialogue or interview clips, helps match action between two disparate takes and truly helps hide edits. Split edits work in either direction and are usually done only to the video track with a roll edit, moving the video edit before the cut (an L cut) or after the cut (a J cut). Why not involve the audio? It's because you get the "radio edit" right first with the Ripple tool. Messing with the audio at this point is likely to ruin all that hard work.

The quickest and easiest way to create a split edit is in a sequence. Normally, if you use the Rolling Edit tool on a linked clip, both the video and the audio will be trimmed together. Although this default behavior is often useful, you'll sometimes want to create a split edit; doing so is easy.

1. Select the Rolling Edit tool or use any of the other roll techniques that we've already discussed.

2. With your technique of choice (or in this case, the Rolling Edit tool), place the tool over the edit you're trying to manipulate.

3. Before clicking and dragging, hold down the Option (Alt) key, and then click and drag.

4. By holding down the Option (Alt) key while trimming, you'll temporarily unlink audio from video, allowing you to quickly create a split edit or L cut between adjacent clips (FIGURE 9.15).

FIGURE 9.15 By temporarily unlinking audio from video in a linked clip, you can use trim tools in Adobe Premiere Pro such as the Rolling Edit tool to create split edits.

5. After making a split edit on a sequence, simply deselect any clips. This way, further trims will affect both audio and video.

 Trim Mode: Roll and Split Edits
Check out this video to see using the new Trim Edit functionality in Adobe Premiere Pro to make a roll edit while also creating split edits.

 Making Splits Using Locked Tracks
Another method you can use to make a split edit is to lock either video or audio tracks. When tracks are locked, you can trim an unlocked track and create a split edit. Just be aware that depending on the type of trim that you perform, you might push audio and video out of sync with each other.

Split Edits in the Source Monitor
If you have a good idea for creating a split edit before editing a clip into a sequence, you can create split edits in the Source Monitor by right-clicking the mini Timeline and choosing Mark Split. Then select whether you want to mark video/audio in or out.

 Asymmetrical Trims and Split Edits
Check out this video to learn more about making asymmetrical trims split edits.

Splits from the Keyboard
If you like the new trimming functionality on the keyboard in Adobe Premiere Pro CS6, you can use it to also create split edits. But for that to work properly, you must untarget (deselect) the tracks you don't want to take part in the trim.

Slipping Edits

For some editors, the concept of a slip edit can be a little confusing. Here's a simple example of what slip edits can do for you: You've marked a clip (In and Out points) and edited it into a sequence, but something is not right. Where it cuts into the action, the shot feels off, and where it cuts out of the action, it feels off too; however, the duration or timing of the clip feels just about right.

When you perform a slip edit, you don't change the duration of a clip; rather, you simultaneously adjust the In and Out points of a clip so that the action better suits your needs. You can make slip edits in a few different ways in Adobe Premiere Pro. Let's work through a few slip edit exercises.

Slipping an Edit in the Source Monitor

Many editors find making slip edits in the Source Monitor to be the most straightforward and the easiest way to visually perform this type of edit. The reason is that you can easily view your In and Out points and how they relate to one another.

1. Open the sequence 06_slip. This a short sequence that you can use to practice slipping edits.

2. Play back the sequence. You can see that the edits flow OK, but on many of the shots, the action seems to be wrong, showing dead space while the camera is panning or adjusting zoom.

3. Look at the first clip in the sequence.

   Notice that the camera is focused on the background (bushes) for far too long before panning over to the subject. But the overall timing seems good. Let's slip this clip so you can see less of the background and more of the subject. Double-click this clip to load it into the Source Monitor.

   Note that there are In and Out points on the clip, and the clip is 6:06 in duration. Also, a green bar is visible on the mini Timeline in the Source Monitor, showing you the duration of the clip. You may have to zoom out to see the entire duration of the clip.

4. Place your cursor in the middle of the green bar (where there are four vertical lines). When you do, your cursor will become a hand (**FIGURE 9.16**). You can also hold the Option (Alt) key to turn the cursor into the Hand tool. Either way, after you've activated the Hand tool, click and drag to the right. Notice the following things:

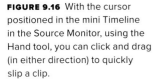

FIGURE 9.16 With the cursor positioned in the mini Timeline in the Source Monitor, using the Hand tool, you can click and drag (in either direction) to quickly slip a clip.

- The clip has been replaced in the Source Monitor with a four-up view (**FIGURE 9.17**).

- The top-left image shows you the clip before the one you're slipping. In this case, it's just black because you're slipping the first clip in the sequence.

- Below that is the In point of the clip you're slipping.

- The upper-right image shows you the clip after the clip you're slipping.

- Below that is the Out point of the clip you're slipping.

5. Drag to the right, until just before the subject appears in frame.

6. Release to make the edit. After making the edit, notice that the clip duration is exactly the same.

   Also, the sequence duration hasn't changed at all, and the clips surrounding the clip you just slipped are unaffected. Play back the first clip to check your work. All of the dead space has been removed, and you can now see more of the subject.

Slipping on a Sequence

Although slipping in the Source Monitor is easy to do, the fact is that it requires the extra step of double-clicking a clip to load it into the Source Monitor. As an editor, you know that even small extra steps can burn valuable time in a project. Therefore, you might find it faster to slip a clip within a sequence.

1. With the same sequence open from the previous exercise, navigate to the second clip.

   This clip has a similar problem as the one you fixed in the previous exercise—the shot is uninteresting and has some wild camera work at the top; plus, you don't see very much of the subject. The clip would probably work better if you slipped the clip so that the action happened a bit differently.

2. In the Tools panel, select the Slip tool or press Y (**FIGURE 9.18**).

3. With the Slip tool active, place it over the second clip, and click and drag to the left.

   In the Program Monitor, you now have a four-up view similar to what you saw in the previous exercise. But this time, you have the added benefit of seeing source time-code on the In and Out point of the clip.

4. Slip the clip about -8:12 so that the new In point is right before the subject comes in frame. Release the mouse to make the edit.

Linked Audio Slips Too!
When you slip a clip with linked audio, that linked audio will slip as well. Keep in mind that if you've unlinked a clip and slip either the video or the audio, you can potentially unsync a clip.

FIGURE 9.17 The four-up view displayed when slipping a clip is a great way to visualize the edit.

A Clip before the clip you are slipping

B In point of clip you are slipping

C Clip after clip you are slipping

D Out point of clip you are slipping. Note that this screen shot is from the second shot in the sequence. The first clip, because there is no prior clip, will show black in the previous clip part of the four-up view.

FIGURE 9.18 You can find the Slip tool in the Tools panel or use the keyboard shortcut Y to activate it.

Slip in Larger Chunks

If pressing the keyboard shortcut a thousand times to make a slip doesn't sound appealing to you, you can adjust how big your Large Trim Offset is by opening Preferences and then choosing the Trim category. The Large Trim Offset parameter is at the top.

Slipping More Confidently

As you slip with the keyboard shortcuts, neither the Program Monitor nor the Source Monitor will display a multiple view display. Therefore, you might find it difficult to slip in this fashion. However, you can always open the clip into the Source Monitor by double-clicking. Then, as you use the keyboard shortcuts, you should see the In and Out points of the clip moving in tandem. Opening a clip into the Source Monitor also has the added benefit of allowing you to see the handles you have on a clip.

FIGURE 9.19 You can find the Slide tool in the Tools panel or press U to activate it.

5. Navigate to the third clip in the sequence. Now that you have the hang of slipping in Adobe Premiere Pro, you can go to the next level.

   This is a nice shot, but unlike the two clips you fixed earlier, this clip could benefit from having a bit *more* of a camera pan. So, you'll slip it by using keyboard shortcuts.

   Using keyboard shortcuts can make you a faster editor, so to perform a slip edit on a sequence, use the following technique.

6. Press Command+Option+left/right arrow (Ctrl+Alt+left/right arrow) to slip the clip backward or forward by a single frame at a time. If you want to slip five frames at a time, just add the Shift key to the shortcut. For this clip, we slipped it forward 2:15 to add more pan to the start of the shot.

Additional clips are provided in this sequence so you can practice slipping using any of the methods from the previous sections.

Sliding Edits

A specialty type of trim operation is the slide edit. Although you'll certainly use the Slide Edit tool from time to time, most likely you'll use ripple and roll or even a basic trim more often. With that said, let's look at an example of when a slide edit is perfect.

Let's say you have three shots of a basketball dunk contest. The first shot shows a player dribbling the ball and approaching the basket, the middle shot shows the actual dunk, and the third shot shows the player celebrating and the crowd going crazy. The sequence of shots is working OK, but the timing feels off. You'd like to see more celebration after the shot and less of the lead-in to the actual dunk. The middle shot of the actual dunk is perfect as is.

You could use other trim tools to make this happen, but you can make this trim all in one step using the Slide tool. The Slide tool works by leaving the duration of the clip you're sliding the same while adjusting the Out point of the clip to the left and the In point of the clip to the right. When you slide, it's also important to remember that the duration of your sequence doesn't change.

Using the Slide Tool

Let's perform a simple slide edit. Using the Slide tool makes slides easy to do because the sequence will update as you drag.

1. Open the sequence called 07_slide.

2. Play back the sequence to review its content.

   Although the sequence is working OK, you can make it a bit better by using a slide edit. The middle clip is working, but the first clip seems a little short, and the third clip seems a little long.

3. In the Tools panel, select the Slide tool or press U (**FIGURE 9.19**).

4. Place the Slide tool over the middle clip, and then click and drag to the right.

As you drag, you'll notice below the clip that there is a yellow timecode box showing you how far you're sliding the middle clip. Additionally, the Program Monitor changes to a four-up display. The clip you're sliding is on top (its In and Out points shown), below on the left (with source timecode overlays) is the Out point of the first clip, and on the right you see the In point of the third clip (**FIGURE 9.20**).

FIGURE 9.20 When you slide a clip, the Program Monitor will show a four-up display, making it easy to see where in the preceding and following clips new edit points will be positioned.

5. Slide the middle clip by +2:00 to the right to make the first clip longer and the third clip a little shorter. This should help the sequence flow a bit better.

6. Play back the sequence to see the results.

Sliding with the Keyboard

Like slipping edits, you can improve your speed by sliding using keyboard shortcuts. The same issues of visualizing a slide hold true, but by looping playback (by pressing the Loop button in the Program Monitor), you can quickly judge the effectiveness of the slide.

1. Undo the previous slide.

2. Select the second clip with the Selection tool to slide it again. This time, you'll use keyboard shortcuts to do it quickly.

3. Try the following keyboard shortcuts to nudge the clip and slip it:

   - Press Option+ , (comma) (Alt+, [comma]) to slide the clip backward (left).

   - Press Option+ . (period) (Alt+. [period]) to slide the clip forwards (right) by a single frame at a time.

   - If you want to slide five frames at a time, just add the Shift key to the shortcut.

4. Make the same slide as before or to your liking.

Keep in mind that neither the Program Monitor nor the Source Monitor will display a multiple view like the one you saw when you used the Slide tool. However, you'll be able to see the two edit points on either side of the clip you're sliding move.

Maintaining (and Breaking) Sync

If you're anything like us, you might be a little obsessed about sync. Nothing is more embarrassing than watching a project with a client and realizing that footage on a sequence is out of sync. However, sometimes you might purposely need to make footage out of sync for stylistic reasons (such as lifting room tone from a clip) or to fix issues often associated with productions that use dual-system recording.

In this section, we'll discuss sync in detail in Adobe Premiere Pro.

Linking and Unlinking Audio and Video

When you ingest a clip that has video and audio, Adobe Premiere Pro automatically links the audio and video. Generally, this is a good thing, but sometimes you'll want to unlink video from audio. Also, sometimes you'll want to link two clips that weren't ingested together. Let's look at how this works in Adobe Premiere Pro.

- **Unlinking clips.** To unlink video from audio, select the clip and either choose Clip > Unlink or right-click the clip and choose Unlink.

- **Linking clips.** To link clips, reverse the procedure for unlinking clips. That is, choose Clip > Link or right-click the clip and choose Link.

- **Linking disparate clips.** If you want to link clips that weren't ingested together, you can. For example, if you spent time lining up a sound effect with a clip, you can then link them, so when or if you move the new pair around the sequence, the clips will stay together. To do this, select the first clip and then Shift-click the other clip(s) you want to link. Then choose Clip > Link or right-click one of the clips and choose Link.

- **Unlinking disparate clips.** To unlink multiple clips, reverse the procedure for linking them together. Either choose Clip > Unlink or right-click part of the linked clip and choose Unlink.

Moving and Slipping Clips into Sync

If part of a clip (either audio or video) has gone out of sync, one option you have to make the clip in sync again is to move the offending out-of-sync portion back in sync.

When a clip goes out of sync, a sync flag appears on the upper-left corner of the clip. If you right-click this flag, you'll be presented with two options—Move into Sync and Slip into Sync—to get the clip back into sync (**FIGURE 9.21**).

Move clips into sync

If you choose the option Move into Sync, Adobe Premiere Pro moves the out-of-sync portion back into sync with the other part of the clip. This means that clips are physically repositioned in the Timeline.

Slip clips into sync

If you choose the option Slip into Sync, Adobe Premiere Pro slips the out-of-sync portion back into sync. Slipping the clip won't move the out-of-sync portion. It will remain on the same part of the sequence as it was when it was out of sync. Instead, Adobe Premiere Pro will slip the part of the clip you selected to slip (as long as there is adequate media) back into sync.

Next Steps

Now that you've refined an edit, the next step is to finish an edit. In the following chapters we'll discuss color correction and grading, audio mixing and repair, effects, quality control, and finally publishing.

FIGURE 9.21 When a clip is out of sync with linked audio or video, a flag appears on the clip indicating how far the clip is out of sync. Right-clicking the flag will bring up the two options to get the clip back into sync.

 Out of Sync? Work with Video

If you notice on a sequence that footage is out of sync, even though Adobe Premiere Pro is telling you that footage is in sync, a good strategy is to get your audio edits correct and then slip or otherwise trim video to match. If you start moving or slipping out-of-sync audio and video, you can quickly go crazy!

CHAPTER 10

Audio Mixing and Repair

AS A VIDEO editor, you're often focused on the visual side of a project, making sure that clips work well together and a story is being told. However, many editors (we've been guilty of this from time to time) simply don't pay enough attention to their audio. Audio that is mixed well and is free of problems like noise can really improve the overall project.

Unlike video where viewers are more apt to chalk up technical issues as stylistic choices, when it comes to audio, viewers are pretty attuned to problems. Fortunately, Adobe Premiere Pro (as well as Adobe Audition) can help you get your audio to sound its best. In this chapter, you'll leverage many of the tools in Adobe Premiere Pro and Adobe Audition so you can utilize them in your own work.

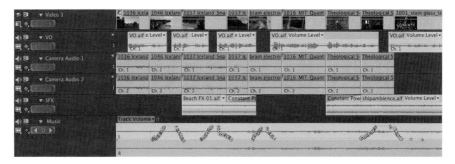

Where Are the Audio Master Meters?

When switching to the Audio workspace, the audio master meters seem to disappear. Just choose Window > Audio Master Meters to bring them back. You can position the meters anywhere you want or dock them to any existing panel so that they're always in view.

FIGURE 10.1 The Audio workspace optimizes the screen to work with audio.

Setting Up the Interface to Work with Audio

Before you start working with audio in Adobe Premiere Pro, it's important to adjust the interface so it's better suited to work with audio. Sure, you can work with audio regardless of how panels are arranged, but taking an extra moment or two to configure your workspace will allow you to work more efficiently.

The Audio Workspace

As with other tasks, such as editing and color correction, Adobe Premiere Pro has a workspace dedicated to working with audio. This workspace moves panels around on-screen to optimize the layout of the application for working with audio.

1. Navigate to Lessons and Media > Lesson 10, open the project 10_audio.prproj, and then open the sequence called 01_Audio Setup from the Sequences bin.

2. Choose Window > Workspace > Audio; note you can also use the keyboard shortcut Option+Shift+1 (Alt+Shift+1).

    When you choose the Audio workspace, a few panels will shift around a bit, but most important, the Source Monitor and Program Monitor panels will become a whole lot bigger (**FIGURE 10.1**). The Audio Mixer comes into view as well. You'll also have a lot more room to display the Audio Mixer, which is useful if you have several tracks to view. With the Audio Mixer selected, you may find it helpful to press the grave accent (`) key to toggle into full-screen, especially if you have a lot of tracks.

3. Feel free to keep exploring and adjusting the audio interface to suit your needs.

One very welcomed improvement in Adobe Premiere Pro CS6 is the redesigned Audio Meters panel. The audio meters now have several options that really make them flexible and add functionality.

- **Resizable.** You can now resize the audio meters to any size you want, even super jumbo! Because of this and the dynamic panel docking system, you can size and then position the audio meters anywhere. Our personal favorite is to have horizontal meters underneath the Timeline panel, allowing us to have a slightly wider sequence panel.

- **Solo Output Channels.** You can now solo individual channels or pairs of channels directly on the audio meters by clicking the Solo button (with the small s) at the bottom or low end of the meters. This makes it very handy to QC that output tracks are being routed properly with adaptive tracks, submixes, and direct output assignments.

- **Peaks and Valleys.** Right-clicking the audio meters brings up a new menu (FIGURE 10.2) that gives you a plethora of options including the scale range and whether the meters are displayed as a gradient.

Also included in this list of options is the ability to show static peaks or dynamic peaks. With the Static Peak option, the highest value attained by a channel will be held by a visual indicator, so you can easily see where a channel had its max peak. With Dynamic Peaks (the default), peaks are held only momentarily. In addition, you can also now view the lowest point of a channel (a valley). Combined peak and valley indictors make it really easy to see the dynamic range in your audio.

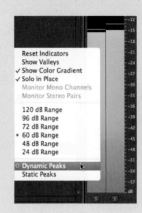

FIGURE 10.2 A new options menu that can be found by right-clicking the audio meters provides increased flexibility for the audio meters in Adobe Premiere Pro.

Master Track Output

As discussed in Chapter 3, "Setting Up a Project," the time to properly configure audio for your sequence is when you first create it. At the creation point, you have the ability to choose the type and number of tracks for a sequence. In addition, you can set up the master output. It's important to think ahead whenever possible; in other words, know your output when you start the edit.

Let's review how to set the Master track output.

1. Press Command+N (Ctrl+N) to create a new sequence.

2. Click the Tracks tab, and then click the Master menu in the Audio section. Don't worry about the preset or settings for this sequence; you're creating it to simply illustrate creating a sequence with a Master track of your choosing.

   Here are the Master track types you can choose from:

   - **Mono Master.** When a sequence is set to Mono, all audio will be output as a single channel. Although not often used, this is an option for some projects, such as those targeting low-bandwidth Web delivery.

   - **Stereo Master.** The default and most common master audio setup, audio will be output in stereo. Individual tracks can be panned within the Stereo sound field.

 Need to Change the Master Track?
After you've created a sequence, its Master track type is locked. If you need to make a change, the best option is to create a new sequence that matches all of the settings except for the Master Track option. You can then copy and paste to move items from one sequence to another. New to CS6, with multichannel master tracks, you can switch the number of output tracks on the fly.

 Hearing Multichannel Output
When creating multichannel or 5.1 master tracks for a sequence, you may not be able to hear all channels depending on your audio setup. You can configure audio hardware in preferences. Additionally, other pieces of outboard gear such as scopes and decks may allow you select different channels for listening.

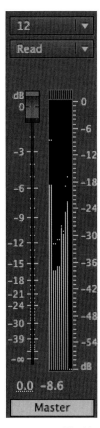

FIGURE 10.3 The Master track of a sequence that uses the Multichannel option. In this case, there are 12 output tracks. A new feature in CS6 is the ability to switch the number of multichannel outputs on a Master track after creation. Note that there are 12 individual audio meters for the output channel, but only 10 are actually in use in this figure.

Working Hot
Although the -10 dBFS rule for peak levels for broadcast has been a golden rule for some time, "working hot," or mixing levels at a higher level for broadcast, is a growing trend. Many broadcasters are OK with peak levels of -6 to -3 dBFS. Be sure to consult the broadcaster you're working with to make sure these "hot" levels are acceptable.

- **5.1 Master.** If you want to mix in surround, setting up a sequence to 5.1 master is the choice you want to make. When using 5.1 as a master, you can pan Mono and Stereo tracks anywhere in the 5.1 sound field, as well as adjust center channel percentage and the LFE (low-frequency effect—that is, subwoofer) volume of those tracks.

- **Multichannel Master.** The Multichannel Master option (**FIGURE 10.3**) allows you to create between 1 and 16 audio tracks for your master track. You can route tracks (including adaptive and submix tracks) to the Master track output channels.

3. For this exercise, choose the Multichannel Master track option, and then in the number of Channels menu choose 12. Twelve channels matches the very popular HDCAM SR tape format that is used in many broadcast workflows. Name the new sequence 12 Channel Master Track. Feel free to add as many tracks of various types that you want (we added 12 standard tracks), but make sure you're using a multichannel master. Then click OK to create a new sequence.

Monitoring Audio Levels with the Audio Mixer

When you switched to the Audio workspace, the Audio Mixer panel became a dominant fixture. Within it you'll find multiple audio meters, arranged in vertical strips, which will help you monitor your audio levels. There are two ways to monitor audio levels in the Audio Mixer.

- **Individual tracks in the Audio Mixer.** With the Audio Mixer open, you can view levels for each track in a sequence (**FIGURE 10.4**). Depending on how you have set up your tracks, meters can appear as mono, stereo, 5.1, or multichannel as can be the case with adaptive tracks.

FIGURE 10.4 No matter the track type, you'll see audio meters for each track in the Audio Mixer. Pictured are mono, standard (which can be both mono or stereo), 5.1, and adaptive tracks. Note the routing icon on the adaptive track indicating what kind of track it is.

- **Master audio output levels in the Audio Mixer.** To the right of all the individual tracks is the Master Audio Meter. Depending on how your sequence is set up, the master audio meter will show mono, stereo, 5.1, or multichannel (1 to 16 tracks) of output. This meter is the same as the main master audio meters outside of the mixer.

Adjusting Audio Levels on a Sequence

One of the main tenets of audio mixing is adjusting levels between various pieces of audio so that they "mix" well together. For example, you don't want to drown out an important bite from an interview with music that is too loud. You can adjust audio levels in Adobe Premiere Pro in a few different places, but because you'll probably spend lots of time in the Timeline panel, let's start by adjusting audio levels there.

Showing Audio Waveforms

When you start to work with a lot of audio, you'll quickly discover that simply seeing a clip on a sequence is not very useful. When you're trying to find a specific bite or key-frame volume in a specific section of a clip, it's very difficult to do that just by looking at a block on a sequence.

By default, Adobe Premiere Pro displays audio the same way it displays closed video tracks. But there are a couple of things you can do so that your audio clips will display audio waveforms. Let's check how you can view audio waveforms in Adobe Premiere Pro on the Timeline.

1. With the project 10_Audio.prproj still open, open the sequence called 02_Audio On A Sequence. This is a rough-cut sequence from the PBS Show *Closer To Truth: Cosmos. Consciousness. God.*

2. On each audio track is a small triangle called Collapse-Expand Track next to the name of the track (**FIGURE 10.5**).

   Click the triangle next to the first track, called VO, to expand the track. When a track is expanded, you'll be able to see audio waveforms on a clip. On the audio wave-forms is a yellow line that you can use to adjust clip volume (the line displayed is viewable because the default view on audio tracks is to display clip keyframes).

3. Resize the track to make it easier to view the waveform for that track (**FIGURE 10.6**). Place your cursor on the dividing line between the VO track and the Camera Audio 1 track in the track controls area to resize the VO track by dragging down.

FIGURE 10.5 Clicking the Collapse-Expand Track triangle lets you quickly view audio waveforms for a given audio track.

FIGURE 10.6 By placing your cursor between expanded audio tracks, you can easily resize a track so the waveforms are easier to view.

 Changing Levels from a Bin We're sure its happened to you: Music or other audio comes in too loud or too soft, and after editing it onto a sequence, only then do you realize the problem, and you end up making the same volume adjustment countless times. The solution? Select the tracks you want to be the same level in a bin or in the Project panel choose Clip > Audio Options > Audio Gain, and then use the Set Gain To option to get the desired level.

Adjust Audio Channels Default Track Format If you want to adjust how Adobe Premiere Pro handles audio channels from imported media, choose Preferences > Audio, and in the Default Audio Tracks area, choose between Use File, Mono, Stereo, 5.1, and Adaptive, for mono, stereo, 5.1, and multichannel mono media. Choosing Mono for stereo media, for example, will treat the clip as a mono pair.

No Waveforms? If audio waveforms are not being displayed, be sure to click the Set Display Style button on the track. Just choose the Show Waveform option. Conversely, if you don't want to view waveforms, you can turn them off using the Display Style button.

Audio Track Icons Audio tracks on a sequence can have icons on them to help you quickly determine what type of track you're looking at. A standard track will have no icon after the track name, a mono track will have a small single speaker, an adaptive track will have a routing icon (indicating you can route source channels to master output channels), and a 5.1 track will have the text 5.1 after the track name.

FIGURE 10.7 You can easily make volume changes on the Timeline by dragging the yellow line on each audio clip.

 Gearing Down on Changes
One problem you might find frustrating as you start to adjust audio levels is that it's difficult to be precise. However, "gearing down" can help. Start moving the yellow volume line; then, by holding down the Command (Ctrl) key, you'll make adjustments up or down for audio level much slower. The key is to start moving first. With respect to keyframes, holding down the Option (Alt) key while trying to move a keyframe will constrain that adjustment to a vertical (level) move and not allow you to move the keyframe side to side.

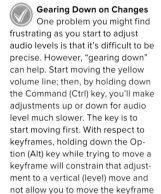

FIGURE 10.8 Adding keyframes to a clip allows you to dynamically adjust volume level on a clip. For a volume change to happen, you'll need two or more keyframes on a clip.

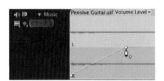 **Resizing Multiple Audio Tracks at Once**
Do you want to adjust the size of the waveforms for multiple tracks? Make sure the disclosure triangle is open for all the tracks you want to resize. Then hold down the Shift key as you drag to resize.

Adjusting Overall Clip Levels

While looking at audio waveforms for your audio clips, you can control the volume of those clips by adjusting the yellow line that is overlaid on each audio waveform.

1. Continue working with the sequence 02_Audio On A Sequence.

2. Place the cursor over the yellow line on the expanded waveform on the first track, called VO, and on the first VO bite. The cursor will change to a white cursor with two small up and down arrows next to it.

3. Click and drag up and down to adjust the overall volume of the clip. As you do, a small yellow box appears informing you of how much you're adjusting the clip levels by (FIGURE 10.7).

4. Adjust this clip until its volume as been raised slightly by 2 dB.

5. For the rest of the clips in the sequence, feel free to experiment by adjusting audio levels up (2 dB for the VO clips) or down to suit your taste.

Keyframing Clip Volume Changes

Although you use static volume changes on a clip all the time, at other times you'll need to dynamically change volume over time. One of the easiest ways to control volume is within keyframes.

1. With the same sequence open as in the previous exercise, let's create an audio fade up on the music clip on this sequence by using keyframes. Make sure you've expanded the Music track to see its waveforms.

2. Select the Pen tool (P).

3. Similar to adjusting overall volume, simply place your cursor over the yellow level line on the clip. The Pen tool changes a bit and shows a plus sign next to it.

4. Click to add a keyframe at the very start of the clip. Although we used the Pen tool, you can also use the Selection tool (V); however, to add a keyframe, you'll need to Command-click (Ctrl-click).

5. Add a second keyframe a little later in the clip. To make any volume change, you need two or more keyframes.

6. After you've made the keyframes, place the cursor over the first keyframe to adjust its value. For this first keyframe, drag down until the value of the keyframe (as shown in the small yellow box) shows infinity; the second keyframe should be set to 0 dB, which it should be already when you added the second keyframe in the previous step (FIGURE 10.8).

7. Feel free to add additional keyframes to adjust audio levels on this clip and the other clips in this sequence. You can keyframe the music to create rises and dips so that the voice and music play off one another. Also, you can add slight fades to the beginning and end of each bite on the VO track.

Smoothing Volume Between Clip Keyframes

One of the features we love in Adobe's products is the smoothing and easing between keyframes. Audio keyframes in Adobe Premiere Pro are no different. You can add Bezier handles to audio level keyframes so that you can smooth a transition between two keyframes (FIGURE 10.9).

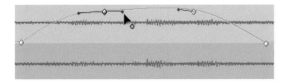

FIGURE 10.9 By adding keyframes to an audio clip, you can then adjust the transition between keyframes by adding Bezier handles.

1. Open the sequence called 03_Smoothing Keyframes. This is a duplicate of the previous sequence you were working with in the previous exercise, but keyframes are already applied to the clips.

2. Make sure either the Pen or Selection tool is active.

3. Place the cursor over an existing keyframe on any of the clips and hold down the Command (Ctrl) key.

   When you do, the cursor changes to a triangle-shaped tool (called the Convert Vertex tool).

4. Click an existing keyframe. Bezier handles will appear on the keyframe.

   Only keyframes that exist between two other keyframes will have Bezier handles on both sides. Keyframes with another keyframe on only one side or the other will have Bezier handles only on the side with the adjacent keyframe.

5. Drag a handle to adjust the velocity of the curve.

6. Experiment with adding Bezier handles and adjust them to taste. Be sure to listen to the audio between adjustments to hear the differences.

Drag and Drop for iTunes
If you use iTunes to organize your music libraries and sound effects, you might not know that you can simply drag files from iTunes directly into the Project panel to begin working with them.

Importance of Smoothing Keyframes
While linear audio keyframes (a straight line between keyframes) are used all the time, for more organic fade-ups and fade-downs consider using Bezier handles on keyframes. By smoothing keyframes with Bezier handles, you can achieve more natural volume changes.

WHAT'S THE AUDIO TARGET?

Now that you can view actual levels for a track or for a sequence, you might be wondering what the proper levels are. How you mix your individual tracks is up to you, but here are some suggestions on overall peak levels for a project that you should keep in mind as you're working with audio in Adobe Premiere Pro:

- **Nonbroadcast.** For nonbroadcast, a peak audio level of -3 dBFS is a good target; average levels are around -12 dBFS.

- **Broadcast.** For broadcast work, peak audio levels should be -10 dBFS; average levels should be around -20 dBFS. Be sure to check with your broadcaster because requirements may vary from broadcaster to broadcaster.

Track Keyframes

Because we are talking about keyframes, we need to make an important distinction that is unique to Adobe Premiere Pro and explain the difference between Track keyframes and Clip keyframes.

- **Clip keyframes.** In the previous exercises, you created Clip keyframes. Clip keyframes exist independently from other clips and have no interaction with the Audio Mixer. It's these keyframes you've adjusted in previous exercises.

- **Track keyframes.** The use of Track keyframes lets you affect several clips at once. These keyframes control all of the clips on one track in the sequence. Additionally, any Track keyframes that you make on a sequence will appear as automations in the Audio Mixer. Likewise, any automations that you create in the Audio Mixer will appear as Track keyframes on a sequence.

For this exercise, you'll use the same sequence as in the previous exercise but this time without any keyframes. You'll adjust the audio levels with Track keyframes.

1. Open the sequence called 04_Track Keyframes.

2. Expand all tracks, and then click the Show Keyframes button in the track header area for any track. Choose Show Track Keyframes (**FIGURE 10.10**).

   A yellow line now runs through the entire audio track.

3. Select the Pen tool. You can add Track keyframes just like you added Clip keyframes by using the Pen tool.

   There are three additional types of Track keyframes you can use.

4. In the upper-left corner of the track is a floating gray box called the Effect menu. Click to choose a keyframe type (**FIGURE 10.11**).

   - **Track > Volume.** You can use keyframes to control the overall mix of an entire track.

   - **Track > Mute.** You can use keyframes to keyframe silence or muting through the entire track.

   - **Panner > Balance.** You can use keyframes to adjust the panning of a track to a particular speaker or to center audio tracks.

5. On this sequence keyframe the music track so it fades up in between audio bites and fades back out after the audio bites. Repeat this throughout the entire sequence.

FIGURE 10.10 Choosing to display Track keyframes allows you to make keyframe adjustments to the entire track. These keyframes are also tied to Audio Mixer automations.

FIGURE 10.11 After enabling Track keyframes, you can keyframe a few different parameters.

Using the Audio Mixer

Using the audio controls in the Timeline panel is a quick way to adjust audio on a clip or a track, but sometimes you'll need more control. That's where the Audio Mixer panel comes in. In this section, you'll explore the Audio Mixer so that you can then use it to make your audio sound its best.

Overview of the Audio Mixer

We have to hand it to it to Adobe—the Audio Mixer in Adobe Premiere Pro far exceeds other NLEs. Maybe it's because it closely mimics traditional hardware mixers or because it's very flexible, allowing you to easily work with multiple types of tracks. In fact, you can use submix tracks as well as add effect inserts and record very complex automations.

Before we dive into the details of using the Audio Mixer, let's take a quick tour of its features (FIGURE 10.12). We'll work our way up from the bottom of a channel strip to the top so you can get a complete view of the controls in the Audio Mixer. To begin, make sure the sequence called 05_Exploring the Audio Mixer (Stereo Master) is open.

Yes, the Mixer Works Differently

If you're a Final Cut Pro or Avid editor, you'll quickly realize that the Audio Mixer panel in Adobe Premiere Pro works differently than in Final Cut Pro 7 or Avid. That's because in Adobe Premiere Pro, the mixer works at the track level and not the clip level like the mixer in those apps does. Although this might initially seem like a limitation, we like the ability to control tracks from the mixer and clips from a sequence. You can, of course, combine track- and clip-level control.

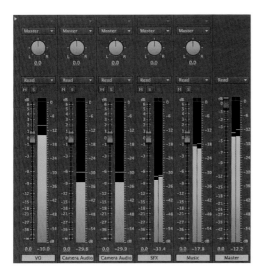

FIGURE 10.12 The Audio Mixer in Adobe Premiere Pro allows you to quickly adjust audio level, pan, create effect inserts, track sends, and assign output tracks.

Track names and channel strips

Each track in your sequence is organized into a channel strip. At the bottom of each strip is a text box for the name of the track (which defaults to the Audio 1, 2, 3 naming structure). Click in this box to use a custom name. For example, you might rename a track to call it VO. Renaming a track in the Audio Mixer also renames it in the Timeline panel.

Volume fader and track meters

Above the name of each track you'll find a numeric volume control (yellow text) as well as a volume fader for each track and submix. Depending on the type of track you're working with, in the fader section, you'll also be presented with an audio meter(s) for that track (FIGURE 10.13). In Adobe Premiere Pro CS6, there are some enhancements to the volume faders and track meters.

- **Double-click to reset.** You can quickly reset a volume fader by double clicking the fader itself to return its value to 0 db. Just keep in mind if the track has had automations recorded, it might not stay at 0db. We'll talk more about automation modes later in this chapter.

- **Two scales.** Each track now has two dB scales. The one on the left for each track and that is attached to the volume fader shows plus or minus decibel adjustments for that particular track. For example, if you dragged up to 3 dB, you would have made a track 3 dB louder than its original volume, which is represented as 0 dB. The dB scale on the right that is attached to the actual audio meter for a track shows track output level.

- **Right-click for additional options.** Like the main audio meters, you can right click the meters for a given track (including the master track) and choose from additional options, including choosing from different decibel ranges for each track, showing with visual indicator peaks as static or dynamic, showing valleys with a visual indicator, and showing the meters as a gradient, or if deselected, as stepped.

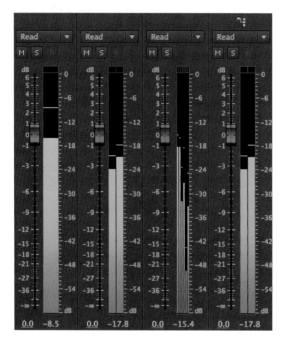

FIGURE 10.13 Depending on the track type, each channel strip will display audio meters for a given track. Additionally, the Master audio track will display meters based on your master output type. From left to right in the figure are Mono, Stereo, 5.1 and Adaptive tracks. Note the Stereo track is a standard track.

Mute, Solo, and Record controls

The next controls you'll encounter are the Mute, Solo, and Record controls. It should be obvious how these controls work, but put simply, the Mute button mutes audio for that channel while it's active. The Solo button mutes all other tracks except the one(s) you've soloed. The Record button allows you to arm a track record audio, such as voice-over, directly to a track via supported hardware. Be sure to watch video #17 about recording voice-over in Chapter 4.

Automation mode menu

Above the Mute, Solo, and Record controls you'll find the automation mode menu. You might be thinking what are automation modes? Put simply, automation modes control how Track keyframes (called *automations* in audio speak) are written, read, and updated. You have a choice between five different modes. If you don't have any experience with automation modes, you'll find they're extremely powerful for mixing quickly and efficiently every major audio tool such as Adobe Audition, Avid ProTools, and so on, has automation modes. Later in this chapter in the "Using Automation Modes" section you'll explore the different automation modes in more depth.

Pan controls

If you're working with standard (either mono or stereo) or mono-only tracks and a stereo master output track, you'll find a traditional pan control to pan audio left or right or somewhere in between. 5.1 tracks on a sequence with a stereo master output track do not have panners. If your master track output is set to 5.1, you'll find a surround panner with additional controls for adjusting center channel percentage and low-frequency effect (LFE) level. Finally, if your master output is set to multichannel, you will find that you have traditional panners and an additional menu between the automation mode menu and the panner for each track called the Direct Output Assignment menu. This menu allows you to direct a track to a pair of output tracks, and using the panner for a given track, you can pan between the different output tracks in the pair.

If you're thinking, hold on a second, there has got to be a better way to route tracks to a master output channel, you're correct. We'll talk about a couple of those ways later in this chapter when we discuss adaptive tracks and submixes.

Toggle between the sequences, 06_5.1 Master and 07_Multichannel (16) Master (we omitted Mono Master because it's not commonly used), to see the panner differences between tracks with these master settings (**FIGURE 10.14**). Please keep in mind that depending on your audio setup, you might not be able to hear all of the tracks in the 07_Multichannel (16) Master sequence. You can adjust the Direct Output Assignment menu back to 1 +2 (assuming you have only stereo output) to route tracks back to those channels. Play with the different combinations of the Direct Output assignment menu and panning tracks to see how they're routed to different Master tracks.

> **The Master Track**
> For all intents and purposes, the Master track in the Audio Mixer acts just like a normal track when it comes to meters and the volume fader. However, you can't assign effects or sends to the Master track. But you can keyframe it!

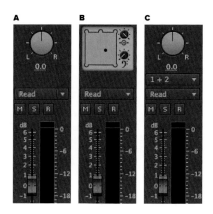

FIGURE 10.14 Depending on your master track output setting, the panner controls and the visibility of the Direct Output assignment menu for tracks will differ. Note the panner is not different in the Multichannel master, but there is now the appearance of the Direct Output assignment menu.

A Stereo Master track
B 5.1 Master track
C Multichannel Master track

Control Supersized
It can be a little annoying to have to tweak an effect added to an insert on the Audio Mixer by using the effect Control knob and toggling through the different parameters in the Effect Properties menu. Instead, simply double-click an effect in the insert section of the Audio Mixer to bring up the VST Editor, which allows you to tweak effect parameters in a floating window. Just note that not all effects are compatible with the VST Editor.

FIGURE 10.15 The effect inserts section of the Audio Mixer allows you to insert effects and bypass or adjust parameters of a given effect.

Submixes or Track Output Assignment?
What is the difference between sending a track to a submix vs. assigning the track output with the Track Output Assignment menu? Well, with submixes, you can control the level of the track sent to the submix, which allows you to (for creative reasons) control what is feeding the submix. Submixes are often used for audio effects work.

Effect inserts

Switch back to the sequence called 05_Exploring the Audio Mixer (Stereo Master). You can skip over the next menu above each pan control called the Track Output Assignment menu. You can use this menu in lieu of using a send. We'll discuss sends in the next section.

Effect inserts allow you to insert audio effects at the track level and affect all the clips on that track, which can be very useful for effects such as limiting, reverb, and so on. To reveal the Effects Inserts and Sends area, click the small triangle in the upper-left corner of the Audio Mixer. When you do that, you'll reveal an LCD-like panel. In the uppermost section, you can insert effects on a channel, and in the lowermost section, you can tweak effect parameters when an effect is selected (**FIGURE 10.15**).

A Effect menu. The top section of this display allows you to easily apply audio effects in sequence to one another on a given channel. With 24 effects to choose from, you can quickly eliminate errors and imperfections in a track.

B Effect Bypass button. If you need to disable an effect (without removing it), use the Bypass button.

C Control knob. You can adjust controls for an effect with a knob similar to that on a mixing board.

D Effect Properties menu. With this menu, you can switch to view different properties for the effect. You can see only one property at a time. The control knob updates for each property.

Channel sends

Directly below the effects section, you can choose to send or route a track somewhere else. Most commonly, this would be used to send a track to a submix, where it's easy to group audio tracks (such as all your music and sound effect) to be adjusted from a single submix control. If you set up your sequence with existing submixes, you can choose an existing submix to send to, or by clicking one of the five available sends for a track, you can create a new mono, stereo, 5.1, or adaptive submix (**FIGURE 10.16**).

FIGURE 10.16 The channel send section in the Audio Mixer allows you to route a channel to another place on the Audio Mixer, such as a submix.

A Send Assignment menu. You can assign a track to the master as well as create submixes for mono, stereo, adaptive or 5.1 tracks.

B Send Mute button. Much like using the Effects Bypass button, you can disable the patch using the Send Mute button.

C Control knob. You can adjust controls for a property with a knob similar to that on a mixing board.

D Send Properties menu. You can control the volume of how much of the track is being sent, as well as adjust the pan of the send by selecting pan in the menu and then using the Control knob.

Additional controls

At the very bottom of the mixer are additional controls, including navigation controls, timecode fields (for current location and sequenced duration), a loop control, and a Record button (**FIGURE 10.17**). With a recording enabled for a track, clicking the Record button and beginning playback will allow you to record audio to a track (such as for voice-overs). Thanks to the "never stop playback" technology found in Adobe Premiere Pro CS6, you can continue to manipulate any control in the mixer without ever stopping playback. Very cool!

Understanding Automation Modes

Now that you know how to manipulate and keyframe audio on a sequence and you've learned about the anatomy of the Audio Mixer, let's explore one of the most useful features of the Audio Mixer—automation modes.

Automation modes in the automation mode menu that we mentioned earlier enable you to record automations (keyframes) and then update those automations for parameters such as volume, pan, effects, and sends. A good way to understand the process of automation modes is you usually "write" an automation (or keyframes) first and then during playback "read" that automation (or keyframes); then you can update it by "latching" onto or by "touching" an existing automation.

You'll examine all the automation modes in the following sections, but first open the sequence called 08_Mixer Automation. This is the same basic sequence that you've been using, but you'll use it again to delve into the four automation modes.

Write

With the sequence 08_Mixer Automation open, play the sequence. In this sequence, you'll notice that the music is competing quite heavily with the voice-over. You might be tempted to keyframe the music clip using Clip keyframes around the voice-over bites, which is OK, but let's fix this sequence with the Audio Mixer (thus creating Track keyframes). You'll first use the Write automation mode to "record" volume changes. Keep in mind that the technique that follows works for pan, effect, and even send volume parameters.

1. Click the Audio Mixer panel, and locate the track called Music, which is track 5.

2. Set track 5 using the automation mode menu to Write (**FIGURE 10.18**).

3. Move the playhead to the beginning of the sequence.

4. Start playback of the sequence; when the music hits breaks in the voice-over, drag the fader for the Stereo music track up to increase its volume. After the break, drag the fader back down to decrease the volume for the track. The breaks in the voice-over are short, so just try to be as accurate as possible.

    Repeat this process for the entire sequence, lowering the volume where the voice-over occurs and raising the volume after the voice-over.

After writing automation data and stopping playback, notice that the automation mode for that channel changes to Touch. This is normal behavior because it allows you to then update the automation data for that track. See the "Touch" section later in this chapter to understand that mode. To see the automation you created on the Timeline, click the Show Keyframes button and choose to show Track Keyframes on the music track.

FIGURE 10.17 The additional controls at the bottom of the Audio Mixer allow you to control overall playback and recording for enabled tracks.

39 **Audio Automation Modes in Action**

The automation modes in the Audio Mixer panel are useful tools to quickly mix tracks. In this video you'll explore the differences between the four modes.

FIGURE 10.18 The Write automation mode allows you to "write" automation data or keyframes to a track.

Fine-Tuning Automations
If you find the process of updating automations in the mixer to be a bit clunky, have no fear. After recording automations with the mixer, you can show Track keyframes on the track you're working with. Your automations will appear as keyframes. You can then click a keyframe and further refine it as you see fit. Also, if you have too many automation keyframes, you can thin them out by choosing Preferences > Audio > Automation Keyframe Optimization.

Updating Automations On-Screen
You may have noticed that after updating an automation with Latch or Touch it doesn't seem like anything happened. This is usually just a screen-redrawing issue; simply move the playhead, and the automation should visually update on the sequence when viewing Track Keyframes.

Read

The Read mode automation behaves as its name implies; it reads previously recorded or "written" automation.

1. Click the Audio Mixer panel, and place the track called Music into Read by choosing that option in the automation mode menu.

2. Start playback of the sequence.

   Notice that the fader for the Stereo track in the mixer now follows the automation you created in the previous exercise.

A cool aspect of the Read mode is that if you attempt to make changes to a parameter in the Audio Mixer, you can't because of the previously written automation.

Latch

The name of the Latch automation move probably doesn't make a lot of sense if you're not an audio engineer. However, Latch is a very useful automation mode. Latch respects existing automation until you actually make a change to a parameter in the Audio Mixer panel.

When you change a parameter in the Audio Mixer, the change will "latch" on or continue overwriting existing automations. Latch is a useful mode when you want to make a change to an audio section on which you've made an automation mistake while in Write mode, and you don't care about overwriting existing automation after the update to a parameter.

1. Click the Audio Mixer panel.

2. Set the automation mode for the Music track to Latch mode.

3. Move the playhead to the start of the sequence and begin playback.

4. When you reach the section where you previously raised the music, move the fader to adjust the volume for that track.

5. Don't make any additional changes and continue playback. Notice that the new levels you made overwrite the previous Write automation on the rest of the track when you stop playback and listen again.

Touch

The Touch automation mode is similar to the Latch mode in that it respects existing automations until you make a change. But unlike the Latch automation mode, after you "touch" to make a change, the Audio Mixer will automatically adjust parameters back to previously written automation data instead of continuing with the change that you've made. This means you could nudge a section of the mix up or down, but when you release the fader, the previously recorded mix will be used.

1. Click the Audio Mixer panel.

2. Set the automation mode for the Music track to Touch mode.

3. Move the playhead to the start of the sequence and begin playback.

4. When you reach the section where you previously raised the music, move the fader to adjust the volume for the track.

5. If you continue playback without additional changes, you'll notice that at the point you made a change, the change takes effect. But after the change, the automation resumes previously made changes (keyframes) (**FIGURE 10.19**).

6. Feel free to experiment with the different automation modes on the rest of the tracks on this sequence.

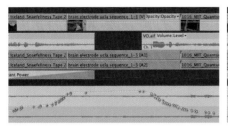 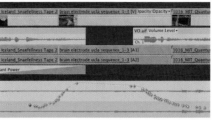

FIGURE 10.19 The Touch automation mode allows you to quickly update existing automations. But after you're done, the automation continues to use previously created keyframes. Original automation data (left); with Touch on, only the fade up automation was affected after the change (right); the original automation continues.

Submixes and Bussing

When setting up a sequence, you can also create submix tracks. These special track types serve as an intermediate step between audio tracks and the Master track. Essentially, you can group multiple audio tracks together into a new track and apply effects and alter volume and other parameters.

There are several uses of submixes.

- **Controlling volume as a group.** Individual tracks can be routed to a submix by using the submix control volume knob; you can then control the volume of a group of tracks all at once on the submix track. In addition, you can also control pan in the same way. When you route an individual track to a submix, you can control the pan of that track to the submix as well as the pan of the submix track itself.

- **Keyframing.** Submix tracks, like regular tracks, can have volume and effect keyframes. So, instead of having to keyframe individual tracks, you can keyframe as a group.

- **Effects.** A very popular use of submixes is to use effects such as compression and reverb on a submix. Instead of having to apply effects to individual tracks, you can apply an effect to the submix track.

The act of sending a channel to a submix is also known as *bussing* or *sending*. Let's look at how submixes and bussing (sending one track somewhere else) works in the Audio Mixer.

1. Open the sequence called 09_Submixes.

   This is the same sequence you've been working with; as a reminder, the first track is a mono voice-over track, the second and third tracks are camera audio (mono pairs), the fourth track is a standard (stereo) sound effects track, and the fifth track is a standard (stereo) music track.

   The sequence has a basic mix that uses Clip keyframes, but you want to create a submix in this sequence so you can give the sound effects and music a bit more of an airy feeling.

How Many Submixes?
How many submixes should you set up a sequence with? You don't need to decide up front. At any time, you can add a submix track to an existing sequence. We'll typically create submixes for things that go together, such as music and effects, dialogue and VO, and so on.

Submixes for Tape Output?
In the previous edition of this book, we detailed how to use submixes to target specific Master track output channels so you could be specific about where audio goes for things like outputting back to tape. There is a much easier way to accomplish the same task now using adaptive tracks, which we'll talk about later in this chapter.

2. Right-click in the track header area on any of the audio tracks, and choose Add Tracks. In the dialog that appears, be sure not to add any additional video or audio tracks, but add an additional stereo submix track (FIGURE 10.20).

FIGURE 10.20 (Left) When you add tracks to an existing sequence, you also have the ability to add mono, stereo, 5.1, or adaptive submixes. Note adaptive submixes work in tandem with adaptive tracks.

FIGURE 10.21 (Right) By using sends on a track, you have the ability to route tracks to submixes, which can be (as in this case) used for control multiple tracks on one submix for effects. After creating the send, you can adjust the send volume by using the Send Properties menu; you can also adjust pan in this menu.

3. If it's not already active, click the Audio Mixer panel. Notice the Stereo submix in the mixer. Click the name section of the submix and name this submix Music & Effects.

4. Click the disclosure triangle on the left side of the mixer to reveal the effects and sends area for each track (the LCD-like panel). On the Sound Effects Track, click in the middle section on the first send (denoted by the down triangle) and then choose the submix Music & Effects. Repeat this process for the Music track (FIGURE 10.21).

5. You can control the volume of the send for both the Sound Effects and Music tracks. You'll have to select each send first and then change its send volume in the Send Properties area. This control defaults to infinity; in other words, no signal will be sent to the submix, so change this value to 0 dB for both the Sound Effects and Music tracks using the Control knob. You can also click the Send Properties menu and adjust the pan of the send, which is useful for adjusting stereo positioning.

6. Right-click each send and change the send to prefader. In combination with a send value of 0 dB (no change) and a prefader setting, any adjustment you make to a track fader or muting will not affect the volume of the channel going to a particular send. Instead, that volume is controlled by the volume Control knob on a particular send.

7. On the Music & Effects submix, click the first insert or effect selection, which is the topmost LCD-looking area at the top of the mixer. From the list of available effects, choose Reverb. Although you can control the different parameters for the Reverb effect using the Effect properties menu (the bottommost LCD looking area), it's far easier to simply double-click the name of the effect to open the VST Editor so that you have visual controls over manipulating the effect (FIGURE 10.22).

8. Adjust the size parameter up to around 48%, change the Pre Delay parameter to around 38ms, and finally adjust the Mix control up to 85%. You may find it most useful to solo the Music and Effects submix as you adjust the parameters.

Adding a Submix Changes Track Assignment Menu?

As of this writing, there may be a small bug in Adobe Premiere Pro CS6 depending on your sequence settings that occurs when adding a submix from the Add Tracks command or from the sends area in the Audio Mixer. When you add the submix, it changes the track output assignment to the submix. The fix is to undo adding the submix and add it again or create a new sequence and paste media into the new sequence. This issue will probably be resolved in future versions of the application.

FIGURE 10.22 Adding an insert or effect to a submix is a quick way to quickly affect a group of clips at one time. Additionally, double-clicking an effect brings up the VST Editor where you'll have visual control over effect parameters.

9. Play back the sequence. You may have noticed that the sound effects and music tracks are much louder now. That's because they're playing back in addition to the audio being sent to the Music & Effects submix. To fix this additive effect, drag the volume faders for the sound effects and music tracks down to infinity, you can also mute the tracks for the same effect. Signal is still sent to the submix because you changed each send to prefader. Play back the sequence, and now you should hear just the submix with the Reverb effect. Feel free to control the volume of the submix to your liking, including automating it, as you learned about earlier in this chapter.

Routing with Adaptive Tracks

In many broadcast workflows, it's essential to be able to route source tracks and their respective channels to output or Master track channels. For example, you may need to create a tape that has a stereo mix of the program on tracks 1 and 2; VO, dialogue, and nat sound on track 3; and music and effects on track 4.

In the previous edition of this book, we suggested creating this "split master" using submixes. New in in Adobe Premiere Pro CS6 are adaptive tracks and adaptive submixes. These innovative track types allow you to quickly route source tracks to Master track channels. With adaptive submixes, you can also route tracks to a submix for effects work, and so on. In this section, let's take a quick look at how adaptive tracks can help you quickly route source channels to output channels for the purposes of creating a split master.

 Adaptive Tracks and Dashed Lines

With the tracks for this sequence expanded, you'll notice that, for example, on the VO track there appears to be three dashed lines. What are these? Well, this is just a visual indicator that the sequence in this case is set up to a Master track of four channels and the VO track is only a mono track with audio only on one track.

Adaptive Track Routing Icon

FIGURE 10.23 The routing icon for adaptive tracks indicates that you can route the track to any output channel including multiple output tracks.

FIGURE 10.24 (Left) The Channel Output Mapping dialog allows you to quickly route source channels to output channels. Note your source channels will always match output channels, so in the case of a mono track, you'll need to route only source track 1 to an output channel.

FIGURE 10.25 (Right Top) Clicking the triangle for an output channel lets you determine how a source channel is mapped to output channels. After selecting channels to route to, your choices are reflected in the Channel Output Mapping dialog (Right Below).

1. Open the sequence called 10_Adaptive Routing in the current project.

   This is obviously the same sequence you've been working on previously throughout this chapter; however, this time all of the audio tracks have been set up as adaptive tracks. Since all of the tracks are set up as adaptive, you can route each one to the four channels of the Master track of this sequence. Why four channels? Many tape formats including HDCAM use four channels of audio.

2. Notice each track on the sequence has a small routing icon after the name of the track. Also in the Audio Mixer for this sequence, you'll notice the same routing icon above the automation mode menu; this icon indicates that these are adaptive tracks (**FIGURE 10.23**). The cool thing is that adaptive tracks can be routed to any output track and can even be routed to multiple output tracks.

3. Double-click the routing icon for the VO track (it's the first track) in either the sequence or the Audio Mixer. When you do, the Channel Output Mapping dialog will open (**FIGURE 10.24**).

4. Since this track is only a mono track, click the dark downward-facing triangle for Output Channel 1 (**FIGURE 10.25**) because it's the only channel you need to route for this track.

5. In the menu that appears, you can choose to route the source track to any output channel; you can also choose to route it to multiple output channels or none at all. For this track, click the triangle and also choose to route the clip to output track 2 as well as track 1 by selecting 2. Click the triangle again, and notice that output tracks 1 and 2 have check boxes by them indicating that the VO track is being routed to both output channels 1 and 2, which is what you want. You want all of the tracks of this sequence to be routed to channels 1 and 2 to create a stereo mix on output channels 1 and 2.

6. Repeat step 6 for the Camera Audio tracks in this sequence, routing each one to output tracks 1 and 2. Just note for the Sound Effect and Music tracks, you won't actually have to do any routing because the source channels 1 and 2 are by default routed to output channels 1 and 2.

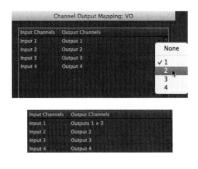

7. Finally, go back to all the tracks and route the source channels one more time as follows: for the VO track add channel 3 as an output channel for input channel 1; output channel 3 will be the VO and Camera Audio track on tape. For the Camera Audio tracks, also add channel 3 as an output channel for input 1. For the Sound

Effect and Music tracks, add channel 4 for both source channels 1 and 2. Channel 4 will be the Music and Effects track.

8. Play back the sequence, and check out the channels have been routed. Note that the camera audio tracks have been panned hard left and right.

Using Audio Effects

As with video, Adobe Premiere Pro has a plethora of effects for working with audio. These effects range from those that allow you to repair or "fix" the audio in some way to those that allow you to control audio dynamics. For example, you might apply compression to an audio track to control its peak volume. Other effects allow you to create "special" effects. For example, if you have recorded voice-over, you might add a touch of reverb to give the voice-over a feeling of space. Although it's outside the scope of this chapter to discuss all of the audio effects and their practical uses, we did want to mention a few important things about audio effects.

Two Ways of Adding Audio Effects

If you've used other NLEs, like Final Cut Pro, you're probably used to applying audio effects to individual clips, which you can also do in Adobe Premiere Pro. But two features we love in Adobe Premiere Pro are the ability to add track-based effects and the ability to add effects to submixes. Let's take a look at adding audio effects in these two ways.

Clip-based effects

Adding a clip-based effect is simple. Browse the audio effects in the Effects panel until you find one you want to use. Then just drag it from the Effects panel onto a clip. To adjust properties for an effect, select the clip, and then click the Effect Controls panel (FIGURE 10.26).

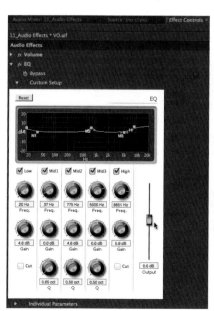
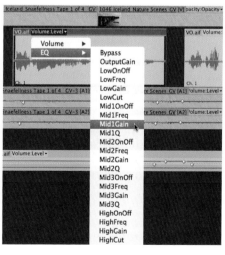

FIGURE 10.26 Clip-based audio effects parameters are adjustable in the Effect Controls panel (left) as well as on a sequence when the Show Clip Keyframes option is selected (right).

Additionally, after an effect has been applied, try selecting the Show Clip Keyframes option. Click the Show Keyframes button in the track header area and select Show Clip Keyframes. Then click the gray box in the corner of the clip to view properties of the effect. You'll then be able to keyframe an effect's parameters directly in the sequence.

Track-based effects

By utilizing the effect inserts in the Audio Mixer, you can also apply audio effects on the track level. What's even cooler is that you can create a submix (essentially, multiple tracks mixed into one as we did earlier in this chapter), send tracks to a submix, and then add an effect to all of them at once.

For example, you might route all VO and primary audio tracks to a submix. You could then apply a compressor (or limiter) to that submix to limit all dialogue to a certain level. Keep in mind that if you add an effect to a track, the options for that particular effect will be available in the Effect Properties section of the channel in the Audio Mixer (**FIGURE 10.27**). Additionally, you can keyframe effects on the Timeline when the Show Track Keyframes option is selected.

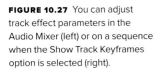

Some Effects
If you'd like to see some effects in action or want to experiment applying effects on your own, be sure to open the sequence called 11_Audio Effects.

FIGURE 10.27 You can adjust track effect parameters in the Audio Mixer (left) or on a sequence when the Show Track Keyframes option is selected (right).

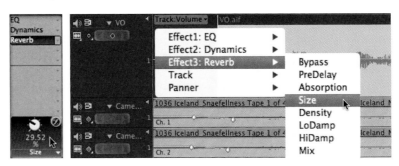

Working with Adobe Audition

You probably think of Adobe Premiere Pro as an editorial application, which it is, but it happens to have some quality audio tools as well. With that said, there are times when you'll want to lean on a dedicated audio application. Here are some examples:

- When you have very detailed and complex mixing audio work to do
- When you need to make severe repairs to audio clips
- When you retime audio to change pitch or speed
- When you perform noise reduction and dialogue matching

What About Other Audio Applications?
Although we strongly urge you to check out Adobe Audition, the fact is that you might use another audio application or have to interact with another person who uses another audio program, like Avid ProTools. In those situations, you can export your audio as an OMF or AAF file. With your sequence selected, choose File > Export > OMF or AAF. Just be sure to find out the best settings your recipient wants you to use for those formats.

The Adobe Creative Suite bundles that ship with Adobe Premiere Pro also include Adobe Audition. You'll find that Adobe Audition is a full-featured audio postproduction application that is suited to deal with even the most complex of audio issues. In this section, you'll learn how Adobe Premiere Pro and Adobe Audition interact, as well as a couple ways to utilize Adobe Audition in your workflow.

Sending Audio from Adobe Premiere Pro to Adobe Audition

Before you can utilize the power of Adobe Audition, you need to actually get a clip or sequence into Adobe Audition. Depending on what you're trying to do, there are several ways of transferring clips to Adobe Audition. Let's take a look at a couple of ways.

Sending individual clips

If you need to send an individual clip to Adobe Audition, you're only a right-click away. With a clip selected, right-click and choose Edit Clip in Adobe Audition. The Render and Replace dialog appears. This dialog will help you render and then replace the audio on your sequence with extracted audio that is sent to Adobe Audition.

The Project panel will then contain the new extracted audio clips. In addition to right-clicking, you can select a clip in your sequence or Project panel and choose Edit > Edit in Adobe Audition > Clip. On the OS level, these extracted clips are placed in the same location as your Adobe Premiere Pro project file.

Sending entire sequences

Although you'll need to send individual clips to Adobe Audition from time to time, the most exciting workflows involve sending an entire sequence to Adobe Audition. By sending an entire sequence from Adobe Premiere Pro to Adobe Audition, you can leverage many of the advanced audio toolsets that Adobe Audition offers.

With a sequence selected in the Project panel, choose Edit > Edit in Adobe Audition > Sequence or right-click the sequence in the Project panel and choose the same option. You'll be presented with a dialog that allows you to configure several options before sending the sequence to Adobe Audition (**FIGURE 10.28**). You'll explore these options in the following exercise.

Tick Tock—Exporting Preview Video to Adobe Audition
If you decide to export video to Adobe Audition, just keep in mind that depending on the length of your project, it can take some time to actually render the video, so plan accordingly.

FIGURE 10.28 When exporting a sequence to Adobe Audition, there are some choices you need to make for different properties of the export.

Let's practice sending a sequence from Adobe Premiere Pro to Adobe Audition. You'll use this sequence for the exercises later in this chapter while we're working in Adobe Audition.

1. With the same project open as earlier in the chapter (10_audio.prproj, open the sequence called 12_Adobe Audition from the Sequence bin. This sequence has two clips with problematic audio. The sequence is not meant to be cohesive but rather contains two clips that need help. Just note if you can also use this sequence to practice sending the clips individually to Adobe Audition.

2. With the open sequence selected in the Timeline panel, choose Edit > Edit in Adobe Audition > Sequence.

3. In the Edit in Adobe Audition dialog, you can leave the name of the sequence at the default.

4. In the Path section, click Browse, and navigate to a location of your choice. Just keep in mind that not only is the Adobe Audition project file saved to that location but also additional files are such as previews and extracted audio. We find it best to often create a new folder within our project folder and choose that as the location.

5. In the Selection menu, you can choose to send the entire sequence or only your active work area. In this case, choose the entire sequence. When using handles, Adobe Premiere Pro will send only the material that you actually used.

6. Specify that you want to add zero seconds of handles. These clips don't actually have handles (we did this to save space on the DVD). But in your own projects, you can add handles.

7. Select the Export Preview Video option to export a video preview, which is useful when mixing and sound designing to picture.

8. Deselect Render Audio Clip Effects.

   When exporting to Adobe Audition, any effects on your audio clips will be "baked in" when this option is selected. Deselecting this option is a better choice, because you can re-create effects in Adobe Audition, and you'll have more flexibility once in Adobe Audition. However, if you're sure of the audio effects you've created in Adobe Premiere Pro, you can leave this option selected.

9. Select Send Clip Volume Keyframe Metadata to send any volume keyframes you've created on clips in Adobe Premiere Pro to Adobe Audition. Once in Adobe Audition, you can further refine these keyframes.

10. Select the Open in Adobe Audition option to automatically open Adobe Audition and the project when you click OK in the dialog.

11. Click OK to send the sequence to Adobe Audition.

    Because you selected the Export Preview Video option, it will take a moment for Adobe Audition to open.

In the next few sections, we'll explain a few different ways to utilize Adobe Audition with Adobe Premiere Pro. Although these exercises will provide you with a peek into some of the features of Adobe Audition, by no means do they show all or even a fraction of what Adobe Audition is capable of.

Noise Reduction

Nothing is as annoying as an audio clip that has excess noise in it. Extraneous noise can come from an HVAC unit, tape hiss, or even ambient noise. Regardless, you'll often want to reduce noise in a clip so audio is more comprehensible and clear.

1. Open the Adobe Audition project that you created in the previous exercise (if it's not already open). If you didn't send a project to Adobe Audition from Adobe Premiere Pro, go back to the previous exercise and do so.

2. When you send a project to Adobe Audition from Adobe Premiere Pro, the default workspace is set to Edit Audio to Video, and the Multitrack Editor is open.

3. Select the first clip, and then in the toolbar at the top of the interface, click the Waveform button to switch to the Waveform Editor (FIGURE 10.29). You can also double-click the clip to enter the Waveform Editor.

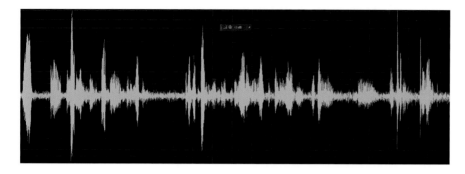

FIGURE 10.29 By enabling the Waveform Editor, you'll get a close-up view of a selected clip.

You're presented with a large waveform of the first clip. You need to select part of the clip that is noisy to define the noise; then you can reduce that noise.

4. Play back the clip again and notice that right after the phrase "work in..." is a section where the subject isn't talking, but there is clearly noise. Using the Time Selection tool (the I bar tool in the toolbar), click and drag to highlight the section of noise you just identified.

5. With the selection active, choose Effects > Noise Reduction/Restoration > Capture Noise Print. You can also press Shift+P. You may be presented with a dialog informing you that the noise print will be captured; if so, click OK to acknowledge the message.

6. You've defined the noise, so click anywhere in the waveform to deselect the selection you've made, and then choose Edit > Select > Select All to select the entire clip.

7. Return to the Effects menu and choose Noise Reduction/Restoration > Noise Reduction (process). You can also press Shift+Command+P (Shift+Ctrl+ P).

8. A new dialog opens (FIGURE 10.30).

From here you can use the Noise Reduction and Reduce By sliders to remove noise from the clip. One option you'll find particularly useful is to select the Output Noise Only check box. Selecting this option allows you to hear *only the noise* you're removing, which is helpful so you don't remove audio you want to keep. Be sure to deselect this option before committing to the noise reduction. At the bottom of the dialog, you can also play/stop the audio as well as loop the clip, so you can refine your adjustments as you're playing back.

Spectral Views
If you want to visually see where noise is located in the frequency range, then use the Spectral Frequency Display. The easiest way to access this view is by dragging the gray bar underneath the waveform in the Waveform Editor. This is useful when a sound is constant like a beep or a hum. You can also use the Spectral Pitch Display, which is useful to see pitches visually when working with music.

Don't Remove Everything!
When noise reducing clips, be careful not to remove 100 percent of the noise, especially if the shot was recorded outside or another environment where a viewer would expect some background noise. If you do remove most of the noise, you may need to layer room tone underneath the clip to have it sound more natural.

FIGURE 10.30 The Noise Reduction dialog contains many parameters that allow you to quickly reduce noise in an audio clip.

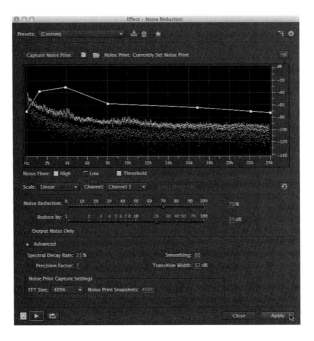

EQ After Noise Reduction
After performing noise reduction, your audio might sound a bit thin or a bit hollow. A good trick is to apply EQ after noise reduction to tweak the results.

Healing Audio
We get it, you're a visual editor. So, why listen to your audio when you can see the problem and fix it? Check out this video to learn more about the spectral view in Adobe Audition and learn more about the Spot Healing brush.

Zooming in Adobe Audition
When you need to fine-tune a selection, you'll find it useful to zoom in to the audio waveform. The easiest way to do this is to position the current-time indicator near the area you want to zoom in to and use the equals (=) and minus (–) keys to zoom in and out of the current-time indicator position. Additionally, you can use the other zoom options at the bottom of the Waveform Editor.

9. If you want to be very detailed when performing noise reduction, you can set control points in the noise graph to dial out noise at a specific frequency. Noise is represented on the graph as a scattered set of points. The closer together and bunched the points are, the more noise (either high frequency in yellow or low frequency in red) at a particular frequency. Volume of the noise is measured on the y-axis; the more points toward the top of the graph, the louder the noise floor at that frequency. Looking at the graph, low frequencies are on the left, midfrequencies are in the middle, and higher frequencies are on the right. By adding a control point and dragging up at a particular frequency, you effectively reduce noise at the frequency; dragging down lessens the noise reduction.

10. Additionally, by clicking the triangle next to the Advanced section, you can further refine the noise reduction. Be sure to try the Spectral Decay Rate if your audio sounds too much like you're listening to a "telephone call from underwater."

11. After you're satisfied with the amount of noise reduction, click the Apply button in the lower-right corner. Figure 10.29 shows how we reduced the noise in this clip. Use this as a guide, but feel free to tweak the noise reduction to your taste.

You may have noticed in the Noise Reduction/Restoration category that there is another type of noise reduction called Adaptive Noise Reduction. What's the difference?

The normal noise reduction is a processed effect. It cannot be placed in an Effects signal chain on the Effects Rack panel, which can be critical if you want to feed the result of one effect to another. In our testing we've found adaptive noise reduction to be very good at removing background sounds, such as wind noise, whereas the regular noise reduction effect is very good at removing constant noises like HVAC sounds and other hisses and hums.

Amplitude Reduction

You've probably listened to a clip at one point and thought it sounded great; then, all of a sudden, a consonant sound such as *p* or *b* causes a giant "plosive" at the start of a word. In the past, making this type of fix was, well, a pain. Using Adobe Audition, you can easily make the fix.

1. With the same project open from the previous exercise (the one you created when you sent an Adobe Premiere Pro project to Adobe Audition), click the Multitrack button to get back to the track layout of the Adobe Premiere Pro project.

2. Navigate to the second clip in the sequence. Double-click it to open the Waveform Editor.

3. Play back the clip by pressing the spacebar, and notice midway through the clip that there is a large plosive on the word "pleasure." Let's fix this.

4. Place the current-time indicator near the plosive (you can see the plosive because of its large amplitude on the waveform in that area). Using the = key, zoom in to the current-time indicator.

5. Using the Time Selection tool, click and drag to highlight the part of the waveform where the plosive is.

6. When you highlight the waveform, that section will be highlighted in white. At the top of the highlighted section, you'll see a control, which you can use to adjust the level of the selected waveform (**FIGURE 10.31**). Using this control, change the level to a value of -22 db. As you make your adjustment, the waveform redraws itself.

7. Click in the waveform outside of the selected area, and play back the clip. The plosive has been essentially eliminated.

You can use this technique for other fixes, such as lavaliere microphone rub and other audio "hits."

Getting Audio Back to Adobe Premiere Pro

We've only touched the surface of what Adobe Audition can do; therefore, we urge you to check out Adobe Audition to perform sophisticated mixes and sound design in your projects. However, if you've sent an individual clip or a sequence to Adobe Audition, you'll probably want to get it back to Adobe Premiere Pro.

Return an individual clip

If you sent an individual clip to Adobe Audition after making fixes or processing it in some way, all you need to do is simply *save* the clip in Adobe Audition. The changes will link back to Adobe Premiere Pro.

Return a sequence

If you've sent an entire sequence to Adobe Audition, to get the updated Adobe Audition sequence back to Adobe Premiere Pro, choose Multitrack > Export to Adobe Premiere Pro. A dialog opens (**FIGURE 10.32**), allowing you to configure what you'll send back to Adobe Premiere Pro.

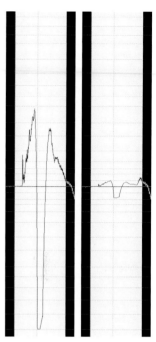

FIGURE 10.31 By highlighting a section of a waveform, you can quickly reduce its amplitude by adjusting the level of the selection. While making the adjustment, the waveform will be redrawn. Before the adjustment, notice the spike in the waveform (left); after reducing the amplitude of the "plosive" (right).

 Finished Adobe Audition Project File

If you're following along with the exercise files and want to see the finished Adobe Audition project that contained these two fixes you'll find it in Lessons and Media > Media> 12_Adobe Audition > 12_Adobe Audition.xml.sesx. This folder also contains the extracted audio and video that was sent to Adobe Audition as well as the bounced track from Adobe Audition that was sent back to Adobe Premiere Pro in the next section. The project 10_audio_finished.prproj references items in this folder so you can listen to the fixes in that project.

FIGURE 10.32 When exporting an Adobe Audition project back to Adobe Premiere Pro, you can configure several options for the export.

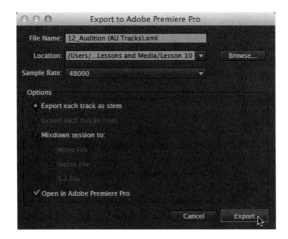

Loudness

Check out this movie to learn how to match loudness or perceived volume. Adobe Audition CS6 features a new algorithm for matching loudness that adheres to international standards bodies.

Retiming Audio with Adobe Audition

If you need to retime audio while maintaining pitch, check out this video. You'll learn how to retime audio with Adobe Audition, which oftentimes does a better job than Adobe Premiere Pro at retiming clips.

FIGURE 10.33 After exporting an Adobe Audition project to Adobe Premiere Pro, you can choose to add the new audio to existing or new tracks on the active sequence.

You'll also be asked where to save the exported XML of the sequence and to specify the sample rate of the new clips. In addition, you have several options: You can export each track individually (a stem); export each submix (bus) individually; or create a mono, stereo, or 5.1 mixdown of the project. Often, we find that exporting individual stems is the best choice, making it easy to do last-minute adjustments or send out a split track master. In addition, you can choose to automatically open Adobe Premiere Pro when you click Export.

When Adobe Premiere Pro opens, you have the option to copy the Adobe Audition tracks to an existing track on the active sequence or create a new track (**FIGURE 10.33**). Just keep in mind that a new bin will be created with the suffix (AU tracks). Inside this bin is a sequence that contains all of your audio tracks from Adobe Audition. This sequence can be useful if you made a mistake placing tracks when exporting them back to Adobe Premiere Pro. Also, after adding the new track(s) to your sequence, you should disable the original audio tracks so you don't hear the fixes along with the original audio.

Next Steps

Now that you're more comfortable with audio in Adobe Premiere Pro, in the next chapter you'll take a look at the powerful color correction tools in Adobe Premiere Pro including video scopes, color correction effects, and Adobe's new addition to the color correction toolkit in CS6—Adobe SpeedGrade.

CHAPTER 11

Color Correction and Grading

A PROJECT IS NOT done until it's finished is an old adage in postproduction. Finishing in postproduction has various meanings, but most pros agree that it means color correction and grading as well as mixing and sound design. In the previous chapter, you learned about the technical process of mixing audio in Adobe Premiere Pro as well as sending clips and sequences to Adobe Audition.

In this chapter, we'll move over to the video side of things and explore color correction and grading. We'll start with the essentials of mastering the scopes, which will help you spot issues within the footage. We'll then look at approaches for adjusting color within Adobe Premiere Pro. You'll also find some advanced options within the Creative Suite with applications such as SpeedGrade, After Effects, and even Photoshop.

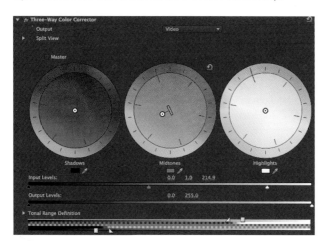

Using Video Scopes

Before we get into the fine details of color correction and grading, let's first look at using video scopes. If you have been editing for a while and have performed some color correction, you likely have some experience using video scopes (but you might be a little foggy about exactly how to use them).

Video scopes measure the video signal in some way (much like a thermometer reads temperature). For example, in Adobe Premiere Pro, using the YC Waveform scope, you can easily measure the lightness or luma in a particular clip to see whether a shot is too bright, is too dark, or has poor contrast. Adobe Premiere Pro has several scopes that you can use to evaluate the video signal in different ways.

You might think that you know what looks good, so why do you need to use scopes? Well, simply put, your eyes lie. Many factors, such as your environment, how much sleep you got the night before, or even your stress level, can influence what your eyes are telling you when color correcting and grading.

Video scopes, on the other hand, don't lie. They give you a technical snapshot of what's really going on with a particular clip when it comes to contrast and color. This section breaks down the different scopes you'll use to color correct and grade your projects so you'll know exactly what's going on with your footage.

Accessing Scopes and the Color Correction Workspace

Here's how to access video scopes in Adobe Premiere Pro:

- **Source Monitor.** Click the Settings button at the bottom right of the Source Monitor (the wrench icon) or right-click the picture area and choose Display Mode. Then choose an appropriate scope or combination of scopes (**FIGURE 11.1**).

- **Program Monitor.** Click the Settings button at the bottom right of the Program Monitor, or just like with the Source Monitor, you can right-click in the picture area and choose Display Mode. Then choose an appropriate scope or combination of scopes.

- **Reference Monitor.** Choose Window > Reference Monitor, and then load a scope or a combination of scopes by clicking the Settings button at the bottom right of the window, and just like with the Source and Program Monitors, you can right-click in the picture area and choose Display Mode.

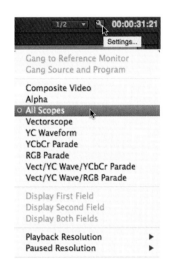

FIGURE 11.1 By clicking the Settings button in the Source, Program, and Reference Monitors, you can choose to display different scopes or video in each monitor.

Another option for viewing the scopes is to switch to the Color Correction workspace (**FIGURE 11.2**) by choosing Window > Workspace > Color Correction. After loading the Color Correction workspace, you'll notice that the interface has shifted around a bit. In the lower-right corner (using the default Color Correction workspace) is the Reference Monitor; from here, if they're not already visible, you can load the video scopes. You can change what scopes are displayed in the Reference Monitor by clicking the Settings button (the wrench icon) in the lower-right corner of the Reference Monitor and choosing a different scope or combination of scopes. As discussed in Chapter 1, you can create a custom workspace and position the scopes where you see fit along with other panels.

It's important to note that when scopes are used in the Reference Monitor, they *will not update in real time when you click Play* in a sequence. The scopes will update in the Reference Monitor only if you scrub through the mini Timeline on the Reference Monitor (or if you scrub the Program Monitor's Timeline when ganged). This limitation makes it impossible to see scopes that reference the sequence during live playback while at the same time watching the playback of the sequence in the Program Monitor on your computer. However, note that if you load scopes in the Program Monitor, they will update in real time, but then you can't see video playing in the Program Monitor. So, what to do? Well, if you're using an I/O device such as an AJA or Blackmagic card, you can view the scopes in the Program Monitor and view your output all in real time through the Mercury Transmit technology in Adobe Premiere Pro CS6.

Scope Essentials

When you start to look at all your scopes, it can feel a bit like looking at the control panels of a 747. In the following sections, let's take a closer look at how scopes measure the video signal in Adobe Premiere Pro.

1. Navigate to Lessons and Media > Lesson 11, open the project called 11_color.prproj, and then open the sequence called 01_scopes. You can use this sequence to see how the scopes work in Adobe Premiere Pro by looking at the different clips (labeled for each scope and what they can measure) and how information is displayed about them on the scopes.

2. Choose Window > Reference Monitor to open the Reference Monitor; or, if you'd prefer, load the Color Correction workspace so that the Reference Monitor is in view.

FIGURE 11.2 The Color Correction workspace optimizes the layout of Adobe Premiere Pro for color correction and grading tasks.

The Importance of a Physical Reference Monitor
Because of variances in computer monitors, try to avoid using your computer monitor to judge contrast and color when correcting footage. Instead, you should use a calibrated external video monitor (also called a Reference Monitor) that is capable of reproducing the color space and black/white levels of video. We highly recommend the options from FSI (Flanders Scientific) and the DreamColor displays available from HP (either stand-alone or on portable computers).

Composite Video Option from the Settings Button
To switch back to video after selecting a scope option, click the Settings button again and choose Composite Video. You can then view the clip loaded into the Source Monitor or the frame underneath the playhead in the Program Monitor or Reference Monitor (if the Reference Monitor is ganged to the Program Monitor).

3. Click the Settings button in the lower right of the Reference Monitor and choose to display the YC Waveform.

The first thing to keep in mind is that each scope (it doesn't matter which one) uses a scale, and this scale is traditionally called a *graticule*; each sets a range of values that a scope measures.

The video signal is displayed on each scale as a collection of pixels known as the *trace* (FIGURE 11.3). On some scopes, such as the YC Waveform, and RGB Parade, the trace actually mimics the picture on-screen from left to right. So, if there was a bright window on the left side of the screen, you'd expect to see trace on the YC Waveform that matches the brightness of the window on the left side of the YC Waveform. Other scopes (such as the Vectorscope) don't actually mimic the picture, instead giving you an overall representation of what's happening in the clip.

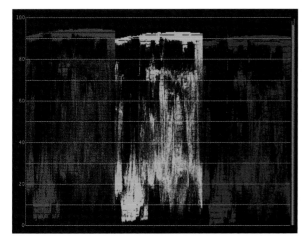

FIGURE 11.3 Trace is displayed on a scale (graticule) on the RGB Parade.

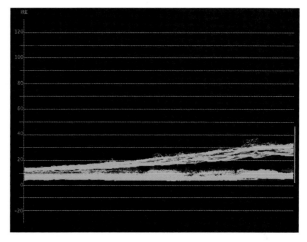

FIGURE 11.4 The YC Waveform allows you to easily measure luma levels in a clip. Trace toward the top of the scope represents lighter pixels; trace toward the bottom represents darker pixels. Trace in the middle of the scope represents midtones. The trace on this YC Waveform is showing a pretty dark shot.

Saturation on the Waveform in Final Cut Pro
If you've used a composite waveform scope or utilized the Saturation parameter of the Waveform scope in Final Cut Pro, the chroma option on the YC Waveform provides the same functionality.

YC Waveform

The YC Waveform (FIGURE 11.4) is the principal scope you'll use to measure lightness or luma (the Y or grayscale part) in a clip. It also allows you to measure the intensity or lightness of the chroma (the C part). Reading a YC Waveform (FIGURE 11.5) is easy once you understand how it works.

The scale that the scope measures is from black at the bottom to white at the top or from dark to light. In technical terms, this is -20 IRE to 120 (Institute of Radio Engineers [IRE]), where 0 IRE represents black and 100 IRE represents white. Values less than 0 IRE or greater than 100 IRE are known as super blacks and super whites. Generally speaking, signal below or above these values is illegal for broadcast. These signals are reserved to provide headroom when shooting and are also used for special purposes like luma-keying graphics.

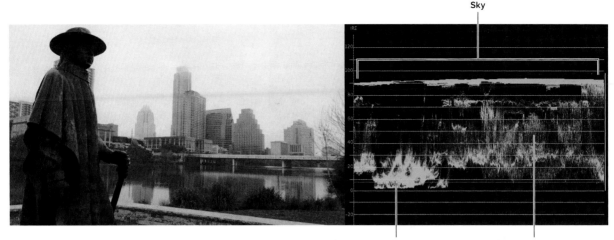

Sky

Dark Statue   Buildings & Lake Reflection

FIGURE 11.5 The YC Waveform mimics the actual picture from left to right.

Adobe Premiere Pro has a few different configurable options for the YC Waveform.

- You can change the intensity of the trace that is displayed, making it easier to view based on your preference. Simply drag the intensity slider at the top of the panel as needed to match your preference.

- You can change the setup (reference black level) that the scope uses. For analog video in NTSC countries using the Beta SP format, black is represented as 7.5 IRE. However, there is no setup in digital video, so the vast majority of people should make sure this option is deselected to get an accurate representation of black in the footage.

- You can choose to display a chroma trace by selecting the Chroma check box (shown overlaid on the luma or Y trace in blue). This is useful for seeing the intensity of the color in footage, which can sometimes make footage illegal for broadcast.

 Contrast Ratio on the YC Waveform

The YC Waveform displays the video signal from black to white; therefore, it's the perfect tool to allow you to judge the contrast ratio of a clip. When trace is closely bunched together, it indicates a low-contrast ratio. Trace that is spread out across the entire scale on the YC Waveform indicates a high-contrast ratio.

Vectorscope

The Vectorscope measures hue and saturation for a particular clip. It's most often used to analyze overall color casts and saturation in a clip. The Vectorscope doesn't mimic the actual picture but instead maps hue and saturation on different angles called *vectors* (**FIGURE 11.6**). The angle that the trace is displayed around the Vectorscope represents hue. Around the Vectorscope you'll see different targets representing primary video colors (red, green, blue) and secondary video colors (yellow, magenta, and cyan). So, if someone in a scene is wearing a red shirt, you'd expect to see some of the trace pushed toward the red target.

The center of the scope is white (or no color). The trace distance from the center of the scope to the edge represents saturation. So, using the previous example in which the subject is wearing a red shirt and the shirt is very saturated, you'd expect to see the trace pointed toward red and toward the outer boundaries of the scope.

Another point of reference on the Vectorscope is the line that intersects the yellow and red targets. This line is commonly known as the *flesh tone line*. Flesh tones, regardless of race, should generally fall somewhere on or near this line.

 Skin Tones, Memory Colors, and Grading Essentials

If you're new to the science and aesthetic concerns of color correcting and grading, we highly recommend our colleague's Alexis Van Hurkman's excellent Color Correction Handbook (Peachpit Press, 2009).

To match your preference, you can adjust the intensity of the trace. You set the scope to
match up to 75% or 100% color bars using the Percentage menu. For most cases, having
the Percentage menu set to 75% (which Adobe Premiere Pro defaults to) is the correct
option. When set to 75%, the outside targets become the reference for "safe" saturation levels (the inside targets would be safe for 100% color bars). Any trace past these
targets (closer to the edge of the scope) may be illegal for broadcast.

RGB Parade

The RGB Parade is similar to the YC Waveform scope, but instead of measuring luma
and chroma, it breaks down the video signal into the lightness of the Red, Green, and
Blue channels (**FIGURE 11.7**). The best way to use the RGB Parade is to view the overall
color balance in a clip. If the blue trace is elevated over the red and green traces, you
know that you have an overall blue color cast in the clip.

Because the RGB Parade traces are displayed on a scale like the YC Waveform, you can
also see where in the tonal range a color cast is occurring. For example, if the RGB traces
are mostly the same but the top of the blue trace is elevated over the red and green
traces, you can infer that there is a blue color cast in the highlights of the clip. How?

Just like the scale on the YC Waveform, the RGB Parade goes from black to white or dark to light. The bottom of the scale represents black, the top represents white, and everything in between represents midtone values.

So, with the blue trace elevated over the red and green traces but especially at the top (toward the brighter/whiter portions of the clip), you know that the color cast occurs mainly in the highlights.

YCbCr Parade

A specialty scope that's often used to calibrate video tape decks, the YCbCr Parade is useful when comparing levels of the video signal (**FIGURE 11.8**). Most digital video uses a color space referred to as YCbCr where Y is the luma component and Cb (Luma minus blue) and Cr (Luma minus red) are known as the *color difference channels*.

The Scopes in Action
Do you want to see the scopes in action? Check out this video for more detail about the practical application of using the scopes.

Here's how to read this scope:

- Y or luma is displayed as the leftmost waveform. The Y trace is displayed vertically from black to white or dark to light (0 to 100 IRE) and is identical to the YC Waveform.

- The middle trace is the Cb (luma minus blue trace).

- The far right is Cr (luma minus red).

Combination views

Often, when color correcting and grading footage, you'll want to view more than one scope at a time to get a more comprehensive view of color and contrast in a clip. At any time you can view multiple scopes (**FIGURE 11.9**) by clicking the Output button at the bottom of the Reference Monitor, Program Monitor, or Source Monitor and choosing one of the combination views.

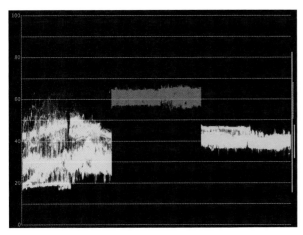

FIGURE 11.8 The YCbCr Parade displays the signal in its luma and chroma channels.

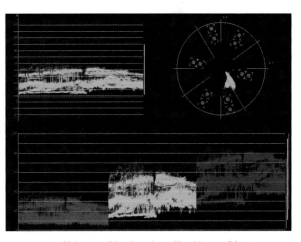

FIGURE 11.9 Using combination views like this one (Vectorscope, YC Waveform, RGB Parade) can be a great way to get an all-inclusive look at the video signal.

Video scopes come in a few different configurations: software scopes like those found in Adobe Premiere Pro, rasterizers that use a separate computer that then displays scopes on a monitor attached to that computer, and hardware-type scopes that are self-contained units. Why might you step up from those included in your nonlinear editor?

Well, here are a couple of reasons:

- **Higher resolution.** Rasterizers and hardware-type scopes tend to be far more accurate than their software counterparts, because the trace is presented on a scope at a far higher resolution.

- **Real-time performance.** Rasterizers and hardware-type scopes perform in real time, reading every pixel in the video signal. The Adobe Premiere Pro scopes sample a smaller amount of pixels and sometimes lag during playback.

But performance has its cost. These external scopes have dedicated video and audio inputs. You'll need some sort of video I/O device to output video from your Adobe Premiere Pro machine to the scopes.

More About the Reference Monitor

FIGURE 11.10 By disabling the Gang to Program Monitor button, you can easily compare video as well as scopes of two different locations in your sequence.

Ganging the Reference Monitor and Program Monitor
By ganging the Reference Monitor to the Program Monitor (with the Gang to Program Monitor button), both monitors will update as you scrub through a sequence. This is great for when you want to see the same frame in each monitor or display scopes in the Reference Monitor for a particular frame while watching video in the Program Monitor. This ganging works only when scrubbing, however, or when you pause playback.

Besides being a home to video scopes, the Reference Monitor is a valuable tool in any color correction workflow. By disabling the Gang to Program Monitor button (**FIGURE 11.10**) at the bottom of the Reference Monitor, you can scrub the mini Timeline of the Reference Monitor to a particular frame and then set the playhead of the sequence (and thus the Program Monitor) to a different frame. This makes color correction more efficient in a couple of ways.

- **Comparing frames visually.** By placing the playheads of the Reference and Program Monitors on different frames, you can visually compare shots. This is particularly useful when matching different angles of the same subject—specifically, comparing skin tone and other memory colors (colors our brains recognize, like skin tone, skies, grass) between shots.

- **Comparing scopes.** As mentioned earlier, your eyes lie! By parking the playhead of the Reference Monitor on one shot and the Program Monitor on another, you can then switch each monitor to display scopes, which lets you compare scopes of each shot to make sure each shot matches perfectly.

Primary Color Corrections

Color correction is generally broken down into two main areas: primary correction and secondary correction. Let's first take a look at primary correction. A good way to think about primary color corrections is to think of them as corrections that affect the entire picture. For example, if you had a shot that was very dark and you wanted to lighten the entire clip, that would be a primary correction. Similarly, if you were to adjust the overall saturation of a clip or give the clip an overall warm look, you'd be performing a primary color correction. In this section, you'll fix some common issues using primary color corrections.

Exposure Problems

It's a fact of life that at some time you'll produce or receive underexposed footage. Shooting at night or in a dark concert venue can cause underexposure problems. Underexposed footage can also be the result of the aperture on the camera not being adjusted. Like its overexposed counterpart, underexposed footage can be tough to work with. The trouble with underexposed footage is that lightening a clip can often introduce excessive video noise, so you may have to employ a third-party noise reduction effect or use tools in Adobe After Effects to remove that noise.

Likewise, colorists will tell you that overexposed footage is also a tough pill to swallow. Depending on how overexposed the shot is, highlight detail can be lost, and in general the clip will look washed out. Sometimes extremely overexposed clips aren't worth using. However, you can fix many overexposed clips quite easily.

Before we actually correct a couple of clips with exposure issues, let's use the scopes to verify some underexposed and overexposed footage.

1. In the current project, open the sequence called 02_under_overexposed.

   This is a simple sequence with only two video clips. Make sure you choose Window > Workspace > Color Correction so the Reference Monitor is in view.

2. Examine the two clips in the Timeline. One has an obvious underexposure, and the other is overexposed. However, it's always best to double-check this by viewing the scopes.

3. In the Reference Monitor, click the Settings button and then choose to display the YC Waveform. Make sure the options for Setup and Chroma are disabled at the top of the scope (there is no setup in digital video).

ADJUSTMENT LAYERS

If you've ever worked in Adobe Photoshop or After Effects, you may have become a fan of using adjustment layers (FIGURE 11.11). The idea with adjustment layers is that instead of affecting the actual clips you're working with, an adjustment layer is placed above the shots you're working with and affects the clips below.

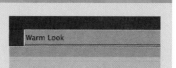

FIGURE 11.11 Adjustment layers are a welcomed addition to Adobe Premiere Pro that give you another option for grading footage.

Well, now in Adobe Premiere Pro CS6 you have adjustment layers! While their uses are many, one way adjustment layers can be used is for color correction. By placing an adjustment layer over a scene or even an entire sequence, you can then add color correction effects to it. Effects added to the adjustment layer will affect all clips below it. The cool part is that an adjustment layer acts like other clips, so it can be trimmed, and so on. You'll learn more about adjustment layers in Chapter 12.

 Static vs. Motion Grading
As you begin to color correct and grade footage, it's important not to just park the playhead on a single frame or clip to judge your corrections. Most clips change in some way for the duration of the clip, so it's essential that you play back a clip and make corrections based on the clip in motion. In Adobe Premiere Pro CS6, you can even color correct while a clip is playing back. Keep in mind that in some clips you may need to keyframe a color correction effect to compensate for changes in exposure and color over time.

 Three-Way Color Corrector in Depth
Check out this video to learn more about the newly redesigned Three-Way Color Corrector. The most full-featured of the Adobe Premiere Pro color correction effects is comprehensive, but in this video, we break it down in more depth so you can utilize it for even your most difficult shots.

Sequence Settings for Color Correction
If you're color correcting source material that is 10-bit or greater, be sure to choose Sequence > Sequence Settings and select Maximum Bit Depth. Selecting this option will allow you to access the full range of information for material that has a high bit depth.

4. Park the playhead on the first clip. Notice that the trace on the YC Waveform only goes from about 0 IRE to about 40 to 45 IRE. This indicates a dark clip (trace bunched toward the bottom of the waveform indicates a dark clip) **(FIGURE 11.12)**.

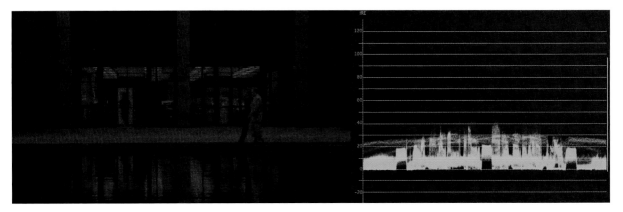

FIGURE 11.12 The dark nature of this clip is verified by looking at the YC Waveform.

5. Move the playhead to the second clip in the sequence.

The trace is elevated on the scale with some of it over 100 IRE, and then it bottoms out around 25 IRE. This elevated trace indicates that the clip is overexposed and is contributing to the general washed-out nature of the clip **(FIGURE 11.13)**.

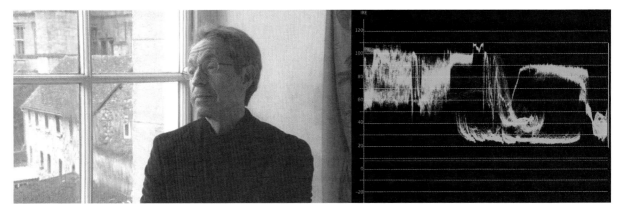

FIGURE 11.13 The overexposed nature of this clip is verified by looking at the YC Waveform.

Adobe Premiere Pro Effects to Fix Exposure

Although it's ultimately up to you how to fix exposure problems with clips in Adobe Premiere Pro, we'd like to suggest a few of our favorite effects for fixing exposure or contrast problems. This list of effects is by no means the only way you can fix exposure or contrast problems but rather represents go-to effects that we like to use. In your own projects, you might find a personal favorite or even combine these effects depending on the situation.

Auto Contrast

The Auto Contrast effect is a straightforward choice that can easily fix contrast issues in many clips. You can find the effect by choosing Video Effects > Adjust > Auto Contrast. Like many auto effects, it can't work miracles, but if you're in a rush, this effect can for sure help you out. Use the Temporal Smoothing option so the effect doesn't radically change from frame to frame.

Luma Corrector

The Luma Corrector effect is extremely useful for situations in which you need to affect the contrast of a clip. The cool part is that you can treat the entire clip (lightening or darkening it overall) or use the tonal range controls to treat only shadows, midtones, and highlights. In addition, using the Tonal Range Definition parameter, you can actually define the shadows, midtones, or highlights of the clip. This effect also allows you to preform secondary color correction discussed later in this chapter.

Shadow/Highlight

Another great effect to use to treat exposure and contrast in a clip is Shadow/Highlight. Choose Video Effects > Adjust to access this effect. The effect allows you to adjust shadows and highlights independently. The auto settings do a pretty amazing job, but for more control, click the More Options triangle to control tonal width and clipping and even color correct your adjustments.

Luma Curve

If you've used the Curves adjustment in other applications (such as Photoshop), you'll be right at home making contrast corrections with the Luma Curve. The idea behind Curves is simple: The entire tonal range is mapped along the curve left to right, black to white, or dark to light. By clicking the curve, you add a control point at that part of the tonal range. With the Luma Curve, if you add a control point and drag up, you'll effectively lighten that part of the tonal range. Add a control point and drag down to darken that part of the tonal range. The Luma Curve is an effective tool for fine-tuning contrast corrections made with other color correction effects or for correcting a shot on the whole. The Luma Curve also has a Secondary Color Correction section where you can target luma corrections to a specific part of a clip (we'll discuss secondary corrections a bit later in this chapter).

Levels

Levels is a very granular effect found in the Adjust bin within video effects that allows you to adjust RGB, black/white input and output levels, and RGB midtone (gamma) levels. Additionally, you can control black, midtone (gamma), and white levels for each channel.

Fast and Three-Way Color Correctors

While primarily thought of as a "color" correction tool, these two effects have similar controls for controlling contrast with the Input and Output level sliders. Additional controls in these tools include auto controls for black, white, and overall contrast. These are probably our most used effects for controlling exposure simply because we use them so much for affecting the color of a clip as well. We'll discuss using these effects for color correction in a later section.

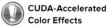

CUDA-Accelerated Color Effects
Although we discuss many of the Adobe Premiere Pro effects for color correction in this section, keep in mind that some of these effects are accelerated for modern systems using graphics card CUDA acceleration. You can filter effects for acceleration by clicking the Accelerated Effects button under the search field in the Effects panel.

Find That Effect
Need an effect fast? You can type its name into the search field of the Effects panel.

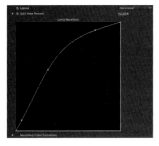

FIGURE 11.14 The original clip (left), Luma Curve (above), and the corrected clip (right)

Fixing Underexposed Footage

An effective way to repair underexposed footage is to use a Curves adjustment. For this first clip in the 02_under_overexposed sequence, you'll use the Luma Curve effect.

1. Select the first clip in the sequence.

2. Type **Luma Curve** into the search box of the Effects panel, and drag it onto the first clip on the sequence.

3. Click the Effect Controls panel.

   Remember that the Luma Curve maps the tonal range from left to right and black to white. Clicking the curve adds a control point to effectively remap luma values along the tonal range.

4. Add a control point in the upper 75% (toward the top) of the curve. Drag up slightly until the top of the trace on the YC Waveform is about 60 IRE. It's an evening shot, so it's OK if it's still on the darker side.

5. Click to add a control point about midway on the curve, and drag up to lighten the midtones of the clip. Drag up until the middle part of the trace is between 30 and 40 IRE.

   On the YC Waveform, the trace has moved up the scale considerably. However, the clip now has a slightly washed-out look.

6. To fix the washed-out picture, add another control point in the lower 25 percent of the curve, and drag down slightly to restore some shadow detail.

7. Toggle the effect on and off by clicking the effect visibility button next to the name of the effect in the Effect Controls panel or use the Split view controls to compare before and after. When you're satisfied with the results, select the Timeline and click Play to watch the corrected clip (**FIGURE 11.14**).

Fixing Overexposed Footage

Fixing an overexposed clip is a similar procedure to fixing underexposed footage. Although you could fix the second clip in this sequence with the Luma Curve (or any number of other color effects), let's use the Luma Corrector effect.

1. Select the second clip in the current sequence.

2. Locate the Luma Corrector effect, and drag it to the second clip in the sequence.

3. With the second clip in the sequence selected, switch to the Effect Controls panel.

   On the YC Waveform, the trace above 100 IRE has automatically been clipped. So, just by adding this effect, the clip is now technically legal for broadcast, but there is more work to do.

4. Make sure the Tonal Range parameter is set to Master, and then adjust the Pedestal parameter until the bottom of the trace is just touching 0 IRE. We used a value of -.21.

   This ensures that parts of the clip (like the subject's black jacket) will be shown as black. The Pedestal parameter performs an offset to the signal and in this case darkens the entire clip.

5. Using the Gain parameter, drag to the right until the top of the trace is right at 100 IRE. We used a value of 1.26. The Gain parameter affects lighter pixels (highlights) more than midtones and shadows. Raising this parameter to 100 IRE is OK because a bright window is behind the subject.

6. Adjust the Gamma parameter up slightly (we used a value of 1.04) so the subject's jacket doesn't look crushed.

   Notice that the bottom of the trace has moved away from 0 IRE. This is because of the overlapping nature of the controls on the tonal range. In this case, it works well because it gives the black jacket a little more detail. With color correction, you'll often need to go between controls adjusting parameters a few times to get the right look in the shot.

7. Toggle the effect on and off. You should clearly see the results of the correction. The corrected clip doesn't look overexposed and has clearly defined blacks without looking washed out.

8. Select the Timeline and click Play to view the corrected clip (**FIGURE 11.15**).

 Footage and the Printed Page
As you flip through the rest of this chapter, just note that the problems and corrections in figures may look slightly different than when working with the footage in the lesson files because of the ways the printed book (or ebook) and video show color and contrast.

 Expanding Contrast
Often, clips are not underexposed or overexposed but just lack "pop." By expanding the contrast ratio in a clip, you can greatly improve a clip's look. While looking at the YC Waveform, try to expand contrast so that part of the trace is touching 0 IRE or black. As a result, black objects on-screen are shown as black, and trace (depending on the desired brightness of the clip) moves toward 100 IRE.

FIGURE 11.15 The original clip (left), Luma Corrector (top), and the corrected clip (right).

Fixing Color Casts

Let's face it, color casts happen. Most are because of improper white balance or a strong light somewhere in the room. Fixing color casts is at the heart of color correction. Before you can fix a color cast, you need to know how to identify one. Fortunately, you have the scopes to help you!

1. In the current project, open the sequence called 03_colorcast. The sequence contains a clip with an obvious blue color cast.

2. In the Reference Monitor, load the Vectorscope (if the Reference Monitor is not visible, choose Window > Reference Monitor or switch to the Color Correction workspace if you're not already using it) to see the hues and saturation in the video signal. You should notice (just like your eyes told you) a strong push of trace toward blue/cyan (**FIGURE 11.16**).

3. Right-click the Vectorscope and choose Display Mode > RGB Parade.

    In this clip, you'll notice that the blue trace is well elevated above the other traces (particularly toward the middle to the top of the scale). From this scope, you can tell that most of the color cast is happening in the midtones and highlights of the clip (**FIGURE 11.17**).

FIGURE 11.16 (Left) The color cast in the clip is verified on the Vectorscope with a large push of trace toward the blue target.

FIGURE 11.17 (Right) The RGB Parade shows overall color balance in a clip. Elevated trace in the Blue channel toward the top of the Parade shows an imbalance mainly in the midtones and highlights. Remember that trace toward the top of the scale represents lighter signal.

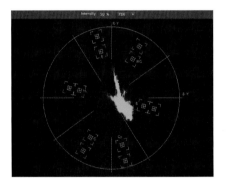 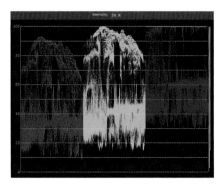

Before fixing a color cast

You know that a color cast is happening mainly in the midtones and highlights from the previous steps, but there are two more important factors to be aware of prior to attempting any type of correction.

- Make a contrast correction first. As you change contrast, you potentially change where in the tonal range a color cast is actually occurring.

- To neutralize any color cast, you must add color from the opposite side of the color spectrum (the opposite side of the color wheel) at a particular part of the tonal range. This example shows a blue color cast in the midtones and highlights. You'd neutralize it by adding yellow to the midtones and highlights controls of the color correction effect in use.

Adobe Premiere Pro Effects to Fix Color

So, you've identified a color cast, and you know that you need to fix contrast first, but what tools do you use? Let's take a look at some commonly used effects that can be used to effect the color in a clip; as a bonus, almost all of these effects also allow you to adjust exposure or contrast too, which is an important first step before color correcting a clip. Just like we mentioned when discussing commonly used effects for fixing exposure or contrast, this list of effects is by no means the only way you can fix color problems in Adobe Premiere Pro; rather, it represents go-to effects.

Auto Color and Auto Levels

If you're in a rush, you can let the Auto Color and Auto Levels effects do the heavy lifting for you! Found in the Adjust bin (Video Effects > Adjust > Auto Color), Auto Color automatically adjusts contrast and color in a clip. Auto Levels, which is also found in the Adjust bin, corrects highlights and shadows (and potential color casts in each) by adjusting the individual RGB channels. You can use them individually or in tandem with each other. Additionally, the Temporal Smoothing option (found in Auto Color and Auto Levels as well as the previously discussed Auto Contrast) allows these effects to not vary greatly from frame to frame.

RGB Curves

The RGB Curves (**FIGURE 11.18**) operate in the same way as their Luma Curve cousin. But instead of one curve, there are four curves: Master, Red, Green, and Blue. The Master Curve is similar to the Luma Curve. The color curves obviously affect that particular color.

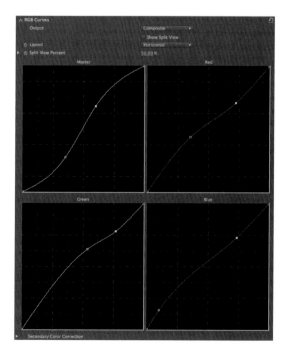

FIGURE 11.18 The RGB Curves give you very granular control on a clip by having the entire tonal range mapped to each curve.

With the RGB Curves, it's important to remember that when you add a control point and drag it up or down, you're essentially adding or subtracting that color at that part of the tonal range. Why subtract color?

When you add a control point and drag down on one of the RGB Curves, you're removing that color but adding color from the opposite side of the color wheel. An easy way to visualize this is by looking at the Vectorscope. When you subtract red, you add cyan; subtract green, you add magenta; and subtract blue, you add yellow. The RGB Curves are a fantastic way to tweak color corrections made with other color effects or to provide lots of granular control for making color corrections with a stand-alone tool.

Fast Color Corrector

The Fast Color Corrector allows you to adjust not only contrast (using the input and output level controls) but also overall color balance and saturation in a clip using the Hue Balance and Angle controls (the color wheel). A good way to think of the Fast Color Corrector is as a one-way or overall color corrector.

Unlike the Three-Way Color Corrector with which you can adjust hue and magnitude of a hue across three areas of tonal range influence (shadows, midtones, and highlights), the Fast Color Corrector affects the entire tonal range. You can also make large hue shifts by using the Hue Angle parameter (or by rotating the outer wheel on the color wheel). This effect is a good tool to use as a quick fix for color casts.

Three-Way Color Corrector

The Three-Way Color Corrector is the workhorse of the Adobe Premiere Pro color correction effects, and for CS6 its interface and usability have been streamlined and enhanced. You'll probably use the Three-Way Color Corrector (**FIGURE 11.19**) more than any of the other color effects. The Three-Way Color Corrector gives you three controls for adjusting hue and magnitude of that hue across three distinct (but slightly overlapping) areas of the tonal range—shadows, midtones, and highlights.

FIGURE 11.19 The redesigned Three-Way Color Corrector is a full-featured color correction effect that splits color correction into three areas of influence in the tonal range—shadows, midtones, and highlights.

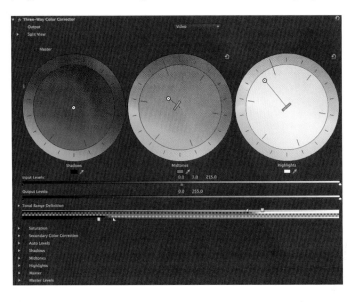

With this control, you can easily fix color casts that might appear only in the shadows, midtones, or highlights, or in a combination of all three areas of the tonal range. The Three-Way Color Corrector also provides color pickers for black, gray, and white balance, making it easy to get the correct blacks, grays, and whites without having to manually adjust the controls.

Fixing (Exposure) Contrast First

For this clip, you'll use the Three-Way Color Corrector because it gives you the most control over correcting the different tonal ranges present in the clip. The goal is to have a balanced clip (where traces on the RGB Parade are all equal). In the real world, however, this is next to impossible, because there is no such thing as a truly neutral clip.

1. Apply the Three-Way Color Corrector effect to the clip called colorcast.mov in the sequence.

2. Select the clip in the sequence, and then click the Effect Controls panel.

3. Right-click in the Reference Monitor (it should currently be showing the RGB Parade), and choose Display Mode > YC Waveform. Double-check that you don't have Setup selected on the YC Waveform, because there is no setup in digital video.

4. Use the Input Levels slider (right below the color wheels) for the darker portions of the clip (the small triangle on the left of the Input Levels graph). Drag right and adjust the contrast in the clip until part of the trace on the YC Waveform is touching 0 IRE.

   Notice that the highlights are already touching 100 IRE, so you shouldn't need to adjust the contrast any further.

Tackling Color

Now that the contrast is under control, let's fix the color cast in this clip. As you previously saw, this clip has an obvious blue color cast that you verified with the Vectorscope and RGB Parade. Correcting this clip to look more neutral is pretty straightforward.

1. Switch the Reference Monitor to RGB Parade. Because the RGB Parade shows the relative color balance between the color channels, you can use the scope as a guide for creating a balanced clip. A clip that is in balance will have all three channels (RGB) in relative balance with each other across the different parts of the tonal range.

2. Above the color wheels in the Three–Way Color Corrector effect, check the Master button. This will "gang" all three color wheels for the different parts of the tonal range together. Next, in whatever color wheel you'd prefer, drag the small circle (called the Balance Magnitude control) toward yellow/orange, and notice that all three color wheels move in tandem.

3. Use the Balance Gain slider (the horizontal bar attached to the Balance Magnitude control), and gently drag toward the outer part of the handle.

   You should notice that the trace on the RGB Parade is now in more balance.

The clip is starting to look better but still looks a bit off. You can correct color casts with the Master option selected, which gangs the color wheels for the different parts of the tonal range together, essentially transforming the Three-Way Color Corrector into the Fast Color Corrector. Unchecking this option will allow you to use all three color wheels independently, which allows you to adjust color balance between shadows, midtones, and highlights and have much finer control of neutralizing a color cast. Just don't be surprised when turning off the Master option makes it look like your previous correction has disappeared; it hasn't. If you look in the Program Monitor or select the Master button, you'll once again see your previous corrections.

You're probably wondering why we didn't tell you to just use the three color wheels to balance the image instead of checking the Master option in the first place. You could certainly do that, but often for extreme color casts such as the one found in this clip, it's often easiest to check the Master button to neutralize the color cast in a broad stroke and then fine-tune your correction by turning off the Master button and using the separate controls for shadows, midtones, and highlights.

4. With the Master button not checked and using the highlights wheel, drag toward yellow/orange.

   You should be trying to get the top of the traces on the RGB Parade as even as possible.

5. Use the midtones wheel, and drag toward yellow/orange to balance out the trace on the RGB Parade for the midtones. Again, you're trying to get the middle part of the traces to look the same.

6. Repeat this procedure using the shadows wheel to try to get the bottom of the trace on the RGB Parade even and in balance (**FIGURE 11.20**).

FIGURE 11.20 Using the three color wheels for shadows, midtones, and highlights, you can fine-tune a color correction for different parts of the tonal range.

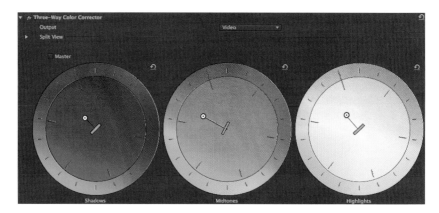

The color should look pretty good, and the trace for each channel should now be in good balance. Just remember that it's almost impossible to get "perfectly" balanced traces; simply get as close as you can and use your eyes to judge what looks good. Open the Vectorscope and notice that the large amount of trace that was pushed toward blue is no longer there (indicating that you neutralized the color cast) (**FIGURE 11.21**). Play back the clip on the sequence to check out your work. Continue to adjust the Three-Way Color Corrector as needed.

FIGURE 11.21 The original and corrected clip with corresponding RGB Parades and Vectorscopes

Secondary Color Corrections

While primary color corrections affect an entire clip, secondary color corrections affect only part of the clip. Let's say you had a clip that looked pretty good, but after primary correction, the skin tones of the actors were still a little red. You could, with secondary correction, target only the skin tones, leaving other parts of the clip unaffected. Additionally, secondary correction is useful when shots of the same subject are intercut from different cameras or when the same shots are used in different scenes and skin tones don't match.

Adobe Premiere Pro Effects for Secondary Color Corrections

Many of the Adobe Premiere Pro effects that you would use for adjusting contrast (exposure) or color also have secondary color correction controls, meaning they allow you to target a portion of a clip and then correct that selected portion. With that said, there are also dedicated effects specifically designed for secondary color corrections. Let's take a look at some of our favorite effects for performing secondary corrections.

Leave Color

Although you can use the secondary controls in other effects, the Leave Color effect is a simple way to achieve very stylized results. The effect allows you to choose the color you want to leave in the clip by using an eyedropper. You can then adjust how much of the other colors in the clip are desaturated by using the Amount to Decolor parameter. You can tweak the effect by using the Tolerance, Edge Softness, and Match Colors parameters. This type of look has been popular over the years in films like *Schindler's List* and *Pleasantville* and in numerous commercials.

Change Color

Essentially, the Change Color effect lets you target a specific color by using the Color to Change parameter and keys that color in the clip. Then, by using the Hue, Lightness, and Saturation Transform parameters, you can change the hue of the selection, how light it is, and how saturated the selection is. By using the Matching Tolerance, Matching Softness, and Match Colors parameters, you can tailor your selection to target just the part of the clip you want. This effect is useful for tackling subjects such as gray skies or faded grass.

RGB Curves

If you're more of a Curves person and prefer using the RGB Curves, you're in luck when it comes to secondary corrections. The RGB Curves effect has tools similar to the other secondary controls in other effects that allow you to perform a secondary correction.

Three-Way Color Corrector

The Three-Way Color Corrector also has a dedicated toolset for making a secondary color correction (by using an HSL key). Because we're often using the Three-Way Color Corrector for primary corrections, we also like to use it for secondary corrections.

Using a Secondary Correction to Fix Skin Tone

Using secondary color correction, matching skin tone is pretty straightforward. Let's first open another sequence to get set up to make a secondary correction.

1. With the project 11_color.prproj still open, open the sequence called 04_skintone. Then choose Window > Workspace > Color Correction if your interface is not already configured in that workspace.

   In the open sequence is a clip that looks OK and is pretty well-balanced, but the subject's face is slightly red. Look at the Vectorscope in the Reference Monitor, and note that there is a bit of trace pushed toward the red target, indicating the skin tone is pushed that way as well. Ideally, skin tone on the Vectorscope will fall on or near the flesh tone line, which is the line that intersects the yellow and red targets (**FIGURE 11.22**).

FIGURE 11.22 The Vectorscope shows the subject's red skin tone. A large amount of trace is pushed toward the red target. Skin tone should fall on the line that intersects the yellow and red targets.

2. Select the clip in the sequence.

   The Effect Controls panel shows that a Three-Way Color Corrector is already applied to this clip. This effect was used to perform primary color correction (a slight contrast correction) on the clip; however, the person's face is still pretty red.

3. Add another Three-Way Color Corrector to the clip. You'll use this second Three-Way Color Corrector to perform a secondary correction targeting the subject's face.

4. In the Effect Controls panel on the second Three-Way Color Corrector, click the triangle to expand the Secondary Color Correction properties.

5. Next to the Center parameter, click the first eyedropper. This eyedropper allows you to sample the subject's face (we clicked the subject's forehead). The other two eyedroppers add to the selection (+) or subtract from the selection (-). Although it looks like nothing really happened, something actually did.

6. At the top of the secondary controls, click the Show Mask button.

   The Program Monitor contains a white-on-black image. The white is the subject's face. With this view, you want to have everything you want to correct (the face and skin tone) to be white and everything else to be black (**FIGURE 11.23**).

FIGURE 11.23 With the Show Mask button enabled in the Program Monitor, you can see a white-on-black image. The white portion denotes the part of the clip that has been selected, or targeted, for the secondary correction. This mask needs further refinement.

After the initial selection (which isn't so good), you could click again on the face with the + eyedropper to add more values, but it's far easier to use the Hue, Saturation, and Luma (also known as HSL) controls to fine-tune the selection.

1. Click the triangle next to Hue, Saturation, and Luma.

   These graphs (also called *qualifiers*) show the color spectrum (hue), saturation (less saturation on the left; more saturation on the right), and luma (black on the left; white on the right). The two square blocks in the middle bar of each graph let you control the "range" of the selection for hue, saturation, and luma. The two outer triangles let you feather or soften the selection.

2. Adjust each qualifier until you've selected all of the face (the white part). If you're more comfortable with adjusting the qualifiers with numeric controls, you can do that below each graph for Hue, Saturation, and Luma.

   Remember that you can see your selection in the Program Monitor (**FIGURE 11.24**). Don't worry if you get a little of the background in the selection or the hot spot on the subject's head is not completely white. This shouldn't be noticeable in the final shot.

Correcting Skies
Correcting and grading skies is a task you'll often do to fix flat skies or to add a layer of style to a clip. Check out this video to see how we color correct and grade skies.

 Ignore the Skin? That's a Sin
One of the most important details to match while grading is skin tone because our minds process skin as a memory color. This means that people know what skin tone should look like.

Memory Colors
Grass is green, and skies are blue, right? When performing primary and secondary color correction, keep in mind that some colors (the combo of hue and saturation) are known as memory colors. Over the years our minds have developed a keen sense of what certain objects such as grass, skies, and skin tone look like. Always pay careful attention to memory colors when grading.

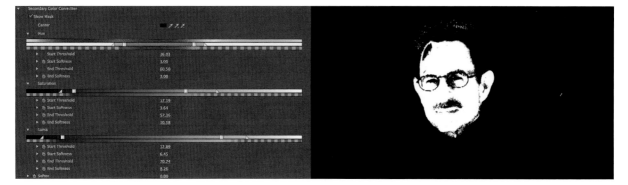

FIGURE 11.24 Using the HSL qualifiers, you can refine the selection to better target the subject's skin tone. Adjust the qualifiers until you have as much skin tone as possible selected.

Vignettes or Shapes

Common among dedicated color correction applications are vignettes, shape, or windows tools. You can use vignettes to isolate a particular part of a clip. For example, you could use a circle vignette around a subject's face to lighten it. Although you can manually build vignettes in Adobe Premiere Pro by duplicating a clip and using a garbage matte or using the title tool, SpeedGrade and After Effects offer more precise masking control.

3. When you're happy with your selection, use the Soften parameter to blur the selection a bit (this helps with ringing edges). A value between 4 and 5 should work well. You can also use the Edge Thinning parameter to refine the edges of the selection; in this case, use a value of 5.

4. Go back up to the top of the secondary controls, and uncheck Show Mask. In the Program Monitor, notice that you're once again looking at the uncorrected clip.

    Now that you've made the selection, you need to make the correction.

5. Use the midtones color wheel in the middle of the effect, and drag the control down toward yellow/green (to neutralize a color cast, you add color from the opposite side of the color wheel). On the highlights color wheel, also drag down toward yellow/green a touch.

6. Check the Vectorscope in the Reference Monitor. Using the flesh tone line as a guide, adjust the midtones and highlights until there is trace falling near or on the line (**FIGURE 11.25**).

7. Using the Input Levels control directly below the color wheels, drag the rightmost point slightly to the left to lighten the subject's face a touch.

8. Toggle the effect on and off to see the result of the secondary correction. Then play back the sequence and check your results; tweak the correction as you see fit (**FIGURE 11.26**).

FIGURE 11.25 Remember that the flesh tone line is a guide, not an absolute rule. Use your eyes and best judgment to determine what looks good.

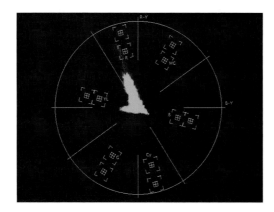

FIGURE 11.26 The original and corrected shots

Secondary Corrections for Special Effects
Check out this video to learn more about using the Leave Color effect to create a very stylized look where everything in a clip is desaturated except for one color.

Getting Projects and Clips to SpeedGrade
In this video, learn about the various ways to get clips and projects into SpeedGrade.

Using Adobe SpeedGrade

A new and welcomed addition to the CS6 lineup is Adobe SpeedGrade. With Speed-Grade, Adobe now has a full-featured dedicated color correction and grading tool. It can be used to really bring your projects to life—color and contrast wise, that is.

Although we could write an entire book on SpeedGrade, let's take a look at the basics. It's important to know how to send a project to SpeedGrade. You'll also learn more with movies provided throughout this section (**FIGURE 11.27**).

FIGURE 11.27 SpeedGrade is an exciting new dedicated color correction tool in Creative Suite CS6.

There are a few main workflows to get footage and projects to SpeedGrade; which one you use really depends on what best works for your project.

Importing

If you simply have a collection of clips that you'd like to color correct, such as a bunch of clips on a tapeless media card that you've transferred and you don't care about how they're edited together, you can import them directly into SpeedGrade. Once they are in, you can correct them and then render them back out. This workflow is often used for on-set dailies work.

That Name Sounds Familiar!
If you're scratching your head thinking the name SpeedGrade sounds familiar, that's probably because before Adobe purchased the product, it was called IRIDAS SpeedGrade. SpeedGrade has long been seen as one of the best grading applications around. The best part is that it used to cost tens of thousands of dollars and is now included in Production Premium. You're welcome!

Getting to Know the SpeedGrade Interface

In this video, learn about the SpeedGrade interface. While initially intimidating, this movie will quickly get you up to speed on the interface.

Primary Corrections in SpeedGrade

In this video, learn how to create primary color corrections in SpeedGrade.

Secondary Corrections in SpeedGrade

In this video, learn how to create powerful secondary color corrections in SpeedGrade.

Get Organized!

If you're going to use the EDL workflow with SpeedGrade, it's important that you prep your sequences. Flatten your sequence to as few tracks as possible. If you have multiple tracks, you can export an EDL for each track that you can then conform in SpeedGrade.

Rendering Clips from SpeedGrade

In this video, learn how to render clips back out of SpeedGrade so you can get back to Premiere Pro.

Using Scene Cut Detection

Oftentimes you won't have an Adobe Premiere Pro project, EDL, or other instruction set that tells you how a self-contained file should be cut up. In those cases, you can import one self-contained file into SpeedGrade and use the Scene Cut Detection feature to automatically cut up the longer clip into separate clips that you can grade. Is it perfect? No, but you have controls for adjusting sensitivity to what SpeedGrade thinks is a cut, and, you can manually create cuts or delete false ones that the Scene Cut Detection might make.

Sending to SpeedGrade

If you have a sequence in Adobe Premiere Pro that you'd like to work with in SpeedGrade, getting it there is easy. Just make the sequence active, and choose File > Send to Adobe SpeedGrade. Keep in mind is that when you choose this option, each clip is rendered out as a DPX image sequence. This does several things. First, it converts all your footage to DPX files, so if you were using a mixed format Timeline, all codecs are rendered to DPX. In addition, if you were using RAW formats such as RED or ARRIRAW, you will lose access to that raw metadata in SpeedGrade. Second, DPX image sequences are really big, so you'll need quite a bit of additional hard drive space in addition to the space that is currently being used to store your original media. For DPX sequences to play back properly, you'll also need pretty fast storage. Third, sending to SpeedGrade also bakes in effects applied in Adobe Premiere Pro.

Conforming a Sequence with an EDL

We know what you're thinking, an EDL? Although EDLs are an older exchange format, they are pretty reliable. In this workflow, you load an EDL and then connect to media. The EDL can come from Adobe Premiere Pro, Final Cut Pro, or other NLEs, but it's important that the EDL be in the CMX 3600 format, which is the most common EDL format. Using this workflow, you can easily and instantly reconnect to mixed format sequences including RAW video files and have access to RAW controls inside SpeedGrade.

Using After Effects and Photoshop for Correction

Although the tools in Adobe Premiere Pro are quite effective for most color correction and grading tasks, you don't have to stop there. If you are using the Production Premium or Master Collection of Creative Suite, you have two great options. Photoshop Extended offers a comprehensive suite of image correction tools. Plus, you can easily turn to After Effects for versatile masking tools and advanced effects.

Sending a Clip to After Effects

After Effects has secured its place as one of the preeminent motion graphics and compositing applications in the world. Both Adobe Premiere Pro and After Effects share many user interface elements as well as commands. Several features make it worthwhile to send a clip to After Effects to be corrected and graded.

- **Color Stabilizer.** The Color Stabilizer effect samples the color values of a reference frame and then adjusts the colors of other frames so they remain consistent. This works well for sources shot under flickering light and can also compensate for flicker inherent to speed effects, time lapse, and stop-motion footage.

- **Colorama.** The Colorama effect allows you to easily remap and animate colors to quickly create dynamic color effects. We often use this effect to quickly stylize a shot or create interesting-looking background elements. When combined with an adjustment layer and blending modes, it can create some very nice duotone and sepia tone effects as well as dramatic contrast.

- **Black & White.** If you need to create custom grayscale or duotone looks, this effect is perfect. Use the color channels to weight the grayscale conversion.

- **Vibrance.** If you need to selectively adjust the saturation in a clip, the Vibrance effect is very useful. Colors that are less saturated in the original image are affected with greater magnitude than those that are already saturated in the original image. This effect is ideal for boosting blue skies and green vegetation. It even offers an option to protect skin tones to keep skin looking natural.

- **Remove Grain.** If your footage has a lot of grain or noise, color correction can make it worse. Fortunately, After Effects offers a handy effect to smooth out the problem areas.

Exporting a clip to After Effects is simple thanks to Dynamic Link.

1. Select the clips in your Timeline panel.

2. Choose File > Adobe Dynamic Link > Replace with After Effects Composition.

   A new After Effects composition is added to your Timeline and Project panels.

3. You are automatically switched to After Effects. Name the project, and click Save.

   Store the project with your Adobe Premiere Pro project file so that your media path structure is easy to preserve. Any additional clips sent to After Effects from your current Adobe Premiere Pro project will join this linked After Effects project.

4. Modify your footage as needed in After Effects.

5. Save your After Effects project file to capture your changes.

6. Switch back to Adobe Premiere Pro, and your project is updated.

   To update a linked After Effects composition, just press Command+E (Ctrl+E) to invoke the Edit Original command.

Correcting a Clip with Photoshop

Although most think of Photoshop as mainly geared toward photography and graphic design, it also excels at working with video (which really is just a bunch of stills played back quickly). If you're comfortable with Photoshop or want to use some of its exceptional tools, it's easy to send a clip to Photoshop. Depending on what you're trying to do, you have a few options:

- If you know you want to take advantage of Photoshop's toolset prior to using a clip in Premiere Pro, you can simply open it in Photoshop.

 Grading in After Effects
To see how you can use After Effects to color correct and color grade, check out this video.

 Using .look Files in After Effects
One nice benefit of SpeedGrade being added to CS6 is that you can use .look files created in Speed-Grade. These small files contain all the corrections for a shot and you can easily apply those corrections to a clip in After Effects or Photoshop. This makes collaboration quick and super easy and also reduces how many times you need to render.

 Color Finesse
After Effects includes Color Finesse—a dedicated color correction plug-in that gives you ample control to color correct and grade your project, especially when shots are part of a motion graphics workflow. If you spend a lot of time in After Effects, it's a go-to tool for color correction and grading.

 But Wait, There's More
There's lots more to Dynamic Link. You can import entire Premiere Pro projects into After Effects as both layered compositions or linked video tracks. You can even copy and paste clips between applications. Be sure to explore this versatile relationship.

Creative Suite Workflow
If you'd like to learn more about workflows available between Adobe Premiere Pro, After Effects, and Photoshop, check out *Motion Graphics with Adobe Creative Suite 5 Studio Techniques* (Adobe Press, 2010).

53

Photoshop Can Fix It

To see how you can use Photoshop to color correct and color grade, watch this video. You'll also learn how to save or render your clips for use in Adobe Premiere Pro.

- You can matchframe a clip in your Timeline to find it in the Project panel. You can then right-click the clip and choose Reveal in Adobe Bridge. One more right-click, and you can choose it in Adobe Bridge and then choose to open the clip in Photoshop.

- If you're already working with a clip in Adobe Premiere Pro, select the media either in the Project panel or in a sequence and choose File > Export > Media. Save the file to the desired location, and then open the file in Photoshop.

After you're done editing the clip, you'll need to export your changes from Photoshop, reimport the clip into Adobe Premiere Pro, and then reedit the clip into your sequence.

1. With a corrected clip in Photoshop, choose File > Export > Render Video.

2. In the Render Video dialog (**FIGURE 11.28**), choose a location to render the corrected clip to. You can also choose to create a subfolder.

FIGURE 11.28 You can configure video export from Photoshop using the Render Video dialog.

3. In the first menu, choose the Adobe Media Encoder option. In the Format menu, you can choose between H.264, DPX and QuickTime. While you can use H.264 in Premiere Pro, we often choose DPX or QuickTime. If you choose QuickTime, you can then choose between Uncompressed, JPEG 2000, and Animation Codecs.

4. The options in the rest of the dialog default to match the clip you're working with. You can change these as needed.

5. Click Render to export the clip.

54

Get the Most from Photoshop

Learn how to process video clips in Photoshop including the very useful Adaptive Wide Angle and Lens Correction effects in this video.

Next Steps

Now that you have the basics of color correction and grading down in Adobe Premiere Pro, you can move on to the next stage in finalizing a project. Up next you'll learn about essential effects that you'll need to refine your program.

CHAPTER 12

Essential Effects

IF YOU TALK to 10 editors and ask them for their top 10 effects, you'll likely end up with a 75-item list. The reason is because there are a lot of strong opinions as well as varied needs that drive the use of effects by video editors. Depending on the genre you edit, effects can range from simple blurring to more elaborate effects, such as complex keying and compositing.

Fortunately, Adobe is well known for its visual effects capabilities. Adobe Premiere Pro has a versatile effects engine that allows you to create complex effects right in the video Timeline. Making tasks even easier is the close relationship between Adobe Premiere Pro and Adobe After Effects.

In this chapter, you'll learn some of the most commonly requested effects you'll be expected to generate. You'll also learn how to seamlessly work between Adobe Premiere Pro and After Effects to cut down on processing time.

The Effects Workflow

Ultimately, you want to make postproduction run as smoothly as possible, minimizing delays and unexpected costs. Adobe Premiere Pro is known for its speed thanks to the Mercury Playback Engine. Fortunately, a well-tuned system will add speed boosts to other applications in the Creative Suite as well. As an editor, you know there are important workflow considerations when it comes to approaching effects.

- **Solo or team?** If you are the only postproduction person on the project, you have a lot of flexibility to determine your own workflow. If you're part of a team, you'll need to balance your needs with others on the project.

- **Pure Adobe workflow?** Thanks to technologies such as Dynamic Link and the Edit Original command, you have many more workflow options. Because you can seamlessly jump back and forth between After Effects and Adobe Premiere Pro, you can integrate effects throughout the editing process.

- **Third-party tools?** Certain effects may be critical to your finished project. Although Adobe Premiere Pro and After Effects have a great deal of similar effects, there is hardly feature parity. Your workflow may be impacted by requirements for third-party filters and effects.

Applying Effects in Adobe Premiere Pro

When it comes to video effects, the choices in Adobe Premiere Pro can be a bit overwhelming. You'll find more than 100 effects built into the application with far more available via third-party plug-ins. It's important to have a clear understanding of how Adobe Premiere Pro treats the use of effects.

Fixed Effects

Every clip that you edit into a sequence already has certain Fixed effects preapplied. Fixed effects can be thought of as controls for the standard geometric, opacity, and audio properties that every clip should have. All Fixed effects can be modified using the Effect Controls panel.

Here are the default effects (**FIGURE 12.1**) that are preapplied to clips in the Timeline panel:

- **Motion.** The Motion effect allows you to animate, rotate, and scale a clip. You can also use advanced Anti-flicker controls to decrease shimmering edges for an animated object. This comes in handy when you scale a high-resolution source and Adobe Premiere Pro must resample the digital image.

- **Opacity.** The Opacity effect lets you control how opaque or transparent a clip is. Additionally, you can access multipurpose blending modes to create special effects and real-time composites.

- **Time Remapping.** This property lets you slow down, speed up, or reverse playback, or even freeze a frame. We explored its uses in Chapter 7, "Additional Editing Skills."

- **Volume.** If an edited clip has audio, the Volume effect is automatically applied. You can use the effect to control the volume for the individual clip.

FIGURE 12.1 The Fixed effects are applied to each clip. For video, these control the Geometry, Opacity, and Speed aspects of the selected clip.

Need to Break the Chain?
You can't reorder Fixed effects, but you can bypass them and use other effects, which are similar. For example, you can use the Transform effect instead of the Motion effect or the Alpha Adjust effect instead of the Opacity effect. Although these effects are not identical, they are a very close match and behave similarly. You may choose to use them when you need to reorder effects that perform these actions.

The Effects Workspace
This lesson uses the Effects workspace that makes working with effects easier. Just choose Window > Workspace > Effects.

The Effects Browser

With more than 100 effects, there's quite a bit to choose from in the Video Effects group. To start, effects are grouped into 16 standard categories (third-party effects may add more choices). These categories group the effects into logical tasks such as Color Correction, Keying, and Time. This makes it easier to choose which ones you want to apply.

To search for an effect, you can simply type its name into the search field in the Effects panel. You can also twirl open a category folder to see its contents. As you work through the options, you'll notice several icons next to many of the effects names (**FIGURE 12.2**). Knowing what these icons represent will influence which effects you choose.

Which Effect Is Where?
With so many Video Effects subfolders, it's sometimes tricky to locate the effect you want. If you know an effect's name, start typing it in the search box at the top of the Effects panel. Adobe Premiere Pro immediately displays all effects and transitions that contain that letter combination, narrowing the search as you type.

No Effects Menu?
Unlike Final Cut Pro 7, there's no Effects menu to browse. We recommend keeping the Effects panel open. You can also press Shift+7 to quickly select it.

FIGURE 12.2 The icons denote the special functions of each effect. The first icon is GPU acceleration, the next indicates that an effect supports 32-bits per channel, and the last means an effect is optimized for processing in the YUV color space without shifting color.

Stay True to 32
When using 32-bit effects, try to stick with all 32-bit effects in the chain for maximum quality. If you mix and match, the effects will have to switch back to 8-bit space to process, which reduces the overall precision. Also be sure to select the Maximum Bit Depth option in the sequence settings. If using the software-only version of the Mercury Playback Engine, a single 8-bits-per-channel effect can ruin a sequence. Those using hardware acceleration get clip-level processing.

When Is YUV Not YUV?
It turns out that the YUV effects don't actually work in YUV. Instead, they function in the more accurately named Y'CbCr color space. The YUV naming is simpler to say and is frequently used (although technically inaccurate).

Creating Favorites
Want to organize your most used effects? Check out this video to learn how you can create a Favorites folder for easy access.

Color-Grade Approach
One way to grade color is to combine adjustment layers with standard effects. Use essential color correction techniques to neutralize and issues with individual clips. Then use an adjustment layer across the entire scene to grade or stylize. This makes it easier to iterate different looks or refine an adjustment.

- **GPU-accelerated effects.** These effects can take advantage of a certified graphics card to accelerate rendering. Thanks to CUDA or Open CL and the Mercury Playback Engine, these effects often offer real-time performance and need rendering only on final export. A supported video card makes a huge difference in performance.

- **High-bit-depth effects.** Certain effects support a higher bit depth than traditional video effects (which offer only the standard 8-bits-per-channel video). These effects are best suited for video shot with 10 or 12 bits per channel formats (such as RED or ARRI) or to maintain greater image fidelity when multiple effects are applied. Additionally, 16-bit photos or After Effects files rendered in 16 or 32 bits per channel color space can take advantage of high-bit-depth effects. Make sure your sequence has the Maximum Bit Depth video-rendering option selected in the New Sequence or Sequence Settings dialog.

- **YUV effects.** For most effects that rely heavily on color transformations (such as the Three-Way Color Corrector), Adobe Premiere Pro offers YUV-enabled effects. Most effects in Adobe Premiere Pro process in the RGB space, which can make adjusting exposure and color less accurate. The YUV effects break down the video into a Y (or luminance channel) and two channels for color information (without brightness). These filters make it easy to adjust contrast and exposure using the native space without shifting color for RGB conversion.

Applying Effects in Adobe Premiere Pro

There are several ways to apply an effect to a selected clip or clips. The method you choose is really a matter of personal preference (just make sure the clips are slected in the Timeline panel).

- Drag and drop from the Effects Browser onto the Timeline clip.

- Double-click an effect in the Effects Browser.

- You can select an effect from the Effect Controls panel, choose Edit > Copy, select the Effects Controls panel of a destination clip, and choose Edit > Paste.

- To copy all the effects from one clip so you can paste them to another clip, select the clip in the Timeline panel and choose Edit > Copy, select the destination clip, and choose Edit > Paste Attributes.

Using Adjustment Layers in Adobe Premiere Pro

If you need to apply an effect to multiple clips at once, an adjustment layer can really come in handy. Experienced After Effects or Photoshop users may already be familiar with the technology that makes its debut in Adobe Premiere Pro CS6.

The concept is simple; you create a new specialty layer that can hold effects and sit above other video tracks. Everything beneath the adjustment layer will be processed by the effect. Adjustment layers can have their trim handles and opacity modified to further refine the effect and its placement. An adjustment layer is often easier to to modify since it is a single effect, rather than multiple instances applied to several clips.

To use an adjustment layer, follow these steps:

1. Click the New Item button at the bottom of the Project panel, and choose Adjustment Layer. Click OK to create the adjustment layer to match the dimensions of the current sequence.

2. Locate the new adjustment layer that was added in the Project panel. You can rename it or move it to a bin to make it easier to track.

3. Drag the adjustment layer to a higher track in the Timeline. Trim its handles to cover just the portion of clips you want to affect (**FIGURE 12.3**).

Adjustment Layers
Learn how adjustment layers in Adobe Premiere Pro can speed things up when designing custom effects.

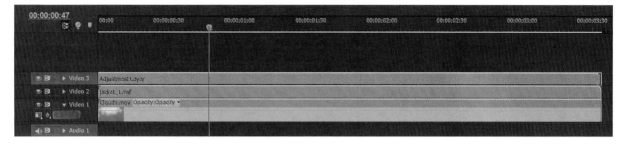

4. With the adjustment layer selected, drag an effect on to it from the Effects Browser (or simply double-click the effect).

5. Adjsut the effect using the Effect Controls panel.

Using Effects Presets in Adobe Premiere Pro

If you create a custom setting for an effect you like, you can save it as a preset. You can also save a combination of multiple effects. If your effect uses keyframes (such as an animated blur), those will also be stored with the preset. This can significantly improve speed and consistency.

One of the most common uses for presets is color correction tasks where a preset is saved for an instance of a subject. Presets can come in handy for stylized looks and special effects as well.

You'll find a collection of built-in presets in the Presets bin (**FIGURE 12.4**). If you twirl open the folder, you'll find numerous nested folders. These contain effects that are ready to use. To use a preset, just drag it onto a clip in the Timeline. You can also select multiple clips in the Timeline to affect several clips at once.

You need to follow a few rules to apply presets.

- If no clips are selected in the Timeline, only the targeted clip is affected when you drag and drop the preset.

- If a selection is made but you drop the preset on a nonselected clip, the targeted clip and any linked track items become selected (whereas the originals are deselected). The preset is applied only to the targeted clip (and linked track items).

- If there are clips selected in the Timeline and the targeted clip is part of the selection, the preset will affect all of the selected clips when you drop it.

FIGURE 12.3 The adjustment layer should cover only the clips you want to affect. All clips beneath it will be processed. Be sure to trim the start and end of the layer as well to match your needs.

Be Sure to Blend
Blending an adjustment layer can significantly change the behavior of an effect. This is a great way to create new looks from existing plug-ins.

Get Organized
You can create new bins by clicking the New Custom Bin button at the bottom of the Effects panel. Nest bins together, and use descriptive names to create a collection of organized presets.

A Better Drag
If you drag an effect preset to the Effect Controls panel, you'll have better control over standard effects. You can precisely position the presets within the processing order (hierarchy) as needed.

FIGURE 12.4 Be sure to twirl open each Effect Preset category to fully explore the many choices available.

Saving Effect Presets in Adobe Premiere Pro

Hands-on Practice
You can open the sequence A_Effect Presets to try saving presets and removing effects.

Although there is a good assortment of effect presets to choose from, you'll ultimately want to create your own. This process is easy and creates a preset file that you can easily move between computers. The process comes down to selecting exactly what you want.

1. Select a clip in the Timeline panel that has one or more effects with customized settings that you want to store as a preset.

2. Switch to the Effect Controls panel. Select one or more effects that you want to store by Command-clicking (Ctrl-clicking) (FIGURE 12.5).

3. Click the Effect Controls panel submenu and choose Save Preset (FIGURE 12.6).

FIGURE 12.5 A custom color grade was created here for a high-contrast duotone with a cool blue tint. This can be stored as a preset for future use.

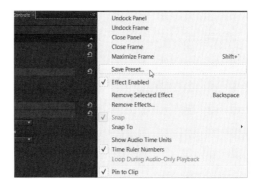

FIGURE 12.6 To store a preset, click the submenu in the upper-right corner of the Effect Controls panel, and choose Save Preset.

4. Give the preset a descriptive name.

5. Choose one of the following preset types to specify how Adobe Premiere Pro should handle keyframes in a preset:

   - **Scale.** Proportionally scales the source keyframes to the length of the target clip. Any existing keyframes on the original clip are deleted.

   - **Anchor to In Point.** Preserves the position of the first keyframe as well as the relationship of other keyframes in a clip. Other keyframes are added to the clip relative to its In point.

   - **Anchor to Out Point.** Preserves the position of the last keyframe as well as the relationship of other keyframes in a clip. Other keyframes are added to the clip relative to its Out point.

6. Click OK to store the affected clip and keyframes as a new preset (**FIGURE 12.7**).

Removing Effects in Adobe Premiere Pro

If you change your mind about an effect, it's easy to remove. You can get rid of them one at a time or take a more aggressive approach and remove them from several clips.

To remove an individual effect, follow these steps:

1. Select a clip in the Timeline panel.

2. In the Effect Controls panel, select the effect you want to remove.

   If you want to select multiple effects, hold down the Command (Ctrl) key as you click.

3. Press the Delete or Backspace key.

You can also remove all effects from one or more clips at once.

1. Select one or multiple clips in the Timeline panel.

2. Choose Clip > Remove Effects, or right-click a clip in the Timeline panel and choose Remove Effects.

   The Remove Effects dialog opens (**FIGURE 12.8**).

3. Select the type of effects you want to remove, and click OK. You can remove intrinsic (Fixed) effects, which include Motion and Opacity, as well as any applied video effects.

   All Standard effects are removed, and Motion and Opacity can be reset to their default values.

Applying Effects in After Effects

As good as effects are in Adobe Premiere Pro, there's no denying that After Effects is a powerful companion (hey, the word *effects* is in its name). Video editors and motion graphics artists have long relied on After Effects for its versatile compositing, robust keying, and footage enhancement effects. Thanks to the close relationship between Adobe Premiere Pro and After Effects, you can seamlessly integrate the two tools much more easily than any other editing platform.

Render In to Out
The option to render between In and Out points may seem disabled at first. To start, click the Timeline's panel menu (in its upper-right corner) and uncheck the option to show the Work Area Bar. You can now mark In and Out points to define a range. Then choose either Sequence > Render In to Out to render any frame rate or speed changes (as well as effects) or Sequence > Render Effects In to Out to only process effects in the range.

FIGURE 12.7 Be sure to give the effect a unique name and accurate description. When you mouse over the preset in the Effects panel, the description will display as a tooltip.

FIGURE 12.8 Think about which effects you want to remove. You can remove all added video or audio effects as well as the Fixed (or Intrinsic) effects.

FIGURE 12.9 Dynamically linked assets appear in the Project panel with unique icons and label colors to make them easier to identify.

Dynamic Link Revisited

We've mentioned Dynamic Link a few times already in this book. It's not that we like repeating ourselves; we just want to burn the term into your brain. Dynamic Link is revolutionary and will totally change how you approach working with media throughout the postproduction process.

Before Dynamic Link, you needed to render and export media to hand it off between two applications. This used disk space inefficiently and was very time-consuming. If you wanted to change an original asset, you needed to render and export it again. This resulted in many versions of assets to keep track of as well as all sorts of file-management challenges.

When you use Adobe Premiere Pro as part of the Production Premium or Master Collection, you gain the ability to create Dynamic Links between After Effects, Adobe Premiere Pro, and Adobe Encore (**FIGURE 12.9**). When working with After Effects, you will frequently send selected clips from Adobe Premiere Pro into After Effects as a composition or nested composition. The original clips in your Timeline are replaced with a dynamically linked After Effects composition.

Dynamic Link can join Adobe Premiere Pro and After Effects to each other in three ways. The first method lets you send clips from Adobe Premiere Pro to a new After Effects composition.

1. In an open sequence, select the clips you want in an After Effects composition.

2. Right-click any of the selected clips.

3. Choose Replace With After Effects Composition.

   A new composition is created and inherits the sequence settings from Adobe Premiere Pro.

The second method allows you to create a new, empty After Effects composition within your Adobe Premiere Pro project. This is useful when you need to create generated media, such as a background or title treatment.

1. In Adobe Premiere Pro, choose File > Adobe Dynamic Link > New After Effects Composition.

2. If the After Effects Save As dialog appears, enter a name and location for the After Effects project, and click Save.

   If After Effects is already running, it creates a composition in the current project. The new composition is named based on the Adobe Premiere Pro project name, followed by Linked Comp [#].

The third way to use Dynamic Link is to link to an existing composition that's already been created in After Effects. This will ensure that you always have the latest version in your sequence that reflects any changes made in After Effects.

Here are several ways to create this link:

- In Adobe Premiere Pro, choose File > Adobe Dynamic Link > Import After Effects Composition. Navigate to and select an After Effects project file (.aep), and then choose one or more compositions to import.

- Drag one or more compositions from the After Effects Project panel to the Adobe Premiere Pro Project panel.

- Drag an After Effects project file into the Adobe Premiere Pro Project panel. If the project has multiple compositions, the Import Composition dialog opens. Select the compositions you want to link.

Browsing After Effects Animation Presets

To get you started, After Effects offers several useful animation presets for treating footage as well as generating motion graphics content. To make tasks easy, After Effects lets you browse presets in the Effects & Presets panel. At the very top of the list is the Animation Presets folder. You can interact with these presets in a few ways.

- **Open each folder.** Twirl open the folder to view several categories. You'll find a variety of options, including Backgrounds, Special Effects, Text animations, and Transitions. To view the contents of a folder, just click the disclosure triangle next to a folder.

- **Use the Search field.** You can also enter a keyword into the search field at the top of the panel to quickly find effects based on their name. If you want to save a search for easy recall, just Shift-click its name. You can then click the magnifying glass to call up a list of saved searches.

> **What Makes a Preset Tick?**
> If you want to see the controls that are being animated with an effect preset, simply press U or UU to reveal only the animated or modified layer properties. By seeing only the controls that are being used, it is easy to tweak the effect.

LINKING TO AND FROM

Dynamic Link is very useful, but Adobe doesn't stop there. You'll find six additional ways to move media to and from Adobe Premiere Pro. Be sure you understand all of the following options so you can make the right decision for your workflow:

- **Copy and Paste.** The easiest way to move media between After Effects and Adobe Premiere Pro is the standard Copy and Paste commands in the Edit menu. If you copy from the Timeline panel, In and Out points as well as editing order are preserved (plus handles). If you copy from the Project panel, the entire clip is transferred.

- **Export PRPROJ.** From After Effects, you can choose File > Export Adobe Premiere Pro project to send media to Adobe Premiere Pro.

- **Import PRPROJ.** You can import an entire Adobe Premiere Pro project into After Effects. This brings an individual sequence or all sequences in as media files. All edits are preserved, but After Effects treats the Adobe Premiere Pro sequence as a single media file.

- **Pro Import After Effects.** The popular tool Automatic Duck has been woven into After Effects CS6. This makes it easier to import Final Cut Pro and Avid projects into After Effects.

- **XML.** Using the XML format, Adobe Premiere Pro can import and export an XML file that links to media assets. This is a useful way to exchange Adobe Premiere Pro projects with other editing and color grading tools (including SpeedGrade). See the book's appendixes for more details.

- **AAF.** You can import the Advanced Authoring Format from Avid editing systems. You can also export using this format to send a project to Avid. See the book's appendixes for more details.

- **Browse with Adobe Bridge.** If you'd prefer to visually browse the presets, you can turn to Adobe Bridge (**FIGURE 12.10**). Click the submenu in the upper-right corner of the Effects & Presets panel, and choose Browse Presets. Adobe Bridge launches, and you can navigate through folders to see icons for each preset. Click an icon to see a preview of the effect. If you double-click a preset, you will switch back to After Effects, and the preset will be applied to the selected layer.

FIGURE 12.10 Browsing presets is easy with Adobe Bridge. It lets you view animated previews of each preset.

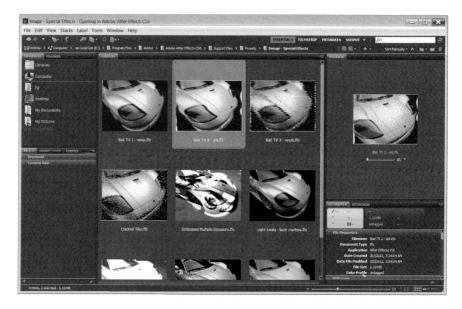

Applying Effects and Animation Presets in After Effects

It wouldn't be After Effects if there weren't multiple roads to the same destination. There are several ways to apply animation presets to your footage. In addition to the aforementioned Effects & Presets panel, here are a few more useful ways to get the job done:

- To apply an effect or animation preset to one or more layers, select the layers in the Timeline. You can then double-click the effect or animation preset in the Effects & Presets panel.

- To apply a recently used animation preset, select the layers in the composition's Timeline. Choose Animation > Recent Animation Presets, and then choose the animation preset from the list.

- To reuse the most recently applied effect, select the layers, and then press Command+Option+Shift+E (Ctrl+Alt+Shift+E).

- You can also copy effects from one layer to another. Select the effects in the Timeline panel or the Effect Controls panel, and choose Edit > Copy. You can then select the target layers and choose Edit > Paste.

Want More Presets?
You can browse and download several presets from the Adobe Web site by visiting www.adobe.com/go/learn_ae_cs3additionalanimationpresets. Most of the ones posted are free. This is also an excellent way to explore the larger After Effects community.

Saving After Effects Presets

Using effect combinations designed by others is certainly useful, but nothing beats making your own (except saving time by storing your own creations for future use). After Effects makes it simple to store several properties into a preset (including animation).

1. Select any combination of properties for a layer. These can include animation properties, such as Position and Scale, or property groups, such as Paint and Transform. You can also select any effects in either the Timeline panel or the Effect Controls panel.

2. Choose Animation > Save Animation Preset.

3. Name the preset and specify a location for the file.

4. Click Save.

Removing Effects in After Effects

Removing an effect is simple. You can click to select it in either the Timeline or Effect Properties panel. You can then press the Delete key to remove the effect. If you want to simply reset the effect's controls, click the Reset hyperlinked text next to the effect's name.

Understanding Keyframes

The concept of keyframes is likely familiar to you as an editor who's used effects. The term has its roots in traditional animation where the lead artist would draw the keyframes (or major poses), and assistant animators would animate the frames in between (a process often called *tweening*). These days, you're the master who sets the major keyframes, and the computer does the rest of the work as it interpolates values in between the keyframes you set.

Adding Keyframes

The process of keyframing is very similar between Adobe Premiere Pro and After Effects. You'll use keyframes to control most properties, including motion, audio, and video effects. The decisions you need to make before you animate is to determine the desired result and the duration for the effect.

Let's explore the animation process in Adobe Premiere Pro (it's virtually identical in After Effects).

1. Place the playhead (Adobe Premiere Pro) or current-time indicator (After Effects) at a point in the Timeline where you'd like the effect to begin.

2. Select the desired clip.

   - In Adobe Premiere Pro, double-click a clip to load it into the Source panel, and then click the Effect Controls panel.

   - In After Effects, select the clip in the composition and choose the Effect Controls panel.

Where to Store Presets?
If you want an animation preset to appear in the Effects & Presets panel, it must be saved in the Presets folder. This folder is located in the Applications/Adobe After Effects CS6 folder on a Mac. For a Windows PC, navigate to Program Files\Adobe\Adobe After Effects CS6\Support Files. The correct location should be chosen by default when you save the preset.

Don't See Your New Presets?
If you've copied in new presets or saved your own, they may not show up in the Effects & Presets panel. Click the submenu in the Effects & Presets panel and choose Refresh List.

Removing Keyframes
To remove a keyframe, you can click on a keyframe and then press the Delete key. You can also remove all keyframes for a layer by turning off the layer stopwatch.

Hands-on Practice
You can open the sequence C_Keyframes to see keyframes in action. Feel free to modify or experiment with this sequence.

3. Click the stopwatch icon next to a property's name (**FIGURE 12.11**).

FIGURE 12.11 When you turn on a stopwatch, an initial keyframe is added for the property (which you can modify by typing a new value or dragging to scrub its value).

Can't See the Effects Timeline?
If you don't see a small Timeline in the Effect Controls panel, click the small, light gray triangle just above the scroll bar for the panel. This button will toggle between Show/Hide the Timeline View for the panel. This will show a small Timeline just for navigating effect keyframes.

Navigating Keyframes
You can easily move between keyframes using the two arrows located next to a property's name. Just click the left arrow to go to the previous keyframe and the right arrow to go to the next keyframe. In After Effects you can also press the J and K keys to perform the same function.

After Effects Auto Keyframes
If you're working in After Effects, you'll find that it offers an Auto Keyframe mode. Simply click the large stopwatch at the top of the Timeline panel. When activated, new keyframes will be automatically added for a property when it's modified. You will either love or hate this feature.

Control Handles
To view the control handles for a keyframe, you need to view a value graph. In Adobe Premiere Pro, twirl down the effect's property using the disclosure triangle next to an effect's name (make sure the Timeline view is displayed on the right). In Adobe After Effects, you select the property and then click the Graph Editor button in the Timeline panel.

4. Move the playhead or current-time indicator to a new point in the Timeline.

5. Change the values for any property whose stopwatch is enabled. A new keyframe is added.

6. The in-between values are automatically interpreted for you by Adobe Premiere Pro (or After Effects).

   The method used for interpolation will vary based on the keyframe style chosen (more on this next).

Keyframe Interpolation

The concept of keyframes makes sense to most editors, but there is still more to explore. One of the greatest untapped controls when animating is the use of keyframe interpolation. You'll find five different methods in Adobe Premiere Pro and After Effects that control the interpolation process. Changing the method used can create a very different animation.

The easiest way to access interpolation methods is to right-click a keyframe. In Adobe Premiere Pro, you'll see all five listed (some effects offer both spatial and temporal categories). In After Effects, choose Keyframe Interpolation to access a floating window for advanced controls.

TEMPORAL VS. SPATIAL INTERPOLATION

Some properties and effects offer a choice of temporal and spatial interpolation. You'll find that all properties have temporal controls for time and some properties offer spatial interpolation as well. Here are the essentials of each method:

- **Temporal interpolation.** Temporal interpolation deals with changes in time. It's an effective way to determine the speed at which an object moves across a motion path. For example, you can add acceleration and deceleration to a motion path with Ease or Bezier keyframes.

- **Spatial interpolation.** The spatial method commonly deals with changes in an object's shape. It's an effective way to control the shape of the motion path. For example, does an object create hard angular ricochets as it moves from keyframe to keyframe, or does the object have a more sloping movement with round corners?

Keyframes have five styles (**FIGURE 12.12**).

FIGURE 12.12 Keyframes can be identified by their shape: (from left to right) Linear, Bezier, Auto Bezier, Continuous Bezier, and Hold Interpolation.

- **Linear interpolation.** The default method of keyframe interpolation is linear. This method creates a uniform rate of change between keyframes. It often looks a bit mechanical because the software calculates in-between values or each keyframe pair, while the other keyframes in use in the Timeline panel are ignored. When using linear keyframes, changes begin instantly at the first keyframe and continue to the next keyframe at a constant speed. At the second keyframe, the rate of change switches instantly to the rate between it and the third keyframe.

- **Bezier interpolation.** If you want the most control over keyframe interpolation, choose the Bezier interpolation method. This option provides manual controls so you can adjust the shape of the value graph or motion path segments on either side of the keyframe. If you use Bezier interpolation for all keyframes in a layer, you'll have a smooth transition between keyframes.

- **Auto Bezier interpolation.** The Auto Bezier option attempts to create a smooth rate of change through a keyframe and will automatically update as you change values. This option works best for spatial keyframes that define position but can be used for other values as well.

- **Continuous Bezier interpolation.** This option is similar to the Auto Bezier option, but it also provides some manual controls. The motion or value path will have smooth transitions, but you can adjust the shape of the Bezier curve on either side of the keyframe with a control handle.

- **Hold interpolation.** The Hold style is an additional interpolation method that is available only for temporal (time-based) properties. This style of keyframe allows a keyframe to hold its value across time without a gradual transition. This is useful if you want to create staccato-type movements or make an object suddenly disappear. When used, the value of the first keyframe will hold until the next hold keyframe is encountered, and then the value will instantly change.

Selected Effects

With the combined power of Adobe Premiere Pro and After Effects, you literally have hundreds of effects at your disposal (add third-party plug-ins, and you could say an infinite number of effects). Entire books could be (and have been) written about effects. However, we'll shine the spotlight on five essential effects that we use to keep clients happy. By looking at the possibilities, you'll have a better appreciation for the options that lie ahead.

To bring these effects to life, we've provided a sample project. Navigate to Lessons and Media > Lesson 12 > 12_effects.prproj. You'll use the same project for all the exercises in this chapter.

Adding Ease
If you want to create inertia (such as a ramp-up effect for speed), try using Ease. Right-click a keyframe, and choose from a variety of options. In Adobe Premiere Pro you can choose Ease In or Ease Out (for approaching and leaving a keyframe, respectively). In After Effects, you can choose Keyframe Interpolation where you'll find the additional option of Easy Ease, which applies resistance in both directions of movement.

Interpolation Illustrated
To see how each interpolation method works (as well as get an overview of Ease), be sure to watch this video.

The Effects Handbook
Instead of wasting pages to cover every effect, we'll point you to an excellent reference—the Help menu (we know you've been led to believe that true geeks don't open the Help menu). To access the good stuff, just press F1. In After Effects, you can even choose Help > Effect Reference to jump right to documentation on every effect in After Effects.

Maximum Quality
If you want maximum stabilization quality, you can choose the Detailed Analysis option under the Advanced category. This makes the Analysis phase do extra work to find elements to track. This option is much slower than others but produces superior results.

Faster Stabilization
If you've ever used Smooth-Cam in Final Cut Pro 7, it can be a lengthy process, because the effect must analyze the entire source file from first frame to last. The Warp Stabilizer effect, on the other hand, limits itself to analyzing only the frames in use.

Image Stabilization and Rolling Shutter Reduction

With the release of After Effects 5.5, Adobe introduced an entirely new method for stabilizing footage that can also be useful to video editors. The Warp Stabilizer can remove jitter caused by camera movement. The effect is very useful because it can remove unstable parallax-type movements (where images appear to shift on planes). The effect proved so popular that it's now moved directly inside Adobe Premiere Pro CS6.

An extra benefit for those shooting with CMOS-type sensors (such as those on DSLR cameras) is the ability to compensate for the rolling shutter, which can lead to an optical bending of material that has strong vertical lines.

Let's put the effect to use.

1. Select one or more clips in an Adobe Premiere Pro Timeline panel that you want to stabilize.

    For this exercise, you can use the sequence 01_Stabilize in the 12_effects.pproj. Use one or both shots.

2. In the Effects panel, locate the Warp Stabilizer effect in the Distort category.

3. Double-click the Warp Stabilizer effect to apply it to the selected clips.

    The Warp Stabilizer effect is applied to the layer. The footage is immediately analyzed between its In and Out points (**FIGURE 12.13**).

FIGURE 12.13 The analysis process takes two steps, and you'll see a banner across the footage as it's being analyzed. You can also see a progress update in the Effect Controls panel. While the analysis is in progress, you can keep working in the project.

4. You can enhance the effect with several useful Stabilization method options, such as:

    - **Result.** You can choose Smooth Motion to retain the general camera movement (albeit stabilized), or choose No Motion to attempt to remove all camera movement.

    - **Smoothness.** You can use this option to specify how much of the original camera movement should be retained for Smooth Motion. Use a higher value for maximum smoothness.

- **Method.** You can use the four methods available. The two most powerful, because they warp and process the image more heavily, are Perspective and Subspace Warp. If either method creates too much distortion, you can try switching to Position, Scale, and Rotation, or just Position.

5. You can also control how the borders are drawn for the effect. With the Framing menu, you can choose to simply stabilize the shot. You can also tell Adobe Premiere Pro to automatically scale or even synthesize new edge content.

6. If you see vertical distortion or warping in the shot, select the Rolling Shutter Ripple option under the Advanced category (**FIGURE 12.14**).

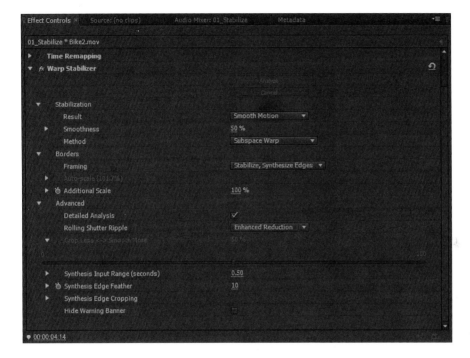

FIGURE 12.14 To use the Advanced options, you need to use either the Subspace Warp or Perspective method for Stabilization. Be sure to experiment with both methods because the choice may vary based on your source footage.

If the stabilization problem is still not solved, select the Detailed Analysis option, and choose the Enhanced Reduction method to avoid warping.

7. Play the effect to preview the effect as needed.

You may need to render this effect to see it play back smoothly because it is very processor intensive.

Timecode Burn-in

Many editors find it useful to apply a Timecode effect to clips when making stringouts for review by team members or clients. Some will apply the effect to individual clips (such as for reviewing performance takes or interviews). Other times, you can just apply it to the entire duration of a sequence. Both ways allow others to precisely refer to timecode to pinpoint scenes. You can control the display's position, size, and opacity, or the Timecode display as well as its format and source.

Don't Scale a Stabilized Clip First!
With all the analysis, scaling the clip manually can cause problems; after you've performed the stabilization, add a Transform effect so the transformation comes later in the effects chain.

Just the Rolling Shutter
The Rolling Shutter repair effect has been pulled out into its own effect. Simply use the Rolling Shutter Repair filter to tackle only waviness and distortion in any clips.

FIGURE 12.15 In most cases, you can just click OK because the settings of the adjustment layer will match the sequence you currently have open.

Let's try using an adjustment layer to apply the effect to an entire sequence.

1. Open the sequence 02_Timecode in the file 12_effects.pproj.

2. In the Project panel, click the New Item button, and choose Adjustment Layer.

3. A new dialog opens to modify the size, timebase, and pixel aspect ratio for the adjustment layer (**FIGURE 12.15**). The default settings match the current sequence automatically, so click OK.

   A new adjustment layer is added into the same bin as the sequence.

4. Rename the adjustment layer to Timecode, in case you want to use it again in another sequence.

5. Drag the adjustment layer to track V2 and trim it so it fits the duration of the sequence (**FIGURE 12.16**).

FIGURE 12.16 You can use the trim tools or commands to adjust the duration of the layer. Be sure to not use the Rate Stretch tool, however, because adjustment layers do have a timebase.

Starting Timecode
If you want to modify the starting timecode for a sequence, just click the Timeline panel menu (in the upper-right corner) and choose Start Time.

Fixed Effects and Adjustment Layers
If you want to adjsut the Fixed effects for a clip such as Motion (Potion, Scale, Rotation) or Opacity, adjustment layers won't work. In this case, the Fixed effects would modify the adjustment layer itself and not the clips below. If you need to adjust several clips at once (such as a picture in picture effect), try using the Clip > Nest command that you learned in Chapter 7.

6. In the Effects browser, locate the Timecode effect (Video Effects > Video) and drag it on to the adjustment layer.

7. Choose a timecode source.

   In this case, the Generate option is best so you can create a timecode that matches the sequence timecode (which in this case starts at 1:00:00:00).

8. Enter a starting timecode of **01:00:00:00** into the Starting Timecode field.

9. Adjust the Position, Opacity, and Size settings for the effect (**FIGURE 12.17**).

   It's a good idea to move the timecode window so it is not blocking critical action in the scene or obscuring any graphics.

10. Leave the Field Symbol check box marked to show whether the footage is progressive or to show which field is displayed.

11. Choose a format to display. SMPTE timecode is the standard, but you can also show frame numbers or feet and frames for 35mm or 16mm film.

12. Choose the Time Display option for your source. Be sure to match the frame rate of your footage.

FIGURE 12.17 If you'll be posting to the Web, be sure to increase the size of the burn-in so it's more readable when the video is shrunk down.

Got Several Angles?
If you're using multiple angles, be sure to use the Label Text option in the Timecode effect. You can identify the camera angle for multicamera shoots for Camera 1 through Camera 9.

What's My Key?
By switching the Output menu to Alpha Channel, you can easily see any problem areas with the matte. Look for areas with lots of specks in them or gray patches to indicate rough transparency spots. Just switch back to Composite when you're finished cleaning up.

Vector Keying in Adobe Premiere Pro

After Effects gets a lot of attention for its compositing abilities, but you'll find a very good keyer in Adobe Premiere Pro. The Ultra Key effect is a GPU-accelerated chromakey effect. You can use it as a placeholder key when working out the timing of effects. You can also use it as a final key in many situations right inside the editing Timeline. Ultra is particularly effective when keying heavily compressed footage such as DV, HDV, and H.264.

1. Select the first clip in your Adobe Premiere Pro sequence that you want to key. This clip should usually fall on V2 or higher in the Timeline.

   For this exercise, you can use the sequence 03_Keying in the file 12_effects.pproj.

2. Apply the Ultra Key effect to the clip on V2.

3. In the Timeline, move the playhead over a frame that contains the color you'd like to key.

4. Double-click the keyed clip and switch to the Effect Controls panel. You can now control the effect with the Output and Setting menus.

5. Click the eyedropper and select a key color (**FIGURE 12.18**).

6. Click the Output menu and change it to Alpha Channel to view the grayscale matte that is generating the transparency.

   Black is transparent while white areas are opaque. Shades of gray equal partial transparency.

FIGURE 12.18 Be sure to select an area close to the subject you are trying to key to ensure a cleaner key along the edges.

Pedestal Down
The higher the quality of your source image, the lower you can set the Pedestal value in the Ultra Keyer. Use Pedestal to filter out noise in the image, but be sure to not overdo it.

A Better Composite
You can use the Color Correction properties in the Ultra Keyer to create a better balance between the foreground and background images. Use the Hue, Saturation, and Luminance sliders to match color and luma values for a more realistic effect.

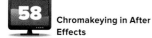 **Chromakeying in After Effects**
You'll find an award-winning keying plug-in called Keylight in After Effects. The effect performs a color key and removes any color spill. Learn how to use it in this video tutorial.

7. You can tweak several other parameters. Twirl down all of the categories to see your control properties. The following are the most essential to get a good key:

- **Transparency.** The default value is 45, but subtle tweaks can affect the transparency of the source layer over the background.

- **Highlight.** The Highlight transparency can also be controlled separately. This is useful for areas that contain specular highlights (such as transparent objects like glass). The default value is 50.

- **Shadow.** You can use the Shadow control to correct any dark areas that have become inadvertently transparent because of color spill. The default value is 50.0 (which does not affect the image).

- **Tolerance.** To remove keying artifacts or spill with skin tones and shadows, adjust the Tolerance property.

- **Choke.** The Choke property shrinks the alpha channel matte by eroding its edges. The default value is zero, and you can increase in small amounts as needed.

- **Soften.** You can blur the edge of the matte with a Box Blur filter. The default value is 0. A little goes a long way here.

- **Contrast.** After blurring the matte, you can actually restore additional contrast into the edge. This two-step combo can help remove artifacts while still preserving some crispness to the edge (**FIGURE 12.19**).

- **Spill Suppression.** Although multiple properties to remove color spill in the image are available, the most useful are Spill and Range. Make small adjustments at a time as needed.

8. Toggle the Output menu back to a Composite view. Adjust the properties as needed.

   It's also a good idea to make sure the Set Playback Resolution menu is set to full for best results. To accurately see the key, change the Select Zoom Level to 100%. You can then use the Hand tool to pan around the image or temporarily maximize the window by placing the mouse pointer over it and pressing the grave (`) key.

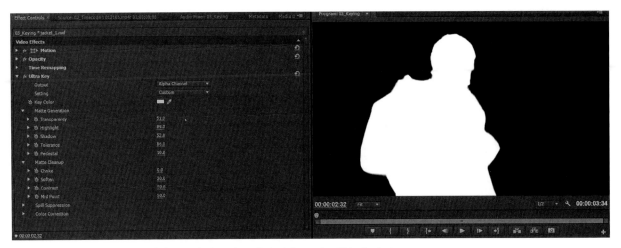

FIGURE 12.19 Keying is a gentle balance of crisp edges that retain a natural blur for fast movement. Be sure to drag through the clip and evaluate several frames.

9. Play the clip at this high-quality, 100 percent view and decide whether the key is good (**FIGURE 12.20**). If needed, adjust the settings you previously learned about.

FIGURE 12.20 The most accurate way to see a key is to view it at full-quality and 100 percent zoom level. If needed, you can render the effect for the ultimate confidence.

Camera Lens Blur Effect

It seems these days that everyone loves bokeh blur. Perhaps it's the DSLR revolution or the rise in popularity of cameras from manufacturers like RED and ARRI. Large sensors and shallow depth of field is hot, but of course images aren't always shot this way.

Fortunately, After Effects lets you create realistic camera blurring that adds subtle highlights and natural blurring. This effect can be used on its own or combined with the Roto Brush for enhanced depth of field with interviews (more on that in the next section).

Let's send a clip from Adobe Premiere Pro to After Effects to adjust its blurring.

What About Lens Blur?
The Camera Lens Blur effect replaces the very slow Lens Blur effect. The new effect works in 32-bits-per-channel space and is much faster than the original. The old Lens Blur effect has been deprecated but will be used when opening legacy (CS5 and earlier) projects.

1. Select the first clip in your Adobe Premiere Pro sequence that you want to blur.

   For this exercise, you can use the sequence 04_Lens Blur in the file 12_effects.pproj.

2. Right-click the shot you want to fix, and choose Replace with After Effects composition.

   Send the shot to After Effects via Dynamic Link, as you learned earlier in this chapter.

3. Switch to After Effects, and select the clip you want to blur in the corresponding composition you created with Dynamic Link.

4. Choose Effect > Blur > Camera Lens Blur.

5. Adjust the following properties to get the desired blurring (**FIGURE 12.21**):

FIGURE 12.21 The Camera Lens Blur effect is a great way to stylize background plates from chroma key effects. You can also animate the blur as a rack focus.

Blur Map in Action
To see how you can use a blur map, open the file 12_Blur_Map.aep in the Lesson 12 folder.

- **Blur Radius.** Use the radius to control the size of the blur.

- **Iris Properties.** Use this property to control the shape of the blur, which is especially visible when you push the blur to create a Bokeh effect, because this is the shape of the actual "blobs" that are created. Additionally, the Roundness property can soften the shapes, and the Aspect Ratio can stretch them. You can also use the Diffraction Fringe to create a halo that shows light wrapping.

- **Blur Map.** A blur map can be used to set a layer to signify the depth of field (**FIGURE 12.22**); you'll explore this option in a separate movie. By using a gradient layer, you can create a gradual falloff. This layer can also be created using Adobe Photoshop. Place the layer below the footage in your composition, and select it using the Layer menu. You can set the Blur Focal Distance to control where pixels are in focus. You can also invert the layer to reverse its direction.

FIGURE 12.22 The original footage (top left) is mapped using a grayscale blur map (top right). The end result shows greater control over depth-of-field blurring (bottom).

- **Highlight.** You can add specular highlights as needed to the bright areas of the footage. Increase the Gain to boost the brightness. To set which areas bloom, lower the Threshold value. You can also use Saturation to boost the original colors in the shot.

- **Edge Behavior.** Be sure to select the Repeat Edge Pixels check box so you don't see a gap around the outside edges.

- **Use Linear Working Space.** This option forces the effect so it behaves as if the project was using a linearized workspace. This increases the realistic properties of the effect.

Enhanced Depth of Field (with the Roto Brush)

In many situations, the background of an interview can be distracting. It might be too bright or too in focus. It might also be an unwanted person walking through the scene or perhaps an ill-placed C-stand. Traditionally, these sorts of problems could be solved with *rotoscoping*—a challenging process of separating a foreground object from the background using animated masks or brush strokes.

Adobe changed the task forever with the invention of the Roto Brush. The Roto Brush requires only a few strokes; thereafter, the tool can calculate transparency. You merely need to indicate to After Effects the foreground and background. After Effects can then intelligently propagate your strokes throughout the entire clip.

Best Blur Possible
To get the highest-quality blurs (especially Bokeh highlights), be sure to set your project to 32 bpc and use a linear workspace.

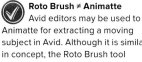

Behold the Roto Brush
For a detailed workflow showing the Roto Brush, be sure to watch this video tutorial.

Roto Brush ≠ Animatte
Avid editors may be used to Animatte for extracting a moving subject in Avid. Although it is similar in concept, the Roto Brush tool requires much less work. Thanks to edge detection and the ability to track motion, you'll find jobs go much quicker with the Roto Brush tool.

Don't Skimp When Using Roto Brush

Your layers must be in Full Quality mode for After Effects to make accurate strokes.

Dial It In

As you refine your strokes for the Roto Brush, switch to a smaller brush.

FIGURE 12.23 Make sure that your subject is clearly in the frame with as little cut off by the edges as possible. Footage courtesy of the National Foundation for Credit Counseling (www.DebtAdvice.org).

For this exercise, you can use the sequence 05 Roto Brush and send the two clips to After Effects. You can also use the project 12_Roto in the Lesson 12 folder. The Roto Brush is a multifaceted tool with several options. Here are a few suggestions for an efficient workflow:

1. **Find a good frame.** Double-click a clip to open the layer. Drag the current-time indicator so you can see that the desired subject is fully in the frame. Try to minimize overlap (**FIGURE 12.23**). This frame is called the *base frame*. This frame should represent the primary subject well so After Effects can detect all of the edges it needs to extract.

2. **Add your first stroke.** Activate the Roto Brush tool (its icon is a paintbrush and person silhouette in the Tools panel). You can also press Option+W (Alt+W). Drag down the center of the object to create the first stroke (**FIGURE 12.24**). When you release the mouse, After Effects takes a moment to update the first stroke. A magenta outline appears to signify the foreground object (**FIGURE 12.25**).

FIGURE 12.24 Use a large brush to quickly paint the initial stroke.

FIGURE 12.25 The Roto Brush typically produces a fairly accurate edge on the first try.

FIGURE 12.26 Red strokes define the area to be subtracted.

FIGURE 12.27 Take the time to get a good edge. You'll further refine it with the Refine Matte properties in a moment.

3. **Add a background stroke.** Define the background to let Adobe After Effects know what information to discard. You can Option-drag (Alt-drag) to create a background stroke (**FIGURE 12.26**).

4. **Add more strokes.** Keep drawing foreground and background strokes until an accurate selection is made. Try to make the segmentation on the base frame as accurate as possible. It serves as a guide for all the other frames, so getting it right is important (**FIGURE 12.27**). Try to use as few strokes as possible to reduce render time.

5. **Fix more frames.** Press the Page Down key to move forward a frame (you can also use the 1 and 2 keys on the main keyboard to go backward or forward a frame). After Effects will keep building the Roto Brush effect using motion tracking, optical flow, and other techniques to propagate the information between frames. As needed, use more strokes to refine the matte as you move through time. Try moving in smaller amounts (like 5 or 10 frames) to check the progress along the way and calculate the new strokes.

6. **Define the range.** The Roto Brush effect is applied for only part of the clip (20 frames forward and 20 frames backward). This is indicated by small arrows that appear in the span bar. As you add more corrective strokes, the effect's duration expands. You can also drag the range in the span bar to increase it (**FIGURE 12.28**).

Freeze It
In the Layer panel, when viewing the Roto Brush tool, you'll find a Freeze button. This can cache and lock the Roto Brush for the work area, which will preserve the matte and save it with the project. This prevents the effect from recalculating the segmentation when you open the project again or make changes to the layer. You'll see a blue bar in the span view, which indicates frozen (cached and locked) frames. To unfreeze Roto Brush segmentation, click the Freeze button again.

Cut the Chatter
The Reduce Chatter option can minimize erratic changes from frame to frame. A higher value includes more frames in the calculation of edges.

7. **Adjust Propagation.** Twirl down the Propogation category and experiment with the options. Adjusting the Search Radius, Motion Threshold, and Edge Detection options can really help build a more consistent track to the edges.

8. **Refine the matte.** The Roto Brush effect offers a Refine Matte option (**FIGURE 12.29**). You can have After Effects compensate for motion blur (for faster-moving objects) as well as decontaminate colors at the edges. Press Option+5 (Alt+5) to toggle the alpha boundary and view your results.

FIGURE 12.28 By default, the Roto Brush effect lasts for only 40 frames. Be sure to define the proper range for your shot. You may need to create new spans for parts of the clip that are significantly different.

FIGURE 12.29 Adjusting properties like Smooth, Feather, and Refine Matte can clean up your edges. Viewing the frame over the transparency grid can make it easier to see your edges. (Just click the Toggle Transparency Grid button at the bottom of the viewer.)

Tracking Cameras

Learn how to track cameras in After Effects CS6 for a variety of effects.

When you're finished with the Roto Brush, click the Freeze button in the Layer panel. You can then click the tab to switch back to your desired composition. There are several things you can do with the extracted clip. You can place the clip over a new background or into a graphic sequence. You might also want to modify the original background by desaturating or blurring it to give more precedence to the subject (**FIGURE 12.30**). The Roto Brush is memory intensive, so you'll likely need to render your Dynamically Linked comps in Adobe Premiere Pro for smooth playback.

FIGURE 12.30 The left image shows the original footage, whereas the right has been further processed. The background was further darkened and defocused to minimize distraction from the subject.

Next Steps

Now that you understand how to use keyframes and effects, you're ready to continue the finishing process. In the next chapter, you'll explore the titling process. You'll learn how to use Adobe Premiere Pro, After Effects, and Photoshop to create lower-thirds and animated titles.

CHAPTER 13

Creating Titles

BECAUSE VIDEO PROJECTS benefit from both sound and picture, it may seem strange that you'll still depend on text. Video editors and motion graphics designers frequently need to use text on-screen to quickly convey important information. The text might offer the viewer important facts about who is speaking (through a lower-third graphic) or acknowledge the creative team behind a project (through end credits). The truth is that there's just no getting around the use of type.

Unfortunately, video professionals often lack formal training in typographic design. Making matters worse, there are often styles or presets in the titling tools that do more to distract the viewer than enhance comprehension. With this in mind, let's explore a foundation for typographic decisions so you can make the right choices in Adobe Premiere Pro and throughout the Adobe Creative Suite.

Further Reading on Type
A great book to truly understand type is the oddly named *Stop Stealing Sheep & Find Out How Type Works* (Adobe Press, 2002) by Erik Spiekermann and E. M. Ginger.

Missing Templates
The title templates (as well as several CS6 demo projects) are not part of the default installers. Be sure to visit http://bit.ly/cs6content to get access to several assets that improve the Adobe Premiere Pro Titler as well as After Effects and Encore.

Video Typography Essentials

Proper use of type is crucial in designing effective graphics for video. Often, the text you create will be composited over moving footage, which can make it even more difficult to read. As you design type for video, it is necessary to balance legibility with style, fitting enough information on the screen but not crowding it. If you can combine this functional purpose with a better sense of style and control, you can improve the professional appearance of your designs.

Font Choice

Selecting the right font can be a tough choice (**FIGURE 13.1**) (of course it might already be made for you by an art director, producer, or client). Chances are your computer has hundreds if not thousands of fonts. You can easily become overwhelmed with the sheer quantity of options. To simplify the process, you need to approach this decision with a triage mentality and consider a few guiding questions.

- **Readability.** Is the font easy to read at the point size you are using? Are all the characters in the line readable? If you look at it quickly and then close your eyes, what do you remember about the text block?

- **Style.** Does the font convey the right emotion for your video? Type is like a wardrobe; picking the right font is essential to the success of the design.

- **Flexibility.** Does the font mix well with others? Does it come in various weights (such as bold, italic, and semibold) that make it easier to convey significance when using that font?

FIGURE 13.1 Although the font choice on the left certainly says American Southwest, it does not capture the same emotional sensitivity as the choice on the right. Always take the time to explore several options when choosing a font family.

How you answer the questions for each of the three guiding principles will steer you toward good design. It's also a good idea to work with your clients, producer, or art director. Instead of scrolling through a list of fonts for hours, interview your clients about the style and mood they want to evoke. If they suggest a boring font, direct them toward an alternative that looks similar but may be better optimized for video.

Serifs

When it comes time to classify fonts, there are two major distinctions: serif or sans serif (FIGURE 13.2). Serifs are the hooks that distinguish the details of letter shape. Sans serif fonts tend to be more uniform in shape.

Serif

FIGURE 13.2 The small hooks on a typeface are referred to as *serifs*. The presence or lack of serifs is a major distinguishing property when classifying fonts.

vs.

Sans Serif

For instant clarity, the shape of individual letters in serif fonts tends to be easier to distinguish. Many clients prefer serif fonts because they are more traditional. Often, there are more serif fonts to choose from because serif type has a long history. Serif fonts are modeled after many handwritten texts as well as the initial type used in printing presses.

A potential drawback, however, is that serif fonts can shimmer or vibrate on-screen because they often come to thin or small points. As an alternative, consider sans serif fonts, which can have a cleaner style and are composed of generally even-weighted lines.

Color Choice

Making the right text color choice can be surprisingly tricky. The truth is that typically only a few colors work well for text and remain clear to the viewer. The task is made difficult because you need to constrain color choice to meet broadcast standards and because text is often laid over a busy moving background (FIGURE 13.3).

Finding Fonts Online
Here are a few of our favorite Web sites that offer free and affordable fonts:

- **Chank**
  www.chank.com
- **Fonthead**
  www.fonthead.com
- **DincType**
  www.GirlsWhoWearGlasses.com
- **Fontalicious**
  www.fontalicious.com
- **Blue Vinyl**
  www.bvfonts.com
- **Acid Fonts**
  www.AcidFonts.com

Font Overload
If you have too many fonts loaded, it can make it difficult to find the right font. It also can lead to serious performance issues, such as an unstable operating system and slow launch times. Consider using a font manager to group fonts into sets for clients as well as activate and deactivate fonts on the fly (without having to relaunch a program).

FIGURE 13.3 The use of a contrasting edge makes it easier to read text when laid over moving video.

Although it may seem a little boring, the most common color for text in video is white. Not surprisingly, the second most popular color is black. If a color is used, it tends to be in very light or very dark shades. Lighter colors that work well include light blue, yellow, gray, and tan. Darker colors that hold up include navy and forest green. Remember to keep your text toward the very dark or very light range, or contrast will become an issue when the text is placed over a motion background.

Kerning

As you work with text, you'll often need to modify the space between letters. Adjusting the space between individual letter pairs is called *kerning* and is typically adjusted one pair at a time (**FIGURE 13.4**). Why all the fuss? Well, design pros *always* check their kerning, because kerning the space between letter pairs produces a better optical flow, which can greatly improve the appearance and readability of your text. Knowing how to kern is often best learned by studying examples of professionally laid out text.

In Adobe Premiere Pro and other Adobe applications, kerning is simple to adjust.

1. Click inside the text block to place your cursor or move it using the arrow keys.

2. When the blinking I-bar is between the two letters you want to kern, hold down the Option (Alt) key.

3. Press the left arrow key to pull the letters closer or the right arrow key to push them farther apart.

4. Move to the next letter pair and adjust as needed.

Tracking

Similar to kerning is *tracking*, which is the overall space between all letters in a line of text (**FIGURE 13.5**). You can use tracking as a way to condense or expand a block of text so it better fits the on-screen space (after all, you can't scroll a video monitor to read more). You might choose a loose track to improve readability (especially if you're using all caps or need to apply a stroked border). Tracking is typically done in the Title Properties panel in Adobe Premiere Pro or the Character panel in other Adobe applications. Tracking, like kerning, is subjective, and you can learn best how to do it by studying professional examples and looking for inspiration and guidance.

Diplomat
improper kerning

Diplomat
proper kerning

FIGURE 13.4 The top line of text has irregular gaps between letters, which creates a challenge when reading the line.

t r a c k i n g
loose tracking

tracking
tight tracking

FIGURE 13.5 The top line is too loosely tracked, whereas the bottom line is too tight. Be sure to experiment with tracking when you need to fill in space on the screen or to make stroke text more readable.

Leading

Another property you'll frequently adjust is *leading* to better fit your text. Pronounced *led*-ing as in the metal, not *lead*-ing as in sheep, leading is the space between lines of type. The name is derived from when strips of lead were used on a printing press to space out lines of text (**FIGURE 13.6**).

By default, the leading should be set to Auto; however, you can adjust as needed to fit text into your design. If you need to fit more text on the screen, you'll tighten the leading to produce less space between lines of text. Be careful to avoid setting the leading too tight; otherwise, descenders from the top line will cross ascenders from the lower line. This collision will likely result in a negative impact on readability.

FIGURE 13.6 The left image has too much leading and creates an unwanted visual break between the two lines. The right image has tighter leading, but care was taken to avoid a collision between the ascenders and descenders.

Alignment

When it comes to video, there are no hard and fast rules for alignment. As a general practice, however, lower-thirds tend to be left or right justified (which leaves room for a logo or bug on the opposite side). Centered or force-justified text is more commonly used for titles or bumpers.

You'll find alignment buttons within the type interfaces of Adobe software (**FIGURE 13.7**). The Alignment buttons attempt to align text left, right, or centered. They also add support for justification, which forces the text to align to both margins through the adjustment of spaces between words.

Point Text vs. Paragraph Text
When setting text in an Adobe application, you often don't just want to click and type (called Point text). Instead, you can click and drag using the Type tool to define the paragraph area first. This is called Paragraph text and offers greater control over alignment and layout.

FIGURE 13.7 The alignment controls in Adobe Premiere Pro, After Effects, and Photoshop are all quite similar in appearance and function.

When using text for video, it's very common to use type that is too small. Because video seems to have two distinct paths these days—traditional and Web—we've developed two quick tests that check for readability.

- **Traditional.** When we build graphics for the television screen, we'll often stand up and step back a few feet from the monitor to view our work. This is because TV viewers rarely sit 3 feet from the screen.

- **Web.** Video on the Web has a different set of problems. The two biggest issues you'll face are playback size and data rate. Most Web video is played back with a width of 320 or 640 pixels. This means that up to 83 percent of your information is being discarded (1920 vs. 360 pixels). Additionally, most Web video is compressed to a significantly smaller data rate. We recommend staying in your desk chair but reducing the playback window to 50 percent (or even 25 percent) magnification. You can also change the resolution of the Program Monitor to quarter or half quality.

Safe Title Area

When you're designing text in an Adobe application, there's almost always the option to turn on guides for the safe title area. In Adobe Premiere Pro and After Effects, you'll find these guides built into most windows, while in Photoshop they appear as guides in the video-ready preset documents (**FIGURE 13.8**).

Essentially you have a series of two nested boxes. The first box shows you 90 percent of the viewable area, which is considered the action-safe margin. Things that fall outside of this box may get cut off when the video signal is viewed on a television set. Be sure to place all critical elements that are meant to be seen (like a logo) inside this region.

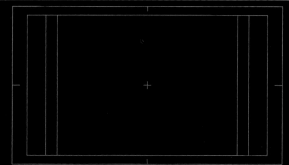

FIGURE 13.8 Clockwise, the safe title margin in Adobe Premiere Pro, the title/action-safe overlay in After Effects, and the preset guides on a Photoshop document created using a video preset.

The second box, which is 80 percent of the viewable area, is called the *tile-safe title margin*. Just as this book you're reading has margins to keep the text from getting too close to the edge, it's a good idea to keep text inside the innermost or title-safe margin. This will make it easier for your audience to read the information.

Using the Titler in Adobe Premiere Pro

Many editors are most comfortable using the built-in titler that's included with their nonlinear editor. Two primary benefits drive this workflow. First, they never need to leave the editing application (reducing new apps to learn, which saves time). Second, they don't want to have to track and manage referenced files and prefer that their titles simply become part of their project file.

The good news is that the Titler in Adobe Premiere Pro (**FIGURE 13.9**) is more robust than those found in other editing applications. It offers precise control over text, layout, and style, which is to be expected given Adobe's long history with computer typography.

- **Title Tools panel.** These tools define the boundaries for text, set text paths, and create geometric shapes.

- **Title Designer panel.** This is where you build and view text and graphics.

- **Title Properties panel.** Here you can adjust options for text and graphic such as font characteristics and effects.

- **Title Actions panel.** Use these to align, center, or distribute text and groups of objects.

- **Title Styles panel.** This panel contains several preset text styles. You can choose from several libraries of styles as well.

> **A Bigger View for the Titler**
> You may have to expand the window to see all the Titler's panels.

> **Restrain Yourself**
> The Titler features several title styles that are overdone and are in fact garish. Unless you're cutting a slasher movie or an over-the-top infomercial, remember to take it easy on the glows, bevels, and gradient fills (these went out of style in the early 1990s).

FIGURE 13.9 The Titler in Adobe Premiere Pro offers advanced options such as shapes, custom fills, and drawing tools. You can also align, rotate, and distribute shapes for precise alignments. Here's a quick rundown on the Titler's panels:

A Title Tools panel
B Title Designer panel
C Title Properties panel
D Title Actions panel
E Title Styles panel

Rearrange the Titler
You can drag the panels in the Titler into a new position or close them if they are unwanted. You can dock a panel to another or to other parts of the interface. The purple highlight indicates where the panel will dock. By rearranging your panels, you can create a more useful workspace that matches your need and screen layout.

Safely Save Those Titles
If you want to capture changes to a title as you design, just save your project to save the title. Titles are automatically stored in the data of your project file.

Use a Title in Another Project
If you want to make a title available for use in another project, select the title in the Project panel. Then choose File > Export > Title, give your title a name, choose a location, and click Save. You can then import that title file the same way you would import any other asset.

Creating and Editing Titles

The Titler in Adobe Premiere Pro is a collection of related panels that are all associated with the tasks of creating text and basic graphical shapes. You can use the Titler to create static as well as animated titles. All titles you create are added to the Project panel. To keep your project clean and easy to navigate, we recommend using bins to hold and organize your titles by style and subject.

To create a new title, do the following:

1. Place your playhead in the Timeline panel over a frame of video that you want to design for.

    For this exercise, you can use the sequence 01 Planes in 13_titles.prproj.

2. Choose Title > New Title > Default Still.

    Alternately, you can click the New Item button in the Project panel and choose Title. The New Title window opens.

3. Confirm that the title's width, height, timebase, and pixel aspect ratio match your needs. By default, these settings are autofilled with your current sequence's settings.

4. Enter a descriptive name for the title, and click OK.

    Titles do not need to have a unique name because no actual files are created on your drive. But sticking with a unique name is still a good idea for practical project management.

5. Design your title using the Text and Shape tools.

    We provide a detailed overview on using these tools in video #61.

6. Close the Titler when you are finished to save the current title.

7. Edit the title into the Timeline, and place it above the desired clips (**FIGURE 13.10**).

FIGURE 13.10 Place the new title above the video clips you'd like it to be superimposed over.

8. If needed, press Return (Enter) to render the effects in the Timeline panel (the video footage has the Warp Stabilizer and Three-Way Color Corrector applied).

9. If you need to make changes to a title after you've closed it, double-click it in the Project or Timeline panel. Titles automatically load in the Titler, not the Source Monitor.

Entering Text

When adding text to a title, you can use any font loaded on your system, including Type 1 (PostScript), OpenType, and TrueType fonts. Make sure the font is loaded before you launch Adobe Premiere Pro for maximum compatibility and application stability.

The Titler offers three styles of Type tools with a vertical and horizontal option for each.

- **Type tool and Vertical Type tool.** Use these tools to create Point text. Text emanates from the point at which you click in the window. You can choose to align the text to the left or right of the insertion point, or even center it. Typing places all characters on a single line (until you press Return [Enter]) unless you enable the Word Wrap option (Title > Word Wrap). Word Wrap moves characters to a new line when it reaches the edge of the title-safe area.

- **Area Type tool and Vertical Area Type tool.** Use these tools to create a text box for Paragraph text. This approach lets you define a box that controls when text automatically wraps. Area type offers more precise control over text wrapping than any other method.

- **Path Type tool and Vertical Path Type tool.** Use these tools when you need to create text along a curved path. Click to define where you want text to start, and then click to add additional points (you can click and drag to adjust the shape of the curve). When the shape is how you want it, start typing to add text along the path.

Formatting Text

The Titler offers precise controls to format text. These controls are all easy to use and interactive, so you can see your updates right in the Titler window as you make tweaks (**FIGURE 13.11**). Here's where to find the essential controls:

- **Titler panel.** In this panel you'll find controls for font, font style, and type alignment above the drawing area. You can also adjust tracking and leading in the bar. The bar was designed for quick access to key controls.

- **Title Properties panel.** All of the formatting controls in the Titler panel are repeated in this panel (along with advanced controls). You'll also find several more controls, including style options such as Fill, Stroke, and Drop Shadow.

The Titler in Adobe Premiere Pro
Learn how to create custom titles quickly as well as use good typographic design in this video tutorial.

Avoid Spelling Errors
Always insist on getting an approved graphic list from the client or producer that has been proofed. Also, we strongly recommend copying and pasting the text from an e-mail or word processor document to reduce the likelihood of spelling errors caused from rushing through data entry.

A Different Kind of Drag
If you drag the corner handle of a Point text object, the text scales larger or smaller. Dragging the corner of a text box reflows the text inside.

Need More Space?
It's possible when working with text to have more characters than room on-screen. If a text box is too small, you can resize it to reveal the hidden text. Look for a plus sign (+) on the right side of the box, which indicates the box contains hidden characters.

No Auto Wrap
If you were to continue typing a long title, you'd notice that point text does not wrap automatically. This will cause your text to run off the screen to the right. To make text wrap automatically when it reaches the title-safe margin, choose Title > Word Wrap. If you want to force a new line to start, press Return (Enter).

FIGURE 13.11 You can use the Titler and Title Properties panels to format text inside a title.

Stylizing a Title

Several options are available for stylizing your text with the Titler in Adobe Premiere Pro. In fact, the controls are quite extensive (so it's easy to overdesign and end up with text that is hard to read). Design for the current decade and leave the thick bevels, rainbow gradients, and giant glows back in the 1990s (**FIGURE 13.12**).

FIGURE 13.12 You can use the Title Styles panel to quickly format text with presets. You can then modify the results using the Title Properties panel.

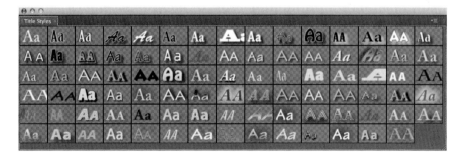

What's That Exclamation Point?

If you see an exclamation point next to the color you've chosen, that's the Adobe Premiere Pro way of warning you that a color is not broadcast-safe. Just click the exclamation point to choose the closest color that is still safe.

Here are some of the most useful tools for modern typographic design:

- **Fill Type.** You have several choices of fill type, but the most useful are Solid and Linear Gradient (just use a subtle gradient, though).

- **Color.** Set the color for your text. You can click the swatch or enter numerical values in the Adobe Color Picker, or you can use the Eyedropper tool to sample from your video clip. Most editors favor white, gray, black, light yellow, or light blue.

- **Sheen.** A gentle highlight can add depth to your title. Be sure to adjust the size and opacity so the effect is subtle.

- **Stroke.** You can click to add an inner stroke and an outer stroke. Strokes can be solid or gradient. Adjust the opacity of a gradient to create a gentle glow or soft edge. A stroke is commonly used to help keep text legible over a video or complex background.

- **Shadow.** The use of a drop shadow is a common addition to video text because it makes the text easier to read. Be sure to adjust the softness of the shadow. Also, be sure to keep the angle of shadows identical for all titles in a project for design consistency.

 Choose a Color from Your Video
Instead of using the Color Picker to change the color-stop color, you can use the Eyedropper tool (located next to the color swatch) to select a color from your video. Click the Show Video button at the top of the Titler panel, move to a frame you want to use by scrubbing the timecode numbers left or right, select the Eyedropper tool into your video scene, and click a color that suits your needs.

CUSTOM TITLE STYLES

To speed up your workflow, you can store a combination of color properties and font characteristics as a style. Styles are shown as descriptive thumbnails in the Title Styles panel. You can use a style by just clicking its thumbnail. All the properties of the text update to match the preset.

To create a style, follow these steps:

1. Select a text block or object that has the properties applied you want to save.

2. In the Title Styles panel menu, choose New Style.

3. Enter a descriptive name, and click OK. The style is added to the Title Styles panel.

4. To view styles more easily, you can click the Title Styles submenu and choose to view the presets as Text Only, Small Thumbnails, or Large Thumbnails.

5. To manage a style, right-click its thumbnail. You can choose to duplicate a style to modify a copy, rename a style so it's easier to find, or delete a style if you want to remove it.

To create a style library, follow these steps:

By default, a style library with 89 title styles loads with the Titler. Many of these do an excellent job of showing what the Titler can do but in truth are not very practical (lime green text and the Hobo font won't win you any design awards). To make the Title Styles panel more useful, we suggest creating your own style library.

1. All styles visible in the panel are stored in the library. Be sure to delete any you don't want to store by right-clicking and choosing Delete Style.

2. To save a style library, choose Save Style Library from the Title Styles panel submenu.

3. In the new window, give the style library a descriptive name, and click OK. Adobe Premiere Pro chooses the correct location and saves style library files with the extension .purls.

In the future, you can click the Title Styles panel submenu to load additional styles to the already loaded styles by using the Append Style Library option. You can also remove the loaded styles and see only the newly loaded ones by using the Replace Style Library option.

You can find additional title styles for download online. You can also save your own and move them from computer to computer by copying the library files. If you want to load additional style libraries, copy them into your presets folder for easier access. Custom styles are stored in the following locations:

- **Mac OS.** Documents/Adobe/Premiere Pro/[version]/Styles

- **Windows.** My Documents/Adobe/Premiere Pro/[version]/Styles

Looking for More Titler Presets?

For a free collection of Titler presets, browse to www.stevengotz.com/templates. You can download these presets and then load them into the Title Styles panel. You'll also find a useful collection in the Lesson 13 folder on the DVD or digital downloads for this book.

Reuse a Title

If you need to create a new version of a title, make sure you create a new version (otherwise, every version in use will be updated in your project). Open the title you want to use as a starting point, and then choose Title > New Title > Based on Current Title.

Vector to Raster

If you place a vector graphic into a title, Adobe Premiere Pro converts it into a bitmap graphic. The image will appear at its original size. You can scale it smaller; if you make it larger, the image may become pixelated.

Change Your Workspace

If you need to do a lot of type, consider changing to the Typography workspace using the Workspace Switcher in the upper-right corner.

 Creating Rolls and Crawls

In this video you'll learn how to create rolling credits in Adobe Premiere Pro. You'll also discover how to make stock market–style text crawls for the bottom of the screen.

Creating a Template

Creating good-looking titles takes a bit of time as you try to find the right combination of font, color, size, and position that pleases your client. Wouldn't it be great to store all that hard work and reuse it as many times as needed? Not a problem; you just use templates.

1. With a title open, click the Templates button or press Command+J (Ctrl+J).

2. Click the Templates menu button in the upper-right corner of the panel.

3. Choose Import Current Title As Template.

4. Enter a descriptive name for the template and click OK to store the template.

To use a template in the future, choose Title > New Title > Based on Template (**FIGURE 13.13**).

FIGURE 13.13 By storing your titles as templates, you can build future titles in your show quickly. You'll also find several other starter templates in the Templates panel.

Advanced Titling with Photoshop

Although Adobe Premiere Pro offers a capable titler, many choose to use the digital imaging and graphic design powerhouse that is Adobe Photoshop. Photoshop offers several advanced options including anti-aliasing (for smoother text), advanced formatting such as scientific notation, flexible layer styles, and even a spell checker.

The decision to stay in Adobe Premiere Pro or to use Photoshop is really a matter of workflow. You may be faster in one application, or you may want the flexibility of bringing your Photoshop text into After Effects. We use Photoshop more often than Adobe Premiere Pro for titling, but that's because we frequently receive graphics that are designed by motion graphics artists.

Creating a Photoshop Document

If you'd like to make a new Photoshop title, Adobe Premiere Pro removes all of the mysteries. You don't have to guess which size to create or even which preset to choose. Thanks to your project settings and open sequence, Adobe Premiere Pro can make some very intelligent guesses.

To create a new title from within Adobe Premiere Pro, follow these steps:

1. Choose File > New > Photoshop File.

2. Examine the New Photoshop File window. The Video Settings should be correctly set for your project (**FIGURE 13.14**).

3. Click OK.

4. Choose a location to store your PSD file, and click Save.

   A new title is written to disk and added to your project.

5. Photoshop or Photoshop Extended opens, allowing you to edit the title.

When you're finished in Photoshop, you can close and save the title. It will be automatically updated in the Adobe Premiere Pro project. If you'd like to return to Photoshop, just select a title in the Project panel or Timeline panel and choose Edit > Edit In Adobe Photoshop.

The Path to Consistency If you're working on a show with only one kind of title, make it a default. With a title open, click the Templates button and choose a template you want to use. You can then choose Set Template As Default Still from the Templates panel menu. The default template will load every time you open the Titler.

FIGURE 13.14 The settings in the New Photoshop File panel will automatically match your active sequence.

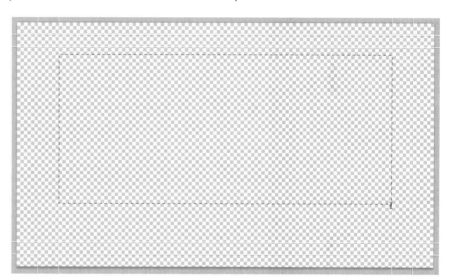

FIGURE 13.15 By using a Paragraph text block, you can precisely control the layout of text in Photoshop.

Photoshop Text Essentials

Much like Adobe Premiere Pro, Photoshop offers both a Horizontal and Vertical Text tool. Similarly, you can click to enter Point text. However, the more useful option is to click and drag with the Text tool to create a Paragraph text block.

1. Select the Text tool by pressing T.

2. Draw a text block, and then click and draw from the left edge of the title-safe area to the right edge (**FIGURE 13.15**). This creates a Paragraph text block to hold the text.

3. Enter the text you'd like to use.

4. Adjust the font and point size to taste.

5. Click the check mark in the Options bar to commit the text layer.

Merged Layers When creating a Photoshop file from within Adobe Premiere Pro, we usually leave the Add to Project (merged layers) option selected. This brings the graphic into the Project panel as a flattened source (with transparency) that will occupy only a single track in the Timeline.

Creating 3D Text in Photoshop Extended In this video you'll learn how to create 3D text designs with Photoshop Extended.

Using the Options bar

The Options bar consists of the most common type controls in an easy-to-access area (**FIGURE 13.16**). When you switch to the Type tool (T), the Options bar automatically displays the most frequently used commands, which can truly speed up your workflow.

FIGURE 13.16 The Options bar provides precise control over text and formatting.

A Tool Presets Picker. Store text presets for quick access. This can include a combination of font, size, alignment, and more.

B Toggle Text Orientation. Switch between horizontal or vertical text alignment.

C Font Family. Choose the font family you want to use.

D Font Style. Choose the weight for the individual font used.

E Font Size. Change the size of the font (measured in points or pixels).

F Anti-Aliasing. Set the anti-alias method to smooth the font's appearance on-screen.

G Alignment. Choose Left, Centered, or Right alignment.

H Text Color. Opens the Adobe Color Picker for the color of the text.

I Warped Text. Allows you to access warping controls for the text.

J Character and Paragraph Panels. Opens the Character and Paragraph panels (docked together) for advanced controls.

Don't Anti-Alias Tiny Text
Very small text (smaller than 16 points) should not be anti-aliased. To improve anti-aliasing on small type, deselect the Fractional Width option in the Character panel menu. This will improve the spacing between letters at small sizes.

Free Transform for Manual Control
If you'd like to freely distort text to the size you need, just select its layer and choose Edit > Free Transform. You can also right-click to access specific transformations when you are in the Free Transform mode.

Using the Character panel

The Character panel provides you with total control over the appearance of text in your graphics. The easiest way to access it is to click the Character and Paragraph panels button in the Options bar, but you can also choose Window > Paragraph.

Many fields are in the Character panel (**FIGURE 13.17**); here are some of the less obvious and most useful choices:

A Vertically and Horizontally Scale. These two fields enable you to stretch your text to force it to fit. Horizontal scaling set at 75 to 95 percent is another useful way to compress a line of text that cannot wrap to another line.

B Type Enhancement buttons. These buttons display modifications that used to be buried in menus. Avoid overusing these effects. Options like Small Caps and All Caps are popular choices to improve the readability of small text. You can also use Subscript and Superscript for scientific notation and positioning special typographic marks like the registered symbol (®).

C Language Selection menu. To harness the power of Photoshop's spell checker, you must set the language on the selected characters. This also drives the automatic hyphenation. To invoke the spell checker, choose Edit > Check Spelling.

D Anti-alias menu. Large font sizes generally benefit from anti-aliasing because it gently blurs the edges of the type, making it appear smoothly composited with the background layers. You'll need to experiment with anti-aliasing because it varies with the fonts chosen and the user's taste. Generally, the None option does not work well, but the other four options can dramatically improve text appearance on-screen.

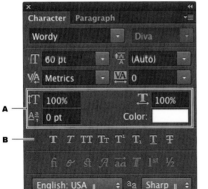

FIGURE 13.17 The Character panel gives you complete control over the individual letters in your text block.

Using the Paragraph panel

The Paragraph panel is generally docked with the Character panel. You can call it up individually or tear it free from the Character panel. The Paragraph panel works on a limited basis for point text. To access full control over type, you must use Paragraph text.

Like the Character panel, many controls are in the Paragraph panel too (FIGURE 13.18); here is a quick overview:

A **Alignment buttons.** You can specify alignment as well as justification. Left justification is the easiest alignment to read.

B **Indent fields.** You can specify how much to indent a particular paragraph or the first line of a paragraph. These controls enable you to have fewer text blocks by giving you better control.

C **Spacing fields.** You can specify how much space you want after each hard return. This enables you to space out paragraphs without needing to insert hard returns.

D **Enable Hyphenation.** To fill more horizontal space, words are often broken across lines at a suitable point within the word. If you want to use this option, select it. Photoshop uses the installed dictionary for the language you specify in the Character panel. This ensures that words are properly hyphenated.

Layer Styles

Photoshop has a number of ways to enhance text with both subtle and dramatic effects (FIGURE 13.19). The three primary advantages of using styles are no render times, easy editability, and portability to After Effects.

> **Better Hyphenation and Line Breaks**
> If you will be using paragraphs or multiple lines of text, be sure to try the Adobe Every-line Composer option. Click the Paragraph panel submenu and choose the correct option.

FIGURE 13.18 Remember the Hyphenate option to fit a large block of text more tightly. The breaks for hyphens are determined by the dictionary chosen with the Language menu in the Character panel.

FIGURE 13.19 The bevel, stroke, drop shadow, and even colors were added using the Adobe Photoshop layer style engine.

To access layer styles, try one of the following:

- Choose Window > Styles to access several presets. Even more presets can be loaded from the panel's submenu.

- Choose Layer > Layer Style and select a particular effect. A new panel opens with precise control over options such as texture, bevel, drop shadow, fill, and glow.

In nearly all cases Adobe Premiere Pro will properly read the native transparency in a Photoshop file. With that said, it's still a good idea to know how to create an alpha channel if you'd like precise control over transparency.

Here's how to create a perfect alpha channel:

1. Make sure all background layers are either discarded or not visible. Place the Photoshop graphic over the transparency background (shown as a light gray checkerboard pattern).

2. Choose Window > Actions. The Actions panel opens. Click the submenu in the panel's upper-right corner and choose Video Actions. Actions automate the process of repeating several commands.

3. Choose Alpha Channel from Visible Layers (the first action in the set), and click the Play button. Read the dialog, and then click Continue. Photoshop creates an alpha channel for you (FIGURE 13.20).

4. If you want more precise control over the Save command, choose File > Save As to store your file. Target a location to store the file. You can overwrite your original file if needed.

5. Choose PSD from the Format menu. Make sure the Layers and Alpha Channels check boxes are both selected, and then click OK. Photoshop's alpha channels are always premultiplied when saving a still image. It will be with white when saving over a transparency grid or whatever color you had loaded in the background.

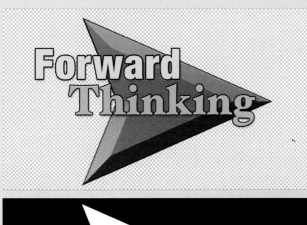

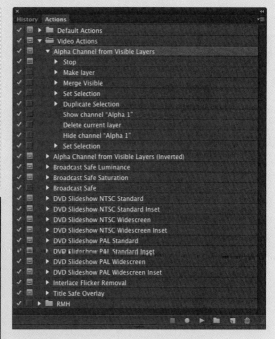

FIGURE 13.20 An alpha channel is an optional step, but it ensures accurate transparency for your Photoshop graphic.

Animated Titles with After Effects

So far we've limited the discussion to using mostly static text in both Adobe Premiere Pro and Photoshop. We find that it's always best to master typographic design before you add the complexity of animation. The truth is that it's a bit too easy to get sucked into text animation presets and go overboard. Of course, that won't stop clients from asking for text animations.

In the Adobe workflow, nothing beats After Effects for animated titles. You'll find a very deep animation engine with 17 different animation properties ranging from Scale and Position to Blur and Skew. We find its controls to be the most exact and varied but also the most difficult to learn.

Setting Text

Fortunately, text controls in After Effects are virtually identical to Photoshop for creating text layers. You can even convert Photoshop text into After Effects text by importing a file and converting it to editable text.

Let's create a new composition from within Adobe Premiere Pro using Adobe Dynamic Link.

1. Choose File > Adobe Dynamic Link > New After Effects Comp.

2. The New After Effects Comp window is automatically filled in with settings that match your project settings (**FIGURE 13.21**).

FIGURE 13.21 The settings loaded for the new After Effects composition will automatically match the current sequence.

A new After Effects composition is added to both your Timeline and Project panels.

3. You are automatically switched to After Effects. Name the project, and click Save.

   Store the project with your Adobe Premiere Pro project file so that your media path structure is easy to preserve. Any additional clips sent to After Effects from your current Adobe Premiere Pro project will automatically join this linked After Effects project.

4. Select the Text tool and click in the After Effects Composition panel to enter text (**FIGURE 13.22**).

Warping Text
Warped text is a cool feature to reserve for special occasions like show titles. The Warped Text command allows you to distort text to a variety of shapes, including Arc, Bulge, Flag, Squeeze, and Twist. Just select a text layer and click the Create Warped Text button (a T above an arc) in the Options bar. Several styles are available in the menu, and you can adjust the options for a more precise effect.

Logos and Bugs
In this quick video you'll learn how to place an Illustrator or EPS file into Photoshop. You can then position and save it as a logo or bug to watermark a video.

Down-Conversion Issues
If you're producing in HD, your show may also be played on an SD television set. After Effects offers a robust title-safe overlay that protects for both 4:3 and 16:9 at the same time.

Animating Text with After Effects
In this video you'll learn how to set up an Adobe After Effects composition and then browse, apply, and customize text animation presets. You'll even learn how to further modify text animations with advanced controls.

FIGURE 13.22 You can click the buttons beneath the composition window to turn on a title-safe grid as well as compensate for non-square pixels. If you are unsure of what a button does, just hover your mouse over it to see a tooltip.

Browsing Presets

To speed up your workflow, After Effects offers nearly 350 built-in animation presets. Experimenting with these presets is a great way to explore what's possible with text in After Effects. Several different options are available to refine text, but it's not that hard to get started.

Want More Presets? You can get several additional animation presets for After Effects by visiting http://adobe.ly/moretext. These are free and created by the talented team behind the original set.

1. Select a text layer in the Timeline panel.

2. Select the Effects & Presets panel (if it's not visible, you can choose it in the Window menu).

3. Click the submenu in the upper-right corner of the Effects & Presets panel, and choose Browse Presets (**FIGURE 13.23**).

   Adobe Bridge launches with the default presets shown.

FIGURE 13.23 To access the Browse command, click the submenu in the upper-right corner of the panel. Most panels in Adobe applications feature a submenu with advanced controls.

4. Select the folder named Text, and double-click to open it. Double-click other sub-folders to audition new animations. Click an FFX file once to see a preview movie in the Preview pane.

5. Press Command+up arrow (Ctrl+up arrow) to go to a higher folder level and browse (**FIGURE 13.24**).

6. Select a preset effect and double-click to apply it to your selected text layer. For this exercise, choose Blurs > Evaporate.

   Adobe Bridge is minimized, and After Effects becomes the active application.

7. Click the RAM Preview button to preview the text animation.

   This animation plays, but depending on where the current-time indicator was positioned, the timings might be off. This can be easily modified.

FIGURE 13.24 Adobe Bridge makes it easy to browse animation options for After Effects. Be sure to download additional animation presets, which are available at http://adobe.ly/aetextpresets.

Retiming Animations

As you work with text animations, you'll often find that they may not be the right duration or need subtle changes. Fortunately, modifying text animation presets is straightforward. You can simply adjust keyframes or make more elaborate changes to additional properties. Let's modify the recently applied animation.

1. Press U to see all your user-added keyframes (**FIGURE 13.25**). Then press J or K to move through keyframes in your composition.

FIGURE 13.25 Keyframes are used to control the timing of After Effects text animation. Spread the frames apart to slow down an animation.

This animation uses two keyframes to define its start and end.

2. Select both keyframes by lassoing around them.

   Drag the first keyframe to the right to approximately 0;00;04;00 to delay the start of the animation.

3. Click in an empty area to deselect your keyframes, and then reselect the second keyframe and drag it to 0;00;08;00 to slow down the animation for dramatic effect (**FIGURE 13.26**).

FIGURE 13.26 Keyframes will snap to the current-time indicator when you hold the Shift key.

A Different Random
Random isn't really random in After Effects, because the effect will repeat the same animation each time it is used. If you want to create a different look when reusing a text animation, simply change the Random Seed number.

66 **Creating 3D Type in After Effects**
Learn how to extrude text for 3D effects in After Effects CS6.

Animator groups include a default Range Selector. This property specifies which characters or section of a text layer are animated. Let's randomize the effect a little more.

4. Click the disclosure triangle next to the Range Selector to close it; then click it again to open it and show all the animation properties. Click the triangle next to Advanced to see all those properties as well.

5. Experiment with the different Advanced properties to see the results. In particular, experiment with the following properties, and click RAM Preview occasionally to view the changes.

   ■ **Randomize Order.** Randomizes the order in which the property is applied to the characters affected by the Range Selector.

   ■ **Random Seed.** Affects the method used to calculate randomness. Try inputting a different value to produce a varied animation.

   ■ **Shape.** Affects the shape used to select characters between the start and end of the range. Choosing different options will result in subtle but significant changes. You can choose Square, Ramp Up, Ramp Down, Triangle, Round, or Smooth.

6. If you're happy with the animation as is, save your After Effects project and return to Adobe Premiere Pro (**FIGURE 13.27**).

FIGURE 13.27 The completed animation is viewable after a RAM preview.

Next Steps

In the next chapter, we begin the process for completing a project. You'll learn important strategies for performing a final quality check. You'll also learn how to prepare a show for broadcast by legalizing your video and audio signals.

CHAPTER 14

Quality Control and Archiving

SO, YOU'VE EDITED your project, mixed it, and color corrected it. You're done, right? Well, not exactly. You'll obviously need to publish the project in some way, whether it's to DVD, Blu-ray Disc, the Web, or even tape (all are discussed in the next chapter).

However, many people miss a step that is vitally important to the success of any project—quality control (QC). The QC process is meant to ensure that your project is technically correct and to eliminate mistakes that can creep in toward the end of a project.

In addition to finalizing a project in this chapter, you'll also tackle media management from a project closeout perspective. You'll find that Adobe Premiere Pro offers a robust Project Manager, which can make consolidating and copying media a snap. Because you'll often need to bundle all the project files for archiving or handing off to another post professional, we think you'll find these management skills useful as well.

Eliminating Mistakes

It's a dreadful feeling when a client or, even worse, a broadcaster calls to say there is a problem with one of your projects. Sure, content issues, rights clearances, and other issues happen all the time; however, some mistakes such as black holes and flash frames are just downright embarrassing! In this section, you'll explore how you can use Adobe Premiere Pro to avoid some small but preventable mistakes.

Checking for Gaps and Flash Frames

In the course of a complex edit, it's quite common to have small gaps (or *flash frames*) appear in a sequence. Most often, these minor mistakes occur as a result of editors not paying attention as they drag a clip into a sequence and imprecisely place it next to an adjacent clip. Likewise, they can also occur during the editorial process as you move clips around and trim clips.

Regardless of the reason, locating a gap or flash frame is easy using Adobe Premiere Pro: In your final sequence, choose Sequence > Go to Gap. This menu (**FIGURE 14.1**) offers four choices. The first two, Next in Sequence and Previous in Sequence, allow you to find gaps to the right or left of the sequence playhead, covering all the tracks in the sequence.

FIGURE 14.1 The Go to Gap menu offers several ways to find gaps in a sequence.

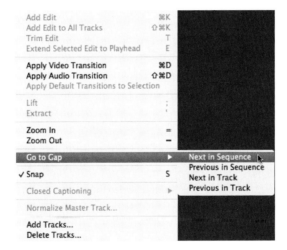

The next two options, Next in Track and Previous in Track, use currently targeted tracks (both audio and video) to locate gaps and flash frames on a particular track or combination of tracks.

Although there are no default shortcuts for any of the Go to Gap functions, you can choose the Adobe Premiere Pro Keyboard Shortcuts option: Premiere Pro > Keyboard Shortcuts (Mac) and Edit > Keyboard Shortcuts (Windows). You can then search or locate the next and previous sequence and track commands (they're located in the Sequence group of Shortcuts). From there, you can map your own keyboard shortcuts to those functions.

Once you've found a gap or flash frame, follow these steps.

1. Select the gap by clicking the gap in the sequence (**FIGURE 14.2**).

FIGURE 14.2 To select a gap, just click it. You can also mark a gap once it's located with In and Out points to perform an extract edit.

2. Press the Delete key to perform a ripple edit to close the gap. Keep in mind that if you select a gap in an audio track or a video track and have Sync Lock on with a corresponding audio or video track, Adobe Premiere Pro will attempt to move the linked part of the clip as well. However, if another clip in your audio or video tracks is in the way, you'll be unable to close the gap. You can disable this behavior by turning off Sync Lock for those tracks, but closing the gap may result in clips that are out of sync with each other.

3. If you prefer to use In and Out points to mark the sequence, you can select the gap and then use the slash (/) key or choose Markers > Mark Selection to mark In and Out points around the gap.

4. In the Program Monitor, after marking a gap, click the Extract button or press the apostrophe (') key to use the Extract keyboard shortcut. This will remove the gap and slide everything on the right of the gap to the left, closing the gap.

Keep in mind that when you mark a gap, the gap will be marked for all selected tracks. You can click the track header for a track to select it—to take part in the extract operation—or to deselect it. But be careful: When you unselect tracks, you can potentially move audio and other tracks out of sync with one another.

Looking for Repeated Shots

Throughout the course of a project, you'll use numerous shots. Often, you'll have a long original clip that you'll slice into dozens of smaller clips. Although this is perfectly normal, some editors and producers absolutely refuse to use the same clip multiple times in a sequence. In Adobe Premiere Pro, you can easily find the number of times that a clip is used in a sequence.

1. In the Project panel, switch to icon view if you're not already viewing the Project panel in that view.

2. In the bottom-right corner of a clip, you'll see one or two orange icons if that clip is being used. The icon that looks like a filmstrip represents video, and the one that looks like audio waveform represents audio. If a clip has only video and no linked audio, you'll see the video icon only, or vice versa (**FIGURE 14.3**).

FIGURE 14.3 The usage icons on a clip in the Project panel when in thumbnail view allow you to quickly see whether a clip's audio or video is being used (orange icons, left) or not (white icons, right).

Trim to Close a Gap
When you close a gap by deleting it, you change the overall duration of your sequence and potentially move audio and other tracks like graphics out of sync with each other. Another way to close a gap is to trim the clip on one side of the gap to close the hole.

X Marks the Spot
If you're a Final Cut Pro 7 editor, you're probably used to using the X key to mark an edit or gap. In Adobe Premiere Pro, when a clip is selected, the slash (/) key performs the same function.

Usage Icons in Action
If you'd like to see the usage icons in action, you can navigate to Lessons and Media and open the project called 14_qc_archiving.prproj. If you open the clips bin and make sure you're in icon view, you'll be able to see the usage icons. Just keep in mind all media in this bin is being used.

Keep in mind if a clip is not being used, you'll see white icons, and in the case of a video clip with linked audio, you'll see only a white icon for the linked audio.

3. The icons are cool, but they don't tell you much other than a shot is in use or not in use. However, what's extremely useful is if you click one of the icons, you can see the sequence that the shot is in and the timecode at which the shot starts. In the case of audio, you can see the sequence and timecode for each channel of that clip (FIGURE 14.4).

FIGURE 14.4 By clicking the usage icons on a clip, you can quickly see in which sequence a clip's video or audio is being used and the timecode where the clip starts.

ADDITIONAL WAYS TO VIEW CLIP USAGE

Besides being able to see whether clips (and which part of those clips) are being used by viewing the usage icons on the thumbnail of a clip, there are a couple of additional ways to see the usage of a clip:

1. In the Project panel, choose the panel menu, and then choose Metadata Display.

2. In the Metadata Display dialog, you'll see a ton of metadata that you can customize and display in the Project panel. The first category is Premiere Pro Project Metadata. Click the disclosure triangle next to Premiere Pro Project Metadata to open this category.

3. About halfway down the list, select the check boxes next to Video Usage and Audio Usage, and then click OK. (You can also save your settings for any metadata that you add or modify as a custom setting by clicking the Save Settings button.)

4. Set the Project panel to list view and then scroll to the right to reveal the Video and Audio Usage columns. If you've used a particular clip multiple times, the counts will appear in these columns. Just keep in mind that this tally takes into account all sequences you have in a project. Clicking the downward arrows next to each usage number reveals which sequence and at what timecode the clip has been placed (FIGURE 14.5).

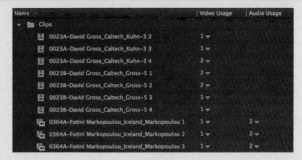

FIGURE 14.5 The Video and Audio Usage columns show whether a clip has been used in a sequence in an Adobe Premiere Pro project and how many times.

5. Additionally, when you select a clip in the Project panel, you can see where it is used in your project. Simply click the clip usage triangle next to the thumbnail and inside the clip Preview pane at the top of the Project panel for either video or audio. For these triangles to appear, the clip must be used in a sequence. If the Preview pane is not being shown for you, simply click in the Project panel menu and choose to enable the Preview pane (FIGURE 14.6).

 0364B-Fotini Markopoulou_Iceland_Kuhn-6 1
Movie, 1280 x 720 (1.0) — video used 1 time
00:00:04:15, 29.97p
48000 Hz – 24-bit – 2 M — audio used 2 times
0364B-DX

Rough Cut : 0364B-Fotini Markopoulou_Iceland_Kuhn-6 1 : 00;00;10;16

FIGURE 14.6 The clip usage triangles in the Preview pane at the top of the Project panel let you see what sequences clips are used on. You can reveal usage for both audio and video using separate buttons.

You might be thinking that it doesn't really matter how many times a particular clip is being used in a sequence but rather whether the same part of a clip is being used multiple times. After all, you may have a 20-minute source clip that you've used different parts of multiple times in a sequence. The various ways of viewing clip usage simply show the number of times the clip has been used but do not account for which parts (in other words, the exact parts) have been used. This missing but desired feature is known as *dupe detection*. Dupe detection allows you to see which parts of a clip are duplicated throughout a sequence. Unfortunately, Adobe Premiere Pro does not offer dupe detection. Our hope is that this useful feature finds its way into future versions of the software.

However, by using subclips (as discussed in Chapter 5, you can create smaller portions of particular bites or portions of action. Then, using the Video and Audio Usage columns, you can determine whether a particular subclip is being used multiple times in the sequence. Although this more manual method is not dupe detection, it enables you to be a little more exact about usage than using the usage methods with a source clip.

Broadcast Legalization

A couple of thoughts may come to mind when you hear the phrase *broadcast legalization*. You might first ask, What the heck is that? Then you might mistakenly decide to skip this section because you think the phrase has something to do with working for broadcast outlets.

Well, simply put, broadcast legalization refers to techniques that are used to adhere to technical specifications for video and audio. Although each broadcaster has its own standards, you need to adhere to some general rules as a content producer.

If you're thinking that broadcast legalization doesn't matter because you're not doing any broadcast work, well, that's a common misconception. By adhering to broadcast specs, you can actually make your footage look and sound its best. By keeping your final project within spec, you'll ensure that processes such as dubs, duplication, and Web distribution go smoothly.

In this section, you'll explore some of the particulars of video and audio legalization.

Video Legalization

Video legalization might seem like an intimidating task, but it's very straightforward. Because you're an experienced editor, chances are you'll be comfortable legalizing your video. But even if you're new to the subject, you can easily ensure that your footage is legal video by using a few techniques and utilizing a couple of Adobe Premiere Pro effects.

Legalizing manually

The process of legalizing video begins with color correction and grading (see Chapter 11). In fact, one of the main goals of color correction is to ensure legality. So, when color correcting and grading footage, you're manually legalizing your video. We'll discuss a few effects in Adobe Premiere Pro to help you legalize footage, but it's always best not

Tech Specs
It's always a good idea to check with a broadcaster about its specific standards for video and audio. Although some variance exists between broadcasters (or distributors, such as for DVD and Blu-ray Disc), you'll find that many broadcasters base their standards on the PBS Redbook standard. You can find the current version of this standard at www.pbs.org/producing/red-book/.

Viewing Saturation on the Waveform Scope

If you right-click the Waveform Monitor in Final Cut Pro 7, you can choose to show saturation. This is the same functionality you get by choosing the Chroma option for the YC Waveform in Adobe Premiere Pro.

External Scopes and RGB Legality

Many external scope setups also have specific tools for measuring RGB gamut legality. Diamond Display (patented by Tektronix) and the Harris/Videotek eye pattern are two useful scopes for measuring RGB legality in combination with the RGB Parade.

to depend on those effects. Try to manually legalize your footage first, and then use the legalization effects to legalize any stray pixels you may have missed.

As discussed in Chapter 11, your eyes lie; therefore, it's crucial that you use the scopes to assist you in ensuring your video is legal. Here are a few guidelines to help you do that:

- **Luma levels.** On the YC Waveform, make sure that no part of the trace is above 100 IRE or below 0 IRE. For most broadcasters, trace above or below these levels is illegal for broadcast. Almost all of the Adobe Premiere Pro color correction effects allow you to adjust luma levels to ensure broadcast legality.

- **Saturation.** Using the Vectorscope as a guide, ensure that no part of the trace extends beyond the outer edges of the Vectorscope. Remember that the distance from the center to the edge of the graticule on the Vectorscope measures saturation of a particular hue. A more conservative approach that is safer for the standards many broadcasters use is to use the hue targets around the Vectorscope as a guide. In tandem with the Vectorscope, you can also measure saturation across the tonal range by choosing the YC Waveform and enabling the Chroma option (**FIGURE 14.7**). Like luma trace on the YC Waveform, with the Chroma option enabled, the blue trace (chroma) that is overlaid on the luma trace should not exceed 100 IRE or go below 0 IRE (for conservative broadcasters; some may allow you to go higher or lower). Using a combination of primary and secondary corrections via an Adobe Premiere Pro color effect such as the Fast Color Corrector or Three-Way Color Corrector, you can guarantee that your footage meets saturation legality.

FIGURE 14.7 By selecting the Chroma option on the YC Waveform, you can see saturation across the tonal range, making it effortless to determine whether you need to desaturate highlights, shadows, or overall saturation.

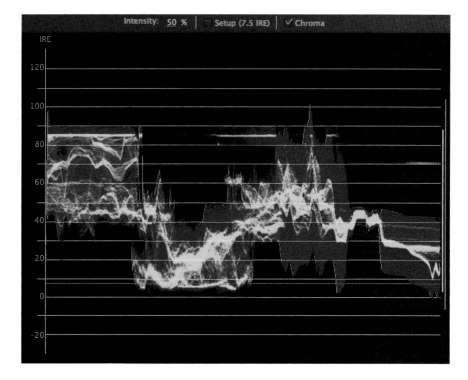

- **RGB levels.** It's important to also check RGB levels using the RGB Parade. Like measuring luma on the YC Waveform, trace above or below 100 IRE or below 0 IRE on the RGB Parade is considered illegal. Unfortunately, in Adobe Premiere Pro, the RGB Parade doesn't make this task easy because it clips RGB values at 100 and 0 IRE. Even with this limitation in mind, you can still judge RGB levels. If you see trace that is excessively clustered at 100 or 0 IRE, there's a good chance that your RGB levels are illegal. Most of the Adobe Premiere Pro color correction effects allow you to legalize RGB levels through contrast and saturation adjustments. For particularly stubborn clips, you can also use secondary correction to manually legalize RGB levels.

Using the Broadcast Colors effect

The Broadcast Colors effect is a simple effect for ensuring that your colors (hue and saturation) are legal (**FIGURE 14.8**). Although the Video Limiter effect (which we'll discuss next) is more full featured because it allows for legalization of both luma and chroma for quick fixes to color only, you can use the Broadcast Colors effect to make sure your footage has legal colors.

FIGURE 14.8 The Broadcast Colors effect allows you to quickly legalize colors in a clip.

To use the Broadcast Colors effect, drag it from the Effects panel to a clip or a nested sequence. Once you've applied the effect, you can then adjust several parameters.

- **Broadcast Locale.** To match the standard for your project, choose either NTSC or PAL.

- **How to Make Color Safe.** This parameter provides four options for making colors safe: Reduce Luminance darkens pixels to legalize them. Reduce Saturation reduces the saturation of illegal pixels. Key Out Unsafe makes a selection via a key, creating transparency in those areas. You can then layer another version of the shot below the shot with the Broadcast Colors effect and treat or affect the lower clip. Those effects or corrections will affect only the keyed areas, much like a dedicated secondary correction. Key Out Safe essentially does the opposite of Key Out Unsafe. Generally speaking, reducing saturation will more noticeably alter the clip than reducing luminance, and the key out options require you to do a bit more manual work to get a shot fixed. With that said, for clips that are very saturated, we find that reducing saturation produces the best results. But for general safety and a less noticeable effect on the clip, reducing luminance works well.

- **Maximum Signal Amplitude (IRE).** A good way to think of this control is as a threshold to which pixels that have an IRE value above this setting will be legalized according to the How to Make Color Safe parameter. Use a value of 100 IRE to ensure the broadest legality.

Using the Video Limiter effect

Although the Broadcast Colors effect works well for legalizing colors, it provides no control over legalizing illegal luma levels. That's why we almost always turn to the Video Limiter effect (**FIGURE 14.9**). We think it provides the most control over limiting the signal.

Broadcast Safe in Final Cut Pro

If you rely on the Broadcast Safe filter in Final Cut Pro 7, the Video Limiter effect will feel similar. The one exception is that the Video Limiter effect doesn't have specific parameters for RGB legality.

FIGURE 14.9 The Video Limiter effect provides a robust set of controls for legalizing both chroma and luma in the signal.

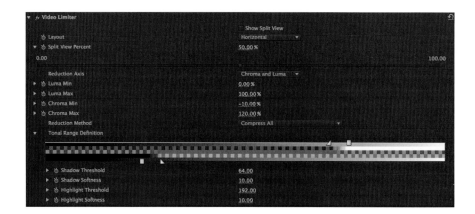

To use the Video Limiter effect, drag it from the Effects panel onto a clip or nested sequence.

To control the effect, you can adjust several parameters.

- **Show Split View.** Sets the Program Monitor to a split view, which allows you to compare the corrected clip to the original clip. This is particularly useful if you want to show a client the difference between versions. You can use the Layout and Split View Percent controls to adjust the split between the original clip and the affected clip.

- **Reduction Axis.** Sets limits for Luma Only, Chroma Only, both Chroma and Luma, or you can use the Smart Limit option to let Adobe Premiere Pro choose the best portion of the signal to reduce. Just keep in mind that depending on which option you choose, there will be different options for setting minimum and maximum levels.

- **Luma Min.** Sets the minimum level for luma in the signal. This option is available if you choose Luma Only or Chroma and Luma in the Reduction Axis menu. The default value of 0% (digital percentage and IRE; although technically different, they are essentially the same thing) is the proper choice.

- **Luma Max.** Sets the maximum allowable luma level in the signal. Like Luma Min, this option is available if you choose Luma Only or Chroma and Luma in the Reduction Axis menu. The default value of 100% is generally correct, although some broadcasters may allow slightly higher values.

- **Chroma Min.** Sets the minimum allowable chroma level in the signal. This option is available if the Reduction Axis is set to Chroma Only or Chroma and Luma. The default value of -30% is a touch too liberal. We find a value of -20% to 0% to be in line with most broadcasters.

- **Chroma Max.** Sets the maximum allowable chroma level in the signal. Like Chroma Min, this option is available only if the Reduction Axis option is set to Chroma Only or Chroma and Luma. The default value of 130% is pretty generous. A value of 100% to 120% offers the broadest legality across broadcasters; however, some broadcasters may allow for higher levels.

Hardware Legalization
If you're working in a tape-based workflow, you may want to consider using a hardware legalizer. These external devices sit in the middle of the signal chain between your Adobe Premiere Pro workstation and a video deck. Hardware legalizers are very accurate, and they provide real-time processing.

- **Signal Min.** Sets the minimum level for brightness and saturation. This option is available only if you choose the Smart Limit option in the Reduction Axis parameter. The default value of -30% is rather low. We find a value of 0% to have the broadest compatibility with most broadcasters when using the Smart Limit option.

- **Signal Max.** Sets the maximum level for brightness and saturation. This option is available only if you choose the Smart Limit option in the Reduction Axis parameter. The default value of 130% is a little dangerous (as far as legality is concerned). A value of 100% offers the broadest legality across broadcasters; however, some broadcasters may allow for higher levels.

- **Reduction Method.** Adjusts the effect based on the preceding parameters as to how legalization will occur. You can choose from Highlights Compression, Midtones Compression, Shadows Compression, or Highlights and Shadows Compression. The default option, Compress All, works well in most situations.

- **Tonal Range Definition.** Sets the ranges and softness for the three areas of the tonal range (shadows, midtones, and highlights).

Audio Legalization

Equally as important as video legalization is audio legalization. As the old adage goes, *audio is half of the picture*. No doubt you've been annoyed from time to time when watching something with over-modulated audio or audio that is too quiet. Well, when it comes to legalizing audio, different broadcasters have different "rules," but knowing a few simple techniques can help you achieve legal audio.

Achieving proper levels

Perhaps the biggest factor to achieving legal audio is to get your levels correct. Levels are measured on the Adobe Premiere Pro audio meters in the Audio Mixer for each track in a sequence as well as the Master audio track, which is also viewable in the mixer or by calling up those meters at any time by choosing Window > Audio Meters (**FIGURE 14.10**).

FIGURE 14.10 The audio meters (both in the Audio Mixer and the stand-alone version) are your principal tool for measuring audio levels for a given track or for an entire project.

It's up to you to decide how to mix your tracks in any given sequence, but your overall master (levels) is what's really important. Depending on your application, different levels are considered legal.

- Before setting your audio levels, you should consider the *reference level* for the project. Reference level is the tone you hear underneath color bars. The color bars represent various colors that will be seen in the rest of the project. The tone is used to represent average or reference levels for the rest of the project. For broadcast work, a reference tone of -20 dBFS is the most common level. For nonbroadcast work, -12 dBFS is common.

- For projects destined for broadcast, peak audio levels should not exceed -10 dBFS. Keep in mind that specific broadcasters may have different requirements. In our experience, this is a typical requirement from most broadcasters.

- If your project is not destined for broadcast, such as a film festival, DVD, or Blu-ray Disc, broadcast peak levels will be pretty low. Peaks for nonbroadcast work should be between -6 dBFS and -3 dBFS. However, when levels hit 0 dBFS in digital audio, noticeable distortion is possible.

Normalization, compression, and limiting

One of your biggest challenges when legalizing audio in Adobe Premiere Pro will be mixing audio to the same overall level. We'll discuss one way to do this in the "Matching volume and loudness" section. But in the course of an average project, you'll want a quick and easy way to make audio the same volume while protecting your peak volume. Peak volume means not having any audio exceed the peak limit for your project (-10 dBFS, -6 dBFS, and so on). Adobe Premiere Pro offers a few methods that allow you to quickly adjust all audio levels to achieve the same level while protecting for peaks.

The first method is called *normalization*. In Adobe Premiere Pro, you can normalize or adjust audio in two ways so that all audio peaks are the same.

FIGURE 14.11 The Audio Gain dialog provides several options for affecting the gain of a clip, including two options for normalizing.

- Normalize Max Peak to / Normalize All Peaks to. Select clips you want to normalize in the Project panel or in a sequence, and then choose Clip > Audio Options > Audio Gain. In the dialog that opens (**FIGURE 14.11**) choose Normalize Max Peak to or Normalize All Peaks to. These functions operate differently depending on whether you're normalizing a single clip or multiple clips. With the dialog set to Normalize Max Peak to, let's say you're normalizing a clip with a peak of -10 dB.

  If you enter a value of -6 dB, the clip will be normalized so that +4 dB of gain is applied and peaks hit -6 dB. If you choose this option with multiple clips, the clip with the highest peak will be adjusted to the value you enter, whereas other clips (with lower peak levels) will be adjusted by the same relative amount but not to the exact level you entered.

  The Normalize All Peaks to option operates in the same way as Normalize Max Peak to for a single clip; however, for normalizing multiple clips, all peaks will be set to the value you enter, not in a relative amount as with the Normalize Max Peak to option.

- **Normalize Master Track.** We find the Normalize Master Track option more useful than normalizing individual clips. To normalize the Master track, select the sequence you want to normalize and choose Sequence > Normalize Master Track.

In the dialog that opens, enter the dB value you want the loudest peak to be (for example, -6dB). The loudest sound will be at that value, and the other peaks will automatically adjust upward or downward to meet the specified value.

Normalization is a good technique to rely on, but it can occasionally cause results you didn't expect because there are often extreme ranges of volume in a clip.

Another method for balancing audio is *compression*. A good way to think about a compressor is as an automatic "turner-downer." A compressor automatically reduces levels that get too high, which allows you to achieve consistent audio levels. Compressors can also be used to raise audio levels and generally to "flatten" dynamic range.

After normalizing and compressing audio to ensure that levels don't go beyond a specified level, you can use *limiting*. Think of limiting as a hard ceiling that a signal can't pass through.

In Adobe Premiere Pro, you can find compression options in two places but the limiting option in one.

- **MultibandCompressor.** Found in the Audio Effects bin, this effect allows you to apply compression across three different frequency ranges (lows, mids, and highs; you can even adjust those ranges). As a result, you can apply varying levels of compression to different frequencies. The effect allows for more granular control while compressing the signal. You can control the MultibandCompressor by using the visual controls that mimic a traditional hardware unit, the numeric controls, or both based on your preference (**FIGURE 14.12**).

Other Level-Changing Options

Two other very useful options in the Audio Gain dialog are Set Gain to and Adjust Gain by. On a single clip or with multiple clips selected, Set Gain to will adjust the gain on a clip to the value you enter, which is useful for quickly changing a VO track, for example. Adjust Gain by with both a single clip and multiple clips changes the clip gain by a relative amount from its current settings.

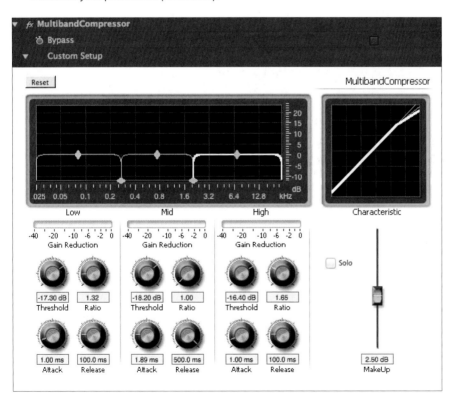

FIGURE 14.12 The Multiband-Compressor is a flexible tool for balancing audio across different frequency ranges.

67

Normalizing, Compression, and Limiting in Action
Check out this video to see the methods of normalizing, compression, and limiting at work on real-world problematic clips.

■ **Dynamics.** Also found in the Audio Effects bin, this effect is actually four effects in one. The AutoGate silences the audio signal if the levels fall below a threshold that you set. This is useful for eliminating background noise—for example, when someone isn't talking or for a voice-over to eliminate unwanted room noise. The Compressor applies compression to the signal. The Expander acts in a similar way to the AutoGate but generally has a "softer," less noticeable effect. The Limiter allows you to set a ceiling for maximum level in a clip (**FIGURE 14.13**). Like the MultibandCompressor, you can use either the visual or numeric controls or a combination of both. Because Dynamics combines many useful options in one, you should strongly consider it as an essential part of your QC workflow.

FIGURE 14.13 The Dynamics effect provides a great deal of control over the audio signal.

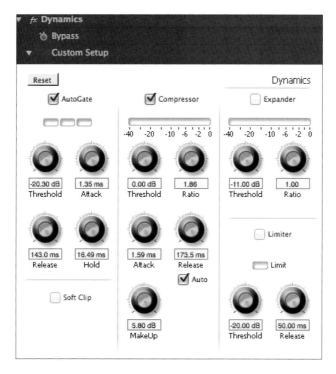

Matching volume and loudness

An important part of audio legalization is loudness. How is loudness different from volume? Simply put, loudness is perceptual volume. Have you ever noticed that different clips that look the same on an audio meter seem to have different volumes? That's loudness. Depending on the frequency of the audio file, you might perceive different volumes even though the clips look the same on a digital audio meter. As you'll see, loudness matching is also a way of matching clips with disparate actual volumes while considering perceived volume.

Measuring Loudness
If you go to any professional broadcast audio house, the mixers there will tell you they rely on the Dolby LM100 Loudness Meter. This external device is the gold standard for measuring loudness. The LM100 features are now also available as a software plug-in for compatible systems. Several third parties make loudness-measuring plug-ins for systems like Avid ProTools.

It's very difficult to use audio meters and your ears to achieve proper loudness within a project. Fortunately, the Adobe Creative Suite provides tools to help you achieve legal loudness levels.

To adjust for loudness, use the following procedure:

1. Navigate to Lessons and Media > Lesson 14, open the project 14_qc_archiving. prproj, and then open the sequence called 01_Loudness. (Note this project also contains two additional sequences that you'll use later in this chapter.) The sequence consists of two clips from the same interview, but the audio in the clips doesn't match both from a true level and from a perceived loudness point of view.

2. Select one of the audio files (they're stereo pairs), right-click, and choose Edit Clip in Adobe Audition. This step replaces the original audio with extracted audio that is sent to Adobe Audition. The extracted audio by default is saved to the same file path as the project.

   Adobe Audition launches, and the audio clips appear in the Files panel.

3. Switch back to Adobe Premiere Pro, and repeat step 2 for the other clip. You must send clips one at a time so that Adobe Audition retains a one-to-one relationship with the original files.

   Adobe Audition again becomes the active application, and the second audio clip appears in the Files panel.

4. Choose Effects > Match Volume. Adobe Audition will automatically switch you to the Match Volume panel if it's open or docked to the interface. If it isn't already opened or docked, the panel will appear as a floating window.

5. Drag the two audio files from the Files panel to the Match Volume panel where it says "Drag and drop files from the Files panel."

   After the files have been added, you'll notice several icons near the top of the Match Volume panel. Click the one that looks like a magnifying glass between the trash can icon and the Match Volume Settings button. Clicking this button will analyze the files in the various methods that Adobe Audition can analyze volume and loudness. Notice that after the files have been analyzed, readings are displayed (**FIGURE 14.14**).

6. Obviously, these clips vary a lot in overall volume, peak volume, and loudness—let's fix that. Click the Match Volume Settings button at the top of the Match Volume panel; the bottom of the panel changes to reveal some controls. The Match To menu offers several options on how to match these files, including to match by Total RMS, File (Total RMS) Peak Amplitude, True Peak Amplitude, Loudness, Perceived Loudness, and now in Adobe Audition CS6 a new option called ITU-R BS. 1770-2 Loudness. Select the ITU-R BS. 1770-2 Loudness option.

   Although all of these options do a decent job of matching the volume of files, the Loudness options will take into account not just level but loudness. We find that using Perceived Loudness as well as the new ITU option to be the most accurate when matching for loudness (**FIGURE 14.15**).

Loudness Scales to Be Aware Of
The main purpose of tools like the Dolby LM100 is to measure dialogue loudness. In recent years, two scales for measuring loudness have been more widely used in audio programs and equipment as the issue of loudness has become more important to broadcasters: Loudness K-Weighted Relative to Full Scale (LKFS) and Loudness Units Relative to Full Scale (LUFS). While there are technical differences between the two scales, they essentially measure a more complete snapshot of loudness.

ITU-R BS What?
Confused about what ITU-R BS.1770-2 means? Don't worry, the ITU is a standards body (International Telecommunication Union), and R is a recommendation by the group. BS is the category of the recommendation, in this case Broadcasting Service (Sound), and 1770 is the actual recommendation number. Finally, -2 just means the recommendation was submitted and then revised.

FIGURE 14.14 Clicking the magnifying glass icon on the Match Volume panel in Adobe Audition allows you to see various volume measurements of clips you're trying to match.

FIGURE 14.15 The Match Volume panel in Adobe Audition allows for several different ways to match volume between clips.

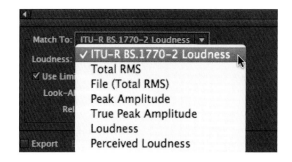

CALM Act
The U.S. Congress passed and the FCC will put into place on December 13, 2012, a law known as the CALM Act (for Commercial Advertisement Loudness Mitigation Act). The CALM Act aims to regulate loudness for commercials and some additional programing. You can find out more by visiting www.fcc.gov/encyclopedia/loud-commercials.

Plus or Minus
When it comes to Loudness most broadcasters will set a target value for average loudness—usually -23 or -24 LUFS/LKFS, however they usually allow for a variance of plus or minus 2 LUFS/LKFS for the average of the measured loudness of a program.

7. With the ITU-R Bs.1770-2 Loudness option selected, Adjust the value of the Loudness parameter to -23 LUFS because the clips in this project will be used in a show for broadcast. This value is recommended by the ITU and EBU, however many broadcasters use a target value of -23 or -24 LUFS/LKFS and allow for a variance of plus or minus 2 LUFS/LKFS over the course of the program so its important you check with your specific broadcaster for their loudness targets.

8. Select the option Use Limiting. For this exercise, the default settings for Lookahead and Release Time are fine as is.

9. To match the volume, click the Run button at the bottom of the Match Volume panel. Depending on your workflow (direct export to another application that's *not* Adobe Premiere Pro, for example), you could also check the Export button and then configure the export by clicking the Export Settings button to save the files with custom prefixes, overwrite existing files, save to a new location, or change the format of the audio file prior to clicking Run (**FIGURE 14.16**). However, you don't need to do that for this exercise.

FIGURE 14.16 By checking the export option and then clicking the Export Settings button in the Match Volume panel, you have total control over saving the processed audio, including changing the file format if needed.

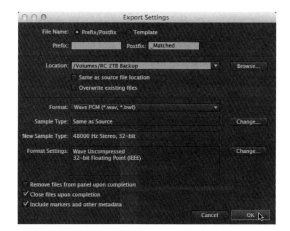

ITU vs. EBU
The ITU and European Broadcasting Union (EBU) both researched and made recommendations about loudness. The ITU study is known as ITU-RBS 1770-2, and the EBU study is known as EBU R128. If you research these studies, you'll find that they seem to compete, with different scales: LKFS vs. LUFS. However, for the end user, many loudness tools can measure on both scales, and while technically different, both standards aim to achieve similar results.

After matching, you'll be able to see in the Match Volume panel that the audio files have been matched as closely as possible for ITU loudness. However, notice the Peak and True Peak levels are now over -10, and in most broadcast workflows, this would be a bit too loud. While we matched the files based on ITU Loudness, the peaks are a touch too high. Let's fix this quickly using the Match Volume panel.

10. At the bottom of the Match Volume panel, change the Match To option to Peak Amplitude and use a value of -10 dB and click Run again. After processing finishes, notice that the peak levels match, while ITU loudness is lower, at -25 LUFS. That's actually OK; most broadcasters allow for a plus or minus 2 LUFS/LKFS variance of the course of the program and since we targeted -23 LUFS the resulting -25 LUFS value is just fine.

11. Choose File > Save All. Then switch back to Adobe Premiere Pro. Notice that the audio clips in the sequence have been replaced with the extracted audio you sent to Adobe Audition (you can also see these new clips in the Project panel). Play back the sequence. Note that the clips now match better in both their peak volume and their loudness.

> **Its all about the average**
> Most broadcasters only care about the average loudness across an entire program called long term loudness and not what it is referred to as short term loudness. Many dedicated loudness measurement tools can measure in short term or long term (average). However, it's the average value that most broadcasters specify on their spec sheets.

SENDING AN ENTIRE SEQUENCE TO ADOBE AUDITION

Sometimes you'll want to work on an entire sequence in Adobe Audition. Fortunately, Adobe Premiere Pro provides a great workflow for getting an entire sequence, including video, into Adobe Audition for more refined audio work.

1. In the Project panel, right-click a sequence, and then choose Edit in Adobe Audition > Sequence to send an entire sequence to Adobe Audition.

2. In the dialog that opens (FIGURE 14.17), choose a name for the new Adobe Audition project and a file path to save files (it defaults to the same file path as the project you're working on but in a subfolder called Adobe Audition Interchange). You can send an entire sequence or just a work area. You also have the ability to choose several additional options, such as adding handles, exporting video along with the audio, rendering audio effects, and sending volume keyframe metadata. In addition, you have the option of automatically opening Adobe Audition.

3. When you're done working on your audio project, you have several options to choose from to get the project back into Adobe Premiere Pro. First, you can export a mix or submix of the entire project. Second, from the Audition Multitrack menu, you can choose Export to Premiere Pro to send the project to Adobe Premiere Pro. For more details on this workflow, be sure to revisit Chapter 10, "Audio Mixing and Repair."

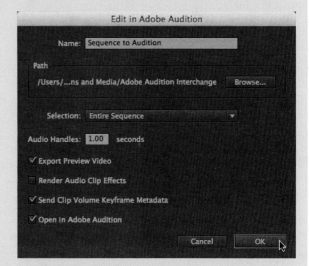

FIGURE 14.17 When exporting a sequence to Adobe Audition, you have several options for how to export that sequence, including the ability to export video and add handles.

Practical Media Management

Media management is part of any project, but media management takes on more importance toward the end of a project when you need to remove unused media or archive a project. In this section, we'll explain how to use the Project Manager to easily eliminate unused media by creating a trimmed project and copying a project from one location to another.

Removing Unused Media

It happens to the best of us: A project becomes bloated with unused clips and media that you have no intention of using. Taking the time to remove unused media streamlines a project and makes it a breeze to find assets.

To remove media, you have a few choices; just note that the first three options that follow do not actually remove media from disk but merely remove asset references from a project:

- Select an item in the Project panel and press the Delete key. Just keep in mind that after removing media from a project, the source files remain on the disk.

- Sort the Project panel by Video Usage or Audio Usage (if these columns are not displayed, in the Project panel menu choose Metadata Display > Premiere Pro Project Metadata and enable those two columns). If a file is not being used, simply select it and press the Delete key. Again, keep in mind that the source file will remain on disk but will be removed from the project.

- Choose Project > Remove Unused. This automated command removes all unused media in a project. Note that used media is media that is being used in any sequence within the project, not just the open sequence. As with the previously mentioned methods, media will remain on the disk.

- If you're serious about removing media from a project as well as from disk, you can right-click a clip and choose Make Offline. Making a clip offline breaks the link the project has to the media file and leaves an offline clip in your Project panel and any sequence that uses that clip. After choosing Make Offline, you'll be presented with a dialog (**FIGURE 14.18**) that asks you if you want the media files to remain on disk or delete them. Note that if you delete them, they will be removed, and any other project that references them will also have those clips appear as offline. After making a clip offline, you can remove the offline reference by simply deleting it in the Project panel.

FIGURE 14.18 Be careful when choosing to make a clip offline. If you remove the clip from disk, it will be permanently deleted, and other projects that reference that clip will have it appear offline in those projects as well.

Using the Project Manager

The principal way to media manage a project in Adobe Premiere Pro is to use the Project Manager (FIGURE 14.19). The Project Manager helps you to accomplish two main tasks.

- **Create New Trimmed Project.** This option allows you to create a new project based on the sequences and the media those sequences use, discarding other media.

- **Collect Files and Copy to New Location.** This option allows you to copy consolidated sequences to a new location.

To invoke the Project Manager, choose Project > Project Manager.

FIGURE 14.19 The Project Manager in Adobe Premiere Pro is the principal tool you use to move media and trim files for media management purposes.

 Media for This Section Uses the PhotoJPEG Codec
Although we've mainly been using H.264 media throughout this book, this exercise uses media encoded with the PhotoJPEG codec. This is because the Project Manager in Adobe Premiere Pro will not trim H.264 media and other long GOP formats. These PhotoJPEG files should play back on a system with Adobe Premiere Pro and Quick-Time installed without the need for further downloads or installs.

 A Sequence or a Project?
In this and the next exercise, you'll be trimming and also collecting a single sequence from a project. You can, however, trim or collect multiple sequences or even an entire project with all the sequences in a project selected in the Project Manager.

Creating a trimmed project

A common use of the Project Manager is to trim a project, which is often referred to as trimming the "fat." This means you can quickly clean up a project by getting rid of media not used in a project as well as getting rid of media not used by a clip in the sequence. For example, let's say you have five clips that are not used in a sequence in Adobe Premiere Pro, and you have 50 clips in a sequence. The clips that are being used in the sequence are all from source clips that are 5 to 10 minutes long; however, each clip in the sequence is only a few seconds in length. Using the Project Manager, you can delete the unused clips while trimming the clips in the sequence so that only the media used (you have the option of using handles) remains.

Creating Offline Clips
Using the Project Manager, select the Make Offline option to make the new project that the Project Manager creates have offline clips. This option is useful if you intend to capture or reconnect "offline" media again in its "online" or full resolution. This works best for tape-based clips, but you can also reconnect tapeless sources to a transcoded or camera original version.

Some Formats Cannot Be Trimmed
If you'll be trimming a project, just be aware that some formats, like H.264, XDCAM, MXF, and HDV, cannot be trimmed. This limitation is because of the frame structure of these formats. While shooting, be sure to avoid unnecessarily long takes.

Trimming a Project with Multicamera Sequences
If your project contains multicamera sequences, Adobe Premiere Pro won't trim the source footage for those sequences.

FIGURE 14.20 Adding handles to a trimmed project is a good idea in case you need to further massage edits or add transitions later.

1. Navigate to Lessons and Media > Lesson 14, open the project 14_qc_archiving. prproj if not already open, and then open the sequence called 02_Trim Project.

   This project contains two sequences (three total) you can use to see how the Project Manager works. Both of these sequences (02_Trim Project and 03_Collect Project) feature footage from an interview segment from the PBS series *Closer To Truth: Cosmos Consciousness God*. In this exercise, let's start with the sequence called 02_Trim Project. This sequence has been color corrected and mixed, so you don't need the surplus of extra handles that are present in each clip. But you do want to create an archived version (with smaller handles) of the segment for potential use in later episodes.

2. Choose Project > Project Manager to open the Project Manager.

3. At the top of the window in the Source section, choose the sequence(s) you want to manage. This project contains three sequences; make sure the sequence called Trimmed Project is selected and the other sequences are not selected (checked).

4. In the Resulting Project section, choose Create New Trimmed Project.

5. Notice that the Exclude Unused Clips is grayed out for this project because there are no unused clips. Also notice that you have the option to create offline clips in the resulting project. For this exercise, you can leave this option deselected, but this is a good choice if you're doing an offline/online workflow and want to recapture or reconnect to high-resolution media after you've created the trim project.

6. In the Options section, select Include Handles. We find that adding 15 to 30 frames is a good number because it allows you to make further edits in the resulting project or to create transitions. For this project, enter **15** frames (**FIGURE 14.20**).

7. Also in the Options section, you can select Rename Media Files to Match Clip Names. This option renames the new media files that will be created to match the clip names used in the project. This is useful if you've renamed clips in the Project panel and want to retain those names. For this project, you can leave this option deselected.

8. In the Project Destination section, click Browse to choose a location for the new project as well as for the new media that will be created from the trim operation.

9. In the Disk Space section, you'll see the amount of disk space available, the original project size, and the resulting project size, which is based on the options you selected previously. After making changes to any of the Project Manager options, click the Calculate button to update the resulting project size. Notice that this project has been trimmed.

10. Click OK to create a new trimmed project. You may be prompted to save the current project. Click OK to continue.

11. After processing has finished, you can navigate to the location where you saved the new project. The folder will have the same name as the original project but with Trimmed as a prefix. Inside this folder is the new project file and associated media for the project.

Collecting a project

Often, you'll want to move a project from place to place. For example, you might want to collect a project so you can hand it off to another editor or even to another facility. In addition, you may want to move a completed project to some sort of archive device, such as a backup hard drive or storage system. By using the Collect Files and Copy to New Location function in the Project Manager, this process is easy.

1. With the same project open as in the previous exercise, open the sequence called 03_Collect Project.

   This sequence is an interview segment that you need to hand off to another team member for color correction and audio mixing—a perfect use of collecting a project.

2. Render the entire sequence by choosing Sequence > Render Entire Work Area. Then choose Project > Project Manager. The Project Manager opens.

   By rendering this sequence when you collect it, you can also move all rendered files along with the media that you process. Note that if you adjusted your work area before starting this exercise, you may need to adjust it to account for all the clips in the sequence.

3. At the top of the Project Manager window in the Source section, choose the sequence(s) you want to manage. This project contains three sequences; make sure the sequence called Collect Project is selected and the others called Trimmed Project and Loudness are not selected.

4. In the Resulting Project section, choose Collect Files and Copy to New Location.

5. For this exercise, you'll notice that Exclude Unused Clips is grayed out. That's because this project doesn't contain any unused clips. In your own projects, this option is OK to use when you know that you don't need unused clips, but if you're trying to make a duplicate of a project, you may want to deselect this option so the resulting project has all the clips of the current project.

6. In the Options section, choose Include Preview Files and Audio Conform Files. If you don't choose these options, effects will have to be rerendered, and audio files will be conformed again to the project. Choosing these options results in more disk space being used for the resulting project and media; however, effects won't have to be rerendered, nor will audio need to be conformed to the project (**FIGURE 14.21**).

7. Deselect the Rename Media Files to Match Clip Names option for this exercise. This option renames files used in the project to the name of the clip used in the project (as named in the Project panel).

 Rename Trim or Collected New Project Files
When you trim or collect a sequence or project, a new folder is created with the prefix Trimmed or Collected; however, the new project file contained in this folder has the same name as the original project file. We find it a good idea to rename the new trimmed or copied project file with a similar prefix or suffix to avoid confusion with the original project file.

 Adobe After Effects Projects and Dynamic Link
If you use Dynamic Link to work with After Effects, be aware that the Project Manager in Adobe Premiere Pro doesn't copy or collect After Effects compositions that are used in an Adobe Premiere Pro project. Clips in a project that dynamically link to an After Effects project will appear offline in a new project after you've used the Adobe Premiere Pro Project Manager to collect a project. You can use the Collect Files command in After Effects, and then after you've managed your Adobe Premiere Pro project, relink manually to the After Effects project.

FIGURE 14.21 The options Include Preview Files and Audio Conform Files are useful when passing off a project to someone else using Adobe Premiere Pro because they won't have to rerender or conform audio files.

An Alternative Approach to Dynamic Link

You can choose to render your After Effects projects to movie files or image sequences. When doing this, choose the option in the Render Queue called Include Project Link. The files created will link to the original After Effects project. Then in Adobe Premiere Pro, you can use the Edit Original command to open the source project in After Effects.

FIGURE 14.22 The folder you choose as the destination folder for the Project Manager will contain a new project file, media used for the project, and preview and cache files.

8. In the Project Destination section, choose a location for the resulting project and processed media. If you have another drive on your system, choose that drive as the location.

9. Click OK to collect all the files and copy them to a new location. You may be prompted to save the current project. Click OK to continue.

10. After processing has finished, navigate to the location where you saved the new project. The folder will have the same name as the original project but with Copied as a prefix. Inside this folder is the new project file, associated media, and preview/cache files (**FIGURE 14.22**). You can now hand off this folder to another team member for the additional color correction and audio work that the segment needs.

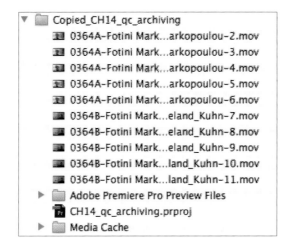

Next Steps

Now that you've taken your final finishing steps, your work is nearly done. Up next you'll learn about the last part of most projects—outputting and publishing to tape, to the Web, and to optical media.

CHAPTER 15

Publish Your Video

YOUR EDIT IS done, and it's time to publish your project. You need to get your finished project out of Adobe Premiere Pro and distributed to a plethora of different deliverables, such as tape, the Web, DVD, Blu-ray Disc, and even portable devices such as iPads and mobile phones.

In this chapter, you'll learn how Adobe Premiere Pro in conjunction with Adobe Media Encoder can speed up your workflow and allow you to be extremely efficient when it comes time to publish your project.

Closer To Truth
Some screen shots and footage for this chapter are from the PBS series Closer To Truth: Cosmos, Consciousness, God. © The Kuhn Foundation. Robert Lawrence Kuhn: creator, executive producer, writer and host. Peter Getzels: producer and director. Find out more about the series by visiting www.closertotruth.com.

Render at Maximum Depth
You may have noticed in the Video panel of the Export Settings dialog there is an option called Render at Maximum Depth. When this option is enabled, bit depth is maintained for media that has a bit depth greater than 8 bits. However, exports that use this option will take longer to render.

Sequence Settings vs. Export Settings
When choosing the Match Sequence Settings option for an export, the Render at Maximum Depth parameter is grayed out. If you need to control this choice, you can access it in the Sequence Settings dialog for a particular sequence.

FIGURE 15.1 The Match Sequence Settings option in the Export Settings dialog allows you to use the same settings as your sequence for an export.

Exporting a Digital Master

Even just a few years ago, a digital master of a project almost always meant creating a master videotape. This tape was the definitive output of the entire project, and as such, it was often cloned to ensure nothing happened to it before it was put on a shelf for long-term storage.

Although this practice still happens, let's face it—it's become far less common in many workflows. In fact, outputting to tape can often be a hindrance (and a costly one at that). More and more projects need to have what we call a *digital master*.

A digital master is simply a self-contained digital file of the entire show at its highest resolution and best quality. Once you've created it, you can then use that file to produce other types of outputs. It also gives you the ability to archive the digital master for later use.

Matching Sequence Settings

When creating a digital master of a project, you'll often want the resulting, self-contained digital file to use the same settings (frame size, frame rate, and codec) as your sequence. The cool thing is when you export from Adobe Premiere Pro, you can match sequence settings, which makes it simple to create a file that matches your edit. No guesswork is involved as long as you chose your original sequence settings correctly. Let's take a look at how this works.

1. Navigate to Lessons and Media > Lesson 15, open the project called 15_publish. prproj, and then open the sequence called 01_Match_Change_Export.

2. With the sequence selected (either in the Project panel or in the Timeline panel), choose File > Export > Media or press Command+M (Ctrl+M).

   The Export Settings dialog opens. It may look a little dense, but we'll break down the interface later in this chapter.

3. In the Export Settings area, select Match Sequence Settings (**FIGURE 15.1**). Click the output name (the yellow text), and name the file Match Sequence Settings.mov. Save the file to a location of your choice.

4. Click the Video and Audio panels midway down on the right side of the Export Settings dialog.

   You'll notice that all options are grayed out because you've chosen to match sequence settings. In the Video panel, the video codec matches the codec chosen for video previews for the selected sequence. Other sequence settings for this project (frame size, frame rate, and codec) also match sequence settings. Likewise, the Audio panel matches the sequence.

5. At the bottom of the Export Settings dialog on the right side you'll notice several additional options, including Use Maximum Render Quality, Use Previews, and Use Frame Blending. These options are important to understand.

   - **Use Maximum Render Quality.** This should be chosen only when scaling your output. Choosing it for creating a digital copy matching sequence settings will only dramatically increase export time.

- **Use Previews.** This can be advantageous if you've changed your sequence to generate high-quality previews and you want to reuse those previews when exporting. With this option unchecked, previews that have been generated during editing will be ignored.

- **Use Frame Blending.** This should be used only when your sequence frame rate doesn't match your output frame rate. This option can create smoother motion when frame rates of a sequence and export don't match.

For this exercise, you can leave all three of these options unchecked.

6. Click the Export button at the bottom of the Export Settings dialog to export the sequence as a digital master.

Choosing Another Codec

Nothing says that you *have* to match sequence settings when creating a digital master of a project (even though in most situations that's a good choice). You can also export a master copy to a higher-quality mastering codec. For example, you might export a project that uses XDCAM-encoded material to the high-quality cross-platform JPEG 2000 codec or another mastering codec of your choice. In this exercise, you'll export a file that uses a different codec than the media used in the sequence.

1. With the same sequence selected, choose File > Export > Media or press Command+M (Ctrl+M).

2. In the Export Settings dialog in the Export Settings area, choose QuickTime as the Format, click the output name (the yellow text), and then name the file Different Codec.mov. Save the file to a location of your choice.

3. Click the Video tab in the Export Settings dialog.

Use the following settings (use the figure for guidance):

- Set Video Codec to JPEG 2000. Keep in mind it may take some time to export to JPEG 2000 (**FIGURE 15.2**).

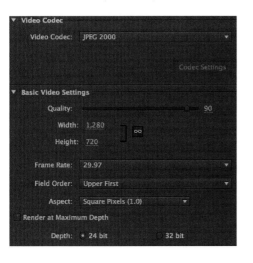

FIGURE 15.2 Options on the Video tab allow you to custom configure your export. In this case, we manually matched sequence settings but changed the codec to the JPEG 2000 codec.

Lossless Output
Video codecs come in two flavors: lossless and lossy. Lossless codecs like the Animation and PNG codecs preserve all data in an encode. Lossy codecs, on the other hand, throw away data in a variety of ways. The trade-off is that lossless exports are much larger than exports that use a lossy codec. Feel free to substitute the Animation or PNG codec in this exercise; for all other parameters, use the same settings.

Mixed-Format Sequences
The mixing of codecs is becoming very common as the variety of digital formats continues to grow. Consider mastering codecs like Avid DNxHD, Apple ProRes, or JPEG2000.

KTOOLS
If you have to output in a different aspect ratio (16 x 9 to 4 x 3, for example), one thing that can be tricky is ensuring that text and action elements are inside the 4 x 3 action- and title-safe zones. In Lesson 15, we've included a zipped file called CS5_KTOOLS, which comes from our friend Tim Kolb. Inside you'll find a number of overlays (PSDs) that you can use as guides to ensure 4 x 3 action and title safety, as well as a few gradients you can use with blend modes to create custom vignettes.

Meet JPEG 2000
JPEG 2000 is a cross-platform codec that is even being used as part of the Digital Cinema Initiative Digital Cinema Package (DCI DCP) delivery system for theaters. It's a very high data rate codec, so it might not play back on all systems (especially ones with slower non-RAIDed drives) but once encoded, it provides outstanding image quality.

- Set the Quality slider to 90.

- Set the frame size to 1280 x 720.

- The frame rate is 29.97, Field Type is Upper First, and Aspect is Square Pixels.

- Uncheck the option Render at Maximum Depth because this footage is 8-bit. If using 10-bit or 12-bit codecs, you can choose this option.

- Set Depth to 24 bits. 32 bit is necessary only to maintain an alpha or transparency channel in the export. This sequence doesn't have any transparency.

4. Click the Audio tab, and choose Uncompressed for the Audio codec. In the Basic Audio Settings section, choose 48000 Hz as the sample rate, Stereo for Channels, and 16-bit for Sample Type.

RECOMMENDED MASTERING CODECS

When it comes to creating a master copy of your project, although it's always a safe bet to create a file that uses the same codec as your project, sometimes you'll want to create a master file in a codec that is more robust. The use of third-party codecs opens up new options for quality (compression ratio, chroma-subsampling, and so on). Here are some codecs that we recommend:

- **Uncompressed.** Depending on your operating system and additional hardware you have installed (like an AJA Kona or Blackmagic Decklink card), you may have the choice to export a project using an 8-bit or 10-bit uncompressed 4:2:2 or 4:4:4 codec. Because of no compression, you'll get the cleanest high-quality file possible, but the downside is your file size will be extremely large and will require a very fast hard drive or disk array to play back without dropping frames.

- **Apple ProRes.** If you're using a Mac with Final Cut Studio/Final Cut Pro X and/or Compressor 5 or Motion 5 also installed, you'll be able to write files to Apple ProRes. This versatile codec comes in a number of "flavors" depending on your needs. Keep in mind that even though a free ProRes decoder is available for Mac and Windows, that decoder allows you only to view or work with ProRes files; you cannot create ProRes files with the decoder.

- **Avid DNxHD.** If you ever need to interact with editors using Avid, another great choice is the Avid DNxHD codec. Similar in quality to other mastering codecs, like Apple ProRes and Cineform, one of the best things about the DNxHD codec is that it's free, and it's cross-platform as both a decoder and an encoder.

- **Cineform.** Part codec, part a suite of utilities, Cineform is a super high-quality wavelet codec that's cross-platform and preferred by many high-end content creators. To use Cineform, you can purchase different Cineform products based on your needs. In addition, Cineform offers a free decoder for Mac and Windows that allows you to play back and work with Cineform-encoded files. But like the ProRes decoder, you will not be able to create Cineform-encoded files.

- **JPEG 2000.** While JPEGs are traditionally associated with still images, the compression can also be used for video. JPEG 2000 is the next generation of JPEG compression and is a good cross-platform choice for encoding. JPEG 2000 is also the codec that is used for Digital Cinema Package (DCP) deliveries to theaters when placed in an encrypted MXF container.

- **Animation and PNG.** Although the Animation codec is only 8-bit and creates very large files, it is truly a universal lossless codec. One warning, though: It's not meant for playback and often stutters even on fast systems. PNG is also a lossless codec. Although commonly used for still image formats, PNG can also work for video, and like the Animation codec, it can support an alpha channel for transparency.

You might be thinking about codecs like DVCPRO HD and SheerVideo, among others. Depending on your workflow, they are perfectly acceptable codecs, but keep in mind that some codecs are platform (Final Cut Pro, Avid) specific and/or even operating system specific.

5. At the bottom of the Export Settings dialog on the right side, you can ignore the additional options of Use Maximum Render Quality, Use Previews, and Use Frame Blending because they aren't necessary for this output.

6. Click the Export button at the bottom of the Export Settings dialog to export the sequence.

Meet Adobe Media Encoder

At the heart of any output or publishing workflow that uses Adobe Premiere Pro is Adobe Media Encoder. You'll find that it is a versatile transcoding and compression tool. You can leverage it to transcode to another editing codec and create files for the Web, DVD, Blu-ray Disc, and even mobile devices. We've found the application to be incredibly fast because it is 64-bit and able to use multiple processors and multiple cores on those processors.

You can utilize Adobe Media Encoder in two ways.

- **Directly from Adobe Premiere Pro.** By choosing File > Export > Media, you'll be presented with the Export Settings dialog (**FIGURE 15.3**). This is essentially the same interface as the stand-alone version of Adobe Media Encoder.

- **As a stand-alone application.** Because Adobe Media Encoder is an application, it can therefore be run as a stand-alone program (**FIGURE 15.4**). You can drop several items into the Adobe Media Encoder, including self-contained files, source clips, and Adobe Premiere Pro or Adobe After Effects project files. You can even utilize the Watch Folder functionality to automatically start encodes when files are dropped into a selected folder.

Why 90 Percent?
While you might want to change this to 100, there is no appreciable quality difference, and the resulting file at 100 percent quality is more than double the size of the encoded file using a setting of 90.

Watch Folders
One handy feature when using Adobe Media Encoder is Watch Folders. When files are placed into a Watch Folder, Adobe Media Encoder can automatically fire off a series of exports. Check out this video to learn more about Watch Folders.

FIGURE 15.3 The Export Settings dialog is where you can configure exports to various formats using Adobe presets or presets that you create.

FIGURE 15.4 You can add Adobe Premiere Pro and After Effects projects directly to Adobe Media Encoder and select a sequence or composition to encode.

Accessing Adobe Media Encoder from Adobe Premiere Pro

As with many features in the Creative Suite, Adobe has put a ton of work and development into streamlining workflow. You can access the power of Adobe Media Encoder directly from within an Adobe Premiere Pro project. Here's how:

- **Individual clips.** With an individual clip selected in the Project panel, choose File > Export > Media or press Command+M (Ctrl+M) to export that clip into the format and preset of your choosing. You can also export the entire clip or set a custom range by setting In and Out points.

- **Sequences.** During the review or delivery stages, you'll often need to export part of a, or an entire, sequence. With the Timeline panel selected or the sequence selected in the Project panel, choose File > Export > Media. You can also drag multiple sequences from the Adobe Premiere Pro Project panel into the Adobe Media Encoder application window.

Overview of the Export Settings Dialog

After choosing to export a clip or a sequence from Adobe Premiere Pro, the Export Settings dialog will open (shown earlier in Figure 15.3). In this dialog, you can customize your export settings, including setting the format, codec, frame size, and frame rate, as well as other options.

The dialog can seem a little intimidating at first, but it's actually straightforward once you get the lay of the land. In this section, we'll deconstruct the Export Settings dialog so you can have total control over your export.

Duplicate a Sequence Before Exporting

If you suffer from an organizational, obsessive-compulsive disease like us, you may want to duplicate the sequence you're working on before exporting. If you name the duplicate in the format Sequence_Export_Date and then continue to work on the sequence, you'll always have a version that matches your export.

Exporting Multiple Clips

If you want to export multiple clips from Adobe Premiere Pro, you'll need to export them one by one. When the Export Settings dialog opens, click the Queue button at the bottom of the window. This will add the clip to the Adobe Media Encoder Queue. Repeat the process until all the clips you want to export are in the Queue. You can customize the clip export settings in the Export Settings dialog or within the Adobe Media Encoder application.

Source and Output panels

Starting in the upper-left corner of the Export Settings dialog are two panels: Source and Output.

The Source panel (**FIGURE 15.5**) allows you to see your original clip or sequence in the center of the panel. Above the preview are cropping controls, which come in handy if you have horizontal or vertical blanking in the clip that you're trying to eliminate or if you're trying to fit a specific aspect ratio.

FIGURE 15.5 The Source panel in the Export Settings dialog allows you to scrub and watch the clip or sequence you'll be encoding, set custom In and Out points, and crop footage for export.

Below the preview is a mini timeline you can use to scrub through a clip or sequence, as well as see source timecode and duration. You can customize duration by setting In and Out points by pressing I and O on the keyboard or using the In and Out buttons. In the Source Range menu, you can set the range (duration) for the entire clip, the entire sequence, the sequence in/out, the work area in the sequence, or a custom range (which you customize by using In and Out points).

The Output panel (**FIGURE 15.6**) shows you a preview based on your settings, including any cropping you may have performed. As you make adjustments to any settings in the Export Settings dialog, it's often a good idea to switch to the Output panel to see the result of your settings, particularly if you do any cropping. Just keep in mind that when it comes to compression artifacts, what you see in the Output panel is an approximation. Above the preview in the Output panel there is a Source Scaling pulldown menu. This menu has several options that determine how any cropping you did in the Source panel is represented in the final output.

Test First, Compress Second
If you want to experiment with different settings to test your footage, it's a great idea to send a 30- to 60-second sample through Adobe Media Encoder rather than your whole project. This way, when you "hit" the right setting, you'll have saved yourself quite a bit of time.

FIGURE 15.6 Using the Output panel is a good way to check the results of any cropping or sizing you may have done. Using the Source Scaling pulldown menu, you can easily change the way cropping is presented in the exported file based on your export settings.

Export Settings

The Export Settings section (**FIGURE 15.7**) on the upper-right side of the Export Settings dialog offers you several options to control your export. Here they are in detail:

FIGURE 15.7 The Export Settings area gives you control over the format your sequence or file will use, the ability to use a preset or create one, the ability to include audio or video in the export, and the ability to choose the name of the exported file and where it will be saved.

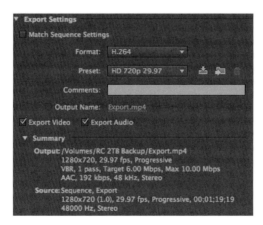

- **Format.** The Format option allows you to choose the format of the resulting file. From QuickTime to Flash, you'll find lots of options here. Keep in mind that Adobe supports more and more formats as time goes on, so this list will continue to grow.

- **Preset.** Depending on the format you've chosen, Adobe has provided presets for common scenarios. Presets are great starting points, but you may want to tweak them further (the preset is changed to custom when it's modified).

- **Comments.** If you create your own preset, you should add comments about the preset so it makes more sense the next time you need to use it. We often enter the frame size, frame rate, and quality information into the Comments field for custom settings.

- **Output Name.** The output name defaults to the current name of the clip or sequence you're exporting. By clicking the yellow text of the name of the file, you can specify a new name as well as change the location where the file will be saved.

- **Export Video and Audio.** Using these two check boxes, you can export video only or audio only, or with both boxes checked, the resulting file will have both audio and video.

- **Summary.** If you toggle the triangle next to the Summary section, you'll be presented with information about your source as well as your output settings. The Output section will dynamically change as you make changes in the tabs covered next.

Filters export settings

Below the Export Settings section you'll find a number of tabs depending on the format you've chosen. First is the Filters export settings tab. Although you might have expected lots of different filters to choose from, you actually have only one choice— Gaussian Blur. By using a slight amount of Gaussian Blur, you can even cut out noise in footage. This allows a compressor to be more efficient and ultimately allows for smaller files. Just be careful *not* to add blur if you're creating a digital master of a sequence or using another high-quality codec because it does soften the footage ever so slightly.

Video export settings

The Video export settings tab (**FIGURE 15.8**) is where you'll probably spend most of your time in the Export Settings dialog. It's here that you control options such as codec and frame size. Depending on the format you choose, this panel and its options will change dynamically. Too many options are provided to cover them all here, but we show you how to use several options in the video tutorials mentioned later in this chapter.

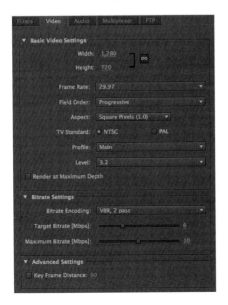

FIGURE 15.8 The Video export settings tab lets you customize options such as frame size, frame rate, and codec, and, depending on the format selected, additional format-specific options.

Save New Presets
The cool thing is that after tweaking settings using the buttons next to the Preset menu, you can save a custom preset or even import a preset if another team member has created one. If you no longer require a preset, you can click the trash can icon to delete a preset.

Single Output
Just keep in mind that if you choose a format that doesn't support video like a WAV audio file, you won't have the option to export video. Similarly, if you choose an image sequence output (like a DPX sequence), you won't have audio choices.

Where's the Deinterlace Filter?
If you choose a format that's progressive and you add an interlaced source, the clip is automatically deinterlaced. There is no need to look for a filter.

Noise and Compression
Noise makes a compressor's job much more difficult and less efficient because it wastes time trying to encode the noise, which ultimately creates a larger file. You can help the compressor by adding a touch of blur on an export. This will "trick" the compressor by evening out noise in the footage, allowing it to compress in a more efficient manner. Just keep in mind this will soften your footage slightly, so be sure to check the results to see whether they're acceptable.

Audio export settings

Like its Video cousin, the Audio export settings tab allows you to customize audio settings. Also like the Video export settings tab, depending on the format you've chosen, you'll have different options to choose from. For example, if you are creating an H.264 file for use on a Blu-ray Disc, you can choose to have your audio encoded as Dolby Digital or PCM (uncompressed) audio.

Multiplexer export settings

If you've chosen a format like an MPEG-based format (such as MPEG-2 for DVD or H.264 for Blu-ray Disc), the Multiplexer export settings tab will appear. Multiplexing controls how the audio and video streams are merged into one. The options here will vary slightly depending on the exact format you've chosen. We recommend sticking with the default settings for most presets, or you may create a file that's incompatible with its intended playback device.

FTP settings

One of our favorite features in the Export Settings dialog and Adobe Media Encoder is the built-in FTP functionality. Instead of having to depend on a third-party FTP tool, file transfer controls are available directly from the FTP tab so you can export a file to an FTP site. This comes in handy for us all the time because we produce a lot of Web video. Having an encoded file go directly to an FTP site saves a bunch of time versus manually having to upload the file after the compression stage.

Additional Options

A few more options are worth your time. Toward the bottom of the right side of the Export Settings dialog are several additional controls (**FIGURE 15.9**).

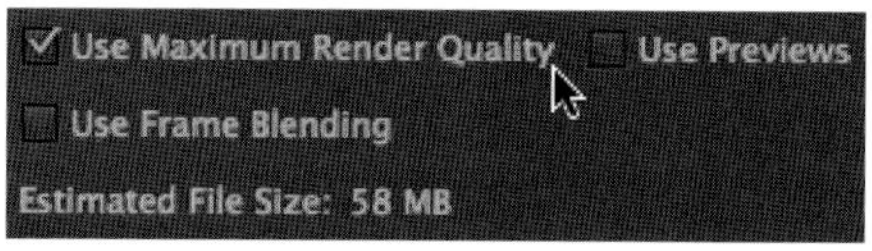

FIGURE 15.9 The additional options at the bottom of the Export Settings dialog can improve the quality (Use Maximum Render Quality) and speed (Use Previews) of an export.

- **Use Maximum Render Quality.** This option controls the quality of scaling for an export. So, if you are scaling a file from 1080p to 480p with this option selected, you'll get the highest-quality file, but be warned; it greatly slows down encoding and definitely requires a high-performance system with a large amount of RAM.

- **Use Previews.** This option is available only if you're encoding sequences from Adobe Premiere Pro. If you've already rendered part of your entire sequence (effects, motion settings, and so on), you can utilize those renders in the resulting output. This greatly speeds up encoding times. However, unless you've customized your sequence settings to use high-quality previews, we don't recommend using this option for final output because by default it uses lower-quality previews.

- **Use Frame Blending.** If your source footage doesn't match your output frame rate, you can toggle on Use Frame Blending to blend frames for smoother motion. This option significantly adds to the render time but is very useful when converting frame rates.

Metadata (or data about data) is an essential way to include additional information about a clip or sequence. Metadata can include copyright information for a file, program information that helps a viewer browse content, or even keywords for search engines. In the Export Settings dialog, by clicking the Metadata button at the bottom, you can customize metadata to an amazing degree. Several options are available in the resulting dialog (FIGURE 15.10). Let's look at a few.

- **Export Options.** Using the menu in this option, you can embed metadata in the output file (this is subject to support by other applications), create a sidecar file (an .xmp file with the metadata info), embed and create a sidecar file, or choose not to include metadata.

- **Source Metadata.** Using the menu in this option, you can preserve all existing metadata in the exported file or exclude all. In addition, by clicking the New button next to the menu, you can create your own rule for what metadata should be included or excluded. You can also include the master speech track and sequence markers as metadata, which can aid other programs as well as possibly allowing search engines to better index the resulting file if it's on the Web.

- **Output File Metadata.** In this section, you can edit any of the existing metadata fields for a given category. You can search for specific metadata fields, and you also have the ability to create a metadata template that uses only the metadata sets and fields that you use most often. Just note that blank metadata fields are not included in the resulting output.

FIGURE 15.10 The Metadata Export dialog allows you to customize metadata (including altering existing metadata) for the exported file.

Exporting Files

After you're done setting up your export, the next obvious step is to export the file. All you need to do is click the Export button. When you do, a dialog appears showing you the progress of the export along with an estimated completion time. Just keep in mind that while exporting, you can't continue to work in Premiere; you'll need to wait for the export to finish.

Another option that you have when exporting files is to add the file to the Adobe Media Encoder Queue (FIGURE 15.11). By choosing this option, you can send multiple clips and/or sequences to the Adobe Media Encoder Queue (Adobe Media Encoder will open). From the Queue you can further refine your settings. The benefit of this workflow is that you can load several items and then walk away while your machine works. In fact, you can even keep working and let the encoding run in the background while continuing to work in Premiere Pro.

FIGURE 15.11 By clicking the Queue button in the Export Settings dialog in Adobe Premiere Pro, you can access the Adobe Media Encoder Queue. Adding files to the Adobe Media Encoder Queue is useful when you need to export multiple formats at the same time.

Exercise Files for Exporting
If you'd like to export to FLV, F4V, DVD/Blu-ray, and H.264, feel free to use the project Ch15_publish.prproj located in the Lessons and Media folder. This project contains a sequence called 01_Match_Change_Export that you can use for testing exports.

Learn More About Flash Video
To learn more about interactive Flash Video, be sure to check out the book *Flash for After Effects, After Effects for Flash* (Adobe Press, 2009).

Importing and Saving Flash Cue Points
You can easily embed Flash Cue Points while encoding an FLV or F4V file, but you can also import Flash Cue Points by clicking the Import Cue Points button above the Cue Points area. In addition, you can save Flash Cue Points as XML files for handing off to a Flash programmer by clicking the Save Cue Points button, which is also located above the Cue Points area.

Creating Flash Content

As a format, Adobe Flash has become ubiquitous on the Web, as well as for media-rich presentations and mobile devices. Because Flash is an Adobe product, creating Flash-encoded video and audio is very easy using the Export Settings dialog in Adobe Premiere Pro (or by using the almost identical Adobe Media Encoder).

Choosing Between FLV and F4V

The thing to know about creating Flash content is you'll need to decide what type of Flash video you want to use. When creating Flash content, you have two choices: FLV or F4V. They are both container formats, meaning they can contain video and audio of various sizes, frame rates, and even codecs. Here is a quick comparison of the two formats:

- **FLV (Flash Video).** This is the original Flash standard. In many ways, it has been replaced with the newer F4V container. The file does offer the unique benefit of an alpha channel, which is helpful when compositing keyed video or graphics into an interactive Flash project.

- **F4V.** The main advantages of F4V are better streaming and metadata support. It also supports the newer codec H.264. This is a popular format for true video content on the Web, but it does require a relatively new version of the Flash plug-in for Web browsers.

For most people attempting to create Flash content, F4V is the best option. But always check with your clients about their exact needs.

Using FLV and F4V Presets

By exporting content to FLV or F4V, you can create Flash-compatible files easily. Like all of the format options available in the Export Settings dialog, there are a number of FLV and F4V presets to choose from when creating flash content. Let's take a look at using a Flash preset.

1. With a sequence or clip selected, either in the Project panel or in the Timeline panel, choose File > Export Media. The Export Settings dialog appears.

2. In the Export Settings section, click the Format menu, and choose either FLV or F4V (we prefer F4V in most cases).

3. In the Preset menu, choose the setting that best matches your needs.

   You can, of course, customize a chosen preset to better fit your needs. Be sure to check out Video #69 for more information on customizing an FLV or F4V preset.

   If you choose FLV or F4V, you can create Flash Cue Points. There are two types of Flash Cue Points. Navigation Cue Points can be used as a way to let viewers navigate to that part of the video, similar to a chapter marker on a DVD. Event Cue Points trigger an ActionScript so that something else happens in a Flash presentation. For example, when the video hits an Event Cue Point, you could have another Web browser window open with content that is germane to the video content.

4. Under the video preview on the left side of the Export Settings dialog, you can add Flash Cue Points (FIGURE 15.12). Navigate to the part of the video you want to add the Flash Cue Point to, and then click the plus button above the Cue Points area. After you've added a Flash Cue Point, in the Type column select the type of Flash Cue Point you desire (Navigation or Event).

Creating FLV and F4V Presets

Check out this video for more information on creating a custom FLV and F4V preset and using Flash Cue Points.

5. After you've selected a preset and optionally added Flash Cue Points, click the Export button at the bottom of the Export Settings dialog to export your sequence or clip.

FIGURE 15.12 When exporting FLV or F4V files, you have the ability to embed Flash Cue Points in the file, which can aid in user navigation or trigger action scripts (written by a Flash programmer) from the Flash Cue Points.

Creating H.264 Content for Devices and Web Delivery

Video and audio are increasingly mobile. If you're anything like us, your life is full of devices like iPads and Android phones, TiVos, and more. These days, those devices almost universally use H.264 files for video content. Additionally, when posting files to our own Web sites and blogs, we're big fans of using H.264. This modern codec produces super high-quality results at relatively small file sizes.

Fortunately, creating H.264 files suitable for devices and the Web is easy thanks to a number of presets available from Adobe. In this section, we show how to use presets available from Adobe to create content tailored to different devices, as well as the Web.

1. With a sequence or clip selected, either in the Project panel or in the Timeline panel, choose File > Export Media. The Export Settings dialog appears.

Using H.264 Presets for Vimeo and YouTube

The video-sharing sites Vimeo and YouTube have become so popular that we'd bet you probably view content from these sites every day. Although Vimeo and YouTube can take most files and recompress them to H.264 files, the compression schemes they use can degrade video quality. In most circumstances, it's best to give those Web sites a high-quality H.264 file to use.

2. In the Export Settings section, click the Format menu and choose H.264.

3. In the Preset menu, choose the preset that matches the device you're trying to export to; if you're exporting to the Web, choose any of the HDTV or NTSC/PAL presets that are appropriate for your project (**FIGURE 15.13**).

FIGURE 15.13 When you choose H.264 as a format, the Preset menu contains many presets, such as those Android and Apple devices as well as YouTube and Vimeo. Please note this screen shot is showing only a partial listing of presets. Yes, there are a lot of them!

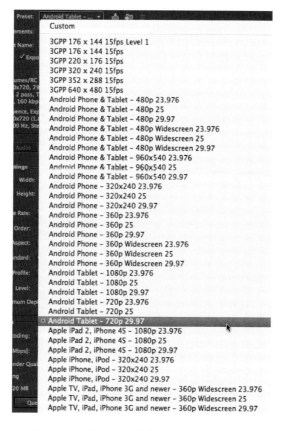

Creating H.264 Presets

Be sure to check out this video for more information on how to customize H.264 presets for devices and for the Web, namely, sharing sites like YouTube and Vimeo.

One word of caution: Although you can customize settings for a preset by using the panels in the middle of the Export Settings dialog, we recommend caution when creating content for devices. Most portable media players and phones have very strict rules on data rate and other options. Deviating from the preset can create incompatible files. Be sure to check out Video #70 for more information about customizing H.264.

4. When creating video for the Web, though, it's important to tailor the video and audio settings for a specific need. Our recommendations are to try lowering the data rate and even shrinking the window size to reduce delivery sizes.

5. After you've selected a preset, click the Export button at the bottom of the Export Settings dialog to export your sequence or clip.

Publishing to DVD and Blu-ray

Let's face it, DVD delivery as a final distribution method and for exchanging cuts has become as common as VHS tape back in the day. The relative high quality of a DVD along with the interactivity and additional playback options (surround sound audio, subtitles, and so on) make it a very attractive choice for publishing your project. The one downside of DVD is that it's standard-definition.

Enter Blu-ray Disc. Although Blu-ray's start as a distribution format was initially slow, it's quickly becoming the format of choice for content producers and postproduction professionals. The best part? Content can be encoded at HD resolution.

It's outside of the scope of this book to cover the authoring in full using applications such as Adobe Encore. But you can encode video and audio for DVD and Blu-ray by using Adobe Premiere Pro and Adobe Media Encoder. In the sections that follow, you'll learn about using presets for DVD and Blu-ray.

Using MPEG-2 Presets for DVD

Like with other formats, Adobe has provided presets for DVD encoding directly through the Export Settings dialog in Adobe Premiere Pro, as well as in the stand-alone Adobe Media Encoder application. The Adobe Media Encoder uses the popular Main Concept encoder for MPEG-2 and is well regarded by professional compressionists. Here's how to use these presets:

1. With a sequence selected in Adobe Premiere Pro, either in the Project panel or in the Timeline panel, choose File > Export > Media.

2. In the Export Settings area of the dialog, click the Format menu, and choose MPEG2-DVD.

3. In the Preset menu, the default choice is Match Source Attributes (High Quality). Notice that there are other Match Source options here too with different quality levels (**FIGURE 15.14**). Choosing one of these presets is a good choice because a lot of the guesswork over quality, frame rate, field order, and pixel aspect ratio is reduced. If you need to fit more content onto a disc, consider one of the lower-quality settings.

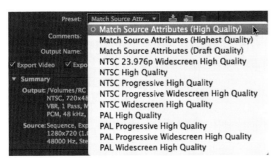

FIGURE 15.14 Adobe includes quite a few useful presets for creating files compatible with DVD authoring that vary the quality of the output file depending on your needs.

You can also choose from any of the other NTSC or PAL presets. Keep in mind that by choosing one of these presets, all the quality controls and other settings available on the tabs toward the bottom of the dialog change.

AVCHD Discs
It is possible to place AVCHD-encoded video onto standard DVD discs to play back HD material. This does require a supported set-top player.

Blu-ray Burners
To author a Blu-ray Disc, you'll need a Blu-ray burner. Many Windows machines come with Blu-ray burning capabilities, but sadly, Mac computers do not have built-in Blu-ray burners. If you don't have an internal Blu-ray burner on your machine, you can install one or get an external unit. We highly recommend the burners sold by Other World Computing (OWC). Check out OWC on the Web at www.macsales.com.

Creating an MPEG-2 Preset for DVD

Using presets can get you only so far. Check out this video for more information about creating your own custom preset for DVD-compatible files.

4. After choosing a preset, you can, of course, tweak settings using the tabs and controls in the Export Settings dialog. Be sure to check out Video #71 for more about creating a custom preset.

5. After you've selected a preset, click the Export button at the bottom of the Export Settings dialog to export your sequence or clip.

Choosing Between MPEG-2 and H.264 for Blu-ray

If you'll be publishing your project to a Blu-ray Disc, you have two main choices as to how the video will be encoded: MPEG-2 or H.264. Like its DVD predecessor, Blu-ray strives to be somewhat backward compatible with support for MPEG-2 (DVDs support both MPEG-2 and the older MPEG-1).

With that said, when creating a Blu-ray Disc, in almost every scenario H.264 is a better choice. Generally, H.264 encoded media will be of better quality compared to MPEG-2 at the same bitrate. In addition, because H.264 is a more efficient codec, you'll actually be able to fit more content on a disc given the same bitrate between encoding standards. However, one downside of encoding footage as H.264 is processing time. We've found that it can take quite a bit more time to encode H.264 for Blu-ray compared to MPEG-2 for Blu-ray.

Even though we're big fans of H.264 encoded media for Blu-ray, the choice is ultimately yours. Try encoding media using both standards to evaluate which you prefer in terms of quality and size.

Using an H.264 Preset for Blu-ray

Creating an H.264 Preset for Blu-ray

Check out this video to learn how to create a custom H.264 preset to create files suitable for Blu-ray.

DVD and Blu-ray Authoring with Adobe Encore

Check out this video to learn the essentials of authoring interactivity for a DVD and Blu-ray using Encore.

If you'll be publishing your project to Blu-ray, you'll most likely use the H.264 for Blu-ray format. As with other formats, Adobe has provided a number of presets that you can use to create H.264 files that will work on a Blu-ray Disc. Let's take a look at using an H.264 preset for Blu-ray.

1. With a sequence or clip selected, choose File > Export > Media.

2. In the Export Settings area of the dialog, click the Format menu, and choose H.264 Blu-ray.

3. In the Preset menu, the default choice is Match Source Attributes (High Quality). We find that choosing a Match Source Attributes preset is a good choice in most situations.

4. You can also choose from any of the other presets (**FIGURE 15.15**) that best match your source. Just keep in mind that the 1440 x 1080 presets are geared to sources like HDV and XDCAM that use a non-square pixel aspect ratio.

5. After choosing a preset, you can, of course, tweak settings using the tabs and controls in the Export Settings dialog. Be sure to check out Video #72 to learn more about creating an H.264 preset for Blu-ray.

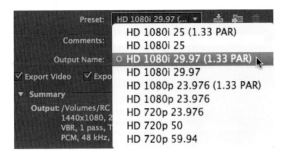

FIGURE 15.15 When working with sources that use non-square pixel aspect ratios, Adobe has provided several Blu-ray presets to work with these sources.

6. After you've selected a preset, click the Export button at the bottom of the Export Settings dialog to export your sequence or clip.

EXCHANGING WITH ADOBE ENCORE

Creating DVDs and Blu-ray Discs are probably the most common ways of delivering a project in addition to the Web and tape. Fortunately, Adobe understands this and has made the integration between Adobe Premiere Pro and Adobe Encore seamless. Here are a couple of ways they can interact:

- **Encore markers.** From a sequence in Adobe Premiere Pro, you can add an Encore chapter marker at a point of your choosing. If you add a marker and then double-click it, you can name the marker, set its duration, add markers, and choose to enable the marker as a chapter marker or as a Web link in the Encore project. Additionally, when configuring a marker, you can configure to create a Flash Cue Point if you're planning to export the project to Adobe Flash through Encore.

- **Sending to Encore via Dynamic Link.** You can also send an entire sequence directly to Encore by choosing File > Adobe Dynamic Link > Send to Encore. The big advantage of using this option is not having to export intermediate files. It also means that your DVD project will update and always have the latest version of your sequence.

Exporting Additional File Types

A lot of one-person shops exist, but when it comes to postproduction, for many, it's a collaborative affair. Quite often you'll need to exchange files and projects with different people to keep the post pipeline moving forward. Whether it's a colorist, an audio mixer, or another editor on a different platform, you'll often need to send others files that they can work with. Fortunately, Adobe Premiere Pro is up to the task.

Edit Decision List (EDL)

Edit decision lists are a common yet antiquated way of exchanging information between different platforms. Originally designed in the days of linear video editing, EDLs are still typically used to exchange information between edit systems, to provide a list of edits from a master file or tape to another creative, and even to provide a network (for legal purposes) the ability to go back and find a source tape because of a legal challenge for a particular show. Exporting an EDL is easy using Adobe Premiere Pro.

1. With a sequence selected, choose File > Export > EDL.

2. In the dialog that opens (**FIGURE 15.16**), you can name the EDL as well as choose from several additional options for formatting the EDL, such as selecting the starting timecode and which tracks to export.

FIGURE 15.16 When you export an EDL, you can customize the settings for the EDL. Be sure to check with the recipient of the EDL to make sure your settings are compatible with the application that person is using.

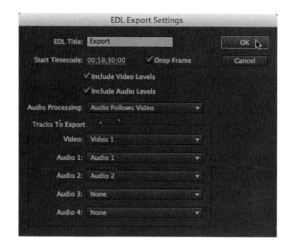

Just keep in mind that it's always a good idea to check with your client or broadcaster for the correct formatting of the EDL. There are several options, and they vary greatly (especially for older hardware systems).

Open Media Framework (OMF)

Open Media Framework has become the standard way of exchanging audio information between systems. Most often, OMF is used to send the audio from a project to a dedicated Audio Mixer. A good way to understand OMF is to compare it to a Zip file. Usually, when you export an OMF, a single file of all your audio tracks is created. Then, when the Audio Mixer opens the OMF in a dedicated audio system, all of the tracks open just as they were in your Adobe Premiere Pro project. To export an OMF file, follow these steps:

1. With a sequence selected, choose File > Export > OMF.

2. In the dialog that opens (**FIGURE 15.17**), you can name the OMF as well as assign a sample rate and bitrate.

    You can also encapsulate (include all media in a single file) or export audio as separate files. Most often, files are encapsulated. In addition, you can use the complete audio files or trim files so only what you're using on the sequence is included in the OMF. If you choose to trim files, you can include handles. We recommend that you include one to two seconds of handles.

As with other exchange formats, always check with the recipient of the handoff to make sure settings are compatible with that person's application.

FIGURE 15.17 OMF is a standard exchange format file type. When you export an OMF, a dialog allows you to configure the settings the OMF will use.

Advanced Authoring Format (AAF)

Advanced Authoring Format is another way of exchanging project information and media between applications. The cool thing about AAF is that it is a relatively modern exchange format and therefore supports several features that other exchange files don't. Choose File > Export > AAF to export an AAF of a selected sequence. First choose a location to save the AAF, and then in the dialog that appears (**FIGURE 15.18**) you can save the AAF as a legacy file, which is compatible with more systems, as well as embed audio into the AAF.

You can then import the AAF into a compatible application. Many professional video and audio applications support AAF including Avid and ProTools systems. So, AAF can be a good format to use to exchange audio and video with users of those systems.

FIGURE 15.18 When exporting an AAF file, you have a couple of options as to how to configure the AAF. Be sure to check with the recipient of the handoff to see whether that person prefers embedded audio in the AAF.

Final Cut Pro XML (eXtensible Markup Language)

Final Cut Pro 7 established itself as a popular postproduction editorial tool over the past decade. Rather than create a closed ecosystem, Adobe has embraced that fact and has provided a versatile option for exchanging projects with editors using Final Cut Pro and even iMovie!

By using XML, you can easily export a sequence for use in Final Cut Pro 7. To do so, select a sequence and choose File > Export > Final Cut Pro XML. Then choose the location to which you want to save the XML file. Final Cut Pro 7 editors will then need to import the XML file into their project. In fact, other tools, such as PluralEyes for audio syncing and DaVinci Resolve, also rely on Final Cut Pro XML to exchange data.

Final Cut Pro X
Final Cut Pro X handles XML differently than previous versions of Final Cut Pro. A great utility that we've found that will let you take the Final Cut Pro XML exported from Premiere Pro CS6 and get that into Final Cut Pro X is 7toX for Final Cut Pro, which can be found on the Mac App Store.

Next Steps

The DVD for this book contains several PDF appendixes of extra content we wanted to share. We encourage you to check out these PDFs for added information on how to get more out of Adobe Premiere Pro and the Creative Suite. As with other software packages, it's through your own exploration of the application that you really start to gain mastery of it. If you hit some speed bumps along the way, notice a missing feature, or see a feature you'd like to see improved, Adobe is listening. You can submit feedback to Adobe from within Adobe Premiere Pro by choosing Help > Adobe Product Improvement Program.

While writing this second edition of *An Editor's Guide to Adobe Premiere Pro*, we've had a lot of fun exploring this fantastic application and updating information for Adobe Premiere Pro CS6, and we encourage you to keep looking for new ways to get your job done with this fantastic tool! If you'd like to keep in touch with the authors of the book as well as a vibrant online community for Adobe Premiere Pro, visit www.facebook.com/groups/premierepro/.

INDEX

Authentic Records is a cultivator of fine musical artists from the heartland and the rest of the country, who may otherwise go "under-noticed." Authentic's goal is to help bring these artists' music to the masses, with a focus on not only building individual careers, but a community of artists helping artists. Music that deserves to be heard and that you deserve to hear. Authentic Records is authentic music by authentic artists.

AUTHENTIC RECORDS

is proud to present....
the Nadas

The Nadas have paved the way for midwest music as Iowa's leading folk rock alt-country band. With over 150,000 records sold, an extensive national tour schedule, and 16 years of experience under their belt- The Nadas continue to masterfully blend flawless songwriting and catchy melodies for a crowd-pleasing experience.

For more info go to:
www.thenadas.com
www.authenticrecordsonline.com
2606 Beaver Ave. Des Moines, Iowa 50310

CLOSER TO TRUTH

COSMOS. CONSCIOUSNESS. GOD.

Some of the footage featured in An Editor's Guide to Adobe Premiere Pro is from the series Closer To Truth Cosmos. Consciousness. God.

Closer To Truth is the definitive series on Cosmos, Consciousness and God, a global journey in search of the vital ideas of existence. It is the most complete, compelling, and accessible series on Cosmos, Consciousness and God ever produced for television.

Closer To Truth explores fundamental issues of universe, brain/mind, religion, meaning and purpose through intimate, candid conversations with leading scientists, philosophers, scholars, theologians and creative thinkers of all kinds.

Find out more.
www.closertotruth.com